Transnational Religion and Fading States

Sponsored by the
Program on International Peace and Security
of the Social Science Research Council

TRANSNATIONAL RELIGION AND FADING STATES

edited by

Susanne Hoeber Rudolph
University of Chicago

James Piscatori
Oxford Centre for Islamic Studies

WestviewPress
A Division of HarperCollinsPublishers

Published in 1997 in the United States of America by Westview Press, 5500 Central Avenue, Boulder, Colorado 80301-2877, and in the United Kingdom by Westview Press, 12 Hid's Copse Road, Cumnor Hill, Oxford OX2 9JJ

Library of Congress Cataloging-in-Publication Data
Transnational religion and fading states / edited by Susanne Hoeber
   Rudolph, James Piscatori.
      p.   cm.
   Includes bibliographical references and index.
   ISBN 0-8133-2767-9 (hardcover).—ISBN 0-8133-2768-7 (pbk.)
   1. Religion and international affairs.   2. World politics—1989–
I. Rudolph, Susanne Hoeber.   II. Piscatori, James P.
BL65.I5T73   1997
291.1'787—dc20   96-35187
                                                                 CIP

The paper used in this publication meets the requirements of the American National Standard for Permanence of Paper for Printed Library Materials Z39.48-1984.

10   9   8   7   6   5   4   3   2   1

Contents

Part Three
Reflections

Preface

This study of the place of transnational religion in world politics arose out of efforts by the Committee on International Peace and Security of the Social Science Research Council (SSRC) to rethink cold war conceptions of security. Those conceptions privileged states by treating them as natural and exclusive actors in international relations; privileged the Western world by treating it as the center and peripheralizing the rest; and privileged the balance of power and deterrence by treating military force as the primary means of self-help in the allegedly anarchical space beyond state frontiers. With the end of cold war bipolarity and the great fear of nuclear Armageddon, such conceptions have become dated, more akin to anachronisms than to universals independent of time, place, and circumstance. In a world of rapid communication, global and local processes can move money and products, images and people, guns and drugs, diseases and pollution, across increasingly porous and irrelevant state frontiers. Because sovereignty within and beyond state borders is not what it used to be, fresh thinking about what security can mean and how it can be approximated seems in order.

The essays in this volume focus on religious formations—sects, "churches," movements, communities, and auxiliary organizations. They show why and how these formations have become an important component of an emergent and relatively recently theorized transnational civil society. Security takes on new meanings and dimensions in the space opened up by the concept, the practices, and the institutions of transnational civil society. That space, although as old as Christendom in the West, is now seen as populated, inter alia, by nongovernmental organizations (NGOs) and movements that are concerned with a wide variety of global issues, such as the environment, human rights, poverty, health, migration, population changes, and weapons of mass destruction. They have given voice and visibility to transnational civil society. NGO forums at periodic United Nations–organized summits—the World Conference on Human Rights, Vienna, 1993; the United Nations Conference on Environment and Development, Rio de Janeiro, 1993; the International Conference on Population, Cairo, 1994; the World Summit for Social Development, Copenhagen, 1994; and the Fourth World Conference on Women, Beijing, 1995—have helped to institutionalize it. The essays in this volume on religious movements and organizations open up a new dimension in the study of transnational society.

Contributors to the volume come from a wide range of disciplines (history, anthropology, political science, sociology), address a broad geographical spectrum (the Middle East, Western and Eastern Europe, Africa, East Asia, Latin America), and address a variety of confessions (Catholicism, Islam, Protestantism, Orthodoxy, Buddhism). Their essays show how religious formations and movements over time and circumstance can generate difference as well as solidarity, conflict as well as cooperation, incivility as well as civility.

This is not a book about the "clash of civilizations." Nor do its essays support the view that religion is a master variable that explains social conflict or threats to state security in the next decade or in the twenty-first century. On the contrary, the essays presented here show how internal differences make conflict within religions as likely as conflicts between them and suggest that shared religion does not shield states from conflict or ensure their cooperation.

The volume owes much to the program officers of the Social Science Research Council, especially Cary Fraser and Steven Heydemann. Cary organized the meetings that gave rise to this volume. Steven provided imaginative advice about how the book could meet its public. Paul Erickson, Allison Lichter, and Jennifer Sime facilitated communications among contributors and production of the manuscript, especially when the editors were far afield. The SSRC's Committee on International Peace and Security funded the meetings that generated the essays, drawing on the grant from the John D. and Catherine T. MacArthur Foundation, which has supported the committee for more than a decade. Andrew Rothman applied his considerable editorial skills to making diverse manuscripts formally comparable. Lloyd I. Rudolph was instrumental in the conceptualization of the volume. Susanne Rudolph borrowed heavily from his seminar, "Rethinking Sovereignty," and he fundamentally revised both ideas in and presentation of the introductory essay.

Susanne Hoeber Rudolph
University of Chicago

James Piscatori
Oxford Centre for Islamic Studies

Introduction: Religion, States, and Transnational Civil Society

Susanne Hoeber Rudolph

Transnational Religion in Liminal Space: Its Demography

Religious communities are among the oldest of the transnationals: Sufi orders, Catholic missionaries, and Buddhist monks carried word and praxis across vast spaces before those places became nation-states or even states. Such religious peripatetics *were* versions of civil society.[1] In today's postmodern era, religious communities have become vigorous creators of an emergent transnational civil society.

Modern social science did not warn us that this would happen. Instead it asserted that religion would fade, then disappear, with the triumph of science and rationalism. But religion has expanded explosively, stimulated as much by secular global processes—migration, multinational capital, the media revolution—as by proselytizing activity. Contrary to expectations, its expansion has been an answer to and driven by modernity. In response to the deracination and threats of cultural extinction associated with modernization processes, religious experience seeks to restore meaning to life.[2]

Religious communities are helping to shape world politics. The language of international relations and security studies on the one hand and that of foreign policy and domestic politics on the other distinguish political life within states from the alleged imperatives of an imagined international system. This distinction and separation deploy a rich vocabulary for "inside" and "outside," to follow Rob Walker's language.[3] Until recently, there were no words and metaphors for designating and populating the liminal space that cuts across inside/outside, a space that is neither within the state nor an aspect of the international state system but animates both.

This liminal and cross-cutting arena is becoming more densely occupied by communities—environmentalists, development professionals, human rights activists, information specialists—whose commonality depends less on coresidence in "sovereign" territorial space and more on common worldviews, purposes, interests, and praxis.[4] Peter Haas has theorized them as epistemic communities.[5] Such communities, including religious communities and movements, have implications for the international system. Their existence has transformed how we understand and explain "international relations," that is, relations among sovereign states in anarchic space. It is possible to theorize these new transnational communities as constituting a world politics that encompasses both transnational civil society and sovereignty-sharing states. The object of this volume is to create a space for religious groups and movements in the consideration of such transnational solidarities.

The communities that populate transnational civil society do not affect the state "system" in the way some wish world governance might. They do not provide a statelike entity to impose order and perhaps justice "outside," in anarchic space, by monopolizing force and supplying universal arbitration and rule enforcement. They do not even supply what transnational regimes are meant to provide—predictable systems of rules that facilitate cooperation.[6] Instead, they create a pluralistic transnational polity. They shape perceptions and expectations that contribute to world public opinion and politics.

Their effects on transnational space are only beginning to be understood. Existential fright about "the coming anarchy" is probably premature.[7] But because a plurality of transnational spaces entails difference as well as commonality with respect to epistemes, identities, and expectations, transnational civil society can be the site of conflict as well as cooperation.

While the fluidity of religion across political boundaries is very old, recent migrations, communication links, and elite transformations joining East with West and North with South have generated unaccustomed flows: Hindus in Leicester, Muslims in Marseilles and Frankfurt, Pentecostals in Moscow and Singapore. Europeans found themselves in a minority at Vatican II, overwhelmed by 200 U.S. and 228 Asian and African bishops.[8] Since the mid-1960s American evangelism has helped to raise the proportion of Protestants to 12 percent of the population of Latin America, formerly a Catholic bastion.[9] In predominantly Chinese Singapore, the Christian population has doubled to one-fifth since 1985. In China proper, optimistic Christian estimates place the number of Christians at 80 million.[10]

It may surprise readers to learn that since the mid-1970s Oklahoma City has acquired five mosques, four Hindu temples, one Sikh *gurudwara*, and three Buddhist temples; that Denver has a similar configuration; that there may be as many as seventy mosques in the Chicago metropolitan area and fifty temples in the Midwest Buddhist Association; and that Muslims outnumber Episcopalians in the United States two to one and are likely to outnumber Jews in the near future.[11]

This explosion of religious formations seems to have been facilitated by the very forces that were supposed to dissolve them: increased print and electronic media, increased literacy—including the higher literacy of postsecondary education—and urbanization. Explaining the increase and intensification in religious discourse in Oman and its entry into everyday life and politics, Dale Eickelman writes:

> The most profound change is associated with the spread of modern literacy and the new media through which ideas can be communicated. Mass literacy came late to Oman. . . . By the early 1980s Oman had a sufficient number of secondary school graduates, members of the armed services and civilian government with in-service training, and university students abroad . . . to engender a transformation in what constitutes authoritative religious discourse. The shift to a print and cassette-based religiosity and the exposure of large numbers of young Omanis to a written, formal, "modern standard" Arabic through schooling and the mass media have altered the style and content of authoritative religious discourse and the role this plays in shaping and constraining domestic and regional politics.[12]

These are the demographics of a new religious transnationalism. In an earlier transnationalism of Islam and Christianity, religion accompanied trade, conquest, and colonial domination. Versions of Christianity continue to flow outward from the West, but reverse flows are now conspicuous as well. Accustomed as we were to controlling the missionary terms of trade, we may be astonished to find "their" products flooding "our" market.

Much of this new transnationalism is carried by religion from below, by a popular religious upsurge of ordinary and quite often poor, oppressed, and culturally deprived people, rather than by religion introduced and directed from above. Well-known transnational structures—especially the hierarchical and bureaucratized Catholic Church, led by an evangelizing Pontiff with global aspirations—are an important component of the new transnational religion. But popular, populist, enthusiastic movements leavened by Pentecostals, Catholic charismatics, and "fundamentalist" Muslims have spread more by spontaneous diffusion.

Rethinking Security

This volume is concerned with the implications of transnational religions for conflict and cooperation, for security, for the future of the nation-state, and for the emergence of transnational civil society. It began as part of an effort by the Social Science Research Council's Committee on International Peace and Security to query the conventional significance of "security." The relevance of transnational religions to security, not obvious in the mid-1980s, came to seem more plausible with the approach of the 1990s, as domestic tranquillity and international peace were increasingly disrupted in the name of religion. Religious formulations of political purposes proliferated, and the political activities of nonstate religious actors became conspicuous. For some, religion promised to become the same kind of summary predictor for peace and war that ideology had been in the 1970s.

But what is security? Whose security, and from whom or what? In American social science discourses the significance of the word, when uttered in the 1960s through the 1980s, was relatively transparent. It had to do with the Western alliance and with the state. For the Western alliance it denoted the security of the United States and its allies in a bipolar world in the context of nuclear threat. For non-Europeans and their states, ambivalent subscribers to bipolarity who doubted the equation of U.S. interests with their own, the word acquired negative and coercive meaning. For the Latin American left, the security state was an authoritarian polity living on U.S. aid and protection. Indians and Indonesians equated security with a bipolarity that reduced their international choices.[13] "Security," then, was a code, at its narrowest, for U.S. security interests, at its widest for the Western alliance and its adherents.

Second, the dominant definitions of security were state-centric. States were the units of action, the definers and guarantors of security. They were the agents that would constitute the international system, entering into alliances or conflict with other state units in pursuit of the security they defined. The state was the critical agent in all transactions governing security. These meanings, security as Western interests in the nuclear balance in a bipolar world and security as a state monopoly, are now increasingly challenged in social science discourses.[14]

Our reading of security turns the lens away from the state as prime actor, focusing instead on civil society as creator and guarantor as well as threat to security. The historical experience of the 1990s provides an empirical backdrop for that different reading. In this decade, the balance of violence has shifted significantly from war "outside," in the anarchic space between sovereign states, to war "inside," between the embodiments of difference in civil society. Whereas war had formerly been embedded in the imbalance of power among states, it now became related to imbalance of status in civil society among ethnic and religious formations. Refocusing on civil society as a locus of security problems is justified by the mortal threat that "civil" wars pose. Even as political developments in advanced industrial democracies make it virtually impossible to engage in interstate wars that create domestic casualties, the fatality counts in civil conflicts rise to figures approximating or overwhelming figures for interstate wars.[15]

Focusing on security as a matter arising in civil society invites a redefinition of the problems that qualify as security issues. Security problems center on physical and cultural survival. The fear of death, Hobbes's ultimate *causans*, and calculations about the probabilities of survival, are implied by the threats of environmental degradation, famine, poverty, population density, disease, and chaos-generating migratory flows.[16] These threats to the physical survival of individuals and particular communities and countries, as well as of the whole human species, loom as large in the 1990s as a nuclear exchange or nuclear Armageddon did in the cold war era.

But the fear of cultural extinction rivals the fear of physical extinction. One doesn't have to carry a New Hampshire license plate ("Live Free or Die") to recognize that physical survival is not enough in a world threatened by the death of meaning. Many of today's conflicts arise from groups' fears that they are culturally endangered species, that enemies seek their cultural, if not physical, annihilation. Such fears drive militant Sikhs, Sinhalese Buddhists, Kurds, Hutus, Andean Indians, and Bosnian Serbs and provide motive and fuel to domestic conflicts in Punjab, Sri Lanka, Guatemala, Turkey, Bosnia, and Rwanda. Identities and the esteem conferred by them are at stake. Religion is one of the prime sources of identity. Its significance has intensified in a post-rationalist world threatened by disenchantment, impersonality, and loss of meaning. Cultural survival, like physical survival, is a critical security problem for the 1990s and beyond.

Religion: Vehicle of Conflict or Cooperation?

The essays in this volume problematize the role of religion with respect to conflict and cooperation. Under what circumstances does religion divide persons and groups? Under what conditions does it bring them together? Religion, as the term is used most of the time by our contributors, refers to practice more often than it does to belief. Although guided and sustained by the meaning systems of transcendent realms, religion as practiced is embedded in everyday life. In countries of the Western as well as of the non-Western world, the most significant form of social organization and source of worldviews for a growing number of people may be religious entities rather than trade unions, political parties, or interest groups. How are these entities related to conflict and cooperation?

"Much recent writing on transnational dimensions of religious change in Latin America has been concerned with overt political acts," writes Daniel Levine, "driven by fears about religion's possible links to revolution (especially in Central America), by false images of a repetition of the Iranian Revolution, or by hopes that religious change would somehow fuel a thoroughgoing cultural and social transformation."[17] The conflict-generating potential of religious mobilizations has received much more attention than their potential for cooperation.

We must remind ourselves that Enlightenment rationalism gave religion a bad name. Religion was false knowledge, the kind of knowledge that Voltaire, Condorcet, and Comte foresaw as disappearing from human consciousness. For Marx, the lingering effects of religions were actively negative, shoring up exploitation and oppression.[18] Modernist social scientists cannot imagine religion as a positive force, as practice and worldview that contributes to order, provides meaning, and promotes justice.

Now that modernity is on trial, in crisis or bankrupt, are there arguments for religion's having a positive role? It can be argued that how people understand their condition affects their sense of security as much as or more than do their objective conditions. If religion can be an opiate that reconciles humans to injustice, it can also provide the vision and energy that engender collective action and social transformation.

Daniel Levine and David Stoll, in this volume, tell of the earnest liberationists and Pentecostal congregations of the Latin American poor empowered by religious self-teaching. It gives them "new orientations, social skills, and collective self-confidence," though less of all of these than the most optimistic liberationism anticipated. Writing earlier of Guatemala, Stoll stresses the role of the new Protestantism among uprooted populations and recent migrants to cities. They construct new institutions and practices to negotiate the shock of transfer, while those living under the surviving Hacienda regime, for whom the old-time Catholicism suffices, remain passive.[19] Ousmane Kane tells of mobile West African Sufis who spawn *zawiyas,* a familiar spiritual and social milieu, in new locations for the migrating faithful, that provide them with the security of identity, food, and education.[20]

Such accounts reveal how religious associations give structure and meaning to human relations, how they create communities and enable action. That the ritual and belief systems of religious communities have a "security" component, that they make possible both physical and cultural survival, is sometimes not visible until they are destroyed. Kane's account of the peaceable transnational trading and kinship networks of West African Sufis provides a benign contrast to the chaotic horrors of Rwanda and Somalia, where both states and civil society contributed to the problem rather than the solution. As Habermas remarks, "Sometimes it takes an earthquake to make us aware that we had regarded the ground on which we stand every day as unshakable."[21] States cannot, without the means of society, construct the ties that bind humans together in obligation.

If practice and belief of religious formations can, at various levels, orient and facilitate collective action and provide security, they can also generate conflict. Religions often provide not only the language and symbols but also the motives for cultural conflict between and within states: Shiite Iran, Orthodox Serbia, Jewish Israel and Muslim Palestine Liberation Organization (PLO), Buddhist Sinhalese and Hindu Tamils in Sri Lanka, Protestants and Catholics in Ireland, Muslims, Hindus, and Buddhists in Kashmir, Sikhs and Hindus in Punjab, Front Islamique du Salut (FIS) Islamists and Secular Socialists (is rationalism a religion?) in Algeria. Rather than reflecting disequilibria in the balance of power, state conflict has taken on the aura of the jihad and crusade. Holy war has joined self-help and ideology as a casus belli "outside," and the confessionally defined "other" has become the enemy within.

The notion that "war" is by definition an encounter between "states" has been shaken by a democracy of weapons that makes Weber's notion of states' monopolizing the use of force into a fairy tale of modernization. Increasingly wars present themselves as conflicts among civilian populations where more civilians than soldiers die. Civil wars like that in Kashmir, which by 1995 was engaging 600,000 Indian troops, more than the 1965 Indo-Pakistan war, and those in Algeria and Bosnia, are likely to be the main sources of violent conflict for the foreseeable future.

Religion is an important component of the identities that define inside conflicts. Low-level conflicts can arise when the practices of an immigrant religious group challenge the prevailing religious conventions and constitution of the host country. This has happened when Muslims in London demanded enforcement of blasphemy laws and those in Marseilles challenged compulsory dress codes in public education. More serious conflicts can arise when a religious minority lays claim to a separate political identity, as Sikhs did in Indian Punjab or Catholics have done in Northern Ireland. Such conflicts are exacerbated when transnational brethren of local religious minorities seeking political autonomy provide help—North American Sikhs in Punjab; Pakistan Muslims in Kashmir; Indian Tamils in Sri Lanka.

Avoiding Domestic Conflict: Assimilation Versus Difference

If modernization can no longer be counted on to erase religion from human consciousness and religion can be expected to trigger some conflicts, what are the possibilities for fewer rather than more domestic conflicts? Processes that foster domestic peace among religious groups have taken a number of forms. Homogenizing assimilation and multicultural pluralism represent contrasting cultural regimes. Neither has wholly succeeded, and neither has wholly failed. The stereotypical American story featured assimilating immigrants who "Americanized," that is, became more alike, more homogeneous. Newcomers were encouraged to emulate the mores of the dominant Anglo-Saxon Protestant cultural forms and to be different in private—for example, to speak Italian or Yiddish at home and not take religious differences into political arenas.

In recent decades multiculturalism has challenged the notion of Americanization and assimilationist homogeneity. Numerous movements recognize and celebrate religious as well as ethnic and racial identities and call for educational diversity. Threats of cultural extinction increasingly drive identity movements. Although threatened in both the United States and Europe by nativist fringe and mainstream backlash, political recognition of difference and pluralist settlements seem harder and harder to oppose or deny. The increase in migration to Europe and North America from non-Christian lands, or to the Middle East from non-Islamic ones, is enabled by the ease with which information technologies and jumbo jets allow immigrants to stay in touch with their home communities. We are likely to see "the indefinite survival of separate collective identities even among groups living in the same place and exchanging goods and services on a daily basis."[22]

In retrospect, the historical ubiquity of "ordered heterogeneity" makes the nation-state's insistence on homogeneity—"one culture fits all"—seem quixotic. The "high level of ethnic uniformity that modern European nations took for granted," writes William McNeill, "was very unusual. Religious pluralism, rather than homogeneity, was the starting point for older civilizations."[23] Mobile peoples moving from rural to urban areas or arriving from distant lands relied on their religious identities and practices to secure them against shocks of transition. Those who brought their religion with them were not perceived as disrupting the homogeneity of a host country. "The great cities of Asia and Eastern Europe adapted to this sort of permanent poly-ethnicity by allowing a series of religiously defined communities to exist side by side. . . . Chinese and Indian cities also accorded extensive autonomy to enclaves of foreigners as a matter of course."[24] McNeill's accounts suggest that homogeneity is not the only mode that can govern how religious communities live with each other.

When and why does religious pluralism foster civility and order and when conflict and disorder? Consideration of the relationship between security and religion has to recognize both possibilities, that is, religious communities as conciliatory components of viable civil societies and as sources of mutual alienation, distrust, and conflict. The dominant path to religious and ethnic civility of most nineteenth-century nation-states was homogenization and assimilation. But this is not the only way to peaceable settlements. The pluralistic guarantees of multinational empires, and the permanent polyethnicity of the older cities in Asia and Eastern Europe represent an alternative cultural constitution. These approaches to conflict resolution are points on a continuum rather than opposites. Future negotiations about cultural security are likely to engage both alternatives.

World Politics in Transnational Space[25]

The challenge by nongovernmental organizations (NGOs) to states in world political arenas is a special phenomenon of the 1990s.[26] World summits on human rights, the environment, population, and women brought states together with relevant and often obstreperous NGO forums and created a new arena for world politics: transnational civil society. The society they began to create had precedents. In place of the anarchy posited by realist theory, Hedley Bull initiated a discussion of state cooperation with his "Grotian" concept of "international society." Robert Keohane, Stephen Krasner, and others elaborated the idea of state cooperation via treaties, international organizations, and regimes. But these precedents differed significantly from the new transnationalism.

The older theoretical discourse of international relations had been carried on mainly via dichotomous oppositions, self-help/anarchy versus world government/order.[27] And it was carried on by dichotomous voices, neorealists versus liberals who, despite their differences, were united by a belief that states are the only meaningful units of action in the global environment.[28] These categories became inadequate for capturing the experience of the 1990s. John Ruggie complained about an "impoverished mindset at work here that is able to visualize long-term challenges to the system of states only in terms of entities that are institutionally substitutable for the state."[29] Since the 1990s, there are the makings of more complex, less dichotomous theorizations that focus on nonstate actors and liminal phenomena, entities operating on the border of "inside" and "outside." Ronnie Lipschutz, for example, writes of "self-conscious constructions of networks of knowledge and action, by decentered, local actors that cross the reified boundaries of space as though they were not there," and of heteronomous networks, "differentiated from each other in terms of specializations: there is not a single network, but many, each fulfilling a different function."[30]

Discussions of neomedievalism had earlier led to an exploration of liminal phenomena and shared sovereignty. Neomedieval discourse drew attention to the possibility of multiple overlapping institutions, organizations, and practices in conjunction with cooperating states that limited and shared sovereignty.[31] As early as 1977 Hedley Bull had noted that neomedievalism "promises to avoid the classic dangers of the system of sovereign states by a structure of overlapping authorities and criss-crossing loyalties that hold all peoples together in a universal society."[32] Though we need not romanticize the medieval, the language and practice of medievalism reminds us that the modern state and the nation-state are recent inventions, not immortal and universal entities independent of time, place, and circumstance nor endpoints of a teleological historical process.[33]

Multiplicity of forms is not the only marker of medieval thought and practice. The medieval Catholic Church was the earliest and has proved to be an enduring constraint on modern state claims to a monopoly on sovereignty and (reason of state) morality. José Casanova, in tracing the career of Catholic globalism in this volume, shows how the Church's universalism, although eclipsed in the era of absolutism and the nation-state, has reappeared as part of the "still undefined global system within which the papacy is attaining once again a central structural role."[34]

Once a nonstate arena is imagined, in which states are significant but not the only players, it becomes possible to specify a space for transnational civil society in global politics. Civil society was a category elaborated in Western liberal thought by social contract theorists. Locke—but not Hobbes—spoke of two realms beyond the "state of nature"—a societal bond that supported civil society and a state that, at minimum, provided a common judge and coercive power. Over the years the role of civil society has been to legitimize a space for nonstate associations, discourses, and practices that can limit or direct state actions. In its Lockean version, civil society has also stood for the idea that society has conventions and regularities that govern human conduct even in the absence of states—the idea that force and coercion are not the only guarantors of order. Finally, civil society is characterized by the way it contrasts with the state. It is the realm of contest, of dispute, persuasion, mobilization, that is, the realm of politics, and the state is guarantor of order, umpire, executor of force, the realm of governance.

Distinguishing civil society from the state is easier than distinguishing it from the private realm. If civil society does not encompass the family, does it encompass neighbors or friends? Probably not. Conventionally, civil society has included "organized"—and in that sense intentional—entities.[35] Are religious identities voluntary and chosen or inherited and predetermined? Are religious formations? As I will suggest at greater length in this volume's conclusion, the distinction between inherited and voluntary may itself be the product of a particular historical moment and may have outlived its significance.

Transnational civil society resembles civil society but also differs from it. First and foremost, civil society is located "inside" states, and transnational civil society "outside." Both provide arenas for challenging states as well as cooperating with them.[36] Just as it is hard to know what should count as civil society, it is hard to establish criteria and parameters for transnational civil society. Candidates include: multinational production, service, and financial firms; Sufi *turuq* and the Pontifical Council for the Promotion of Christian Unity; human rights NGOs; terrorist, drug, and Mafia networks; satellite telecommunication companies.

The idea of transnational civil society, like the domestic variant, invokes resistant and polemical connotations, a space for self-conscious, organized actors to assert themselves for and against state policies, actions, and processes. It is this resistant and oppositional meaning that differentiates transnational civil society from the state cooperation that Hedley Bull designated as "international society." International society, like liberal regimes, was seen as taming and transcending the anarchy posited by neo-realists and creating the conditions for cooperation and conflict in world politics. It was a statelike entity, providing authoritative guarantees. Transnational civil society, by contrast, is a political realm, representing and mobilizing interests and opinions. The religious formations and movements that inhabit transnational civil society engage in the persuasion and collective action of world politics.

The sectors of transnational civil society—including the religion sector—and actors within sectors may conflict or cooperate. Stephen Toulmin invokes the British television serial *Upstairs, Downstairs* to characterize the situation at five major United Nations (UN) organized meetings, world summits, where NGOs formed parallel forums to the official gathering.[37] These occasions have displayed the new world politics on a well-lit stage. By its horizontal, global mobilization of opinion, the NGOs "downstairs" have broken the monopoly of states on the representation of domestic opinion. They bring world opinion to bear on "upstairs," the assembly of official state actors. It so happens that at recent global summits they have cooperated more with each other than they have engaged in conflict.[38] The need for a common front if state-drafted resolutions were to reflect NGO preferences provided a powerful incentive to find and articulate common positions.

However, we cannot assume that transnational nonstate space, transnational civil society, will be "civil." Entities bound by differing norms and interests will not always have strategic reasons to cooperate. Religious formations and movements may share analytic membership in a "religion" sector but will have good reasons to differ. Transnational pluralism is likely to result in both benign and nonbenign outcomes.[39]

Thinning Out Monopoly Sovereignty

Communities constituting transnational civil society may have authority and even power; they do not claim sovereignty. They have authority in that a formally organized religious transnational entity such as the Roman Catholic Church is in a position to license and de-license the activities of its organizational units in particular national sites, such as the National Councils of Bishops. An informally structured movement such as that of the West African Sufis is able to shape the transnational pilgrimages of its adherents across sacred territory; to satisfy, by negotiations with nation-states, its adherents' expectations and claims for free passage; and to regulate, via norms and conventional practice, the associated kinship transactions, market behaviors, and political demands.[40]

Religious networks and communities in domestic and transnational civil society render state claims to monopoly sovereignty problematic. This challenge is less familiar than the challenge from global markets in ideas as well as goods and services. It is now commonplace to show how markets, media, and telecommunications can create transnational arenas by forming networks and solidarities that circumvent the Westphalian state system with its emphasis on territoriality and sovereignty. Thousands of interveners in transnational space have the authority and power to provide an alternative to state activity, not replace it. The process being described here is not the collapse or demise of states but rather the thinning of their effect, function, and finality.

Transnational activity is guided by imaginary maps whose boundaries do not approximate the spaces depicted on political maps—for example, the (large) transnational realm of Catholic Christianity, or the (smaller) transnational realm of the Tijaniyya Sufis. Catholics and Sufis create arenas governed by considerations other than sovereignty. Such arenas do not replace or supersede political maps showing territorially defined states. We can imagine them as transparent plastic overlays, alternative meaning systems superimposed upon the meaning system of political maps. They do not replace state-defined space; they provide alternatives to it. In the nineteenth and twentieth centuries nation-states tried to make the overlays coincide. Ethnic cleansing in Bosnia and Rwanda are merely the pathological expressions of a more general impulse to coordinate linguistic community, religious community, and ethnic community. Such efforts seem increasingly atavistic.

I use the metaphor of plastic overlays as a counter to the zero-sum metaphors that often characterize the challenge that transnational forces offer the state. "The state is waning" suggests that it will vanish and be replaced by other forms of political organization. More likely is a progressive contraction of state activities and claims that would allow nongovernmental phenomena to share functions and meaning now monopolized by states. What this suggests is less a waning of states than a more complex set of interrelations in which rival identities and structures jostle the state. New alliances and goals become possible as domestic civil society joins up with transnational civil society to challenge states and as states in concert employ elements in transnational civil society to limit particular states' sovereignty.

Hierarchy and Self-Organization

Hierarchy and self-organization, the terms used to order the contributions to this volume, derive their meaning from the theory and practice of polity, economy, and organization. Hierarchy invokes rationalization, centralization, and authority from above and can be found in the formal organization of civil society and the state. Self-organization invokes decentralized spontaneity, self-made affinity groups, and agency from below.[41] Hierarchy and self-organization provide the conceptual framework for the diversity of relationships that religious formations introduce in the space between civil society and the state.

Because hierarchical organization exercises control from the top, it can maximize resources by concentration and coordination. But because it tends to require the maintenance of heavy organizational overheads, it is less adaptable to new circumstances and particular locales. When hierarchical structures claim to control and speak for large constituencies, they can act as more powerful counterplayers to states, but they also offer more visible and accessible targets for states seeking to control or officialize societal groupings.

Self-organization, in contrast, implies decentralization and spontaneity rather than centralization and control. Contrary to the concentration promoted by hierarchy, it can entail a dispersal of resources. But this very dispersion reduces costs of entry. It allows amateurs easily to replicate casual organizational forms and to adapt them to locale and circumstance. Ideas and practice diffuse by a kind of capillary action that states may find harder to track, control, and destroy.

Transnational religion makes its appearance in many forms, is propagated by a variety of processes, and generates malign and benign consequences. Our contributors illustrate the range of the possibilities.

Self-Organization: From Society and from Below

Dale Eickelman's account in this volume of Islamic transnationalism, "Trans-state Islam and Security," features the paradox of self-organized activity. Because of the ad hoc, self-made, and loosely structured forms of most Islamic societal organizations—the reverse of a coordinated "Comintern of Islam"—they penetrate deeply and widely and rely on strong commonalities across organizational and state boundaries. Do these Islamic organizations, in Lebanon, Egypt, Iran, Afghanistan, cooperate with each other? The commonalities, Eickelman suggests, are more the result of emulation than cooperation. Islamic activists attend cooperative events, international conferences, but they do so as much to enhance themselves in their locales as to coordinate or conspire with transnational actors. Local praxis replicates common organizational templates of philanthropic and welfare enterprises that facilitate the pious acts of virtuous Muslims and sometimes become the location of political activists. Their claims to solidarity are real and spawn financial and tactical support networks, but they do not spawn sustained cooperation or significant formal coordination.

In a reversal of conventional expectations that education and mass media will be bearers of rationalism and secularism, both forms of communication have strengthened Islamic commitments and commonalities. The proliferation of mass higher education in the 1960s, visible in Muslim as in other developing and developed countries, has created a flood of first-generation students, many of whom have repaired to religion as a way of understanding and supporting their status as educated persons and *nouveaux arrivés*. These young people, says Eickelman, have reimagined religion in ways that replace traditional religious specialists and their formal representation of Islam with simple, easily accessible, attractive, and cheap books, magazines, and cassettes. They consume and communicate in colloquial Arabic rather than the formal medium of the older-style scholars.

In "Bridging the Gap Between Empowerment and Power in Latin America," Daniel Levine and David Stoll report the shift from transnational religious initiative from the top to local structures and networks generated from below. Highly visible transnational actors—liberation Catholics of the left, Evangelicals of the right—transported religious formations to Latin America and across national frontiers within Latin America in ways that paralleled cleavages in the cold war conflict. These transnationally propelled activities for a time led observers to underestimate the role of local and autonomous agency in the spread of religious doctrine and practice.

Latin American Catholicism rests on five hundred years of transnational proselytizing that was deeply intertwined with the colonial experience and the export of culture from Spain and Portugal. In the post–World War II era, the generous social message of Vatican Council II and the more liberal thrust of the Latin American Episcopal Conference (CELAM) effected significant changes in the social base of the Church. The translation into local languages of the liturgy and the encouragement of Bible reading and lay participation created conditions hospitable to the spread of liberation Catholicism and the decentralized and self-ministering networks of base ecclesial communities (CEBs). Catholicism itself became not only a religion for below but also from below.

The Protestant presence in Latin America, which has not only challenged Latin American Catholicism but also moved into the local spaces and religious habits created by liberationism, has grown strikingly, with the number of churches nearly doubling from 28,000 to 54,000 from 1953 to 1985. Whereas prewar Protestantism grew out of European missions, the postwar expansion was encouraged by the entry of U.S. evangelical and Pentecostal churches into the ground that mainline Protestantism had abandoned. Most of the new missions were North American, and they came to fight both communism and the "whore of Babylon." But a focus on televangelism and on U.S. proselytizers can be misleading in attempts to evaluate the significance of the Protestant resurgence. Levine and Stoll write of religion from below as spreading through an "available demography" of mobile persons moving from rural to urban settings and into literacy and education, or stationary rural peoples receiving soteriological communications together with economic intrusions. As Eickelman does in the case of Islam, Stoll and Levine emphasize the casual nature of organizational structures. Such informal networks are easy for amateurs to create and serviceable for the immediate needs of the faithful. They give Evangelicalism its competitive strength and diffusionary power.

Levine and Stoll are more cautious than an earlier generation of social scientists that expected much from Latin American religion from below. This religiosity can create "social capital," laying the foundation for further changes in society and politics. But there are limits on the effectiveness of religion from below. Self-ministered religiosity can empower and spread easily. But without connections to higher and more formal policy levels in civil society and the state, these networks may fail to generate consequential social change.

In Ousmane Kane's "Muslim Missionaries and African States," West African Sufis are found to occupy autonomous space in transnational civil society, but they are also intertwined with states. Regarded by the French colonial state as the embodiment of dangerous pan-Islamic tendencies, the Tijaniyya *tariqa* nevertheless made its peace with that state. The marabouts, spiritual leaders of the Sufi orders, replaced earlier kings as intermediaries between the colonial state and society. They increased their economic power as well as the reach of Islam. The Tijaniyya spiritual influence stretches from Morocco across the Senegambia region and on to Nigeria, with regional and local *zawiyas* sending disciples to the parent *zawiya* at the holy cities of Kano (Nigeria) and Kaolack (Senegal). The movement's transnational sacred geography is concretized by pilgrimage, trade, markets, and marriage networks enabled by sacred cities and by the birthday celebrations of the prophet and of a *tariqa*'s spiritual leader. Its engagement with states is confirmed through the electoral support it offers ruling governments, support that is reciprocated through extraterritorial privileges—customs exemptions, autonomy of holy cities, scholarships to foreign universities for the faithful, and loans.

Sufi *zawiyas*, like other Islamic informal organizations, address issues of physical and cultural survival in contexts where state infrastructure is uneven or weak. They provide both forms of security through centers that offer multiple services, the transmission of religious knowledge, refuge to fugitives, help to the indigent, and political support. *Zawiya* networks provide civil society's hedge against personal insecurity, communal violence, and chaos. The predictable symbolic and economic sociability of the Tijaniyya presents a sharp contrast to the utter collapse of sociocultural networks in parts of East Africa in the mid-1990s.

In "Faces of Catholic Transnationalism: In and Beyond France," Danièle Hervieu-Léger reveals the new, informal, homemade face that is displacing the formal, catechized, and bureaucratized visage of an older Catholicism. She points to a number of contradictory tendencies. On the one hand, we see the decline of the parish and the local *clocher*, of the intimate universe that organized the practicing Catholicism of the French, marked by the diminution of church attendance and clerical vocations. Their place is taken by wide-ranging, loosely structured affinity groups of enthusiastic and emotional young people traveling across state borders to World Youth Congresses, committed at the doctrinal level to a bland, generalized ethical commitment. On the other hand, the Church is moving to strengthen its hold and to universalize its organizational structure. What continental scholars call "integralist" tendencies are on the increase, reasserting more conservative and stringent standards of canonical adherence. The two tendencies, the looser, self-made Catholicism of affinity groups and the growth of a more centralized pattern, represent alternative forms of globalization.

Hierarchy: From a Center and from Above

Ralph Della Cava's "Religious Resource Networks: Roman Catholic Philanthropy in Central and East Europe" is the quintessential account of religious formation from the top, from a center, and via formal organization. He not only demonstrates the workings of religion from above but also argues that "autonomous" and "spontaneous" religious NGOs are heavily and increasingly dependent on sponsors in the developed world. His argument is buttressed by his representation of the ways in which the Holy See, a multiplicity of lay-directed European and American philanthropic organizations, and the German episcopate reached out to the East European churches before and after the decline of communism. The story reveals the Catholic Church's vast and intricately complex bureaucracies—the German *Kirche in Not* alone could function as the department of welfare of a respectable state. The complexity reflects the pluralistic world over which the See of Peter presides.

The conduct of Catholic Ostpolitik from the Danube to Vladivostok posed delicate diplomatic issues for the Church as its multiple but coordinated players approached the states of Eastern Europe and Russia after World War II. The iron curtain proved more porous to church exchanges, and communist states proved more inclined to make concessions, than was then admitted by a Church seen as single-mindedly opposed to godless communism. The more recent, post-1980 encounter in the former Soviet Union between an expanding Rome and Russian Orthodoxy raises questions concerning the relationship between religious and political territoriality. The monopoly of the Orthodox Church, promoted by its earlier alliance with the communist state, is threatened by the new openness to religious diversity. The Russian state, like the East Asian states reviewed by Baker, favors religions that are well insulated from outside influences.

In "World Religions and National States: Competing Claims in East Asia," Don Baker discusses the dirigiste efforts of East Asian states to deny and render invisible domestic religions from below while privileging world religions from above. This policy derives, on the one hand, from an internationally available post-Enlightenment discourse that declares some religions to be superstitious and others not, and, on the other hand, from the propensity of East Asian states to subsume religion. Baker reviews the ways in which external agency has forced Asian states to grant religious freedoms and the uneven distribution of such freedoms across religions. The path to religious autonomy in China, Japan, and Korea was forged by imperialist intruders who established enclaves of extraterritoriality. At the end of the nineteenth century the European powers extracted the privilege of noninterference with their religions and the right to proselytize. With the end of overt European domination, East Asian countries supported freedom of religion as a marker of modern respectability in the world system of states.

The religions that East Asian states are willing to register and recognize for purposes of religious freedom include "world" religions and exclude "unevolved" popular religions, those without high-culture trappings, "scriptures," and recognizable organizational attributes. Thus, in China, Protestantism, Catholicism, Buddhism, Taoism, and Islam are acceptable but "shamanism" and "folk religion" are not. Indigenous privileging of the religions of the intellectuals coincides with evolutionary history and social science classifications that are the legacy of colonial and neocolonial cultural transmission.

These principles of recognition give transnational religions ambiguous significance. They are viewed positively as the bearers of triumphant modern norms and the doctrines and organization of consequential world orders. They are viewed negatively when they contest the monopoly of states accustomed to subsuming religion. The preference for organized religions from above, says Baker, over spontaneous and informal practices below may be dictated by political prudence as much as by a cultural aesthetic. Organized religion is easier to keep track of and control.

In "Globalizing Catholicism and the Return to a 'Universal' Church," José Casanova, addressing the oldest of the Western transnational religions, emphasizes religion from above and the expanding space of transnational civil society. Central to the story is the history of the waning and subsequent revival of Catholic universalism. The claims of the medieval Church to articulate a universal moral realm fell victim to the rise of the nation-state and the consequent nationalization of churches. The Church's adaptation to nation-states protected the faithful and their space to practice religion, but it did so at the cost of upholding universal norms. The settlements with Mussolini and Hitler represented extreme adaptation, whereas the relatively informal exchanges with the East European communist regimes revealed a more moderate accommodation.

The trend is now reversed, claims Casanova. In the post–World War II discourses of the Church, the increasingly robust Catholic defense of human rights contrasts with the earlier, narrow defense of the needs of the faithful. Vatican II's Declaration on Religious Freedom as well as John XXIII's vigorous espousal of universal human rights heralded a shift from *libertas ecclesiae* to *libertas personae*. The Church, Casanova argues, has shown itself prepared to assert freedom of religion in the face of state sovereignty and *raison d'état,* as in its challenges to the authoritarianism of Franco, Marcos, and the rulers of Poland (although the pope's equivocal retrospect in June 1996 on the Catholic Church's inaction with respect to the fate of the German Jews suggests that a few older reticences persist). This process, Casanova argues, has not only made the Church the "First Citizen of Global Civil Society" but also has returned Rome to what he calls the North Atlantic Protestant capitalist system from which it had become alienated.

Cary Fraser's "In Defense of Allah's Realm: Religion and Statecraft in Saudi Foreign Policy Strategy" is an examination of the strategies adopted by Saudi Arabia in its maneuvers for leadership in the Middle East. Here, religion is treated as a resource in interstate competition rather than as a realm in civil society or an autonomous meaning system. Iran exploits the affinity feelings of the Shiite diaspora in Lebanon, Iraq, and Saudi Arabia and the contagious enthusiasm for a radical Islam in order to enhance its international capacities. Saudi Arabia contests Iran's primacy by exploiting its control of Mecca, its standing as guardian of the holy places of Islam, and its representation, via Wahhabi Islam, of an older Islamic legitimacy.

The account is situated in the context of a familiar balance-of-power story in which civil society hardly makes an appearance. All the actors are maximizing states using whatever resources they can—oil prices, support for the PLO, pro- or antimonarchical sentiments, alliances with superpowers, Shia or Sunni affiliation—to enhance their respective interests.

The 1950s and 1960s witnessed a cleavage in the Middle East between pan-Arabist powers and their opponents. The post–World War II modernizers, Gamal Abdel Nasser, Saddam Hussein, and Anwar Sadat, led the secular, antimonarchical, "socialist," anti-Western, and often pro-Soviet pan-Arabism. They faced Islamist, monarchical, anti-Soviet, often Western-allied forces led by the Gulf kingdoms, with Saudi Arabia at their head. The

Iranian Revolution, Fraser argues, redefined the rules of play. The older cleavage was partly superseded by a new one between radical Islam, led by Iran, and conservative Islam, led by Saudi Arabia. These contestants fill the space left vacant by the decline of pan-Arabism's main exponent, Egypt, which suffered Nasser's death, defeat by Israel, and expulsion from the Arab League after signing the Camp David accords.

Fraser's is not an account designed to support the view that Islam is a solitary force marching against the West or that religion is a variable capable of predicting alliances. The Saudi dependence on the West for arms and financing, the Iraqi forces' dependence on the West in the Iran-Iraq War, and the anti-Iraqi forces' dependence on the West in the war over Kuwait together suggest that Islamic states ally across religious/civilizational lines and represent anything but a united civilizational front.

The contributions to this volume do not forecast a more likely future or more successful prospects for hierarchy or self-organization. They suggest that transnational civil society is made up of highly diverse forms that need to be understood and theorized with the nuance and complexity appropriate to a crucial new arena of action.

NOTES

1. Churches may be the oldest creators of civil society in the West. One is reluctant to assert that they have universally had such a role because the very notion of civil society is often considered a product of liberal Western thought. Don Baker's essay in this volume, "World Religions and National States: Competing Claims in East Asia," suggests that the society-state dichotomy is not a "natural" or universal conceptualization. For a discussion of the uses of the concept of civil society, see my concluding essay.

2. "The new mass clientele for Protestant missionary activity ... [arises from] the creation of converging trends in demography, social mobility, and the continuing appeal of religions that stress an intense spiritual life. Dramatic population shifts and accelerated urbanization have drawn Latin Americans to the cities while opening rural life to the outside world via expanded transport and communications." Daniel H. Levine, "The Latin American Experience of Transnational Religious Activism" (paper prepared for the SSRC Conference on Transnational Muslim Missionary Movements, University of Aberystwyth, Wales, October 1992), 8.

3. R. B. J. Walker, *Inside/Outside: International Relations as Political Theory* (Cambridge, England: Cambridge University Press, 1993).

4. This formulation does not make a distinction between ideas and practice but assumes that concept and praxis implicate each other.

5. See Peter Haas, "Introduction: Epistemic Communities and International Policy Coordination," special issue of *International Organization* 46 (1) (Winter 1992):1–35. The general omission of religious movements from the category of such epistemic communities is presumably a replication of the pervasive enlighten-

ment conceit that draws boundaries between "rationalist" and "affective," between positive and imagined, between ascriptive and voluntaristic. For a theoretical critique of these distinctions, see my concluding essay.

6. Stephen D. Krasner, "Structural Causes and Regime Consequences: Regimes as Intervening Variables" in *International Regimes,* edited by Stephen D. Krasner (Ithaca: Cornell University Press, 1983); and Robert O. Keohane, *After Hegemony: Cooperation and Discord in the World Political Economy* (Princeton: Princeton University Press, 1984).

7. Robert D. Kaplan, "The Coming Anarchy," *Atlantic Monthly,* February 1994. The authors of this volume find the positive, motivating, and cooperative impact of religion as significant as it is negative, divisive, and conflictual. By contrast, Kaplan's undiscriminating view of ethnicity and religion, born especially of his perception of conflict in Africa, strikes a single note; all mobilizations are assigned to the negative column. Yet it is precisely the variable potential of religious and ethnic formations that needs to be investigated. For an account that is also pessimistic but more discriminating about Africa and does not assume that Africa is the world, see Aristide Zolberg, "The Specter of Anarchy: African States Verging on Dissolution," *Dissent,* Summer 1992.

8. Although Europeans no longer constituted a majority at the time of Vatican II, two-thirds of the college of Cardinals was still Italian. See José Casanova, "Globalizing Catholicism and the Return to a 'Universal' Church," in this volume.

9. For recent figures, see James Brooke, "Pragmatic Protestants Winning Converts in Brazil," *New York Times,* July 4, 1993. For accounts of this growth, see David Martin, *Tongues of Fire: The Explosion of Protestantism in Latin America* (London: Basil Blackwell, 1990); David Stoll, *Is Latin America Turning Protestant?* (Berkeley: University of California Press, 1992); and David Stoll and Virginia Burnett, eds., *Rethinking Protestantism in Latin America* (New York: Columbia University Press, 1993).

10. Nicholas Kristof, "Christianity Is Booming in China Despite Rifts," *New York Times,* February 7, 1993.

11. Diane L. Eck, "In the Name of Religions," *Wilson Quarterly* 17 (4) (Autumn 1993):99. These figures and estimates were gathered by the Pluralism Project of Harvard University's Committee on the Study of Religion. See also James Brooke, "Attacks on U.S. Muslims Surge, Even As Their Faith Takes Hold," *New York Times,* August 28, 1995. Philip Lewis provides an account for Britain in *Islamic Britain: Religion, Politics, and Identity Among British Muslims* (London: I. B. Tauris, 1994).

12. Dale F. Eickelman, "National Identity and Religious Discourse in Contemporary Oman," *International Journal of Islamic and Arabic Studies* 6 (1) (1989):1–20.

13. Discussants from Latin America participating in meetings held to produce this volume viewed the mission of this group suspiciously insofar as "security" was said to be part of its interests.

14. See, for example, David A. Baldwin's review essay and the volumes he reviews, "Security Studies and the End of the Cold War," *World Politics* 48 (October 1995):117–141.

15. See Stockholm International Peace Research Institute (SIPRI) figures for casualties in domestic wars in twenty-nine countries. The figures are topped by wars in

Sudan (37,000 to 40,000), Angola (122,000), Tajikistan (20,000 to 50,000), and Guatemala (46,000). The compilation does not cite years but acknowledges that these figures are in some cases cumulative over decades. Cited in *Time International*, October 9, 1995, 20.

16. The formulation of the security problems in terms of physical and cultural survival or extinction is borrowed from Lloyd I. Rudolph.

17. Daniel Levine, "Transnational Religious Regimes in Latin America: Social Capital, Empowerment, Symbols, and Power" (working draft presented at the SSRC Working Group on Transnational Religious Regimes, New York, October 1993). This was an early draft of the chapter in this volume by Daniel Levine and David Stoll.

18. The Communist Party of India (Marxist) is debating whether its local cadres should be censured for participating in, even organizing, the festival activities for Goddess Durga, which are a pervasive feature of the October festival season in Bengal, stronghold of the communists in India. The proponents of participation argue that not doing so is to lose a central means of communicating with the people. *Statesman* (New Delhi), October 9, 1995. For interesting neo-Marxian approaches that read religion as a language articulating the life-situation of believers, see writings by Indian historians in the "subaltern" tradition who attempt a new understanding of nineteenth- and twentieth-century "communalism": Gyan Pandey, *The Construction of Communalism in Colonial North India* (Oxford: Delhi, 1990), Shahid Amin, "Gandhi as Mahatma: Gorakhpur District, Eastern UP, 1921–2," in *Selected Subaltern Studies*, edited by Ranajit Guha and Gayatri Chakravorty Spivak (New York: Oxford University Press, 1988).

19. David Stoll, *Is Latin America Turning Protestant?*, 13. For an earlier account, see Emilio Willems, *Followers of the New Faith* (Nashville, TN: Vanderbilt University Press, 1967). The same religious orientations may be associated with a variety of practices, from quietism to activism. Today's Pentecostalism, speaking in tongues and recommending faith healing, may recommend tomorrow the cultivation of self-discipline and the will to seize one's fate. Nineteenth-century Evangelical fundamentalism in Great Britain underwent a shift toward "a social theology that made less of biblical doctrines of inherent personal sinfulness, guilt and divine punishment . . . whilst making more of practical service to others through the discipline of hard work as self-denial." Gerald Studdert-Kennedy, "The Imperial Elite," review of Clive Dewey, *Anglo-Indian Attitudes: The Mind of the Indian Civil Service* (London: Hambledon Press, 1993) in *Economic and Political Weekly*, July 9, 1994, 1722.

20. Ousmane Kane, "Muslim Missionaries and African States," in this volume.

21. Jürgen Habermas, *The Theory of Communicative Action*, vol. 2, *Lifeworld and System: A Critique of Functionalist Reason* (Boston: Beacon Press, 1984–1985), 400.

22. William McNeill, "Project Report: Fundamentalism and the World of the 1990s," *Bulletin of the American Academy of Arts and Sciences* 47 (3) (December 1993):29. For earlier discussions of assimilation in American life, see Milton M. Gordon, *Assimilation in American Life: The Role of Race, Religion, and National Origins* (New York: Oxford University Press, 1964); Nathan Glazer and Daniel Patrick Moynihan, *Beyond the Melting Pot: The Negroes, Puerto Ricans, Jews, Italians, and*

Irish of New York City (Cambridge, MA: MIT Press, 1963); and Will Herberg, *Protestant, Catholic, Jew: An Essay in American Religious Sociology* (Chicago: University of Chicago Press, 1983). For a discussion of the role of cultural extinction in separatist movements, see Lloyd I. Rudolph, "India and the Punjab: A Fragile Peace," in The Asia Society, *Asian Issues 1985: Asian Agenda Report 3* (Lanham, MD: University Press of America, 1986).

23. Religious pluralism may have thrived in part because religion was too serious an aspect of life to be assigned to the private realm, a condition that homogenizing solutions encourage.

24. McNeill, "Project Report," 29–30. For an extended discussion of this type of pluralism, see Benjamin Braude and Bernard Lewis, eds., *Christians and Jews in the Ottoman Empire: The Functioning of a Plural Society*, 2 volumes (New York: Holmes and Meier, 1982), especially the introduction and the essay by Benjamin Braude. For a proposal to institutionalize a form of *millets*, or religious federalism, in India, see Partha Chatterjee, "Secularism and Toleration," *Economic and Political Weekly* 29 (28) (July 9, 1994):1768–1778.

25. For formulations in this and the next two sections, I have drawn extensively on Lloyd I. Rudolph's discussion of civil society in *Political Science* 518, "Rethinking Sovereignty," Graduate Seminar, University of Chicago, Winter 1995.

26. Stephen Toulmin, "The UN and Japan in an Age of Globalization: The Role of Transnational NGOs in Global Affairs" (paper written for a forthcoming, as yet untitled volume of the Peace Research Institute of International Christian University, Tokyo, October 1994).

27. Neorealism emphasizes an institutional version of radical individualism in which each state relies upon its own devices and balances of power provide hope for stability. "A state has to rely on its own devices, the relative efficiency of which must be its constant concern." Kenneth Waltz, *Man, the State, and War: A Theoretical Analysis* (New York: Columbia University Press, 1959), 159. "[U]nits in a condition of anarchy . . . must rely on the means they can generate . . . for themselves. Self-help is necessarily the principle of action in an anarchic order." Kenneth Waltz, *Theory of International Politics* (Reading, MA: Addison-Wesley, 1979), 111. This emphasis is challenged by liberal institutionalism's assertion of conventions and rules: "Much behavior [in international politics] is recognized by participants as reflecting established rules, norms, and conventions, and its meaning is interpreted in light of these understandings." Robert Keohane, "Neo-Liberal Institutionalism: A Perspective on World Politics," in *International Institutions and State Power: Essays in International Relations Theory* (Boulder: Westview Press, 1989). Keohane's analysis continues to focus on states as the main actors but asserts a more rule-governed set of interactions than the radical statist individualism of the neorealists suggests. For the neoliberals, there is an immanent orderliness emerging from the experience of interaction and the convenience of expectable behavior.

28. For an interesting account of the new theoretical players on the epistemological scene of international affairs, see Alex Wendt, "Constructing International Politics: A Response to Mearsheimer," *International Security* 20 (1) (Summer 1995):71–81. See also Stephen D. Krasner, "Power, Politics, Institutions, and Transnational Relations," in Thomas Risse-Kappen, editor, *Bringing Transnational*

Relations Back In: Non-State Actors, Domestic Structures, and International Institutions, Cambridge University Press, Cambridge, England, 1995.

29. John G. Ruggie, "Territoriality and Beyond: Problematizing Modernity in International Relations," *International Organization* 47 (1) (Winter 1993):139–174. Ruggie's doomed flirtation with postmodernism in this essay is also theoretically interesting.

30. Ronnie D. Lipschutz, "Reconstructing World Politics: The Emergence of Global Civil Society," *Millennium: Journal of International Studies* 21 (3):390–391.

31. The medieval metaphor was launched by Hedley Bull under the title "the New Medievalism" as he tried to imagine alternatives to the nation-state system. Hedley Bull, *The Anarchical Society* (New York: Columbia University Press, 1977), 254–255. See also John G. Ruggie, "Continuity and Transformation in the World Polity: Toward a Neorealist Synthesis," *World Politics* 35 (2) (January 1983):273–274.

32. Bull, *The Anarchical Society,* 255. But, adds Bull, the promise was imperfect: "[I]f it were anything like the precedent of Western Christendom, it would contain more ubiquitous and continuous violence and insecurity than does the modern state system." Ubiquitous and continuous, probably; but body counts may be higher for modern warfare. Markus Fischer attempts to subsume the medieval model of international relations to the neorealist paradigm by showing that church discourses and practices that characterized inter- and trans-kingdom relations in the Christian world merely disguise the continuity of self-interested and conflictual motives that always have and always will characterize humankind. Markus Fischer, "Feudal Europe, 800–1300: Communal Discourse and Conflictual Practice," *International Organization* 46 (2) (Spring 1992):139–174.

33. Kenneth Pennington's discussions of shared sovereignty place the problem of state-centered monopoly sovereignty in perspective. See *The Prince and the Law, 1200–1600: Sovereignty and Rights in the Western Legal Tradition* (Berkeley: University of California Press, 1993), especially "Epilogue: The Sixteenth Century and Beyond."

34. José Casanova, "Globalizing Catholicism and the Return to a 'Universal' Church," in this volume.

35. Some would sort religion with "unintentional" entities. Weber provides an interesting introduction to this question when he allots "sects" to the intentional side of the divide and "churches" to the unintentional side. Whether the member has to qualify and be selected is Weber's crucial marker of intentionality. "The Protestant Sects and the Spirit of Capitalism," in *From Max Weber: Essays in Sociology,* edited by Hans Gerth and C. Wright Mills (New York: Galaxy, 1958), 302–322. But this is not an easy distinction to maintain in a day when old "churches," such as Islam or Hinduism, are erecting new qualification boundaries, or when Catholics have the choice of construing their faith according to *Opus Dei* or Liberation Catholicism.

36. In a pre-Grotian world, before political theorists diverged on whether they would regard states or individuals as *the* moral entities of international relations, it was ambiguous as to who the actors were that constituted international society—princes, *res publicae, civitates.* Bull, *The Anarchical Society,* 29.

37. Stephen Toulmin, personal communication. Also his "The Role of Transnational NGOs."

38. Professor Carolyn Elliott of the University of Vermont, in an unpublished report on the Beijing conference on women, contrasts the coordination and consensus at Beijing with the internal conflicts visible at Mexico City, the first UN conference on women. "Women of the world have learned to work together. The shouting matches between women—Arabs and Palestinians, South Africans and Africans, American feminists and Third World critics—that dominated Mexico City were virtually absent in Beijing. Nor was there division between regions of the world." "Elliott Travel Letter," unpublished personal communication, October 1, 1995.

39. For an account that emphasizes the possibilities for incivility as well as for change arising out of "a marked increase in the number of spontaneous collective actions," see James N. Rosenau, *Turbulence in World Politics: A Theory of Change and Continuity* (Princeton: Princeton University Press, 1990), 369. Also Sidney Tarrow, "Eastern European Social Movements: Globalization, Difference, and Political Opportunity" (unpublished manuscript).

40. See Ousmane Kane, "Muslim Missionaries and African States," in this volume.

41. The idea of self-organization has been used as a metaphor to refer to market behavior. Paul Krugman, "City Spaces: Chicago and Los Angeles" (lecture at Dean's Symposium, Social Sciences Division, University of Chicago, April 21, 1995). Krugman used the metaphor to suggest how a series of uncoordinated decisions and acts created the outcome that is each of these cities. I use it here to invoke the spontaneity presumed to characterize market behavior without, however, assuming that the play of spontaneous pluralities produces mutually satisfactory equilibrium outcomes. Like critics of markets, I give equal emphasis to the socially and individually negative effects of market failures.

PART ONE

Self-Organization: From Society and from Below

ONE

Trans-state Islam and Security

DALE F. EICKELMAN

Religious transnationalism has long been part of the Middle East and the Muslim world. Modern forms of travel and communication have accelerated religious transnationalism—the flow of ideologies, access to information on organizational forms and tactics, and the transformation of formerly elite movements to mass movements—rendering obsolete earlier notions of frontier as defined primarily by geographical boundaries.

Islam and Political Activism: Past and Present

Partially in response to political and ideological developments in nineteenth-century Europe, a pan-Islamic movement developed in the late nineteenth century and continues in modified form to the present.[1] Most such movements were initially confined to the educated elite, although this elite claimed to speak for all Muslims. In contrast to older forms of religious movements, including those of the religious brotherhoods that were viewed with caution by colonial officers, the early pan-Islamic movements showed some resemblance to European nationalist movements.[2] In the Middle East in the nineteenth century, French Catholic and American Protestant missionaries opened religious schools in the Levant, and from the 1880s onward, the Alliance Israélite Universelle sent its emissaries throughout North Africa and the Ottoman Empire.[3] Although the work of these missionary enterprises was aimed, respectively, at Christians and Jews, these "minority" communities were widely distributed geographically in the nineteenth century, so that foreign involvement with them had a significant and pervasive impact on the region's Muslim majority. Moreover, these religious missions took place within a wider framework of economic hegemony and political domination in which foreign powers actively sought to protect the interests of Jews and Christians.

By the 1920s and 1930s, Muslim religious movements such as Egypt's Society of Muslim Brothers began to acquire large followings and to develop distinctly modern forms of organization.[4] The Muslim Brotherhood (*Ikhwan al-Muslimin*), Egypt's first genuine twentieth-century organized mass political movement, never fully recovered from the crippling wave of mass arrests and imprisonment instigated by Gamal Abdel Nasser in 1954. Indeed, repression of the movement under Nasser discredited its moderate elements and paved the way for alternative, more radical, religious movements that recruited a generation of younger militants unwilling to compromise with state authorities.[5]

For religious activists, Nasser's prisons and prison camps remain vivid metaphors for the moral bankruptcy of existing governments. In recent years Egypt's Muslim Brotherhood and similar movements elsewhere have regained strength, in no small part due to external private and state support from Saudi Arabia and other Arab Gulf states. However, whatever the radical past of the Muslim Brothers in Egypt and in Jordan, they now constitute the moderate wing of religious activism.

Since the late 1970s, Islamic activisms—in the plural, for these movements are multiple and overlapping—have widened in appeal and shifted in form. Their structure and the basis for their appeal are obscured by labeling them all simply as "fundamentalist" or "radical." They are the result of both conceptual innovations and emerging networks for communication and action that affect virtually all Muslims and profoundly shape the direction of contemporary Muslim thought. Some groups are led by what Olivier Roy disparagingly calls "micro-intellectuals," charismatic individuals largely self-trained as religious intellectuals and who thus constitute a sharp break with the formally trained religious authorities (*'ulama*) of an earlier generation.[6] Other scholars, notably Yves Gonzalez-Quijano, suggest that such self-trained religious intellectuals may be actors in newly emerging religious and symbolic fields. Gonzalez-Quijano argues that the rapidly growing popularity of mass-marketed "Islamic" books—inexpensive, attractively printed texts that take advantage of modern printing technologies and graphics and are accessible to a readership that lacks the literary skills of the educated elite of an earlier era—may be ignored or discounted by traditional intellectual elites because they are trapped within the existing episteme, or symbolic field of possible and imagined discourse.

Islamic activism, notwithstanding its adherents' claims of wishing to restore a "pristine" Islam, is a distinctively modern phenomenon. As such, its appeal is wider than that of the militant secular leftist and nationalist movements that pervaded much of the Middle East and North Africa through the 1960s. More so than secular leftists, its leaders and intellectuals address audiences in writings and in speech in a religious language and style more widely accessible than that used by state authorities.[7] For the "new" Islamic intellectuals and their audiences, these forms rather than sacred texts become central to the religious and political imagination.

There are structural affinities among many activist leaders; most have strongly local roots and act in specific regional and national settings. Examples include Juhayman al-'Utaybi, who led the siege of the Great Mosque of Mecca in November 1979, and Muhammad Marwa ("Ya Tatsine"), the charismatic leader of the uprising in Kano, Nigeria, in December 1980, which resulted in over 4,000 deaths.[8] Algeria's Islamic Salvation Front (Front Islamique du Salut, FIS), formed in February 1989 and declared illegal in March 1992, remained less a unified party than a cluster of loosely associated groups declaring a common goal—the creation of an Islamic state—but subject to schisms because of disagreement over methods, leadership, and what an "Islamic state" might imply.[9] The August 1994 claim of one Algerian group to have established a caliphate in Algeria—an institution formally abolished in Turkey in 1924—only highlights the inherent limits to the universalist claims of radical groups.[10]

The rise in religious activism and militancy since the 1980s has occurred in the context of rapid population growth, worsening economic conditions (including growing perceived inequalities between rich and poor), the stress of accelerated population shifts from rural to urban areas, and the inability of most states of the region to provide adequate housing, health care, and social services. Specific political events, especially the 1967 Arab-Israeli War, contributed heavily to discrediting secular nationalist movements. Although enthusiasm for Iran's 1978–1979 Islamic Revolution had only limited appeal outside of Iran, the idea of an Islamic revolution indicated the wide appeal of an Islamic vocabulary to articulate popular political sentiment. The leaders of some countries, notably Morocco, skillfully co-opt the language and goals of Islamic activism, but the leadership of most countries is less successful in this task.[11]

Islamists claim that they base their lives on core values that have been neglected or ignored by state authorities and established political elites, and in some cases they provide services and support where the state does not and thus buttress the claim that they, not the state, can offer an Islamic justice. In many places—Egypt,[12] Algeria,[13] the popular quarters of Casablanca,[14] the West Bank and Gaza,[15] Kuwait under Iraqi occupation,[16] and Uzbekistan's Ferghana Valley[17]—Islamist groups have provided and in some cases continue to provide basic health and welfare services, housing, even employment opportunities. In some regions, including the Ferghana Valley and Israel's occupied territories, Islamist groups—not the state—provide security against crime, or at least offer "protection" services that merchants and entrepreneurs view as imprudent to refuse.

The rising influence of Islamic political activism occurs at a time when the consequences of an earlier wave of "modernization," notably the widened base of mass higher education, with its implications for a wider political mobilization than prevailed in the past, have taken hold. In contrast to fundamentalist movements in the United States, Islamic activism appeals significantly to the first generation of Muslim youth in the Middle East and Central Asia to have benefited from mass higher education. For most of the Muslim world, mass higher education is a recent phenomenon. In the Middle East, for example, mass education began in earnest only in the 1950s, largely after Egypt's 1952 revolution. Fifteen to twenty years later, large numbers of students had begun to complete the advanced educational cycles, and it is at this point that the consequences of mass education for religious and political action become discernible. In Egypt, the number of primary school pupils more than doubled in the decade following the 1952 revolution. Corresponding increases in secondary and university education began in the mid-1960s. The timing of educational expansion varies for other parts of the Middle East, but throughout the region it has been associated with a rise in religious activism.[18]

Mass higher education in the Muslim world—by which I mean states with a Muslim majority population—has led to a reimagining of religion and politics. Among the implications of this reimagination is that religiously committed activists have replaced traditionally educated religious scholars as sources of authority, so that in both religious and secular matters, patterns of authority have become more diffuse and open. Second, religion has implicitly been systematized and objectified in the popular imagination, making it self-contained and facilitating innovation. Finally, the greater access to education, like access to the mass media, has broadened senses of language and community. Just as the rise of written vernacular languages in Europe since the sixteenth century and the spread of print technology created language communities wider than those of face-to-face interactions, mass education (and mass communications) has played such a role in the contemporary Arab world, transcending the narrow bases of local communities and dialects and creating new bases of religious and ethnic affinity.[19] As Richard Cottam notes, at the time of the British- and U.S.-managed coup d'état against Iran's Muhammad Musaddiq in 1953, no more than 10 percent of Iran's population was politicized.[20] Now that access to education has become almost universal for a younger generation, at least in urban areas, political awareness has significantly increased, lessening the prospects for success of the older pattern of covert foreign intervention, except in facilitating local actions. The repressive policies of many regimes in the Middle East and Central Asia continue to limit political participation and choice, but they cannot mitigate the heightened level of politicization.

In short, Islam is a powerful vehicle for expressing nationalist grievances against the West and for legitimizing opposition to oppressive domestic regimes. Islamist movements appeal especially to a younger, educated cohort, often from the lower middle class, whose social mobility—facilitated in earlier eras through labor migration and education—is increasingly blocked. Religious activism is growing in importance in such contexts, offering people a renewed sense of self and a framework for community action where states appear ineffective.[21] Ironically, activist leaders have often received a Western-style secular education and are familiar, if not comfortable, with Western-style institutions. The influence of religious activists is increasingly felt in the educational systems of the region and, as previously indicated, the ultimate accolade to their success is the effort by regimes in the Middle East and elsewhere to co-opt Islamist slogans and goals. Islamist political success is varied, but Islamist ideologies and activisms are too important for the regimes in Muslim-majority states to ignore.[22]

Variety and Cooperation Among Islamist Groups

All contemporary Islamic movements react to the Iranian Revolution, but none has followed its model of an Islamic revolution from above. The elites of some movements seek to enhance their stature by participating in international conferences, and some states, such as Sudan, pay the expenses of many participants, whose attendance (often accompanied by an honorarium) supports their claim to transnational Islamic credentials. Most radical leaders, though, have mainly regional support, which only occasionally transcends national boundaries. This accords considerable popular strength to activist movements, but it also constrains their expansion.

There is significant diversity in the structure, context, and support of Islamist groups. Some, such as Egypt's Muslim Brotherhood, have formal structures, but most do not transcend national boundaries as popular movements, as opposed to the tactical support, training, and facilities that the leadership of movements can offer to like-minded individuals and groups elsewhere. Thus many older members of Egypt's Muslim Brotherhood have strong ties with Saudi Arabia and the Gulf states, which offered economic and political refuge to many in the years of Nasser's persecution. Likewise, Bangladesh's Jama'at-i-Islami is formally autonomous but retains close ties with the movement's world headquarters in Punjab and appears to accept—although it does not publicly acknowledge—major donations from individuals and institutions in Saudi Arabia and elsewhere in the Gulf for its campaign for Islamicization.[23] In Europe and North America, first- and (to a lesser extent) second-generation immigrant communities offer better bases for the exchange of ideas and information than those available in countries of origin.[24] On August 7, 1994, for example, the Islamic Liberation Party (Hizb al-Tahrir al-Islami) filled greater London's Wembley Stadium with 12,000 people for an international conference that included many leading Islamic activists.[25] Since 1991, Moscow and, to a lesser extent, Istanbul, have played a similar role for Muslims of Central Asian origin.[26]

Public claims of solidarity between movements do not always indicate sustained cooperation. Just as with participation in international conferences, the intent is often to boost the prestige of leaders in specific national contexts. For example, in 1993 a video was circulating in Egypt and among Muslim communities as distant as New Zealand showing Ahmad Sayf al-Islam Hasan al-Banna, the son of Hasan al-Banna, the founder of Egypt's Muslim Brotherhood, preaching to the deportees from Israel's occupied territories in the no-man's-land in southern Lebanon. The presence of the religious leader among the deportees was not associated with any concerted concrete action among Egypt's Muslim Brotherhood to change the status of the deportees, but it sought to assert the international stature of al-Banna's son.[27]

Audiocassettes even more readily cross international boundaries than their video counterparts, although their presence is less a sign of direct intergroup cooperation than the popularity of topics and speakers who have developed a following large enough to allow modest profits to the informal network of kiosk vendors who distribute them. The importation of audiocassettes and videos into Arab countries is almost always prohibited, although clandestine trade in them is lively. It is through contacts in the West—mosques on Chicago's South Side, Tucson, Kansas City, and in London, Bradford, and Birmingham—that Muslim activists are likely to borrow from one another through face-to-face contacts and collect the literature of other like-minded groups. As with the short books and pamphlets that make up what Gonzalez-Quijano calls the "new" Islamic book, these cassettes are simple and direct in style.[28] They use a vivid, colloquial imagery rather than the more formal Arabic of most religious scholars and focus on everyday concerns, giving them a popularity unmatched by other forms of religious discourse. Easy access to photocopy machines and cassette duplicators renders censorship ineffective.[29] Indeed, censors can often be inadvertently subverted when mainstream magazines and newspapers publish content analyses of otherwise forbidden materials. The tone of the article may condemn the contents of radical cassettes or sermons, but many readers may be primarily interested in the content of the sermons, not the opinions of the journalist introducing them.[30]

Islamist groups often emulate one another's organizational forms and doctrines, although such emulation is usually not the product of formal alliances. Nationals studying in other countries formally or informally assimilate doctrines and organization, although such doctrines and organization quickly take on distinctly local forms. This was the case with Morocco's now outlawed Islamic Youth Movement (al-Haraka al-Shabiba al-Islamiya), formed after the 1967 Arab-Israeli War. Modeled in part on Egypt's Muslim Brotherhood and in part on traditional Sufi (mystical) religious orders, the movement had two elements—a public wing, which pursued educational and religious goals, and a "deniable" clandestine wing. The state indirectly supported this and other religious movements in the 1960s and early 1970s to counter the influence of the secular left. The Moroccan government, confident that it could co-opt and control the movement, infiltrated it through an exiled Syrian Muslim Brother working in Morocco as a consultant to a state-supported religious training center. He, in turn, had his daughter join the organization's women's branch.[31] Such experiences of security penetration intensify activist suspicions of transnational connections, and the fear of unwittingly incorporating government agents and provocateurs cripples the organizations' expansion. It was not only in Morocco that Islamist groups benefited from state support in earlier years. Regimes as diverse as those of Israel, Egypt, Jordan, and Algeria saw Islamic activism as a means to counter secular leftist influences, and until the early 1980s many Islamist groups benefited from state support or at least tolerance.[32]

Another example of influence through emulation or educational links that span generations is the formation of an Islamic movement among university students in Afghanistan. Although more than three decades old, the example still suggests how such movements spread. The first organized Islamist movement in Afghanistan, the Muslim Youth Movement (Sazman-i jawanan-i musulman), established at Kabul University in the late 1960s, owed much to advice from faculty members who in the 1950s had studied in Egypt, where they came into contact with the Muslim Brotherhood. These faculty members suggested to their students that they organize along similar lines to make Islam relevant to Afghanistan's political and social transformations and to counter the appeal of leftist student groups.[33]

The role of transnational "educational" missions cannot be sufficiently emphasized. Since late 1991, Turkish-speaking Muslim activists based in Germany, for example, have entered Uzbekistan and the other Central Asian republics as teachers of language and religion. They fund mosques, create religious study groups, and select promising Central Asian youth for further study and training in Germany.[34] Elsewhere, state sponsorship or private donations—notably from Saudi Arabia or the Gulf states—provide missionaries to West Africa and other parts of the Muslim world.[35]

Where formal political activity is strictly controlled, as in the Central Asian republics, religious groups and private voluntary organizations nonetheless often have considerable latitude. They can offer vital community health and welfare services, thus assuring community support and making it difficult for states to separate extremists from moderates.[36]

The clandestine side of activist movements is often modeled after traditional Sufi brotherhoods in which a "hidden" (*batin*) level of organization is legitimated by claims of a higher level of spirituality and commitment to the organization's goals. This use of traditional forms of religious legitimacy is why it is often difficult to separate the informal networks of religious adepts from those with radical political goals, the target of state security services throughout the region. A concurrent organizational template is a network of cells (*khalliyat*) modeled after Marxist organizations. This model is not surprising, as in some parts of the Muslim world former leftists form a significant part of radical Islamic movements: One survey indicates that 60 percent of Hamas activists in Gaza, for example, acknowledged prior membership in Marxist organizations.[37] Similarly, in Pakistan and Bangladesh, Muslim activists have been attracted by the "highly structured, cadre-based" organization of communist movements.[38]

There is a tacit symbiotic relationship between the secrecy of Islamic activist groups and repression by state security organizations. Most religious activists have good reason to fear state repression. On May 30, 1994, Omani authorities made the first of over 300 arrests, including government officials and several members of the security forces. Official sources claim that 47 of those arrested were senior members of the "Muslim Brotherhood structure," and these were among the 120 held in custody pending sentencing by both a State Security Court and a religious court on charges that include belonging to an illegal organization and *fitna*, or rebellion against established authority. Although there were early unofficial reports of arms caches, none had been found and at least some officials eventually acknowledged that none of those apprehended advocated violence. Three were eventually condemned to death on the charge of "misuse of Islam and its tolerant principles." The sentences, announced on November 12, were immediately commuted to life imprisonment.[39]

The Omani leaders of the Muslim Brotherhood movement had been recruited outside of Oman, notably in Britain, the United Arab Emirates, and Saudi Arabia, but especially in the United States and Egypt. An Omani from Dhufar, Oman's southern province, but living in Dubai began recruiting for the movement in the early 1980s. By 1987 he had managed to create an organization within Oman itself, drawing equally on northern and southern Omanis and thus obviating regional differences (although only a minority of those arrested appeared to be Ibadi Muslims, many of whom are located in Oman's northern interior). In Oman, the movement was governed by a council (*shura*) of fifteen members, under which was a six-member Executive Committee. The Executive Committee, in turn, was divided into committees, one of which was responsible for coordinating activities with Muslim Brothers in neighboring Gulf countries. Also under the Executive Committee were regional committees, each divided into "branches," which in turn were divided into cell-like "families" of up to fifteen members each. Recruitment followed a security-conscious process of talent spotting, cultivation, and training, making it difficult for the state to identify all of the movement's potential activists or supporters.[40]

Against such structures, the security forces of regimes coordinate their activities. This can take the form of European cooperation with the states of the region—as with French assistance in Saudi Arabia's internal security, including assistance in ousting dissidents from the Grand Mosque in Mecca in 1979[41]—and intraregional cooperation—such as the January 1989 agreement in Algiers between the interior ministers of the Maghrib states (Libya, Algeria, Tunisia, Mauritania, and Morocco) to coordinate their efforts against Islamic radicalism. The agreement was reconfirmed at a second meeting in Tunis in early January 1993.[42] Given shared networks of cooperation, training, socialization, and tactics, one can speak of a common "security culture" that overrides differences of language, religion, and nationality in dealing with opposition religious groups.[43]

Nonetheless, the lack of formal organizational hierarchy among many Islamist groups contributes to their survival. Lacking a formal chain of command, they are all the more difficult for state security services to disrupt. This appears to be the case for the Algerian groups that came together in 1989 to form the FIS coalition. The amorphousness of many activist groups, formed from networks of trusted neighborhood and school acquaintances and devoid of complex hierarchies, makes them difficult for security services even to monitor.[44]

Intergroup support is tactical and fluid. Lebanon's Hizbullah (Party of God) offers protection and facilities to its Turkish Kurd counterpart in the Beka'a Valley, although the financing of its military and publicity activities is unclear. A May 25, 1993, terrorist attack on the eve of discussions between the Turkish government and Turkish Workers Party (PKK), for which the PKK claimed responsibility in a news release from Lebanon, followed by the announcement of a "peace pact" between the PKK and the Turkish Hizbullah, called into question the identity of those responsible for the renewed terrorist attacks.[45] Following Algeria's January 1992 military coup that annulled the FIS victory in the December 1991 national elections, Moroccan security forces and French journalists noticed an upsurge in drug arrests in Morocco and southern France involving youth with declared FIS connections. Reports in the French press speculated that FIS activists, faced with severe repression by state security forces and the need to raise short-term cash, may have sought a tactical alliance with smugglers in Algeria.[46] Similarly, in August 1994 Moroccan security forces dismantled a terrorist network that had created caches of smuggled arms in Morocco and engaged in attacks against tourists. Some of the captured youth were linked to radical Muslim groups in France, and there was press speculation that elements of Algerian military intelligence may also have wanted to create a political crisis in Morocco at a time when a solution to the Western Sahara crisis appeared close at hand.[47]

Toleration, Repression, and Transnational Links

From the perspective of most Muslims in the Middle East and elsewhere, few religious organizations can be labeled either "moderate" or "radical." Saudi authorities, for example, label any group that challenges the regime's religious credentials as "incendiary" (su'ri) and "wickedly evil" (athimi), and similar groups in Oman have been convicted of fitna, a word with heavy religious overtones implying political and religious sedition.[48] Nonetheless, as "radical" movements seek to secure a broad base of popular support, they often become more moderate or at least come to represent themselves as such, so that a sociological profile of a group at an early stage may not necessarily represent it at later stages.

There is nothing particularly Islamic about the tendency of radical groups to moderate their tone and goals as they aspire to mainstream influence. In addition, as we have seen, many activist Islamic movements, like their counterparts in other world religions, have overlapping public and "clandestine" elements, some of which may be "deniable" or independent of any unified command structure. Thus Hamas in the occupied West Bank and Gaza can be viewed less as a single, coherent organization with a central command than a loosely organized movement in which several independent affinity groups compete with one another for leadership and support. Many of the activities of such groups involve social services and welfare and, as Denis Sullivan has shown for Egypt, many of these groups are sufficiently powerful and popular that they can effectively co-opt government officials entrusted with regulating them.[49] The basis of financing and support for these groups may appear less unusual if they are compared with those who support independence in Northern Ireland or who sustained Meier Kahane's Kach Party, whose supporters had been linked to violent acts under Israeli law but which continued to receive major private funding from Americans and Israeli supporters.[50] Until the 1990 Iraqi invasion of Kuwait, the London-based Committee for the Liberation of the Gulf—predominantly, if not exclusively, Shiite and anti-Saudi and probably run by Saudi dissidents—appears to have been funded first by Iran and subsequently by Iraq.[51] Its inactivity since 1990 suggests the extent to which such groups are dependent on external state funding or major private backing.

The flow of information among groups is rapid and decentralized and does not depend on postulating an Islamic "Comintern." Links between groups are usually forged by personal ties and are often subject to schisms and personal rivalries. Some states or private donors support groups intended to serve as international nodes—Egypt's Muslim Brotherhood, the World Muslim League in Saudi Arabia, and comparable organizations in Iran and Pakistan. They all share the goal of "re-Islamization" or intensified commitment to Islam, but the links are multiple, fluid, and subject to severance at short notice, as was the case during the Gulf War.[52]

State-Supported Sponsorship and Religious Violence

Transnational ideological and logistical support for radical groups that condone terrorism and assassination generally requires a secure, external, state-supported base. There are limiting cases. Areas of Lebanon not under effective governmental control, for example, offer safe havens for both religious and secular groups in neighboring countries—including the Armenian Asala, Hizbullah, and the Kurdish PKK. In Egypt security forces uncovered in 1993 a domestic clandestine arms factory linked with religious extremists and with cross-border smuggling links with Libya and Sudan.[53]

Such transnationalism need not, however, take the form of radicalism or violence. It usually connects militant groups with states or external groups seeking to enhance their influence and interests by supplying weak states with greater networks and increasing their powers and influence. Thus Saudi Arabia, Iran, Sudan, Libya, and Pakistan, and individuals and Islamic charities within these countries, have at various times supported activist Islamic movements elsewhere as a means of extending their own influence and interests. The line between the official sponsorship of radical groups and individual initiative is often difficult to discern, as the case of the wealthy Saudi businessman, Usama bin Laden, suggests. Bin Laden has financially supported "militant Islamic causes from Afghanistan to Algeria," and one Egyptian official accused the Saudi government of "benign neglect" toward the funding of religious "terrorists."[54] Official Saudi attitudes appear ambiguous.[55]

The manipulation of religious groups is not a monopoly of those who work against U.S. and European interests and those of supposedly liberal regimes in the Middle East. After the Soviet invasion of Afghanistan in 1979, Pakistan, Saudi Arabia, and the United States supported Afghan militants, recruiting and training mercenaries from other Muslim countries—including Egypt, Algeria, Sudan, and Saudi Arabia—to fight alongside Afghan refugees operating from bases in Pakistan.[56] In the 1980s, Afghan resistance became a "joint venture" of the Muslim Brotherhood and the Saudis, with tacit U.S. support. 'Abdallah 'Azzam, director of the Muslim Brotherhood Peshawar office, was a Jordanian Palestinian assassinated in 1989. He claimed Egyptian Muslim Brother Muhammad 'Abd al-Nasr as his spiritual guide. The principal financial support for militant activities came from Saudi Arabia. Prince Turki, head of Saudi intelligence services, was the principal contact for the militants, and Pakistan's Inter-Services Intelligence provided local support.

The level of control exercised by state security services over these groups is uncertain, and U.S. security services presumably did not approve of some of the purposes to which training camps were put. One such camp in the Paktya province of Afghanistan served to train Kashmiri militants, Philippine Moros, and Palestinian Islamists. Many of these militants have since offered their services to other militant movements in the Middle East, often in their countries of origin.[57] In earlier times, Jordan allowed anti-Asad Syrian Muslim Brotherhood militants to train in bases in Jordan, as did Iraq, and Syrian exiles in other countries, including Saudi Arabia and West Germany, poured money into anti-Asad militancy, some of which appeared to have covert U.S. approval.[58] In all these cases, external state support, especially in the form of funds and training from security services, inadvertently marginalized religious moderates.

Iran, in particular, has sought to extend its influence throughout the Muslim world by supporting movements elsewhere, particularly in the Arab world. Musa al-Sadr, a Lebanese Shiite cleric educated and raised in Iran, did much to crystallize an activist, political Islam sympathetic to Iran until his "disappearance" during a trip to Libya in 1978. Although he received transnational financial support from Libya, the Lebanese diaspora, and the Shiite establishment in Iran, he was controlled by none of them, and this independence may have led to his disappearance.[59] More recently, the Lebanese Hizbullah has benefited from ties with Iran, but even when Hizbullah activities further the policies of some elements of the Iranian government, it would be difficult to argue that it is merely a client group controlled by Iran. For example, the decision on when to use suicide bombings as a political tactic, beginning in 1982 and continuing for several years, was entirely in the hands of the Lebanese, who locally determined the targets of their violence, both non-Muslim opponents and rival Islamic movements.[60]

The big prize for Iran is securing influence in Sudan, a Sunni Muslim country, where it can claim to transcend the boundaries of Shiite sectarianism. Yet here again, though, it is far from certain that one can speak of Iranian "control" as opposed to support and training for a party or regime—such as Hasan al-Turabi's National Islamic Front, whose interests have at times coincided with Iran's.[61] Similarly, although Sudan may offer support to various North African movements, it is difficult to speak of control over them. Turabi may practice a "double discourse" when he says that it is his presence at international Islamic conferences that gives the appearance of transnational links and a "misunderstanding" of Islam when his activities are linked to terrorist activities. States seeking to enhance their religious credentials and expand their influence sponsor Islamic conferences, and these bring together scholars and activist leaders from throughout the Muslim world, just as several Middle Eastern governments or wealthy merchants in oil-rich states support Islamic outreach centers in the West to further understanding of Islam. The bulk of these activities focus on ideological arguments and religious propagation. They could, in some circumstances, provide a network of sympathizers and a mask behind which political violence can be organized and perpetrated. There are precedents for militants in other religious traditions to act in this fashion.

Conclusion: Islam and State Security

Islamist movements and Middle Eastern states with Muslim majority populations face similar security dilemmas. Many regimes see Islamist movements as major challenges to their legitimacy. They may seek to co-opt or neutralize the leaders of these groups, and all states try to control mosque sermons and restrict the use of mosques for opposition meetings. Even when successful, accommodations with activist groups are usually fragile, and states often risk precipitating a worse situation in repressing them. Few governments in the 1990s contemplate repeating Hafiz al-Asad's 1982 siege of militant Muslim radicals in Hama, which resulted in 5,000 to 10,000 deaths and the destruction of the city's old quarters.[62] Most states—like their Islamist opposition—find a middle ground that mixes formal statements of compromise and toleration ("We seek dialogue with all parties") with indirect or even formally deniable tactics. Or they may undertake the very reforms desired by the religious activists. In Oman one security official, acknowledging the impossibility of identifying all those participating in the Muslim Brotherhood movement, commented that "the arrests had only bought time in which the sources of dissatisfaction could be addressed."[63] The ambiguity of this phrasing, in which the "sources of dissatisfaction" remain unspecified, also indicates the dilemma of political analysis offered by security services. Security services must display loyalty to the regime, but at the same time must alert the regime to its own inadequacies.

Islamist activist movements, for their part, characterize most regimes as corrupt, arbitrary, elitist, Westernized, and despotic, alienated from the majority of the population. Yet to sustain security, the leaders of such groups, even if their decisionmaking units carry labels like *shura* or "family," must themselves be arbitrary, elitist, and despotic, and their compartmentalization of information and responsibility strongly emulates those of the state security services entrusted with holding them in check.

Islamist groups have a significant voice in countries where Islamic parties are recognized or are thought to be significant. Moroccan officials, for

example, estimate that 20 percent of the student body is Islamist in sympa-
thies.[64] Many Islamists realize that democracy can afford them a greater
sphere of action and therefore support democratic movements, although
others vehemently oppose democracy as an atheistic denial of God's sovereignty.[65]

Supporting democratic movements is probably the best way of preventing the growth of political terrorism, and the indiscriminate suppression of
Islamist movements usually cripples moderate elements.[66] Jordan's experience suggests that allowing Islamists to participate in the political process
while dealing firmly with extremists willing to use violence effectively undercuts support for radicalism. A recent survey in Jordan suggests that the
Islamic movement there has lost 25 percent of the support it enjoyed in
1989 because voters have now had an opportunity to see what Islamists
could do in power, and the 1993 elections confirm this trend. As in Morocco, participation in the electoral process in Jordan has also meant an implicit but core concession, as Laurie Brand points out: "[W]hile the expanded realm of political freedoms [Islamists] expected to develop through
the liberalization process might target many things, the overthrow of the
monarchy would not be among them, in exchange for the state conceding a
greater space to civil society."[67] One must also be attuned to shifts in radical movements over time, as even Lebanon's Hizbullah (also cut off from
effective state sponsors) has reverted to its earlier role of providing community infrastructure and statelike respectability.

In open political settings, Islamists are usually forced into greater moderation. Islamic activism professes an anti-Western orientation, but the structure, training, and movements of its advocates suggest considerable famil-
iarity with the West. Some activists find much to admire in the West; others
locate all evil in the West. These attitudes are unlikely to change in the
short term. They have been fueled for generations as the United States, in
pursuit of cold war interests, has espoused "stability" rather than democratic change, sometimes supporting unpopular, authoritarian elites throughout the region.[68] The best we can do is to avoid imputing to Muslim societies in general, or to Muslim political activists in particular, a propensity
for radicalism or terrorism, or to avoid allowing governments of the region,
often with shaky or uncertain claims to "just" rule, to label religious opposition as necessarily undemocratic or uncivil. As Graham Fuller argues,
"For the West, Islam is not the problem. The problem is hardship and frus-
trations born of rapid socioeconomic development in a variety of Muslim
countries—mirroring problems found in the non-Muslim Third World as
well—and a resentment of foreign cultural influence that threatens to en-
gulf their own."[69]

One might add to Fuller's caution a warning against assuming that the
historical developments of the decades since the 1970s, in which we have

seen an ascendancy of religious extremism in many regions of the world, are any more reliable a base on which to predict future developments than the conventional political wisdom of the 1950s and 1960s that Lebanon was a model of "modernization" for the rest of the region to follow. The immediate past is not necessarily a guide to the medium-term future, and both states and Islamist groups are capable of evolution. Indeed, state security structures and Islamic extremist movements have much in common in terms of organizational structure, forms of recruitment, and contradictions between formal ideology and the demands of group loyalty. A current Iranian secondary school text asserts that "whereas the old monarchy required complex security and intelligence gathering services, the Islamic Republic has a thirty-six million member intelligence service."[70] This claim is hyperbolic, but it correctly emphasizes the importance that both states and Islamist movements attach to a popular base. In the context of rising educational levels, and mindful of changing constituencies, both the repressive apparatus of the state and the tactics of radical groups may rapidly evolve, and the possibilities of both acceding to a civic pluralism, while not inevitable, gives cause for cautious optimism.

NOTES

1. Jacob M. Landau, *The Politics of Pan-Islam: Ideology and Organization* (Oxford: Clarendon Press, 1990).

2. See, for example, Octave Depont and Xavier Coppolani, *Les confréries religieuses musulmanes* (Algiers: A. Jourdan, 1897; reprint, Paris: J. Maisonneuve, P. Geuthner, 1987).

3. Youssef Courbage and Philippe Fargues, *Chrétiens et juifs dans l'Islam arabe et turc* (Paris: Fayard, 1992).

4. Richard P. Mitchell, *The Society of the Muslim Brothers* (Oxford: Clarendon Press, 1969), remains the classic introduction to this movement and the point of departure for understanding its organization, including the distinction between its public and clandestine wings. For the introduction of modern bureaucratic forms in Sufi religious orders, see Michael Gilsenan, *Saint and Sufi in Modern Egypt: An Essay in the Sociology of Religion* (Oxford: Clarendon Press, 1973), 92–128. Similar transnational movements developed elsewhere, notably in Palestine and in support of 'Abd al-Krim al-Khattibi's Riffian Republic in Morocco in the 1920s, but these movements, popular in their own regions, attracted principally elite support elsewhere in the Muslim world. For Palestine in the 1930s, see Nels Johnson, *Islam and the Politics of Meaning in Palestinian Nationalism* (London: Kegan Paul International, 1982). For the Riffian rebellion, see Germain Ayache, *Les origines de la guerre du Rif* (Rabat: Société Marocaine des Éditeurs Réunis, 1982).

5. Gilles Kepel, *Muslim Extremism in Egypt: The Prophet and Pharaoh*, trans. Jon Rothschild (Berkeley and Los Angeles: University of California Press, 1993 [orig. 1984]). This updated new edition remains the best survey and analysis of contemporary religious movements in Egypt.

6. Olivier Roy, *L'échec de l'Islam politique* (Paris: Éditions du Seuil, 1992), 118–166.

7. Yves Gonzalez-Quijano, "Les gens du livre, champ intellectuel et édition dans l'Égypte républicaine (1952–1993)" (Ph.D. diss., Institut d'Études Politiques, Paris, 1994), 398–418.

8. Roy, *L'échec de l'Islam*, 146. On Muhammad Marwa, see also Paul M. Lubeck, "Structural Determinants of Urban Islamic Protest in Northern Nigeria: A Note on Method, Mediation, and Materialist Explanation," in *Islam and the Political Economy of Meaning*, edited by William R. Roff (London: Croom Helm, 1987), 79–107.

9. Séverine Labat, "Islamismes et islamistes en Algérie: Un nouveau militantisme," in *Exils et royaumes: Les appartenances au monde arabo-musulman aujourd'hui*, edited by Gilles Kepel (Paris: Presses de la Fondation Nationale des Sciences Politiques, 1994), 43.

10. "Le GIA annonce la formation d'un gouvernement islamique," *Le Monde*, August 28–29, 1994, 3.

11. See Dale F. Eickelman, "Religion in Polity and Society," in *The Political Economy of Morocco*, edited by I. William Zartman (New York: Praeger, 1987), 88–92, and Rémy Leveau, *Le sabre et le turban: L'avenir du Maghreb* (Paris: François Bourin, 1993), 80–83.

12. See especially Denis J. Sullivan, *Private Voluntary Organizations in Egypt: Islamic Development, Private Initiative, and State Control* (Gainesville: University Press of Florida, 1994), and Sami Zubaida, "Islam, the State, and Democracy: Contrasting Conceptions of Society in Egypt," *Middle East Report* 22 (6) (November-December 1992):2–15.

13. Ahmed Rouadjia, *Les frères et la mosquée: Enquête sur le mouvement islamiste en Algérie* (Paris: Karthala, 1990).

14. Nadir Yata, Moroccan journalist, interview by the author, Casablanca, April 17, 1992.

15. Jean-François Legrain, "The Islamic Movement and the Intifada," in *Intifada: Palestine at the Crossroads*, edited by Jamal R. Nassar and Roger Heacock (New York: Praeger, 1990), 176–189.

16. Dr. 'Adnan al-Shati, interview by the author, Kuwait, June 13, 1993. See also Ghazi al-Khalaf, *Intishar al-irada al-Kuwaitiyya* [Propagating the Kuwaiti will] (Kuwait: n.p., November 1991), a profile of the resistance fighters.

17. Abdujabbar Abduvakhitov, "Islamic Revivalism in Uzbekistan," in *Russia's Muslim Frontiers: New Directions in Cross-cultural Analysis*, edited by Dale F. Eickelman (Bloomington: Indiana University Press, 1993), 79–97.

18. For further discussion of the implications of mass higher education for religious thought, see Dale F. Eickelman, "Mass Higher Education and the Religious Imagination in Contemporary Arab Societies," *American Ethnologist* 19 (4) (November 1992):643–655.

19. See Eickelman, "Mass Higher Education," and Stanley J. Tambiah, "Reflections on Communal Violence in South Asia," *Journal of Asian Studies* 9 (4) (November 1990):741–760.

20. Richard Cottam, "United States Middle East Policy in the Cold War Era," in *Russia's Muslim Frontiers*, edited by Eickelman, 19–37.

21. See, for example, Rabia Bekkar, "Taking Up Space in Tlemcen: The Islamist Occupation of Urban Algeria," *Middle East Report* 22 (6) (November-December 1992):11–21.

22. For an excellent account of Islamist movements that stresses their diversity, see Graham E. Fuller, *Islamic Fundamentalism in the Northern Tier Countries: An Integrative View* (Santa Monica: RAND, 1991).

23. Rafiuddin Ahmed, "Redefining Muslim Identity in South Asia: The Transformation of the Jama'at-i-Islami," in *Accounting for Fundamentalisms: The Dynamic Character of Movements*, edited by Martin E. Marty and R. Scott Appleby (Chicago: University of Chicago Press, 1994), 689, 693.

24. Gilles Kepel, *Les banlieues de l'Islam: Naissance d'une religion en France* (Paris: Éditions du Seuil, 1987), 225–312. See also Xavier Raufer, "Islamisme, capital Londres," *L'Express*, August 11–17, 1994, 18–19, especially good for tracing the links between international meetings, publishing, and the violent pasts of some groups that currently represent themselves as moderate.

25. The Islamic Liberation Party (ILP), established in Britain in 1985, claims 2,000 members and cells in fifty universities in Britain itself. Its leader is a thirty-seven-year-old Syrian, 'Umar Bakri Muhammad, who also runs a publishing house. The movement, founded in 1951 by a follower of the mufti of Jerusalem, had members in Egypt, Algeria, Iraq, Libya, and Jordan in the 1970s as well as branches in Europe. In 1974 members of the group were implicated in a failed assassination attempt against Anwar Sadat, and in April 1993 three students at the Jordanian military academy in Mut'a were arrested for plotting the assassination of King Hussein. They were executed in January 1994. Raufer, "Islamisme, capital Londres."

26. Abdujabbar Abduvakhitov, interview by the author, Tashkent, October 12, 1992; Vitaly Naumkin, interview by the author, Moscow, October 14, 1992. The former Soviet Union had the fifth largest Muslim population of any country in the world—55 million, with 500,000 Muslims in Moscow alone. Most Muscovite Muslims remained closely linked with their communities of origin. See Dale F. Eickelman and Kamran Pasha, "Muslim Societies and Politics: Soviet and U.S. Approaches," *Middle East Journal* 45 (4) (Autumn 1991):632.

27. William Shepherd, personal communication, May 25, 1993.

28. Yves Gonzalez-Quijano, "Les livres islamiques: Histoires ou mythes?" *Peuples méditerranéens* 56–57 (July-December 1991):283–292.

29. For a case study of the ease with which censorship can be subverted, see Dale F. Eickelman, "Islamic Liberalism Strikes Back," *Middle East Studies Association Bulletin* 27 (2) (December 1993):163–168.

30. See, for example, "Shra'it al-ta'arruf 'ala al-rasif: Jins, wa-fitna wa-tahrid" [Extremist cassettes on the sidewalk: Sex, rebellion, and incitement], *al-Ishtiraki* (Casablanca), June 21, 1992, 2–3. *Al-Ishtiraki* is the Arabic-language newspaper of one of Morocco's secular leftist political parties. The article's Moroccan author, who drew heavily on material originally published in the Egyptian magazine *Rus al-Yusif*, says that he chose anonymity because of the attacks on journalists critical of radical Muslim thought. Egypt's Faraj Fuda had been assassinated in Cairo several weeks earlier. For further discussion of the importance of videos and cassettes, see Dale F. Eickelman and James Piscatori, *Muslim Politics* (Princeton: Princeton University Press, 1996), 121–131.

31. Muhammad Drayf, *Al-Islam al-siyasi fi-l-Maghrib: Muraqaba wathaqiya* [Political Islam in Morocco: A documentary survey] (Casablanca: al-Majalla al-maghribiya li-'ilm al-ijtima' al-siyasi, 1992), 209–229. For other examples of emulation, see Roy, *L'échec de l'Islam*, 95.

32. Rouadjia, for example (*Les frères et la mosquée*, 36), writes that "from 1976 to 1980, the Islamists succeeded, with the connivance of the regime, to reduce Marxist influence to nothing." In Jordan's West Bank in the 1950s, Jordan's monarch encouraged Islamist movements as a means of fighting Nasser's influence. After Israel seized the West Bank in 1967, occupation authorities tacitly encouraged Islamist movements, especially on university campuses, as a means of containing the secular left, especially the Palestine Liberation Organization (PLO). Thus while Israelis did not tolerate pro-PLO campus demonstrations, Islamist demonstrations, even when they led to violence, were unchallenged. Jean-François Legrain characterizes this tolerance as based not on collaboration but on "an Israeli satisfaction" that they were exacerbating divisions in Palestinian society. See Legrain, "Islamistes et lutte nationale palestinienne dans les territoires occupés par Israël," *Revue française de science politique* 36 (2) (April 1986):231, 246.

33. David B. Edwards, "Print Islam: Media and Religious Revolution in Afghanistan," *Anthropological Quarterly* 68 (3) (July 1995):171–184.

34. Interviews by the author, Samarkand, October 9, 1993.

35. Robert Launay, *Beyond the Stream: Islam and Society in a West African Town* (Berkeley and Los Angeles: University of California Press, 1992), 73–74.

36. On such activity in Egypt, see Sullivan, *Private Voluntary Organizations;* in Algeria, see Rouadjia, *Les frères et la mosquée*, and Rabia Bekkar, "Taking Up Space in Tlemcen"; in Morocco, see Mouna El Banna, "Au Maroc, des islamistes sous surveillance," *Le Monde*, September 1, 1994, 4.

37. Bruce Lawrence, personal communication, January 15, 1993.

38. Ahmed, "Redefining Muslim Identity," 679.

39. Reuters dispatch from Muscat, November 12, 1994.

40. Although observers of the Gulf knew of the arrests as early as June, the first formal word of them appeared in Kuwaiti newspapers in late August 1994. See "Up to 70 Suspects in Omani Islamist Ring to Go on Trial," *Mideast Mirror*, August 31, 1994, 27; and Solidarity International for Human Rights, "Unusual Human Rights Abuses in the Unusually Quiet Sultanate of Oman," Washington, D.C., September 30, 1994 (Report/OMAN9403/94). The prisoners were released in November 1995, just prior to the celebration of the twenty-fifth anniversary of the reign of Sultan Qaboos, although many complain of continued close surveillance and other restrictions. Also Omani observers, interviews by the author in London, Paris, and New York, September-November 1994.

41. The French signed a security agreement with Saudi Arabia in 1980. Since 1982 French police have had an office in Riyadh to implement it. *Al-Rassed* 2 (40) (November 14, 1994), citing Reuters and Compass dispatches.

42. See André Pautard, "Les voisins aux aguets," *L'Express*, August 11–17, 1994, 16–17; and *al-Bayane* (Casablanca), January 7, 1993.

43. See Dale F. Eickelman and Malcolm Dennison, "Arabizing the Omani Intelligence Services: Clash of Cultures?" *International Journal of Intelligence and Counterintelligence* 7 (1) (Spring 1994):1–28.

44. Olivier Roy goes so far as to say that Algeria's FIS lacks a real strategy to take power "in the sense of concerted, organized action, aided by a precise plan." Quoted in Vincent Hugeux, "Olivier Roy: Le 'coup d'état permanent'" *L'Express*, August 11–17, 1994, 20.

45. Anatolian News Agency, "Kurdish Rebels Kill 35 in Attack," May 25, 1993; "Saddam Again?" (Editorial), *Wall Street Journal*, May 31, 1993; *Cumhuriyet* (Istanbul), May 29, 1993.

46. Algerian businessmen engaging in smuggling (*trabando*) generally support FIS because of its promise to impose only "Islamic" taxes, interpreted in Algeria as the elimination of the stiff duties now levied on imported goods. Security officials, interviews by the author, Tangier, June 26, 1992; Jamal Amiar, interview by the author, Tangier, June 27, 1992.

47. The case is summarized in François Soudan, "Barbus ou barbouzes?" *Jeune Afrique*, September 8–14, 1994, 8–11. It also suggests the close working ties between French and North African security services.

48. See "Those Who Spread These Leaflets and Publications, Copy Them, or Distribute Them Commit a Major Evil and Will Be Responsible for Its Evil and the Evil of All Those Influenced by It" (in Arabic), *al-Sharq al-Awsat* (London), November 19, 1994, 1; see also Leslie Cockburn and Andrew Cockburn, "Royal Mess," *New Yorker*, November 28, 1994, 54–72.

49. Sullivan, *Private Voluntary Organizations*.

50. "Arab-American Pleads Guilty in Israel to Aiding Militants," *New York Times*, June 17, 1993, A15; Gideon Aran, "Jewish Zionist Fundamentalism: The Bloc of the Faithful in Israel (Gush Emunim)," in *Fundamentalisms Observed*, edited by Martin E. Marty and R. Scott Appleby (Chicago: University of Chicago Press, 1991), 318.

51. See Dale F. Eickelman and James Piscatori, "Social Theory in the Study of Muslim Societies, in *Muslim Travellers: Pilgrimage, Migration, and the Religious Imagination* (London: Routledge, 1990), 9. At the same time as Iraq was funding Saudi dissident groups, Saudi Arabia allegedly channeled funds into Iraq's nuclear program "on condition that some of the bombs, should the project succeed, be transferred to the Saudi arsenal." Cockburn and Cockburn, "Royal Mess," 61.

52. Roy, *L'échec de l'Islam*, 143–144.

53. See Karim Subhi, "Masani' siriyya li-l-silah . . . wa-l-tujjar taht al-ard" [A secret underground arms factory . . . and merchants], *Rus al-Yusif*, June 14, 1993, 42–45.

54. Youssef M. Ibrahim, "Saudis Strip Citizenship from Backer of Militants," *New York Times*, April 10, 1994. For an overview of Saudi support for militant groups, see Roy, *L'échec de l'Islam,* 150–153. Also see Mouna Naïm, "La 'bonne volonté' du régime islamiste soudanais," *Le Monde*, August 17, 1994, 8.

55. Saudis appear to fund various religious and tribal factions in neighboring Yemen. See Paul Dresch and Bernard Haykel, "Stereotypes and Political Styles: Islamists and Tribesfolk in Yemen," *International Journal of Middle East Studies* 27 (4) (November 1995):403–431. In August 1994, following the kidnapping of an Omani and a Saudi diplomat in Algeria, Algerian security forces reportedly had no indication of the identity of the kidnappers. The Saudi government sent an official delegation to cooperate with the Algerian authorities. Within a day of the delegation's arrival, it

made contact with the militant group responsible for the kidnapping and arranged for the hostages' release. A diplomatic observer in Rabat (interview with the author, September 5, 1994) read the incident as suggesting that the Saudis had not severed their contacts with religious militants in Algeria, as had been widely assumed when these groups declared their support for Saddam Hussein at the time of the 1990–1991 Gulf War.

56. Antoine Jacob, "Les 'Afghans' accusés d'être liés au terrorisme intégriste," *Al Bayane* (Casablanca), April 12, 1993.

57. Jacob, "Les 'Afghans' accusés." See also Tim Weiner, "Blowback from the Afghan Battlefield," *New York Times Magazine*, March 13, 1994, 52–55. Islamic movements are also strong in Kuwait, where Islamists had a strong showing in both parliamentary and municipal elections in the fall of 1992. Public and private contributions to support militants in Afghanistan have provided 20 million Kuwaiti dinars (about US$70 million) since the late 1970s. Mahmud 'Abd al-Wahhab, "20 milyun dinar Kuwaiti li-l-mutatarrifin fi Afghanistan" [Twenty million Kuwaiti dinars to extremists in Afghanistan], *Rus al-Yusif* (Cairo), June 7, 1993, 28.

58. Patrick Seale, *Asad of Syria: The Struggle for the Middle East* (Berkeley and Los Angeles: University of California Press, 1988), 334–336.

59. Fouad Ajami, *The Vanished Imam: Musa al Sadr and the Shia of Lebanon* (Ithaca: Cornell University Press, 1986).

60. Martin Kramer, "Sacrifice and Fratricide in Shiite Lebanon," *Terrorism and Political Violence* 3 (3) (Autumn 1991):30–47.

61. Charles Richards, "Soft Words in Sudan Conceal Face of Terror," *Independent* (London), June 9, 1993, 14; interview with Hasan al-Turabi, *Libération* (Paris), March 17, 1993. But Sudan's tacit support of French efforts to capture international terrorist Carlos (Ilitch Ramirez Sanchez) in August 1994 was widely read as a signal of "moderation."

62. Seale, *Asad*, 332–336.

63. Interview by the author, London, October 1, 1994.

64. Interviews by the author, Rabat, April 15–16, 1992.

65. See Abdelasiem El-Difraoui, "La critique du système démocratique par le Front islamique du salut," in *Exils et royaumes*, edited by Kepel, 105–124.

66. See "Radicalizing Algeria" (editorial), *New York Times*, February 12, 1992, A24.

67. "Jordan: The Subtler Way," *Economist*, April 3, 1993, 43. See also Laurie A. Brand, "'In the Beginning Was the State . . .': The Quest for Civil Society in Jordan," in *Civil Society in the Middle East*, vol. 1, edited by Augustus Richard Norton (Leiden: E. J. Brill, 1995), 148–185.

68. Graham E. Fuller, *Iraq in the Next Decade: Will Iraq Survive Until 2002?* (Santa Monica: RAND, 1993), 77.

69. Fuller, *Islamic Fundamentalism*, 31.

70. Cited in Golnar Mehran, "Socialization of Schoolchildren in the Islamic Republic of Iran," *Iranian Studies* 22 (1) (Winter 1989):39–40.

TWO

Muslim Missionaries and African States

OUSMANE KANE

Should security be conceived of as a mere preoccupation with armaments or nuclear deterrence, or can it be understood in a wider meaning that comprehends the experiences of identity, community, safe residence, and belonging? Conventional scholarship on security, because of its propensity to declare natural the political phenomena of the last two centuries, which brought the rise of the state system, emphasizes the nation-state as the only guarantor of security, therefore taking it for granted that parallel arrangements of political interactions are of little, if any, significance in security studies.

Ronnie Lipschutz draws our attention to the growing number of "networks of economic, social and cultural relations ... occupied by the conscious association of actors, in physically separated locations, who link themselves together in networks for particular political and social purposes."[1] These networks, whose numbers are multiplying, shape what Lipschutz terms "global civil society." When they strive for transnational representation and expansion, Susanne Rudolph argues, "networks of civil society can be conceived of as competing ... which would lead us to expect more conflict. But they can also be conceived of as providing more choice in terms of systems of action and grounding of identities."[2] In any case, the relevance of these networks cannot be ignored altogether in security studies.

In this chapter I focus on contemporary *turuq* (Sufi orders; singular *tariqa*) in West Africa. My argument is that these networks, which contributed a great deal to the spread of Islam in black Africa, make tension less likely, while their absence actually makes it more likely. They perform many of the survival functions—providing community, shelter for the needy, medical support, economic networks—that family or state performs in other societies, and they do so without regard to state borders. Thus they create networks of trust and routines of peaceable interaction that contrast with the experience of distrust, conflict, and violence between ethnic communities that has afflicted some African states. In a world in which civil war is the most common form of conflict, they create the conditions of peace.

Two West African turuq in particular witnessed a remarkable growth in the course of the nineteenth century: the Qadiriyya, which originated in Iraq and was founded by Abd al-Qadir al-Jilani (d. 1166), and the Tijaniyya, which originated in Algeria and Morocco and was founded by Abu al-Abbas Ahmad al-Tijani (d. 1815).[3] In black Africa, these two turuq subdivided into hundreds of branches, which, in the course of time, became totally independent of the Arab turuq whose name they carried.[4] I will show how West African Sufi orders, particularly the Tijaniyya, operate as a set of networks of global civil society. Such networks might have different orientations toward states. Some, says Lipschutz, are antistate, others are oriented toward state reform, and a third set simply ignores the state altogether.[5] In my conclusion I shall attempt to identify which of these ideal-types characterizes West African Sufi networks' orientations toward states.

I will begin by sketching out the context in which the turuq emerged as sociopolitical communities in West Africa. I will then center my analysis on the Niassène Tijaniyya tariqa. I will describe the modus operandi of this tariqa in West Africa in general, and in Senegambia in particular. Following this I will analyze the relationship of the Niassène Tijaniyya tariqa to the Arab states, its proselytizing in the United States, and the consequent creation of a U.S.-Senegal network. Finally, on the basis of this case study, I will conclude by addressing the question of the effect of the operation of these Sufi networks on the issue of security broadly understood.

Turuq as Sociopolitical Organizations in West Africa

In the course of the nineteenth century, West Africa in general and Senegambia in particular witnessed a period of insecurity and profound upheaval. The insecurity was due in large part to the war for the acquisition of slaves, which was Senegambia's main economic activity during the eighteenth and nineteenth centuries.[6] It was in this context of insecurity and instability that the French colonial conquest, which itself brought about major upheavals, took place. The French dismantled the preexisting kingdoms by breaking them up into provinces and cantons. This weakened considerably the sovereigns whose legitimacy had already been undermined by their deep involvement in the slave trade. The French put an end to the slave trade and imposed a "colonial peace," which rendered idle thousands of warriors who had been continually under arms during the precolonial period.

In the face of this upheaval in their social order, the Wolofs—the majority ethnic group in Senegambia—rallied around the marabouts (the leaders of the turuq). The French succeeded, to a large extent, in making these marabouts their intermediaries in the imposition of the "colonial peace."[7] The marabouts enjoined their disciples to respect colonial laws, to pay taxes, and to return to farming, where the energies of many social groupings (e.g., aristocrats, clienteles of weakened kings, professional warriors) were rechanneled.

In exchange, the recognition of the colonial authorities promoted these marabouts to the leadership of their community.[8] Consequently the Senegambian turuq were to become powerful organizations, not only spiritually but socioeconomically as well. From this collaboration, however, it should not be concluded that Sufi turuq were simply agents of the French administration. They had their own agenda, as the Niassène Tijaniyya case well illustrates, which included Islamizing the heathen, spreading their own religious faith, and extending their networks beyond the colonial space.

Thanks to the peace of the colonial period, the turuq contributed enormously to the wave of Islamization that unfolded during this time. Indeed, the percentage of the Muslim population of Mali increased from 50 percent on the eve of the colonial conquest to 80 percent in the present period. Moreover, the French, by encouraging the cultivation of peanuts with the construction of a railway that linked the hinterland to the sea, enabled the marabouts to become an economically powerful force. The disciples of the marabouts dedicated part of their time to the cultivation of the marabouts' fields. In return, the marabouts gave religious instruction and looked after their disciples' interests.

Based in the region referred to as the "peanut basin," the marabouts took control of peanut production, the export of which has long been Senegal's main source of revenue. The marabouts were thus to become a powerful economic force. And last but not least, because they served as a transmission belt between their clientele and the colonial authorities—and, later on, the postcolonial state—the marabouts developed into a powerful political force.[9] However, although Sufi orders acquired strength in French colonial West Africa, this does not mean that before the colonial conquest Sufi orders had no social significance. On the contrary, they have a long history. Following the collapse of the Almohad in North Africa, the loss of Muslim Spain, and the inability of post-Almohad dynasties to halt the progress of the "Christians," Sufi orders spearheaded the "holy war" against the Spanish and the Portuguese. They acquired a powerful influence in North African political life and from there spread south of the Sahara.[10] A good illustration of Sufi orders as a powerful precolonial sociopolitical force is the Sanusiyya tariqa in modern Libya.[11] But the West African Sufi communities, thanks to the backing of the French, came to control communities that had been led by Africans kings before colonial interference.

During the two decades following Senegal's accession to independence, a majority of those marabouts who led the most important religious communities intervened in political life by instructing their clientele to vote for the party in power. These instructions influenced hundreds of thousands of votes at election time. With urbanization and the emergence of secularized elites, strong pressure was put on the marabouts—even by their own disciples—to desist from directly intervening in the political arena. While these pressures led the supreme leadership of the main turuq to abstain from instructing their disciples on how to vote, one must not conclude that the turuq ceased to be an important political force. The rural areas, where Senegal's ruling party draws the core of its support at election time, are controlled by the marabouts, whose backing is essential for any candidate who wishes to be elected.

In exchange for the marabout's tacit or overt support, the state authorities—following the practice of the colonial government—have, for a long time, granted them a variety of benefits (e.g., tax exemption, nonpenetration of state authorities in holy cities,[12] awarding scholarships for study in foreign universities to clients of the marabouts, various generosities in the form of cash grants or [nonrepayable] loans). For example, during the 1970s the Senegalese state guaranteed loans from private banks to marabouts. The banks consented to loans amounting to several millions of dollars—some of which were never repaid—that enabled marabouts to undertake business ventures. Some saw these operations—and with good reason—as a means both for the state more easily to control the marabouts and for the ruling party more solidly to anchor its base of political support. However, it should be recalled here that the Sufi turuq have a double standing with respect to state legitimacy. As far as the colonial state was concerned, the marabouts enjoined their disciples to abide by its laws. In that sense, they can be seen as supportive of that state. At the same time, they were seen to advocate pan-Islamic or pan-African ideologies dangerous to the state.[13] Although they were by and large supportive of postcolonial political authorities, they also challenged the postcolonial state's authority on some occasions when the latter tried to implement decisions that were considered violations of Islamic identity.

The Niassène Tijaniyya as Networks of Global Civil Society

With a firm base in Senegambia, some of these turuq established strong ties with communities beyond the boundaries of the French colonial state. At the same time, they started operating in a space that corresponds not to the political map of the colonial and, later on, the postcolonial state, but to a sacred geography created by pilgrimage routes and centers, enabling the circulation of both goods and people regardless of the regulations of different states. This space in which the Niassène Tijaniyya operates, like other such networks, illustrates the importance of the networks that constitute global civil society.

From its Senegambian base, this tariqa, beginning in World War II under the impetus of the religious leader Ibrahima Niasse (1900–1975), spread throughout West Africa. This tariqa owed its success not only to the charisma of Ibrahima Niasse[14] but also to the fact that its two bases—Kaolack in Senegal and Kano in Nigeria—were important commercial centers. For several centuries Kano had been one of the major centers of trans-Saharan trade. Today it is the largest industrial and commercial center in northern Nigeria.[15] Commerce and trade were the driving forces behind the spread of this tariqa in West Africa. Not only were a fair number of Niassène Tijani missionaries involved in trade, but also to a certain extent trade and commerce can be said to be the foundation of the movement's political economy.

Structures and Ideologies of the Niassène Tijaniyya

The structural base of the movement of the Niassène Tijaniyya is the *zawiya* (lodge). The zawiya is an important institution in the history of Muslim turuq. The works of the anthropologist Sir Edward E. Evans-Pritchard on the Sanusi of Cyrenaica[16] and those of the French colonial administrators Octave Depont and Xavier Coppolani[17] illustrate the different functions fulfilled by a zawiya. These include place of worship, center for the transmission of religious knowledge, place of refuge for fugitives, welfare institution for the indigent, and base for political organization. In varying degrees and according to the context, the West African turuq have fulfilled most of these functions. As for the Niassène Tijaniyya, at the head of each zawiya is a person in charge who is supposed to have received a consecration from the parent zawiya conferring upon him the title of *muqaddam* (representative). The muqaddam is a prayer leader and gives both exoteric and esoteric instruction. The point of departure for Sufi-inspired turuq is the principle that there is a visible aspect (*zahir*) of mundane things, which comes within the province of exoteric instruction, and a hidden aspect (*batin*) of existential realities, the understanding of which is reserved solely for initiates (*'arifun*). The observation of the five pillars of Islam—belief in God, prayer five times a day, fasting during the month of Ramadan, the obligation to give alms, and the pilgrimage to Mecca if one is able—is certainly important for the followers of Sufi-inspired Islam. Nonetheless, it does not alone permit one to accede to knowledge of the mysteries of existence (*ma'rifa*). In Sufi cosmology one only accedes to such knowledge through spiritual education (*tarbiya*) under the supervision of a teacher *(al-shaykh al-murabbi)*. The legitimacy of Sufi leaders and the important margin of maneuver that they hold in the leadership of their communities is explained in part by the central place that Sufi cosmology confers upon them.

The most important zawiya of the Niassène Tijaniyya is located in Kaolack, in the peanut basin of Senegal, where the founder of the order lived and where his descendants live today. Other zawiyas identifying with the Niassène Tijaniyya are spread across the African Sahel, from Senegal to Sudan.[18] The zawiyas may serve as inns offering hospitality to visiting fellow disciples. Considering this, the number of zawiyas—as well as that of their disciples—has multiplied considerably in numerous regions of West Africa where petty commerce is a fundamental aspect of the culture (notably in Nigeria, Ghana, and Niger). The followers are generally linked to the tariqa through the intermediary of a zawiya, which is often the one closest to their place of residence. In principle, the followers make offerings to support both the zawiya and its muqaddam. A part of the offerings, which is not fixed and depends on how much disciples can give, is forwarded to the parent zawiya of the Niassène Tijaniyya, either by the muqaddam or by a representative of the parent zawiya in Kaolack sent periodically to collect the offerings (*hadiya*), which can be given in kind or in cash. These forwarded offerings are used to support the family of the marabout, to construct mosques and other zawiyas, or to benefit the needy.

Various religious ceremonies are organized that allow for the representation of different zawiyas. The most important is the *maulud* ("birthday"), for which several thousand people from different countries, especially from West Africa, gather together. Two types of mauluds exist. The first celebrates the birth of the Prophet and the second that of the leader Shaykh Ibrahim Niasse, a major figure of the Niassène Tijaniyya tariqa. Both of these mauluds are celebrated in Kaolack. The celebrations of the mauluds involve gathering together a maximum number of disciples for an evening of religious chanting and of glorifying the Prophet.

It may be noted that religious gathering around cults of saints exists in almost all Muslim societies. From the religious festivals (*mausim*) at the mausoleums of Muslim saints in the Maghreb to the pilgrimages to the tombs of Muslims saints in India (*dargha*), these festive rituals are a durable component of Muslim societies.[19] In various Muslim societies these rituals draw on Islamic themes as well as on the local religious order. These celebrations are hotly condemned as heretical innovations (*bid'a*) by Muslim reformers who follow a more austere brand of Islam and who tend to reject all local traditions. These reformers, who have a "rational" vision of religion and an individual vision of salvation, have appeared in West Africa as a result of urbanization and the gradual substitution of traditional Quranic instruction by more modern formal education.

For the Niassène Tijaniyya, the maulud, though essentially a religious event, nonetheless has several important economic effects. Numerous pilgrims traveling from different African countries to the parent zawiya in Kaolack often bring with them a variety of goods. Given their good relations with the turuq, the Senegalese authorities might exempt from customs' duties the products transported by the pilgrims. These goods can then be used as offerings to the parent zawiya or sold on the Senegalese market.[20]

In addition to the mauluds, there is another transnational religious celebration: the organization of pious visits (*ziyara*). The ziyara originally took place during harvest periods. The peasants undertook a pious visit to the parent zawiya and offered a part of their millet harvest to the marabout. The ziyara thus responded to the logic of a primarily agricultural society. A second type of ziyara, called the "money ziyara," appeared as a result of the combined effect of urbanization and the birth outside of Senegambia of communities identifying with the Niassène Tijaniyya tariqa. It is an occasion for disciples who are directly involved in the production of goods to commune at the parent zawiya. The actors involved in this second ziyara are disciples from urban areas and from other countries. Their offerings are made in the form of cash. Though not as important as the maulud, the ziyara has nonetheless become a transnational event in the modern period. Whether for the ziyara or maulud, it is the disciples who travel from their place of residence to the parent zawiya, where they are able to commune at the mausoleum of the founder, to be blessed by his descendants, and, for some, to engage in business transactions. Besides the periods of the maulud and ziyara, some disciples from different regions organize periodic visits. These voyages are an occasion to make pious visits, but for some pilgrims it is an opportunity to inquire into the state of the market and, as a consequence, to develop business strategies.

In this respect, the Nigeria-Senegal axis is the one where the circulation of goods and people functions the best, thanks to the increased means of rapid communication. Whereas three decades ago Senegal and Nigeria were linked only by a road and a railway, today the two countries are linked by several weekly flights. Throughout the 1970s and 1980s an enormous gap in prices existed between Senegal and Nigeria. This allowed one to purchase goods in Nigeria and then sell them duty-free for three to four times the price in Senegal. Given the economic effects of these religious events, it is not surprising that they attract numerous pilgrims up to the present day, some of whom are not motivated only by religious reasons.

Despite the importance of commerce, one cannot reduce the movement of pilgrims solely to the search for profit, for the pursuit of benediction is important in these pilgrimages. Some pilgrims come with their children on the occasion of religious ceremonies such as the maulud and ziyara. These children are often left at the parent zawiya for several years, where they pursue religious studies or serve the marabout or his family. The notion of volunteer work for the marabout is called *khidma* in the language of the turuq. The disciples of the turuq believe that by putting themselves at the service of the marabout they will be able to gain benediction (*baraka*), which guarantees salvation and success both in this world and in the hereafter. An important consequence of khidma is that those who carry it out for a certain number of years accede to rank of muqaddam when they leave the parent zawiya. Once home, they have a very good chance of occupying important religious functions.

During sojourns at the parent zawiya, it sometimes happens that disciples from other countries marry young women of the parent zawiya and then return with them to their countries of origin. This circulation of men and women has the effect of reinforcing the links between the parent zawiya and its disciple communities in other countries. An important aspect of this circulation of goods and people is that it favors interbreeding between tariqa followers of different ethnic groups (e.g., Arabo-Berbers from Mauritania; Wolofs from Senegal; Hausas from Nigeria, Niger, and Ghana). The parent zawiya in Kaolack is a cosmopolitan place where a number of foreign languages are spoken, notably Mauritanian Arabic and Hausa. These two languages are spoken there because the Moorish and Hausa communities are the most commercially oriented in West Africa and make up the largest number of foreign disciples in the Niassène Tijaniyya. In the absence of any systematic census it would be hazardous to estimate the number of interethnic marriages, but there is little doubt that hundreds of such marriages have taken place over the past few decades.

A third celebration involving significant movements of people is the Annual Conference of the Gambia. This conference was instituted by Shaykh Hassan Cissé, the grandson of Ibrahim Niasse and *imam* (religious leader) of the main mosque of the parent zawiya. The themes of the conference touch upon the challenges confronting Muslims in the modern world. But like the maulud, it brings together several thousand people. Another remarkable fact is that it takes place in Gambia, a country surrounded by Senegal, and with the blessing of the Gambian authorities. Most postcolonial African states have not favorably viewed the recruiting of disciples within their borders by religious figures based in other countries. But unless the leaders of transnational religious communities support opposition activity to existing regimes, most West African states do not apparently try to hinder the circulation networks of goods, people, and benediction. The Niassène Tijaniyya was subject to restrictions in northern Nigeria in the 1960s. During this time the Northern Element Peoples Union, which opposed the Northern Peoples Congress that governed northern Nigeria, relied on the Niassène Tijaniyya to contest the established order. This resulted in repression against the Niassène Tijaniyya and its disciples and the interdiction of its leader from entering Nigeria. In neighboring Niger, the government of the period led by Hamani Diori, fearing a contagious effect from subversive activities, likewise took measures aimed at preventing the leadership of the Niassène Tijaniyya from entering the country. But apart from these rare cases, the transnational activities of the turuq have not been subject to special restrictions. This might partly be explained by the fact that some political elites identify themselves to some extent with the tariqa and implicitly adhere to the idea of a transnational sacred geography in which turuq operate.

The Relationship with the Arab States

Since the African countries attained independence, the Arab states have taken an interest in West African turuq. But this interest cannot be explained solely by faith and fraternity. It seems to be dictated in equal measure by a wish to instrumentalize the turuq. Given the importance of the turuq in the political life of black Africa, a number of Arab states have tried—often in the context of interstate rivalry—to use them for political ends. Thus during the 1960s, the rivalry between Saudi Arabia and Egypt—both of which sought to extend their influence in the Arab and Muslim world—led their respective authorities to take an active interest in West African turuq. President Gamal Abdel Nasser maintained close contacts with the Niassène Tijaniyya and received Ibrahim Niasse on several occasions in Cairo during that time. Ibrahim Niasse was named a member of the Research Academy of the University of al-Azhar. Moreover, Nasser gave out scholarships throughout the 1960s to Ibrahim Niasse so that the latter's sons and disciples could pursue their education in Egypt. Since then, hundreds of youths from the Niassène Tijaniyya and other Senegalese turuq have been trained in Egyptian universities, notably at al-Azhar.

Nasser's perspective was first and foremost pan-Arab. This pan-Arabism threatened Saudi Arabia, however, and its ruler, King Faisal, reacted by undertaking a pan-Islamist policy.[21] In the 1960s, the Niassène Tijaniyya, which was believed to be the most important Islamic organization in West Africa and which possessed a clientele in all West African countries,[22] was able to help increase the popularity of the Egyptian president in black Africa. Likewise, the Egyptians hoped that African students educated in Egypt would become future elites favorable to the Arabs. Saudi Arabia and the Gulf countries, despite their disapproval of the religious doctrine of the turuq, gave them substantial amounts of money, especially after the price of oil increased in the 1970s. This aid included grants of hundreds of thousands of dollars and scholarships. But since the 1980s the Gulf states have only given scholarships to the youngest students, probably with the aim of influencing them during their studies so that they would adopt the religious doctrine prevailing in the Arabian peninsula. The Iraqi regime, despite its secular character, also indulged the West African turuq, granting scholarships for study in Iraqi universities and subsidies for the construction of religious centers (including several hundred thousand dollars donated in the late 1970s to the leadership of the Niassène Tijaniyya). It should be noted that this generosity corresponded exactly with the outbreak of the Iran-Iraq War. During this period, Iran undertook an intensive propaganda offensive in black Africa against Iraq and the monarchies of the Gulf; Iran counted numerous ardent supporters among young African Muslims, a certain number of whom had spent time in Iran.

Recently there have been signs of a revived interest on the part of Morocco in the West African turuq. Indeed Morocco has always maintained good relations with turuq, giving financial assistance for the building of schools and religious centers in West Africa and scholarships for study in Arab schools and universities. In 1985 a major conference on the Tijaniyya was organized in Fez, where the main parent zawiya of the Tijaniyya is based, by the Moroccan minister of religious affairs. Hundreds of leaders of African turuq were invited to the conference, and afterwards a number of associations were created, such as the Association of Ulema (religious scholars) of Morocco and Senegal and the Association of Ulema of Morocco and Nigeria. Large sums of money were also freed up by Morocco to finance the black African turuq. This conference, which brought together all the leaders of the black African Tijaniyya, was organized precisely at the moment when most of the black African states had come out in support of self-determination for Western Sahara. It seems that the king of Morocco attempted to use the West African tariqa leaders in order to persuade black African diplomats to favor his annexation of Western Sahara.

In 1987 Algeria, whose National Liberation Front government had fiercely combated the Algerian turuq—and, above all, the Tijaniyya, whom it had accused of collaborating with the colonial powers, encouraging obscurantism, and so on—invited hundreds of leaders of African tariqa branches to make a pilgrimage to the holy places of the Tijaniyya in Algeria. The Algerian authorities also accorded generous subsidies to the West African turuq.

One could multiply these examples many times, demonstrating the interest of the Arab countries in the turuq and the generosities lavished upon them, either directly or through various organizations (e.g., the World Islamic League, the Da'wa Movement based in Libya). However, while mutual cooperation may enable such a state or the turuq each to achieve some of their goals, turuq are not tools that states (either Arab or African) can easily manipulate. Moreover, although the Sufi communities still have some authority over their disciples, the latter are now increasingly emancipated. On some occasions, some disciples may refuse to follow their instructions.

The Creation of an American Network

Under the impetus of Shaykh Hassan Cissé, the grandson of the founder of the Niassène Tijaniyya, this tariqa attempted to set up a Tijaniyya network in America. A former student at Northwestern University in Evanston, Illinois, Hassan Cissé became popular with hundreds of African-Americans, responding both to their religious needs and to their search for identity. Cissé developed a following in New York and Chicago and founded variants of zawiyas in Atlanta, Chicago, and New York. This author frequented one of these zawiyas in the Bronx for a few months. Muslims of both sexes adhering to the teachings of the Tijaniyya met there on a regular basis to recite the rituals of the Tijaniyya tariqa. The majority were African-Americans but there were some Africans as well. Since Hassan Cissé founded the first zawiyas more than a dozen years ago, the number of African-Americans attracted to the Tijaniyya has continued to grow. In the absence of any systematic census it would be risky to estimate their actual number. This network has enabled numerous Tijani Africans to immigrate to the United States. They generally marry African-Americans in order to legalize their status in the United States. Until the middle of the 1980s, Tijani Africans were, for the most part, vendors of African objets d'art. According to my informants, this type of activity could easily yield an income of $200 a day.

Whereas at the beginning of the 1980s only workers were part of this network, the vision of the New World attracted numerous Arabic-speaking Senegalese students, who not so long before would have gone to the Arab world to continue their studies. These students came to the United States in order to work while pursuing their studies. They became workers out of necessity, due to the high cost of education in the United States and the need to work in order to survive. This condition was meant to be only temporary but often ended up as a long-lasting vocation. This American Tijaniyya network does not function as a one-way street. Several dozen African-American families have gone to live at the parent zawiyas in Senegal and their children are educated there in an Afro-American school set up exclusively for them. The attraction of African-Americans to the Tijaniyya cannot be reduced to any single factor. Discussions with them suggest that many have a strong sense of racial consciousness, and the affirmation of their identity plays a central role in their conversion to Islam or interest in the Tijaniyya. Moreover, some of these African-American disciples of Hassan Cissé who had originally been converted to Islam by Muslim missionaries from

Pakistan adopted the Tijaniyya tariqa because of its "specifically African character." Some African-American families living at the parent zawiya travel back and forth between Senegal, where they have developed business partnerships, and the United States, where they stay only long enough to sell their merchandise. The Americans who have come to live in Senegal have never been refused visas by the Senegalese authorities. The only exception to this was the denial of a visa—at the request of the U.S. government—to Louis Farrakhan, who had been invited to Senegal by Shaykh Hassan Cissé.

Conclusion

Before addressing the implications of the Niassène Tijaniyya as an exemplar of transnational civil society for security broadly understood, I wish to discuss how much of it is indeed civil society, given the argument in the scholarly literature that affiliation in the turuq is automatic, presumed, or inherited, whereas the major criterion of civil society, at least in its classical definition, is voluntary association.[23] Sufi orders in Senegambia were born in rural areas; their early organization very much followed patterns of rural life; and the maulud celebration, called *Gammu* in Wolof, was a Senegambian pre-Islamic harvest festival before it assumed Islamic significance.

For the rural populations of colonial Senegambia, Sufi Islam was a hegemonic discourse. Affiliation was to a considerable extent automatic. But the Senegambian turuq, particularly when a drought hit the Sahelian countries in the 1970s, went through some measure of urbanization.[24] This no doubt affected patterns of recruitment. For the urban-educated middle class, some of whom are also involved in the Sufi networks and are offered such alternatives as joining other political or cultural associations, affiliation can indeed be said to be voluntary. Therefore, I will argue, Sufi turuq are fulfilling to an ever increasing extent the classic criterion of gesellschaft according to Ferdinand Tonnies—that is, voluntary affiliation. African-Americans are also new members whose affiliation is voluntary and for whom the very fact that the leaders are black men has made the turuq appealing. Though Senegambian Sufi orders originated in the Arab World, they acquired a great deal of emancipation from the Arab Sufi orders.

Earlier in this chapter, I alluded to the question of how the Sufi turuq's orientations correspond with Lipschutz's three ideal-types. The answer is contingent: A tariqa's position oscillates among the three ideal-types. In some situations, turuq, or at least their leadership, cooperate with states; in others, they adopt antistate positions, but more important, they constitute a "community of affinities" operating outside the state.

In a recent study of state-society relations in Senegal with special reference to the turuq, Leonardo Villalòn suggests three models of societal responses towards the state—isolation, engagement, and contestation:

> Isolation covers that range of activities which society can undertake in order to distance itself from the State. . . . Engagement refers to those types of state-society interactions which might be considered complementary. It signals the willingness of social groups to deal with the state in playing within the established rules of the game. Finally, "contestation" includes the confrontational elements of society-based struggle with the state.[25]

Within the third ideal-type, Villalòn suggests that "it may be at times difficult to empirically categorize particular societal activities in this schema—social groups may simultaneously play a game and attempt to change the rules."[26]

These three orientations largely parallel at the domestic level the typology that Lipschutz suggests in relation to transnational civil society. I conclude this chapter with a consideration of the relations between the turuq and states.

Relations between the turuq and states, both colonial and postcolonial, as I showed earlier, have not been zero-sum situations. Much as "colonial masters" were able to develop the monoculture of the cash crop, Sufi leaders, who encouraged the bulk of their rural followers to engage in this activity—to respect colonial laws and pay taxes—acquired economic and political power. As for the postcolonial state itself, without the willing collaboration of the turuq, it would have found it much more difficult to carry out its agricultural policy or even to win elections. These relations fit the concept of engagement.

As for contestation, the turuq had adopted antistate positions on several occasions. During the 1970s the Senegalese state reduced the producer price of peanuts. Following that move, the turuq enjoined their disciples to renounce the cultivation of peanuts and instead to engage in the production of millet as a means of achieving self-sufficiency. Likewise, when the Senegalese state tried to reform the family code in order to restrict polygamy, the turuq totally dissociated themselves from the reform on the grounds that it conflicted with Islamic identity.

Isolation is the third and most important orientation of the turuq as an exemplar of a relatively autonomous transnational civil society vis-à-vis the state. Throughout this discussion, I have emphasized the tariqa as a symbolic community that is shaped by the various meetings that bring together disciples from different regions. These meetings—the maulud and ziyaras of different kinds held in Kaolack and international conferences held in neighboring Gambia—create a sense of a sacred space that transcends the nation-state. These meetings also create a culture in which Sufi beliefs and experiences are important ingredients, although experiences other than Sufi may contribute to its shaping.

What are the implications of the existence of these Tijaniyya networks for the question of security broadly understood? They perform many of the functions associated with a modern welfare state not performed by African states. From the standpoint of individuals, security can indeed be perceived in terms of what assures their survival. The turuq, given their transnational, spiritual, and economic activities as well as the matrimonial alliances they facilitate, offer their clientele a wide variety of survival strategies and means for spiritual development. As the turuq and their number of disciples expanded, the potential resources they were likely to put at the disposal of their clientele gradually increased. The zawiya has been, generally speaking, more than a simple place of worship; it has also been a shelter for the needy and for travelers, a place for economic transactions and for lineage-related activity as well as a supplement to the poor medical infrastructure. Different spiritual events, such as the maulud and ziyara, are an occasion for the leadership to collect the funds that maintain the symbolic institutions, support the leadership, and aid the less well-to-do members of the community. The tariqa networks take responsibility for the welfare of hundreds of thousands of individuals, which many African states lack the means to do.

These, then, are some of the elements that permit one to say that the existence and operation of the Tijaniyya networks are likely to favor the security of those who are a part of them. In a decade that has seen some African states not only fail to preserve security, the Tijaniyya networks have picked up many of the enabling functions performed by states. As agents of civil society, they have created conditions of trust and reciprocity that both facilitate the stability of states and preserve an autonomous sphere for the networks.

NOTES

I am grateful to Susanne H. Rudolph, James Piscatori, and the other participants of the Social Science Research Council's "Transnational Religious Regimes" workshops for their suggestions and criticisms on earlier drafts of this paper.

1. Ronnie D. Lipschutz, "Reconstructing World Politics: The Emergence of Global Civil Society," *Millennium: Journal of International Studies* 2 (3) (Winter 1992):393.

2. Susanne Rudolph, "Toward a Theoretical Framing of the Volume" (note to members of the working group on transnational religious regimes, November 15, 1993).

3. See Jamil Abu al-Nasr, *The Tijaniyya: A Sufi Order in the Modern World* (London: Oxford University Press, 1965).

4. The central role played by Sufi orders in Senegambia in the restructuring of the Wolof social order after the colonial conquest has attracted the attention of many scholars. See, for example, Donal B. Cruise O'Brien, *The Mourides of Senegal: The Political and Economic Organization of an Islamic Brotherhood* (Oxford: Clarendon Press, 1971), 12ff., and Lucy Behrman, *Muslim Brotherhoods and Politics in Senegal* (London: Oxford University Press, 1970).

5. See Lipschutz, "Reconstructing World Politics," 393.

6. See Jean Suret-Canale, *Conséquences sociales et contexte de la traite négrière* (Paris: Présence Africaine, 1964), 91.

7. For a discussion of this point, see Leonardo Villalòn, *Islamic Society and State Power in Senegal: Disciples and Citizens in Fatick* (Cambridge, England: Cambridge University Press, 1995), 202–207. I am grateful to Dr. Villalòn for kindly allowing me to quote the page proofs of his manuscript.

8. See Abd al-Qadir Sylla, *Al-muslimum fi al-sinighal, ma'alim al-hadir wa alafaq al-mustagabal* [The Muslims of Senegal: Characteristics of the present, horizons for the future] (Qatar: al-Wahda, 1968).

9. See Cristian Coulon, *Le marabout et le prince: Islam et pouvoir au Sénégal* (Paris: Pedone, 1981).

10. See Mervyn Hiskett, *The Development of Islam in West Africa* (London and New York: Longman, 1984), 10.

11. See E. E. Evans-Pritchard, *The Sanusi of Cyrenaica* (Oxford: Oxford University Press, 1949).

12. The city of Touba, which constitutes a state within the Senegalese state, is the best example of this. From Senegal's independence up to the present, the Senegalese state has never fully taken control of this city. Many products from abroad, having completely escaped customs' duties, are sold there. Fugitives from justice being pursued by state authorities also have a good chance of being granted refuge there with impunity.

13. As far as the Niassène Tijaniyya is concerned, colonial officers sometimes reported it as respectful of colonial laws and at other times as a vehicle of pan-Arabic, pan-Islamic, or pan-African ideologies hostile to the French. My assumption is that Ibrahim Niasse's orientations toward the colonial state changed during the 1950s. It was during that period that he established close ties with some radical Arab and African leaders (e.g., Gamal Abdel Nasser, Kwame Nkrumah). The anticolonial wind that was blowing in the colonized countries influenced not only political leaders but also religious leaders. With regard to Ibrahim Niasse's anticolonial stance, see his pamphlet, *Ifriqiyya ila al-ifriqiyyin* [Africa to Africans] (Lagos: Time Press, 1959).

14. During a pilgrimage to Mecca in 1937, Ibrahim Niasse met the Emir of Kano (in northern Nigeria). At this meeting Niasse managed to persuade the emir that he was the pole of saints (i.e., a redeemer in Sufi eschatology). Not only was Niasse accepted as such in Kano, but it was from this city that this movement extended its influence throughout all of Africa.

15. See Abdullahi Mahdi, "The Military and Economic Nerves of the Sokoto Caliphate: An Examination of the Position of Kano Emirate Within the Caliphate," in *Kano and Some Other Neighbours*, edited by Brawuro Barkindo, 191–204 (Zaria, Nigeria: Ahmadou Bello University Press, 1989).

16. See Evans-Pritchard, *The Sanusi of Cyrenaica*. For a general discussion of the zawiya in the Muslim world, see my "Zawiya," in *The Oxford Encyclopedia of the Modern Islamic World* (New York: Oxford University Press, 1994).

17. See Octave Depont and Xavier Coppolani, *Les confréries religieuses musulmanes* (Algiers: A. Jourdan, 1897).

18. See John Paden, *Religion and Political Culture in Kano* (Berkeley and Los Angeles: University of California Press, 1973); Hiskett, *The Development of Islam*

in West Africa, 287–288; Mervyn Hiskett, "The Community of Grace and Its Opponents the Rejecters: A Debate About Theology and Mysticism in Muslim West Africa with Special Reference to Its Hausa Expression," *African Language Studies* 17:99–140; Christopher Gray, "The Rise of the Niassène Tijaniyya: 1875 to the Present," *Islam et sociétés au sud du Sahara* 2 (1988):34–60; Ahmed Rufal Mohammed, "The Influence of Niasse Tijaniyya in the Niger-Benue Confluence Area of Nigeria," in *Muslim Identity and Social Change in Sub-Saharan Africa,* edited by Louis Brenner (Bloomington: Indiana University Press, 1993), 116–134; Awad al-Sidi al-Karsani, "The Tijaniyya Order in the Western Sudan: A Case Study of Three Centers, al-Fasher, al-Nahud and Khursi" (Ph.D. diss., University of Khartoum, 1985).

19. These practices have long been characteristic traits of popular Islam. Emile Dermenghem has written a remarkable description of these rituals in the Maghreb. See Emile Dermenghem, *Le culte des saints dans l'Islam maghrébin* (Paris: Gallimard, 1954). For an analysis of similar phenomena in India, see Christian Troll, ed., *Muslim Shrines in India* (Delhi: Oxford University Press, 1989).

20. It should be noted, however, that for a long time nonreligious actors have been involved in cross-border trade networks. See Ebrima Sall and Halifa Sallah, "Senegal and the Gambia: The Politics of Integration," in *Le Sénégal et ses voisins,* edited by Momar Coumba Diop (Dakar: SET, 1994), 117–141.

21. See James Piscatori, "Ideological Politics in Saudi Arabia," in *Islam in the Political Process,* edited by James Piscatori (Cambridge, England: Cambridge University Press, 1983), 59.

22. See Hiskett, *The Development of Islam in West Africa,* 287.

23. See the discussion by Susanne Rudolph in her introductory essay in this volume, "Religion, States, and Transnational Civil Society," under the subheading "Is Religion Part of Civil Society? Theoretical Questions."

24. For a discussion of Sufi urbanization, see Donal B. Cruise O'Brien, "Charisma Comes to Town: Mouride Urbanisation, 1945–1986," in *Charisma and Brotherhood in African Islam,* edited by Donal B. Cruise O'Brien and Christian Coulon (Oxford: Oxford University Press, 1988), 135–155.

25. See Villalòn, *Islamic Society and State Power in Senegal,* 26.

26. Ibid.

THREE

Bridging the Gap Between Empowerment and Power in Latin America

DANIEL H. LEVINE AND DAVID STOLL

Benedicta Serrano lives in El Agustino, a barrio that rises on a bare hilltop amidst the seemingly endless shantytowns of Lima, Peru. Like everyone in El Agustino, Benedicta is poor, but she is neither dispirited nor disorganized. Despite continuous harassment and persistent threats of violence from police and army on one side and leftist insurgents on the other, Benedicta's poverty has led her to community organization rather than isolation, activism rather than apathy. Like many of her friends and neighbors, Benedicta Serrano became and remained an activist through her involvement with the Catholic Church, a church that itself has been transformed, by liberation theology and the organizations it spawns, from unquestioned ally of the old order to prophetic voice of a new one.

Benedicta Serrano is a modest and unprepossessing woman with a long history of activism and leadership, including barrio and citywide programs for community kitchens, glass-of-milk programs, educational efforts, and general social as well as political organization. She has a clear and articulate vision of what her activities in the community are all about. At a 1990 meeting held in Lima to consider the overall situation of liberation theology and the likely challenges it faces in the future, she had this to say:

> For myself, after three years of participating in a Christian community, I have learned how important it is to make a commitment to others and to ourselves.

A commitment that works in this life that God has given us, and *for* this life that we continue to share. . . . Through our groups and our organized activities, we have learned to carry out democracy in practice, in permanent dialogue. It's nothing fancy; [but rather] just part of our daily lives, something we do every day, like cooking or planning daily activities.[1]

Benedicta's story is a hopeful one: We hear fresh voices, we see evidence of confidence, organizational skills, and a commitment to change. But another look shows that after years of activism, many of the ordinary women and men who have been mobilized through grassroots religious groups are arguably worse off than when they began. Their organizations face dwindling resources, declining participation, burned-out leaders, and bitter factionalism. From all sides they must contend with hostility and restrictions. In Peru itself, groups have been trapped between a government that is at best indifferent, a much less supportive Catholic hierarchy that has become wary of activism and anxious to reassert its authority, a vengeful guerrilla movement (Sendero Luminoso or Shining Path), and a popular clientele that is starting to drift away.[2]

The experiences of activists like Benedicta Serrano have counterparts throughout Latin America, where decades of reform and change in religion have laid a foundation for new cultural orientations and social capabilities. Backed by religious personnel (and often by mainline church institutions as well), ordinary men and women have come to activism and reached for a new place in society, politics, and in the churches as well. The role played in these developments by liberation theology and the transformations it promoted and legitimized in the Catholic Church are well known, and it is not our intention to go over this familiar ground here.[3] For present purposes, it suffices to note a few points. The move to activism grounded in new understandings of religion and new uses of religious institutions represents a dramatic shift with significance well beyond the frontiers of Latin America: A radical movement was advanced by a section of the priestly class (and the religious groups they helped to found and direct) using that religion's transnational networks to address a general agenda of social and political change. Further, the experience of activism is not limited to Catholics: Protestants and Protestant groups have also been mobilized, although, as we shall see, with characteristic differences from their Catholic cousins. Finally, Peruvian experiences are echoed not only for their success in bringing new social groups to voice and activism, but also in the contemporary crisis now gripping popular religious groups all across the region. They have lost membership, political allies, and financial support. The resulting organizational decay has been deepened by indifference or hostility from former allies in church, society, and politics. Difficulties of this kind suggest that despite the fact that religious change has clearly empowered ordinary people throughout Latin America, there is a palpable gap between this "empowerment" and "power"—between the new energies and orientations spawned by religious change and the capacity of communities and organized groups to achieve tangible and durable benefits.

Will these energies ever have a decisive impact, and, if so, on what? Or are the obstacles simply too great and the resources too meager to create new kinds of religion, culture, and politics? Why has it been so hard to build enduring and effective organizations on the basis of this new empowerment? Questions like these are of more than academic concern. To be sure, the issues raised here are important to scholarship, and as scholars, we search for answers by linking elements of social theory to the experience of not one but many cases and communities. But we must remember that the questions driving this analysis have relevance and impact beyond the confines of scholarship. They come to scholarship out of the experience of ordinary people throughout Latin America who every day face the challenge of renewing organizations and making them work effectively for the community. These men and women are more than mere objects for our study: They are active subjects. They debate the issues, they weigh the options, and the answers they seek and find are as much a part of our story as the theories scholars craft and the connections they see.

Social Capital and Empowerment

In this chapter we examine the religious energies unleashed in Latin America in terms of the creation and transmission over time of social capital. We use the term *social capital* to refer to a constellation of orientations, social skills, and cooperative experiences that alter the basic landscape of politics by creating and encouraging the spread of trust as a social value.[4] Social capital is built over time in a cumulative process whereby acts of trust reinforce one another, making possible the creation and extension of networks of cooperation and "civic engagement." These networks provide a practical basis for embedding any social activity in a supportive and mutually reinforcing context.[5] In this way, they undergird the construction of democratic politics in which broadly based and pluralistic participation and competition replace manipulation and control from above by an authoritarian state. Without such networks and the heritage of social capital that makes them possible, political systems neither "hear" nor respond to the demands of citizens: Their demands remain inarticulate and invisible.

Our central argument here is that the gap between empowerment and power can best be understood in terms of the lack of social capital, or to be more precise, of its isolated and incomplete formation. The problem has as much to do with concrete problems of experience as it does with exaggerated expectations. Like any historical process, building social capital takes time. Those engaged in the process (group leaders, members, and those promoting such experiences) face dangers, difficulties, and opposition of all kinds. After all, the construction of independent resources and of a culture that promotes their sustained use challenges established arrangements of power and privilege. Opposition, often in the form of violent repression, is not just likely, it is inevitable.[6]

These observations suggest that empowerment and its transformation into power will take a lot longer than liberation theologians thought when they set out to change the world in the late 1960s. In the mid-1990s it is clear that what church social activists and much of the Latin American left saw as a short-term (one generation or less) process of consciousness-raising, political mobilization, and conquest of power can only be understood and perhaps achieved over a much longer term. At minimum, the process requires the constitution of stable social groups, the reworking of gender and family relations over generations, and a sustained effort to institutionalize principles of equity in the day-to-day operation of social movements and political institutions. This means that activism that moves to an early focus on politics and political outcomes is likely to run out of steam rather quickly. In the same way, analysis that restricts its focus to politics and political outcomes distorts the process and misses much of the point.

The social capital that undergirds empowerment and makes power possible is best understood as a by-product of more general activities. In a recent review of U.S. religious and social history, Warner argues that "the empowerment functions of religion are latent. At an individual level, those who seek well-being in religion tend not to find it; those who gain well-being in religion are not those who seek it."[7] Warner's comment suggests that efforts to move from the individual to the collective level are likely to fail when organizations lack the kind of mutual trust and shared experience that only comes with time and repeated experience in an activity that is meaningful. Jumping too quickly from religious origins to political ends short-circuits the process, undercutting the social experience in which new cultural formations get a chance to consolidate and basic attitudes to authority are laid down.[8]

Latin American experience presents many particularities and variations, but for our purposes, these differences are less important than the threads that knit the region together. As we shall see, transnational religious linkages of great historical depth and scope are an important component of this unity.[9] The pattern reaches back to the very origins of what we call Latin America. The missionary orders that worked alongside the Spanish and Portuguese monarchies left a legacy that reached beyond churches and seminaries to embrace schools and universities, courts and legal codes. Their efforts had a profound, long-lasting impact on elite as well as popular culture. More recently, instances of transnational religious activism include human rights networks; development agencies; missionary enterprises and their media networks and Bible societies; seminaries, institutes, and publications that promote new religious ideas such as liberation theology; and church bureaucracies whose lobbying and fund-raising campaigns stretch to the United States and Europe.[10]

Several trends have converged in the past few decades to place the impact of religious linkages like these in a new and often much more conflictful light. The long-standing Roman Catholic monopoly has been challenged throughout the region by the rapid growth of evangelical Protestant churches. At the same time, intense movements for change within Catholicism, associated with liberation theology and the popular groups and movements it supports and legitimates, have brought new kinds of religious groups onto the public scene. The dramatic transformations of the past quarter century, including heavy doses of social mobilization, political violence, and authoritarianism, have provided the setting and audience for change while giving these innovations new and heightened impact.

To focus analysis and keep exposition reasonably brief, we anchor our discussion of Latin America in two countries, Peru and Guatemala. Peru and Guatemala are instructive cases for analysis and comparison. The two countries have much in common. In each case, the bottom of the social pyramid is occupied by an impoverished (mostly indigenous) peasantry, which is now streaming into the cities. Religious change takes place in each case amid extremes of poverty and violence, with a wide range of religious and political groups competing for popular support. There are also important differences, and for present purposes we take Peru and Guatemala as representatives of alternative paths and possibilities of religious and political change. Since the early 1960s, Peru has been one of Latin America's leading examples of progressive Catholicism. Gustavo Gutiérrez, a Peruvian, is often cited as a father of liberation theology, and his influence has helped to make Peru a founding center for liberationist ideas and organizations in the region. Beginning in the mid-1970s, networks of groups and of grassroots activists associated with and inspired by liberation theology played a key role in building a major popular movement. Their actions contributed to the return of civilian rule in 1980. Progressive Catholics played an important role in the construction of a broad coalition of leftist parties that captured the mayor's office in Lima as well as a growing number of seats in Congress. This coalition (Izquierda Unida, or United Left) seemed poised for victory in the national elections of 1985, and despite losing that vote to APRA's (Alianza Popular Revolucionaria Americana, long Peru's dominant political party) Alan García, overall prospects for the progressive movement seemed good. But these hopes soon collapsed. The political allies of popular religious groups proved unreliable as the United Left splintered, leaving many grassroots groups divided and adrift. Progressive Catholics also lost key supporters and protection in the institutional church just as they began to be squeezed between the violence of the Shining Path insurrection and the violence of a fearful and vengeful state. A further blow came in the elections of 1990, when grassroots groups voted for Alberto Fujimori, abandoning the parties of the left, who were promoted diligently by church activists. Similar efforts to turn Guatemalan Catholicism into a platform for progressive social change fell victim to military repression of leftist guerrillas.[11] The Catholic Church in Guatemala has also faced one of Latin America's most successful evangelical Protestant movements, whose hopes for social change provide a fascinating and instructive contrast with those of progressive Catholicism. Liberation theology's importance to hopes for empowerment and its contrasting fortunes in these two countries make Peru and Guatemala particularly useful for examining the dynamics of empowerment, power, and social capital.

Latin America's Experience of Transnational Religion

Transnational religious activism was present at the creation of what we know today as Latin America. Having expelled Islam from Spain with the final defeat of the Moors at Grenada in 1492, the crusading spirit moved on to implant Iberian Catholic culture across the seas. Despite the close alliance between cross and sword that marks this history, fusion has rarely been total: Transnational religious organizations (e.g., missionary orders like the Franciscans) retained considerable autonomy. In remarkably little time, they implanted a network of missions, churches, schools, and related ecclesiastical institutions (including the Inquisition), attacking indigenous religious practices and aggressively spreading the gospel. Conversion to Catholicism was an integral part of the whole experience of domination. The monopoly they established has only lately been challenged, this time by the aftereffects of another wave of transnational religious activism, which not only attacks the religious monopoly laid down over these five hundred years but also a series of cultural assumptions and political practices that have grown up around it.[12]

The effort begun in the sixteenth century was no one-shot effort. After the initial burst of conquest and expansion, missionizing activity settled down to a regular routine, including systematic coverage of territories and establishment of a network of institutions. These included land grants, establishment of territories in which missionary orders in effect were the government (an example being the famous Jesuit reductions in Paraguay), and a provision for the regular, systematic transfer of human and material resources (through the orders) between Spain and the colonies. The relative autonomy that religious congregations enjoy in the structure of the Catholic Church facilitated these transfers, allowing missionaries to exercise independent and occasionally critical roles.[13] These institutional arrangements were substantially consolidated by the mid-seventeenth century, and the region settled down to an established religious monopoly that persisted with little challenge for the next three hundred years. Routine was the order of the day.

The most recent noteworthy wave of Catholic transnational missionary activities came in the years after World War II, and gained force with the developments of the Second Vatican Council and beyond. With the communist victory in China, missionary orders like the Maryknolls, which had originally been created to go to China, turned their attention to Latin America.[14] Growing leftist political activism reinforced Church fears of "losing control" over peasants, workers, and the growing urban middle classes. These concerns sparked a range of efforts that combined evangelization with social and political action—for example, in Catholic Action movements (among labor, peasants, students, women, professionals, and the like) designed to insulate the faithful from ideological and political contamination. Groups like the Cursillos de Cristiandad (Little Courses in Christianity, widely known in English as the cursillo movement, founded in Spain in the 1950s and propagated aggressively throughout Latin America), combined intense religious experience with affirmation of hierarchy and loyalty to the Church. The cursillo movement, explicitly targeted at social elites, was in many ways a precursor of contemporary efforts like Communion and Liberation or Opus Dei.[15]

The Second Vatican Council (1962–1965) and its extended impact in Latin America via Medellín (1968) and Puebla (1979) brought renewed interest in missionizing activity, but now with important differences. The decisions to translate liturgies into local languages and to encourage reading the Bible opened up new and highly popular fields for Church activity. At the same time, emphasis on lay participation and (for a while) on internal democratization in the Church spurred the growth of a series of hitherto unknown forms of organization, including networks of small groups (CEBs, from the Spanish for base ecclesial communities, comunidades eclesiales de base), priests' associations and groups of study centers, some affiliated with the Jesuits, some independent. The emergence of these decentralized networks within the overall structure of the Catholic Church came along with important innovations fusing religious change and efforts to spread the gospel with cultural transformation, a surge of organization, and new forms of social and political action. The growth of liberation theology and its associated networks of centers, publications, and grassroots movements is an important case in point. These informal transnational networks have worked effectively at various levels for over twenty-five years.[16] Their systematic effort to legitimate participation and to facilitate experiences of democracy have the potential to spark a cultural transformation of immense proportions.[17]

Alternative continental networks were also established, building on structural differences in the Catholic Church. CELAM (Conferencia Episcopal Latino Americano, or Latin American Episcopal Conference) coordinates the region's national bishops' conferences. CLAR (Conferencia Latino Americano de Religiosos, or Latin American Conference of Religious) does the same for male and female religious orders. Headquartered in Bogotá, Colombia, the two organizations run networks of publications, conferences, and workshops and provide human and material resources that are central to the legitimation and effective diffusion of alternative positions for the Catholic groups. As CELAM moved in a conservative direction after the mid-1970s, differences between the two groups become more prominent, for example, in the interpretations and kinds of actions they promoted in Central America, and particularly in Nicaragua.[18]

Apart from organizations with direct ties to central church structures, a vast number of "development agencies" of religious inspiration have established themselves throughout Latin America in ever growing numbers since the 1960s. One can scarcely visit a barrio or rural community without tripping over programs started by some French, Dutch, Swiss, Irish, American, or other organization.[19] These groups provide otherwise unavailable resources, and their efforts to promote community development, organizational creation, and new public policies have spurred a kind of citizen awareness and a range of activities that did not exist previously.

Human rights networks, comprising offices created by churches (such as Vicariate of Solidarity in Chile or Tutela Legal in El Salvador), along with groups with loose church affiliations (including the Washington Office on Latin America) and organizations with no explicit religious ties (such as Amnesty International), played a critical role in the 1970s and 1980s. Within individual countries, their defense of human rights saved countless lives and maintained open spaces for resistance to repression and arbitrary rule. In transnational terms, they generated information and helped to diffuse it across frontiers, sharing resources and providing access to international arenas.[20]

Although Protestant experience with transnational missionary activism in Latin America does not go back as far as the Catholic, it is no newcomer. Nineteenth-century antecedents include the activities of Bible societies and a series of measures removing restrictions on Protestant activity that were undertaken by anticlerical governments all across the region. Most early missions were sent by immigrant churches from Europe (e.g., German Lutherans, English Anglicans or Methodists, Scottish Presbyterians) and restricted their activities to servicing their particular clientele. These denominations (so called "mainline churches") for the most part remained small, with limited missionary projection. Substantial change began in the late 1960s, when mainline Protestant denominations started withdrawing from missionary work. They were replaced by evangelical, fundamentalist, and Pentecostal churches and their associated cross-denominational missionary groups, who at this time were beginning to carve out an important space for themselves in North American society. These groups, broadly identified with the "Religious Right," now thoroughly dominate North American church efforts overseas. Between 1953 and 1985, the total number of U.S. missionaries overseas almost doubled (28,000 to 54,000). Once dominated by representatives of the mainline churches, by the 1980s, almost 90 percent of the total came from fundamentalist and Pentecostal organizations.

Although by definition Protestants lack the hierarchically defined center that (at least in theory) characterizes the Catholic Church, they have also created international structures for work in Latin America. Churches and nondenominational groups or alliances maintain their own networks, and several regionwide groups are also active. Liberal main-line churches grouped in the National or World Council of Churches with regional affiliates like CLAI (Consejo Latino Americano de Iglesias, Latin American Council of Churches) or ISAL (Iglesia y Sociedad en América Latina, Church and Society in Latin America) can be distinguished from fundamentalist and Pentecostal churches, which operate, for example, through the Latin American Conference of Evangelicals (CONELA) with strong ties to churches and groups in the United States, ranging from the Assemblies of God and the Campus Crusade for Christ to the Full Gospel International Businessman's Fellowship and the Christian Broadcasting Network. Beginning in the late 1960s, these and other groups (including Mormons, Seventh-Day Adventists and Jehovah's Witnesses, to name only a handful) established vigorous expansion programs targeting Latin America, which they envisioned as a decisive battleground, not only against the Catholic Church (still seen as "the whore of Babylon") but also against communism. When the two were perceived to have been in alliance (for example, with liberationist Catholic support of the Sandinista Revolution in Nicaragua), the stage was set for a volatile mix of evangelization with nationalism and anticommunism, often directly linked to right-wing regimes and to the objectives and instruments of U.S. foreign policy.[21]

These efforts met a highly receptive audience, and since the mid-1970s the encounter has produced spectacular growth, including massive numbers of new members, proliferation of small churches (above all in urban areas), consolidation of large churches linked to denominations (Brazil, Chile, El Salvador, Guatemala), and creation of new ways to spread the word, via revivals, crusades, radio, and especially television. At the beginning, many operated through long-established missionary efforts, infusing them with new resources and energies. There was much disaster evangelism, for example, throughout Central America, where new churches often came to coordinate earthquake or storm relief, then stayed to expand seminaries, schools, and church activities in general.[22] Ties with local military rule and alignment with U.S. policy made the task substantially easier.[23]

The new mass clientele for Protestant missionary activity from the 1960s on was created as a result of converging trends in demography, social mobility, and the continuing appeal of religions that stress an intense spiritual life. Dramatic population shifts and accelerated urbanization have drawn Latin Americans to the cities while opening rural life to the outside world via expanded transport and communications. This made ordinary people available for a range of competitive religious efforts. Most accounts of conversion and church growth confirm that converts and new affiliations to Protestant churches are overwhelmingly drawn from men and women with an intense experience of change and mobility and with hopes for improving personal and family life. This helps to explain the widely noted appeal of fundamentalist churches to the newly educated, including groups with technical training, a phenomenon visible in other cultures as well. The appeal of the message has to do with the general sensation of change, a vision of the churches (and at first, their foreign connections as linked to a more "modern" way of living), the attraction of stress on literacy and unmediated access to the text, personal responsibility, intense spirituality, and health and healing.[24]

Protestant success caught most observers by surprise and left many perplexed. Success has sometimes been attributed simply to the power of the mass media, as if television or radio had some magical quality. Others rest their case on a supposed loss of cultural identity or point to the region's deep and violent social, economic, and critical crises, crises that presumably drive converts to seek solace in religions, especially in those which, like the new wave of Protestants, stress charismatic powers and personal conversion to the apparent exclusion of efforts at collective improvement. These theories distort reality and cloud our understanding; a substantial literature is now appearing that provides a better understanding.[25] This is not the place for a detailed discussion, and it suffices here to emphasize a few points: why the audience was available and receptive in these years; how the particular structure of the Protestant churches and their links with transnational organizations spurred growth; the relation of sustained growth to the coming generation of locally recruited leadership; and the nature and impact of political involvement by transnational groups and local affiliates.

Protestant churches are better equipped to adapt to change of the kind that Latin America is experiencing. Their churches are newer, with an intense presence in the expanding urban periphery. They are not burdened with extensive and complex networks that have to be maintained. All this enables churches and movements to operate and compete more effectively in the religious marketplace now emerging in all of Latin America's big cities. Low thresholds help: It is simple to organize a church and not very difficult to gain recognition as a religious leader. There is a built-in dynamic at work here: The poorer the church, the more it depends on expansion to survive.[26] This reinforces the power of the "Great Commission" (the duty of Christians to carry the message and to make disciples of nations and persons) in the consciousness and practices of members.[27]

The impact of this new wave of transnational religious activism stems from the convergence of agents and audience. Agents here include those who staff programs, stand on street corners, and knock on doors to invite residents to attend meetings.[28] As with Catholicism, many of these agents are foreign, but in this case, sustaining and consolidating early expansion is more likely when a new generation of locally recruited leaders takes over. The evidence suggests that this is beginning to happen, as the relative weight of foreign missionaries and their entourage (crusades, meetings, specialized media networks) yields to that of homegrown talent and resources.[29] These changes stem partly from the economic and political difficulties U.S. groups have experienced in recent years, but it is also important to acknowledge the quality and effectiveness of the new generation of local churches. Innovative use of mass media combined with an intense church life (small meetings, overlapping groups, home visits) powered a "capillary" expansion that is likely to prove more durable than the early wave.[30]

Transnational Regimes, Religious Change, and Social Capital

Most thinking about transnational regimes, religious or otherwise, proceeds from a basic assumption that these are organized and knit together in some overt fashion—projected to a clientele by some group or network of groups that operate together, however loosely. Analysis therefore focuses on the deliberate projection of programs or models by transnational bodies such as private voluntary organizations, development agencies, church-related structures, political and trade union networks. Issues of staffing, finance, and the delivery of ideas and programs through networks, linkages, and the like move to center stage.[31] The assumption of intentionality and deliberate projection often helps in making sense of the behaviors of corporations, private voluntary organizations, or state agencies. It can also help when dealing with specific religious groups. But an exclusive focus on formal organization and intentionality misses much of the action. Transnational influences work in more complex and varied ways. Networks can take many forms, ranging from vertical and hierarchical patterns—the classic Catholic model—to more acephalous models in which emulation, not projection, takes precedence—as in Muslim cases as well as in some of the more recent Latin American experiences that we discuss later in this chapter. All of this underscores the fact that contemporary religious change in Latin America has no unique, explicit, or self-conscious "moment of creation." Change arises instead from simultaneous creation and informal emulation as groups of clergy and ordinary people begin experimenting with new ideas and models for change around the same time all across the region. By themselves, formal documents and official institutional programs provide no direct guide to action or its impact: Religions are more than what elites or institutions do. The relation between leaders and followers, between formal organization and popular understanding, is rarely if ever direct or automatic. The informal side of the process, rooted in civil society— indeed often present at its creation—is central to the potential transformative power of the process as a whole.

We respond to these concerns here by incorporating two mutually reinforcing dimensions into our analysis. The first addresses the construction of civil society as new networks of trust, confidence, and organizational capacities arise out of religious change. The social capital created in this way can lay a foundation for further change in politics as well as religion. The second concerns the process of connecting these new social capacities to the broader exercise of power in enduring and effective ways. The clear and growing gap between empowerment and power throughout Latin America presents a challenge to scholars and activists alike. The empowerment that many expected would result from the religious and social innovations of the past few decades has not translated into the construction of durable instruments of power or into shifts in power relations. Many groups have failed, many hopes have been disappointed.

Hence the inevitable question: If religious change since the late 1960s really has empowered ordinary people by giving them new orientations, social skills, and collective self-confidence, why do these people remain poor and powerless? Why have the relations of power rarely if ever changed in ways that reflect the new social capital being formed? Why have political projects resting on these "new social movements" and assertive new trends in "civil society" so often collapsed? What do the complexities of these relations and the disappointment and defeat of so many hopes suggest about better ways to ask the question if we are to grasp the true possibilities and limitations of empowerment and power that religious change creates?

Religious change contributes to the formation of social capital to the extent that religious groups establish bases for social trust in forms of freely given cooperation with the potential to reach beyond explicitly religious activities to undergird cooperative activity in other walks of life. It is a truism that trust grows and is reinforced with use. The slow construction and reinforcement of relationships of trust among individuals and groups lays a basis for broader arrangements of civic engagement, giving substance to the very notion of a "civil society" founded on organized citizen initiative and independent of the state—a concept that has been little more than a catch-phrase through most of Latin American history.[32]

Recent work on other societies and cultures offers relevant insights into the origins and dynamics of social capital. In a study of Italy's experiments with decentralization and regional government, Robert Putnam and his collaborators discovered that where a program was situated geographically was more important than the specifics of content or implementation in determining success or failure. Exploring the roots of these differences, they uncovered markedly different regional traditions of governance. In the north, a tradition of civic republics rooted in a profusion of autonomous citizen efforts reaches back to the communes and city-states of the Middle Ages. In the south, a tradition of hierarchy and monarchical absolutism prevails, exemplified in the history of Naples. The "civicness" that Putnam found in the north stands in sharp contrast to the "amoral familism" made famous by Edward Banfield in his study of a village in southern Italy. The northern civic pattern grows out of horizontal links of trust and freely given cooperation between individuals and groups; the southern absolutist pattern grows out of a prevailing lack of trust, which makes vertical relations of domination the logical medium for most transactions. In each case, institutionalization of the normative pattern in civic or monarchical arrangements reflects and reinforces the prevailing cultural formations.

Putnam argues that, once established, horizontal networks of civic engagement are more durable and self-sustaining than vertical absolutist traditions. "A conception of one's role and obligations as a citizen, coupled with a commitment to political equality," he states, "is the cultural cement of the civic community."[33] The self-reinforcing and cumulative nature of social capital allows us to speak of circles that are virtuous rather than vicious, that is, series of actions whose self-reinforcing quality promotes the accumulation of resources and supportive experiences in ways that produce growing levels of trust and cooperation, expanding networks of civic engagement, and societies in which "stability" is created from below, not imposed from above. The concept of social capital underscores the mutually reinforcing effect of cultural and social creations, and points our attention to how the moral bases of community are worked out in practice, by embedding them in the structures and routines of daily life. "Trust itself," as Putnam argues, "is an emergent property of the social system, as much as a personal attribute. Individuals are able to be trusting (and not merely gullible) because of the social norms and networks within which their actions are embedded."[34]

Although Putnam demonstrates the importance of social trust and shows why it persists over time, he pays less attention to how and why traditions of trust are established in the first place. Are individuals and societies permanently captive to inherited cultural norms and to the way power is organized? Or can cultures be transformed in ways that leave visible and tangible effects on the social and political order? These questions go to the heart of much recent scholarship on religion in Latin America, which itself responds to a generation of effort by activists and ordinary people to change religion in ways that make culture and politics more democratic. Across a broad range of specific issues—liberation theology and base communities, the rise and spread of evangelical Protestantism, new norms about gender, economic activity, politics, and so forth—the overriding concern has been to understand how religious change can lead to new orientations to self, community, and collective action, as embodied in new kinds of social organizations.[35] The presence of such groups, and the gradual construction of networks among them, changes organized social life as much as it changes religion, making possible the emergence of new norms about activism, equality, and the proper exercise of authority. Social trust is embodied in these new norms and nurtured in everyday activities ranging from study circles to cooperatives and rotating work on community projects. The process is a dialectical one: Norms and structures change together.

Since the 1960s, churches and related religious organizations throughout Latin America have reached out to new clienteles. Inspired by changing ideas about what religion should do and what role it should take in the social order, they carried new messages and sent new kinds of agents to the population. At the same time, this population, set on the move by large-scale demographic and social changes—agrarian concentration, internal migration, war, the spread of literacy and media—came to the churches with urgent, unmet needs. Here, as at other times in history, ordinary people have turned to religion as a path for self-realization, protection, and advancement.[36]

When and how did these changes get under way? It is not easy to sort out deliberate promotion (by pastoral agents or preachers, for example) from emulation and spontaneous, parallel creation. Both are present, and as noted earlier, the evidence suggests that pressures for change began popping up more or less simultaneously in many of the region's Catholic communities in the early and mid-1960s. These early efforts were legitimized by major events in the Catholic Church, including the Second Vatican Council (1962–1965) and the conferences of Latin America's Catholic bishops at Medellín (1968) and Puebla (1979). Although these meetings did not create change ab ovo (agents and audience were already present), nonetheless they played a key role, creating spaces into which local Catholic activists could insert new missions and organizations. New formal and informal networks sprang up, with church institutions and groups of priests in various countries creating study centers, sponsoring publications, and knitting together human rights organizations. Networks of intellectuals and organizers carried the message to the grass roots, sparking the creation of base groups and giving them a place (often literally a room or house, but also, in a broader sense, organizational protection) in which to meet and grow.

These developments lie at the heart of what later became known as liberation theology and served as its connection to the "popular classes." The changes drew the practice of many Catholic groups into line with traditionally Protestant ideals, including the scriptural basis of church life and the importance of conversion and of worship in small, self-governing groups.[37] The new structures, mediating agents, and leadership strata justified by liberation theology[38] were followed by the rapid growth of evangelical Protestant churches that flourished in the same popular classes targeted by liberation theology and assumed by many to be its natural base.[39] These changes helped to create capacities for voice, action, and cooperation of a kind that formerly had been isolated and sporadic in Latin American culture and politics. Challenging the long-familiar Latin American social pyramid with its tiny elite, small middle class, and broad oppressed masses, these new voices sparked hopes for thorough cultural and political democratization.[40]

Although social capital in the sense used here is clearly new, it is important to remember that these new religious networks were never created out of thin air. They arose within enduring social, cultural, and political structures, including the churches. Such continuities provide a valued sense of legitimacy, of belonging to something bigger than self, family, or community. They also open doors to resources and to connections otherwise unavailable to small and weak groups. But in the same measure, they are a source of constraint and weakness, subordinating group interests and agendas to those advanced by larger institutions. Just as once the church had to beg from the rich to give to the poor in charity, in the same way contemporary efforts to "empower the poor" and give them voice depend on support and resources from big structures of power and privilege.

This brings us to the nub of the problem. Most grassroots groups do not begin by spontaneous generation but rather as a result of deliberate efforts by religious agents (including repeated visits, invitations, and promotional campaigns) to draw people into them. The priests, sisters, and lay activists who do the day-to-day work of organization provide continuing connections to larger structures, connections that are anticipated and valued by the men and women who join the groups. The fact of these connections does not negate the reality of change at the grass roots, but it does require us to acknowledge that the long-term impact of social capital created at this level is conditioned as much by the character of these connections—and of the specific agents who implement them on a day-to-day basis—as it is by the new orientations and capabilities themselves. Organizational mediations and linkages are central to the story.[41]

Social capital need not be explicitly political, and for the most part it is not. For many group members, the concept would be remote, and its connection to overtly political projects farfetched. For ordinary people social capital means tools, a house, shares in a cooperative, or a car—concrete resources that people need, not the group per se, or its "project." This makes theoretical as well as practical sense, for the core of any workable concept of social capital is to identify a process that constructs new orientations and capabilities out of everyday life routines and struggles. Networks are strengthened by use, building on small victories, accumulating social resources, and reaching from family, neighborhood, or business to larger structures and institutional arenas. Seen in this light, it is clear that time is needed, perhaps generations, if the process is to have any chance of taking hold. Success is unlikely when efforts are made to leap directly from small-scale actions to "politics" on a grand scale. One longtime observer of peasant groups in Venezuela argues that insisting on beginning with an explicitly political project can be self-defeating. "A political project is something immense. It means nothing less than the pretension to arrive at power, take power and project a new type of organization for Venezuelan society. Very logical for those who work at conceptual levels. But for those working at the practical level, it's like asking a peasant who is making a slingshot to kill birds if he has thought about building an atomic bomb."[42]

Ambitious political goals such as "seizing the state" or changing "the system" can be unrealistic and exhausting for movements that build incrementally from below. Constructing power in civil society is also an immense project, and time alone will not do the job. Success requires sustained effort, with attention not only to the building of networks but also to the whole process of putting together and maintaining linkages among levels. Analysis must devote as much effort to conceptualizing power and studying networks on this level as on the level of national politics and big institutions.

The Case of Progressive Catholicism in Peru

Peru's experience with popular religious and political organization has already been discussed in broad outline, with emphasis on the constraints and defeats of recent years: the harsh effects of Peru's economic and political crisis, the loss of allies in church and politics, the threat and reality of violence from all sides. Before going into detail on the sources and true extent of this crisis, it is worth remembering for a moment how promising it all once seemed. Beginning in the late 1960s, there were clear signs that long-standing patterns of oligarchic domination in Peru were beginning to lose their grip. The "progressive" military regime of General Velasco Alvarado (1968–1976) launched a series of important political and institutional reforms, promoting agrarian reform and encouraging grassroots organizations of all kinds. Internal migration accelerated, mixing hitherto isolated coastal and mountain (Creole and Indian) communities. Responding to these changes, an extensive network of local groups sprang up all over the country, providing new spaces for participation and new opportunities to make that participation effective in political terms.[43] The ideas that later crystallized as "liberation theology" took form in these years, drawing strength and examples from the social and cultural changes taking place in the country as a whole. Through the early 1960s, new ideas were worked out in a wide range of forums, including pastoral weeks, social seminars, and priests' associations, along with a range of student and professional groups.[44]

The movement's early success makes sense as part of the breakup of what had been an exceptionally powerful and long-lasting system of domination, founded on equal measures of racism, cultural hegemony, and the physical isolation of communities, and control of the state by a narrow and self-perpetuating elite. Julio Cotler described Peru as a triangle without a base, noting how classic patterns of power and domination rested on parallel networks reaching down from the elite into a mass in which the dominated were isolated from one another, with few chances for contact, little sense of common interest, and no organization of shared identity.[45] The broad social changes noted earlier, reinforced by the deliberate organizational efforts of progressive Catholics and other groups, mark the beginnings of efforts to fill in the base of that triangle, subverting the hierarchical arrangements of control on which elites had long depended.

Peru's experience with religiously linked popular organization has consistently stressed combining theological reflection with organization and action in groups that, although inspired by liberation theology, remain formally independent of the church. Liberation theology's flagship organization, the Instituto Bartolomé de las Casas, is a case in point. The Institute grew out of earlier initiatives intended to support research, reflection, and publication on issues ranging from theology to literature, community organization to politics. The Institute was organized in its present form in 1980, in a deliberate attempt to professionalize personnel and to put finances on a permanent and independent footing. Independence allows the Institute to sponsor activities that would otherwise come under formal ecclesiastical control. A noteworthy example is the "summer schools of theology," a program that brings together thousands of people every year at various levels throughout the country for courses and promotion programs on theology and on biblical studies.[46] Other examples include the Institute's permanent involvement with grassroots groups across the country. These include women's groups (such as the famous community kitchens of Lima's barriadas), neighborhood associations, teachers, peasant and trade unions, and professional organizations of all kinds. This involvement includes providing training materials, holding seminars and retreats, and helping coordinate local and regional programs.

It is precisely these efforts that have fallen on hard times in Peru. The importance of independent popular organization to both the theory and the practice of progressive Catholicism in Peru requires that we look closely at the causes of the problem. Some have argued that the apparent success of these groups was an illusion to begin with. Luis Pásara asserts that the efforts of what he calls "Peru's leftist angels" was marked from the beginning by a "radical Catholic style" (compounded of utopianism, clericalism, elitism, intellectualization, and verticality) that undercuts the validity of any claim to empowerment of the poor.[47] In this view, progressive Catholicism was just another manipulation of the poor, and Pásara approvingly cites one critic who accused liberation theology of "taking for popular whatever sociology says about the people."[48] In later work, Pásara directs attention to the ambiguous role played by the nongovernmental organizations (NGOs) who organize popular groups and mediate their access to international resources and advice. Because they often advance their own agenda, presenting it as the voice of the people, it should be no surprise that associated groups have only shallow roots in the community and find it difficult to survive any loss of aid, let alone sudden shifts in the interests of their outside supporters.[49] These criticisms deserve serious attention, but their validity is undermined by a determination to attribute all problems to defects inherent in the progressive Catholic project for popular organization. Complete understanding requires us to take a more broadly based look at the issues. Some of the problems faced by groups in Peru are common to Latin America as a whole; others are specific to Peru itself.

As in much of Latin America, the transition from military to civilian rule (1980 in Peru) immensely complicated the panorama for popular groups. There was much unity in the struggle to end military rule, a unity reinforced by the unpopular policies of Velasco Alvarado's successors in what is commonly known as "the second phase" of Peru's military regime.[50] With open, civilian, and democratic politics, that unity began to crack open. Instead of a single common enemy, there were now alternatives, choices, and competition. Popular groups once united around the churches divided, following a variety of political paths; the United Left itself did not last out the decade. These general political trends were reinforced by a tendency to organizational fragmentation with roots in the economic and political crisis of the 1980s. Peru's economic decay, which included the region's first "debt crisis" and a sharp drop in real income and levels of living, was amplified by a bout of hyperinflation at the end of the decade. The result was a desperate search for personal and family survival in contexts that favored scattered small-scale initiatives while punishing large-scale collective action—

small enterprises (*micro empresas*) or street vending as opposed to trade unions.[51] Economic disaster went hand in hand with decay in state capacity and a crisis of leadership and credibility for the established political parties, whose collapse was made manifest in the 1990 presidential elections, when the unknown Alberto Fujimori won a smashing victory over novelist Mario Vargas Llosa, himself an insurgent antiparty candidate. These troubles were compounded by the cholera epidemic that opened the 1990s.

The combined impact of economic, political, and social troubles undermined popular groups at the very moment when changes in the composition of the Catholic hierarchy were beginning to turn the tables against them within the Church itself. Throughout the 1980s, conservative Vatican policies had slowly made their weight felt all over Latin America. In the context of a campaign against liberation theology and what the Vatican sees as undue "politicization of religion," seminaries and publishing houses have been investigated and occasionally purged, censorship has been imposed, and progressive clergy and prelates have been transferred or retired to be replaced by young conservatives. This campaign had particular force in Peru, where by 1988 conservatives had taken a voting majority in the Episcopal Conference. This was a prelude to the 1990 retirement of Lima's progressive Cardinal Juan Landázuri Ricketts and his replacement by a conservative. The resulting loss of ecclesiastical cover meant restricted access to resources or popular organizations, growing competition within the Church, and increased difficulties in mobilizing support.[52] One example suffices to give the flavor of the problem. Women's groups that depended on Church and political allies (in the hierarchy and the mayoralty of Lima) for powdered milk that they then distributed through their own networks of groups now found themselves cut off. When available at all, resources were now channeled through networks controlled from above.[53]

The impact of these factors was magnified manyfold in Peru by the steady escalation of violence and terror throughout the 1980s and into the present decade. This violence, stemming from the Shining Path insurrection and state efforts to suppress it, has had devastating effects on popular groups. As Shining Path expanded and extended the reach and the intensity of its activities, the guerrillas began to clash openly with groups active in popular work, including many linked to the progressive Catholic agenda. These encounters quickly escalated from threats and intimidation to a steady stream of bombings and assassinations in a systematic attempt by Shining Path to eliminate competition for popular support. Shining Path targets have included educators of any kind, rural extension agents, and union organizers, along with priests, sisters, catechists, and so forth. The campaign of terror did not always succeed. For example, Shining Path was effectively blocked in areas with strong preexisting popular organizations, such as the Sur Andino, a region stretching from Cuzco south to Puno.[54]

The general climate of terror and violence nonetheless sparked a massive flow of refugees and disrupted countless efforts. At the same time, the escalating official war against Shining Path marked any organized effort as potentially subversive, leaving popular groups trapped in the middle, their members frightened, their leaders prime targets for violence.[55]

The attacks on popular organization in Peru have been so powerful, and allies of popular groups so fickle and unreliable, that even the strongest networks would have had difficulty surviving, let alone remaining vital and active. That they have survived at all attests to the strength of their own commitment and to the depth of their roots in the population. Survival has surprised many observers, who for some time now have been writing obituaries for both liberation theology and for the popular movement. Indeed, a curious pattern is now emerging in commentary about popular groups. In the mid-1970s, a generation of scholars joined with activists on the left in viewing such groups as bearers of a wholly new politics and culture. But as Peruvian sociologist Teresa Tovar has pointed out, these same intellectuals now commonly paint the same groups as disorganized, irrational, divided, and anomic.[56] The same population provides the raw material for both paradigms: They cannot both be true. But of course the dilemma is false. As we have seen, communities and their circumstances have changed, with the combined effects of economic and political crisis dividing groups and producing an understandable focus on short-term, localized strategies for survival. For our purposes, the point to remember is that grassroots groups must not be reified—identified once and forever with a single organizational form or program. We need to see them in all their complexity and contradiction, made up of individuals trying to chart a course in difficult and changing seas. Thus, as Tovar states, "we need to get away from searching for a historical subject [in the classical Marxist sense] something privileged and sacralized by virtue of its position in the social structure and from whose vantage point one can make sense of society and history as a whole. Instead, we need to see a plurality of subjects, whose identities are created through their own interactions and forms of understanding, and whose positions are therefore changeable."[57]

Much of the difficulty for liberation theology lies in the concepts that theologians and activists have used to identify popular groups and organize their political project. From the outset, liberation theology's social analysis has relied on Marxist categories—above all class, exploitation, and dependency—to make sense of poverty and of the poor. But poor people have identities and concerns that reach beyond class; failure to acknowledge this distorts their interests and puts their support at risk. Reducing popular identity and concerns to class alone created a gap between popular culture and those who opted for the people. Political strategies were also flawed. The underlying notion of politics at work here ran more or less like this: The "people" by definition constitute a majority; unified around class interests, they will grow in confidence and strength, achieving victory for some sort of socialism. The weakness of these ideas became evident in the wake of the 1990 elections, when popular groups all across Peru abandoned parties of the left and voted massively for Alberto Fujimori, who was widely perceived as "one of us"—that is, nonwhite.

The combination of economic decay, political disaster, and organizational weakness noted here has sparked several efforts at rethinking. In 1990, for example, the Instituto Bartolomé de las Casas held a meeting in Lima to evaluate the experiences of the past few decades and set a course for the future. The organizers were blunt: "We have come a long way in Latin America and we have questioned many of the ideas we once held. But we also know that we were not all wrong. Many of our insights were clearly incomplete, and were not exempt from the necessary encounter with history which defeated, modified, or verified them. We want to cast a balance."[58] After several days of discussion and interchange, one of the central conclusions reached was that "for twenty years we've talked about popular groups and made the popular subject central to all our theories, but we've never really let popular groups speak for themselves."[59]

Unfortunately, the admonition to "let popular groups speak for themselves" is not as simple as it sounds. Despite reverses and continued subordination, the popular culture of Peru has changed in significant ways. Based on her studies of Lima shantytown dwellers, Stokes affirms that "the recent history of popular political consciousness in Peru is of interest not only because it demonstrates hegemony at work, but also because it illustrates the flowering of a counterhegemony." She notes the "rise of a counter-hegemonic mentality and counter-hegemonic social movements. As these mentalities and movements grew, the institutions and forces that had helped them to emerge were greatly strengthened; the relationship between the popular movement and the conditions propitious to its growth was dialectical and mutually reinforcing."[60] In some cases, urban or rural popular movements have become sufficiently institutionalized that they have managed to withstand the effects of violence, economic decline, and political abandonment.[61] But one thing we know with certainty about popular groups is that their fate is rarely in their hands alone. To survive and be effective on the political scene, they need allies and connections, and they have to learn to play the political game. This requires jettisoning much of the theory of politics and political action on which the movement has long relied. Popular groups can no longer assume that they are by definition a majority and therefore destined to victory. They need to operate as a minority, one group among many, making deals and playing the game of politics over the long haul.[62]

Our discussion of progressive Catholicism in Peru has underscored the need for a long-term view, one that reaches beyond the agendas of leaders and institutions (political or ecclesiastical) to connect with the concrete needs and the evolving identity of popular groups themselves. Scholars and observers often confuse theological texts and what activists write about the people with what the people themselves think and say. This is understandable; it can be tiresome and difficult to make the effort required to find and listen to ordinary people. Each of the authors has swallowed clouds of dust and waded through seas of mud just to get to communities and attend meetings in the countryside and city neighborhoods. Seemingly endless hours feel like "wasted time": hours spent on the bus, followed by more hours waiting for people to get home from work and slowly gather together. But when the effort is made, things are learned that simply cannot be discovered any other way. Among many lessons, one that is quickly absorbed is that those who "go to the people" are often much more radical than the people themselves.

One regularly hears discussions in Latin America about the Church's role as a "voice for the voiceless," representing and fighting for the oppressed and the excluded. This is an honorable and often risky role: The effort to accompany and defend the poor has meant suffering and death to many. But serving as "voice for the voiceless" retains presumptions of distance and authority that fit easily into traditional directive roles. For those raised in a hierarchical and still paternalistic tradition, being a voice for the voiceless can be a lot easier than standing aside to let the voiceless speak for themselves, hearing what they say, and trusting them to act.[63] Ordinary people have ideas of their own, ideas that are often ignored or simply glossed over by pastoral agents with an agenda to put in place. They are interested in politics, and they want to act in ways that will benefit themselves and their families and communities, but their politics is much less crude, much more nuanced than a simple class-and-politics-first vision would lead us to believe.[64]

The Case of Evangelicals in Guatemala

In Guatemala a military-dominated state crushed the kinds of political mobilization envisioned by liberation theologians and social activists. Catholic pastoral workers organized an extensive network of educational programs and cooperatives in the 1960s and 1970s, but many of these organizations were destroyed when guerrillas tried to turn them to their own purposes and the Guatemalan army responded with kidnappings and massacres. The Catholic Church staged a surprising recovery from the apocalypse of 1980–1982, and a defiant "popular movement" associated with the Catholic left was becoming stronger in the early 1990s. But what was most visible in Guatemala were its flourishing evangelical Protestant churches. In the 1980s evangelical church leaders claimed to represent more than a third of the population; by the 1990s they hoped to be shepherding more than half. Since then, church-growth planners have been obliged to face the realities of revolving-door membership, which could place their share of the population as low as 20 percent.[65] But a neighborhood's evangelical churches still tend to draw many more people than the local Catholic parish does.

The North American genealogy of Latin American Protestantism has made it easy to misinterpret its appeal. Having grown out of sustained missionary activity from a dominant power, born-again religion has often been condemned as an alien cultural invasion. It is true that evangelical visions of reforming family life, restoring moral order, and empowering believers draw on foreign models, most obviously the United States. It is also true that North American missionaries continue to be influential coordinators and financiers of evangelism, mass media, pastoral education, and organization-building. But most evangelical churches are now led by Latin Americans, not foreign missionaries, whose budgets in any case have been dwarfed by the number of people attracted to the new churches. If recent rates of growth continue, a third of the Latin American population could identify itself as *evangélico* in another generation. Latin evangelicals also have their own distinct priorities. Unlike their North American brethren, the majority are Pentecostal. That is, their churches preach baptism in the Holy Spirit, and they practice "gifts of the spirit" such as speaking in tongues, faith healing and prophecy, in ways that may draw on folk Catholic traditions.

Because evangelical leaders tend to political conformism in comparison with their Catholic competitors, they often stand accused of undermining Latin American resistance to the North American juggernaut. Astounded by evangelical success among the poor, Catholic and left commentators have often painted Latin American evangelicals as right-wing conspirators or their dupes. It is true that the U.S. religious right became embroiled in the Reagan administration's war policies in Central America—indeed, the religious right was one of the few enthusiastic constituencies for it. Particularly in Central America, there is no shortage of elites, including military officers, who have taken refuge from the social admonitions of the Catholic Church in a suitably nonjudgmental evangelical congregation. Upwardly mobile people have found born-again religion a useful way to individuate themselves, and poor people find it an eloquent new idiom to express their tribulations.

As a movement, however, Latin American evangelicals do not share the agenda of the North American religious right. In the specific case of Central America, evangelicals show little interest in becoming anticommunist cannon fodder. Research conducted by Ignacio Martín-Baró shortly before he and five other Jesuits were murdered by the Salvadoran army suggests that Salvadoran evangelicals differ little from the rest of their social class in political attitudes.[66] Despite many efforts by evangelicals to get involved in electoral politics and to organize political groups, on the whole these have met with only scattered success to date, and have yet to cohere into stable political vehicles.[67]

Only in moments of crisis have churches pulled together and got behind savior-like political figures. Two well-known cases occurred in Peru and in Guatemala. We have already noted the experience of Peru, where then-unknown candidate Alberto Fujimori got critical backing from the Evangelical Alliance in the 1990 presidential elections. That alliance ended soon after Fujimori took office, when he broke basic campaign pledges and turned autocratic. Guatemala provides an instance of a much longer-term relation. The bulk of that country's evangelical leadership lined up behind Efraín Ríos Montt, a retired general and evangelical convert who seized power in 1982. The alliance was strengthened by the general's campaign to bring morality to government and it remained in force through the brutal counterinsurgency campaign that made Ríos Montt into an international human rights pariah. Ríos Montt remains popular in Guatemala. As an icon of law and order, he combines the appeal of the righteous evangelical with that of the military caudillo. In the 1990 election he was the most popular candidate for president, among Catholics as well as evangelicals, until a constitutional impediment knocked him out of the race. Four years later he won election to the Guatemalan congress along with the single largest block of deputies, from a party that is a personal vehicle, which may enable him to change the constitution.

Evangelical attitudes toward politics may not appear to be very consistent. Whether you wish to flee the corruptions of the world, rebuild the walls of Jerusalem, or fight godless communism, a contradictory justification is always available. The most commonly sounded note among evangelists in Latin America is still probably avoidance, not least because religious minorities have much to fear from the turntable politics of unstable republics. But as churches attract politically active members of the middle and upper-middle classes, these individuals have sought prayerful encouragement for electoral campaigns. As they succumb to the usual fate of politicians, evangelical church leaders draw back again. In the specific case of Guatemala, the emerging dictum is that although church members are free to get involved in politics, they should do so as individuals rather than committing the church as an institution, which ought to remain above politics. After political violence abated somewhat in the mid-1980s and Guatemala returned to elected government, evangelical visionaries tried to translate their growing membership into electoral strength. Yet they proposed little more than electing morally committed brethren, who were to fight corruption and find "Christian" solutions to intractable social conflicts. In Guatemala this is called *la derecha moralizante* ("the moralizing right"). One reason for the lack of a constructive program is that the "moralizing right" includes powerful elite interests who oppose structural change. Even these vague hopes were dashed when the first evangelical to be elected president, Jorge Serrano Elías (1991–1993), proved to be highly corruptible. When he tried to cover up his many transgressions by suspending the constitution, he was driven from office in disgrace.

The apparent futility of political reformism in a situation like Guatemala returns us to the basic question of this chapter: Can the day-to-day discourses and practices of grassroots religious groups have a long-term impact on how power is exercised in an authoritarian society? Whether these groups are Catholic base communities, evangelical congregations, or something else, can they, over decades and generations, work to build reserves of social capital and social trust which can then spill over into other arenas?

One level on which the impact of such groups needs to be studied is that of gender relations, particularly in households and the socialization of children. Evangelical churches have long been understood as a way for women to bring men under control, but how gender politics operates in the milieu of Latin American churches has only recently been identified as an issue.[68] The evils of machismo and the rewards of marital harmony occupy a prominent place in the rhetoric of these groups, but divergences between discourse and practice have yet to receive much attention. It is also likely that Catholic base communities and evangelical congregations approach gender issues in different ways with different implications.[69] Sustained fieldwork is needed to see how changes in gendered behavior, particularly the male exercise of authority, work over several generations, especially how these affect the way children are raised, their social expectations, and their behavior.

In wider social arenas, ambivalent evangelical hopes for "this world" can be understood as a cautiously phrased ideology of empowerment. Consider the discourse of self-improvement for which the Latin American left has so often attacked evangelicals as antisocial opportunists. Allowing ample room for personal failure ("falling" into sin and repenting) and group schism (the Lord's "calling" to start a new congregation), the evangelical discourse of fictive kinship ("brothers" and "sisters" in Christ) should build trust among converts, their families, congregations, and other brethren. For evangelicals accustomed to living under repressive political systems that offer few possibilities for constructive action, the mere activity of prayer, sometimes referred to melodramatically as "prayer warfare" or "spiritual warfare," can become a language of protest. To observers thinking in terms of explicit protest, appealing to the power of prayer may sound like little more than passivity and resignation. Yet it provides a moral language to interpret social crisis, identify underlying causes, and weigh possible responses. The discourse of prayer sets expectations that, because they are sure to be disappointed, can become a foundation for political action in the future.

As a result, evangelical moralizing is not hard to interpret in terms of building social capital and social trust. Perhaps the key premise is the evangelical belief in the power of moral transformation, of individuals being regenerated or "born again." To change society you have to start by changing the hearts of individuals, evangelical leaders argue. Change enough individuals, they believe, and you will change society. More honest officials will inhabit the government, Christian military officers will end egregious human rights violations, businessmen and workers will treat each other with greater respect. Such thinking may seem ingenuous, but taken in its own terms, praying to "raise up a nation" is an attempt to turn a gospel of personal empowerment into a language for building confidence in the possibility of fair play among diverse social groups.

Evangelical visionaries assert that they are constructing a new moral order that will revitalize private and public in societies rife with deceit and distrust. They are seconded by David Martin, the sociologist of religion known for his work on secularization, who has described how separationist, even sectarian evangelical congregations can serve as a cocoon for nurturing new social values, with particular emphasis on domesticating authoritarian, violence-prone males. Were evangelicals as separable from the interactions of daily life as they are in their religious rituals, we might postulate the existence of a moral counterculture, even an alternative civil society. But because evangelical moralists live and work in corrupting and unforgiving milieux, we have to ask exactly how their hopes translate into the poverty-stricken, repressed communities where the majority of Guatemalans live.

For a look at this local level, consider the case of the Ixil Mayas, an indigenous peasant population of about 85,000 in the western highlands. Following the Spanish Conquest, the Ixils reinterpreted missionary Catholicism in terms of their own indigenous traditions, and the clergy gradually became powerless to stop them. The first missionaries to disrupt Ixil syncretism were a new wave of imported Catholic clergy who arrived in the 1950s. In the name of orthodoxy, priests from Spain organized restless youth to break with the ways of their elders. Although radicalized clergy later referred to the resulting groups as "base communities," they were never known as that locally, and most group members had ameliorist, not revolutionary expectations. Evangelical churches boomed only after 1980, when the Guatemalan army defeated guerrilla organizers through a ruthless policy of massacre, scorched earth, and relocation. With the Catholic Church being scapegoated by the army for the arrival of the guerrillas, many Ixils sought refuge in evangelical churches. Although the Catholic Church almost disappeared as an institution in the early 1980s, it has again become an influential presence despite the arrival of twenty-odd evangelical groups, which range from tiny splinters and unstable one-man theocracies to a few large and well-organized denominations.

In Ixil country, both Catholic reformers and evangelical churches have been associated with empowerment. In traditionally gerontocratic communities, rule by elders has been eroded, as have patron-client relationships between Mayan peasants and nonindigenous patrons.[70] New forms of association have set up new channels of communication, including a new consciousness of "rights" vis-à-vis larger political structures.[71] A new class of "promoters" in bilingual education, development projects, and cultural revitalization have made visible progress in advancing themselves, and sometimes their communities. These promoters, who are generally reform Catholics or Protestant, are learning to compete with nonindigenous Guatemalans on their own terms, but without abandoning their indigenous identity. As a result, the more favorably situated Ixils are redefining their relations with ladinos "from below." They do not appeal to laws or government, nor do they even look to transformations at that level. Instead, they construct new rituals of equality in religious services and build new personae as literate entrepreneurs and administrators who can hold their own with previously superordinate non-Indians.[72] By changing the cultural and political landscape, they change the terms in which struggle is understood and engaged.

Like the majority of Guatemalans, Ixils are not trying to storm the gates of Jerusalem. When confrontation looms, they generally try to avoid it, because the consequences can be so devastating. At the level of evangelical churches, political engagement is simply not where they put most of their energy. It is easier to find pastors scorning *la política* than encouraging activism, arguments for which still have to be made in an apologetic tone. What preoccupies evangelical churches on the institutional level is evangelism and the planting of new congregations, and on the personal level the redefinition of self and the reformation of family life. For observers in search of a social and political dimension to the faith, born-again religion continues to be very individualistic, almost private. Although it is not hard to find leaders who enunciate right-wing prophetic visions, while others utter left-wing alternatives, it is very uncertain how much these matter to the vast majority of ordinary members.

The disjunction between religion and politics goes deeper than the disappointments of liberation theology or the hesitancies of born-again Protestants, to a basic distrust of confessional politics. In the Ixil towns, for example, virtually everyone denies voting for political candidates on the basis of religion. These are not people schooled in the fine points of Western secularism, and they make these denials even though two of the last five presidents have been evangelicals who sparked considerable debate over religion and politics. Instead, Ixils stress, they vote on the basis of the personal qualities of the individual person (including whether he belongs to the ruling party, in the hope of attracting the benefits of patronage). When the leadership of a political party is dominated by a particular religious tendency, as sometimes occurs, this fact is mitigated by the recruitment of a religiously diverse ticket of candidates. Catholic bishops occasionally warn against the dangers of "holy war" between Catholics and Protestants, but in the Ixil area there is little sign that anyone wants to shed blood over confessional differences (land and cows are another matter). Ordinarily, Catholics and Protestants manage to work together without apparent friction over religion. Even very committed evangelicals and Catholics are quick to sermonize on the virtue of tolerance. This suggests that Catholic as well as Protestant congregational religion can be viewed as a slow but steady builder of what Ixils call *confianza,* or confidence, which can be taken as their term for social trust or social capital.

In comparison with the Islamic revival of northern Africa and the Middle East, religious structures in Latin America seem to be less state-oriented and less overtly political. When Guatemala's born-again dictator Efraín Ríos Montt threatened the church-state distinction with a prophetic interpretation of his authority, he was lampooned effectively as "the ayatollah" and "Dios [God] Montt." Although many evangelical leaders will probably support him again if they have the chance, they are quick to disavow his theocratic inclinations, which he also denies himself. Because of the strength of these feelings, religion may in any case not be as important a language of politics in Latin America as it has lately become in the Middle East. Not only is the proper role of Catholic bishops and evangelical associations in politics hotly contested. Bishops and evangelical associations are themselves often the first to acknowledge the limits on their role. The absence of overtly confessional groups makes it possible for Catholics and evangelicals to enter the political arena under nonsectarian forms of leadership.

The Gap Between Empowerment and Power

Judging from the experience of Peru and Guatemala, the social capital being generated by religious change in Latin America has some built-in limitations. Even the most optimistic scenarios quickly run up against powerful limits to the scope of any possible action, and ambiguities in how empowerment is experienced and understood. New social capacities and cultural norms have clearly been established, but they are constrained and limited in many ways. Group members understandably focus on local issues and tangible evidence of improvement for themselves and their families and communities. The deployment of new resources is stunted by the authoritarian social relations in the midst of which so many groups have emerged. Leaders and ordinary members of these groups are vulnerable to attacks by their enemies and abandonment by their own self-professed allies.

The gap between empowerment and power, which gives title to these reflections, neatly captures the ambiguities of the situation. The origins of this gap lie in a range of obstacles—cultural, ideological, and structural—to turning new orientations into organizations that last and that accomplish goals that mean something to their members. Evidence of the gap abounds: the continued vulnerability of cooperatives, the short lives of community organizations, the collapse of political alliances between new social groups, the inability of many leaders to nurture new generations of leaders to succeed them, the subsequent burnout of what seemed bright possibilities, and of the whole idea of a "new way of doing politics."[73] To be sure, achievements need not be political, in the sense of "parties, power, and votes." Making politics primary can be self-defeating. The poor can be counted upon to put much of their effort into the usually quiet improvement of their families and neighborhoods, the quest for education, and the struggle for economic success. But whatever the short-term goal may be, in the long run it cannot be realized or even envisioned without the establishment of durable structures that eventually produce new kinds of leaders whose activities spill over into other arenas.[74]

Any effort to understand and to bridge the gap between empowerment and power will be enriched if we can begin to sort out how much of this gap stems from religion itself and how much is derived from the impact of relations with existing structures of power, such as the state or major economic formations. How much of the problem comes from the specific character of religious change itself and from the special role played by churches as institutions? How much is the product of economic weakness, effective repression, circumstance, and fickle allies? Consider the following points:

- Change at the grass roots is often constrained by the very religious agents who set the reform in motion. Anxiety over keeping grassroots groups loyal to the church hierarchy inhibits alliance-building with groups like themselves: Decisions of all kinds are referred to the hierarchy. At best, the results are dense but segregated networks of groups; at worst, potential nuclei of civil society are strangled at birth.[75]
- Such constraints have lately been reinforced in the Catholic Church by the combined effects of a Vatican campaign against grassroots autonomy and the evaporation of external funding and personnel upon which grassroots groups have long depended.[76]
- Change at the grass roots can also be constrained by members' reluctance to move past a local focus for group actions. Goals are

limited to begin with; ordinary members are wary of utopian dreams.

- Prevailing images of what politics is about also do much to hem in grassroots groups. Part of the difficulty lies in liberation theology's emphasis on the "wisdom of the people," which deprecates connections to other social groups and levels. For too long, liberation theologians assumed that "politics" was a simple matter in which "the people" (the majority) would achieve power and implant socialism. That leaves little room for maneuver when socialism has lost its appeal, and it leaves activists helpless when politics requires constant efforts at negotiation and compromise.

- Many grassroots Catholic groups inspired by liberation theology put considerable trust in alliances with left-wing political parties. Peruvian experience suggests how vulnerable such groups can become to manipulation or division at higher levels. The "new politics" being created at the base fell victim to the "old politics"; groups were left adrift and abandoned.[77]

- The result is paradoxical: Bridging the gap between empowerment and power is more likely when power itself is not an initial goal. Groups need to consolidate their own identity and to found their inner life on enduring bonds of solidarity, trust, and the experience of common effort. Reaching for political goals at the beginning undercuts the effort to build ties like these, and guts the very possibility of sustained collective action of any kind over the long haul.

Conclusion

How can the concept of social capital help us understand and perhaps even bridge the gap between empowerment and power in Latin America? Religious change creates a potential for changes on a larger and broader scale. Central to these changes is the creation of networks of new grassroots communities and of a group of newly confident men and women who are their members, whose organized presence and newfound voice alter the landscape of culture, society, and politics. This is where social capital is created; this is the basis for any hope for a new civil society. But the process is shot through with ambiguities, and the potential is constrained by limitations, some self-imposed, others imposed on groups and members by forces beyond their control. Grassroots groups cannot be understood in isolation from surrounding structures. They emerge in close connection to national and transnational institutions. The issue is not to get away from such relations, but rather to reconstruct them so that they can provide the basis for clusters of sustained independent action, not continued arrangements for subordination.

Susanne Rudolph has suggested three questions that should guide any discussion of religious agents as units of transnational civil society: Do they demonstrate the reality of transnational flows? Do they affirm the consequential nature of these for patterns of conflict and cooperation? And can one specify the respects in which transnational civil society organizes itself?[78]

Reviewing our argument in light of these criteria underscores once again the ambiguities of the Latin American experience. The importance of transnational flows in religious change is obvious. New cultural norms have been elaborated, new patterns of organization have been legitimated, and new issues such as liberation theology, human rights, and the resurgence of born-again Christianity have been placed on national and continental agendas. These innovations have had clear impact in community organizing, in cooperatives, and in new political movements, including radical challenges to the existing order. Innovations of this kind rest on the elaboration of new social solidarities, values, and collective bonds that help activists and ordinary people to stay together through tough times, and that connect otherwise innocuous community activities with larger political potential. Seeing these innovations as initial efforts to build social capital permits us to specify how transnational civil society organizes itself. The effort takes place, if at all, through a long-term process in which concrete human needs—not only for material goods but also for spiritual and religious satisfaction—find expression in programs and group structures brought to local audiences by religious activists of all kinds, from Catholic sisters to evangelical preachers.

Perhaps expectations were exaggerated to begin with. Many scholars expected "everyday forms of resistance" to build impetus for structural change. Beneath the surface of everyday group concerns, they searched for utopian longings.[79] Yet the aspirations of ordinary people tend to stay modest, for self-protection if nothing else. Scholars and activists alike were also misled (and misled themselves) by the clamor to "reread history from below." Looking at history as experienced by ordinary people is of course important, if for no other reason than to underscore the importance of popular actions and to avoid the assumption that history is only what elites do and institutions mandate. But more is at stake than rereading history from below, because it is precisely in the fusion of history as experienced from below with power and culture as projected by elites and their institutions that keys to the future are found.

A first step in any effort to bridge the gap between empowerment and power is to acknowledge that building social trust and accumulating social capital take time. What political and religious progressives in Latin America understood as a direct progression from consciousness-raising (*concientización* in Spanish) to mobilization and power is actually a much longer and more tangled process of change that works, if at all, through the constitution of stable social groups, the refashioning of gender relations and the family, the slow strengthening and transformation of community, and the institutionalization of equity in politics. Building social capital is a project for the long haul: Closing the gap between empowerment and power is less a matter of bringing the majority to power than of learning to live and survive as a minority, playing the political game day to day at all levels. For the new politics to have a chance, groups will have to play the old politics more attentively than ever before.

NOTES

The authors thank Cary Fraser, Charles Kenny, James Piscatori, Susanne Rudolph, and Catalina Romero for comments and suggestions on earlier drafts of this chapter.

1. "Nuevos Horizontes de Liberación," panel with Benedicta Serrano, Paulo Freire, Gustavo Gutiérrez, *Páginas* (Lima) 118 (November 1992):60, 71.

2. The Peruvian Catholic hierarchy was once considered one of the most progressive in Latin America. But in recent years the effects of growing Vatican pressure have been amplified by a wave of appointments of young conservatives to key positions. See Ralph Della Cava, "Thinking About Current Vatican Policy in Central and Eastern Europe and the Utility of the 'Brazilian Paradigm,'" *Journal of Latin American Studies* 25 (2) (May 1993):257–282; idem, "Vatican Policy 1978–90: An Updated Overview," *Social Research* 59 (1) (Spring 1992):169–199; and Jeffrey Klaiber, *La Iglesia en el Perú* (Lima: Pontificia Universidad Católica del Perú, Fondo Editorial, 1988).

3. See, for example, Arthur McGovern, *Liberation Theology and Its Critics: Toward an Assessment* (Maryknoll, NY: Orbis Books, 1989); Madeleine Adriance, *Opting for the Poor* (New York: Sheed & Ward, 1986); Marcelo Azevedo, *Basic Ecclesial Communities in Brazil* (Washington, DC: Georgetown University Press, 1987); Phillip Berryman, *Liberation Theology* (New York: Pantheon, 1987); *Religious Roots of Rebellion: Christians in the Central American Revolutions* (Maryknoll, NY: Orbis Books, 1984); idem, *Stubborn Hope: Religion, Politics, and Revolution in Central America* (New York and Maryknoll, NY: The New Press–Orbis Books, 1994); Michael Dodson and Laura O'Shaughnessy, *Nicaragua's Other Revolution: Religious Faith and Political Struggle* (Chapel Hill: University of North Carolina Press, 1990); William E. Hewitt, *Base Christian Communities and Social Change in Brazil* (Lincoln: University of Nebraska Press, 1991); Daniel H. Levine, *Popular Voices in Latin American Catholicism* (Princeton: Princeton University Press, 1992); David Martin, *Tongues of Fire: The Explosion of Protestantism in Latin America* (Oxford: Basil Blackwell, 1990); Jenny Pearce, *The Promised Land: Peasant Rebellion in Chalatenango, El Salvador* (London: Latin America Bureau, 1986); David Stoll, *Is Latin America Turning Protestant?* (Berkeley: University of California Press, 1990), or David Stoll and Virginia Garrard Burnett, eds., *Rethinking Protestantism in Latin America* (Philadelphia: Temple University Press, 1993); Scott Mainwaring, *The Catholic Church and Politics in Brazil:*

1916–1985 (Stanford: Stanford University Press, 1986); Daniel H. Levine and Scott Mainwaring, "Religion and Popular Protest in Latin America: Contrasting Experiences," in *Power and Popular Protest: Latin American Social Movements,* edited by Susan Eckstein (Berkeley: University of California Press, 1989); Scott Mainwaring and Alexander Wilde, eds., *The Progressive Church in Latin America* (Notre Dame: University of Notre Dame Press, 1989). Recent trends in scholarship on liberation theology as well as on religion and politics in Latin America generally are discussed in Daniel H. Levine, "On Premature Reports of the Death of Liberation Theology," *Review of Politics* 56 (1) (January 1995):105–131.

4. For a broad discussion of the concept and uses of social capital, see Robert D. Putnam, *Making Democracy Work: Civic Traditions in Modern Italy* (Princeton: Princeton University Press, 1993) and the sources he cites. The broader foundations of the argument about social capital can be traced back to Alexis de Tocqueville, *Democracy in America,* 2 volumes (New York: Schocken Books, 1961), and to Aristotle.

5. For a discussion of social capital that stresses the relevance of context and embeddedness, see Alejandro Portes and Julia Sensenbrenner, "Embeddedness and Immigration: Notes on the Social Determinants of Economic Action," *American Journal of Sociology* 98 (6) (May 1993):1320–1350.

6. For a detailed account of the violence brought to bear on those promoting such efforts, see Berryman, *Stubborn Hope.*

7. R. Stephen Warner, "Work in Progress Toward a New Paradigm in the Sociological Study of Religion in the United States," *American Journal of Sociology* 98 (5) (March 1993):1070. In his reexamination of the theory of secularization in light of U.S. history, Warner stresses that religion in the United States has been culturally pluralizing, structurally adaptable, empowering, generative of identity, and a powerful source of new voluntarism.

8. Researchers all too often identify political outcomes with religious origins in misleading and distorted ways. The demand is for immediate change, and change confined within narrowly political channels. John Burdick, for example, states: "Conceived thirty years ago in the womb of the Second Vatican Council, the People's Church grew in the 1960s and 1970s under the shadow of dictatorship and reached a kind of maturity in 1979, when priests nourished by the theology of liberation found themselves walking the corridors of power in revolutionary Nicaragua. In retrospect, it now appears that the Sandinista Revolution may have represented the Popular Pastoral's high water mark." John Burdick, "The Progressive Catholic Church in Latin America: Giving Voice or Listening to Voices," *Latin American Research Review* 29 (1) (1994):184–185. On the misuse of Nicaraguan experience by ideologues of Left and Right, see Daniel H. Levine, "How Not to Understand Liberation Theology, Nicaragua, or Both," *Journal of InterAmerican Studies and World Affairs* 32 (3) (Fall 1990):229–246.

9. To be sure, unity has other sources and dimensions. For a more general discussion, see Daniel H. Levine, *Constructing Culture and Power in Latin America* (Ann Arbor: University of Michigan Press, 1993), chapter 1.

10. Most accounts of transnational dimensions of religious change in Latin America do not address the issue of whether or to what extent these constitute a regime in the sense used here. See, among others, Sara Diamond, *Spiritual Warfare:*

The Politics of the Christian Right (Boston: South End Press, 1989); Michael Dodson and Laura O'Shaughnessy, *Nicaragua's Other Revolution*; Phillip McManus and Gerald Schlabach, eds., *Relentless Persistence: Nonviolent Action in Latin America* (Philadelphia: New Society Publishers, 1991); Ronald Pagnucco and John D. McCarthy, "Advocating Nonviolent Direct Action in Latin America: The Antecedents and Emergence of SERPAJ," in *Religion and Politics in Comparative Perspective,* edited by Bronislaw Misztal and Anson Shupe (Westport, CT: Praeger, 1992), 125–147; Brian Smith, *More Than Altruism: The Politics of Private Foreign Aid* (Princeton: Princeton University Press, 1990); Christian Smith, *The Emergence of Liberation Theology* (Chicago: University of Chicago Press, 1991); and David Stoll, *Is Latin America Turning Protestant?* Systematic accounts of Vatican policy to Latin America are rarer, but see Ralph Della Cava, "Thinking About Current Vatican Policy," and E. Hansen, *The Catholic Church in World Politics* (Princeton: Princeton University Press, 1986). David Martin broaches transnational issues, but more in terms of systems of ethos than organized patterns of ideas and action. Martin, *Tongues of Fire.*

11. See David Stoll, *Between Two Armies in the Ixil Towns of Guatemala* (New York: Columbia University Press, 1993), or Phillip Berryman, *Religious Roots.*

12. We refer, of course, to the growth and spread of evangelical Protestantism. On these movements and their significance, see Stoll, *Is Latin America Turning Protestant?*; Martin, *Tongues of Fire;* and most recently, Harvey Cox, *Fire from Heaven* (New York: Addison-Wesley, 1994). Evidence and argument on these issues are reviewed in Daniel H. Levine, "Protestants and Catholics in Latin America: A Family Portrait," in *Fundamentalisms Comprehended,* edited by Martin E. Marty and R. Scott Appleby (Chicago: University of Chicago Press, 1995), 155–178.

13. The same is true today. Catholic religious orders (and church structures generally) continue to be relatively privileged channels for people, ideas, and other resources. Their role in sustaining resistance to military rule, maintaining human rights networks, and promoting development projects throughout Latin America over the last thirty years is a case in point.

14. Religious orders are also subject to change, and many have been dramatically affected by involvement in changing social and political contexts. See Penny Lernoux's posthumously published *Hearts on Fire: The Story of the Maryknoll Sisters* (Maryknoll, NY: Orbis Books, 1994).

15. As these comments suggest, foreign priests (and to a lesser extent, sisters) are also an important presence in Latin American Catholicism. Many churches continue to depend on foreign personnel, who come to the area through direct diocese-to-diocese, church-to-church agreements as well as through connections with missionary orders and movements.

16. Catalina Romero, "Theology of Liberation and Networks in the Catholic Church" (unpublished manuscript, 1992), and C. Smith, *Emergence.*

17. Levine, *Popular Voices.*

18. Levine, *Popular Voices;* Brian H. Smith, *More Than Altruism*; C. Smith, *Emergence.*

19. Brian H. Smith, *More Than Altruism.*

20. Lawrence Wechsler, *A Miracle a Universe: Settling Accounts with Torturers* (New York: Penguin, 1990).

21. Stoll, *Is Latin America Turning Protestant?*

22. Stoll lists eight organizational forms that evangelical missionary activity commonly assumes: the crusade, the relief and development agency, the support mission, the alliance, the conference, the confraternity, the ethnic federation, and the "the Third World Mission." David Stoll, "Characterizing Evangelical Transnational Networks: The Case of the United States and Latin America" (unpublished manuscript, 1992).

23. This is also true in Chile under the military government, and in reverse for the case of the Nicaraguan revolution, where the Sandinistas found strong support from the international networks of liberation theology.

24. Cf. Manuel Marzal's account of reasons given for conversion to new churches in Lima: a general sense of change in life, followed (in order) by access to biblical truth, the desire to find Christ, and the experience of healing and health. Manuel Marzal, *Los Caminos Religiosos de los Inmigrantes a la Gran Lima: El Caso de El Agustino* (Lima: Pontificia Universidad Católica del Perú, Fondo Editorial, 1988), 386.

25. Levine, "Protestants and Catholics"; Marzal, *Los Caminos*; Martin, *Tongues of Fire*; Stoll, *Is Latin America Turning Protestant?*; and Stoll and Burnett, *Rethinking Protestantism.*

26. Bryan Froehle, "Religion and Social Transformation in Venezuela: Grassroots Religious Organizations in Contemporary Caracas" (Ph.D. diss., University of Michigan, 1992), and Levine, "Protestants and Catholics."

27. The "Great Commission" is based on Matthew 28:19, in which Jesus says, "Go therefore and make disciples of all nations, baptizing them in the name of the Father, the Son, and the Holy Spirit." The "Great Commission" undergirds missionary Christianity in general and is particularly important to evangelical Protestantism. Cf. Stoll, *Is Latin America Turning Protestant?*, 3, in which he defines evangelical Protestantism as "a tradition distinguished by three beliefs, including (1) the complete reliability and final authority of the Bible, (2) the need to be saved through a personal relation with Jesus Christ, often experienced in terms of being 'born again,' and (3) the importance of spreading this message of salvation to every nation and person, a duty referred to as the 'Great Commission.'"

28. During the 1990 elections in Peru, Alberto Fujimori, a Catholic, was openly supported by the evangelical churches. His opponent, Mario Vargas Llosa, although an atheist, was strongly backed by the Catholic Church, which mounted a vigorous and ultimately unsuccessful campaign against Fujimori on the theme that "Peru is a Catholic country." That the core objection was to evangelical activism carried by independent popular groups is suggested by the experience of coauthor Levine. During the campaign one aristocratic lady complained to him about all these evangelicals she saw, knocking on doors and urging people to support Alberto Fujimori. She thought it scandalous. Levine replied that that is what people do in elections: They knock on doors and try to convince others.

29. Stoll and Burnett, *Rethinking Protestantism.*

30. In contrast to Catholic agents, who are overwhelmingly female (sisters far outnumber priests), Protestant activists appear to be predominantly male. This is in keeping with their message, which in most cases reinforces male domination in households and churches. Class and ethnicity play an ambiguous role. Although

conversions and affiliations to Protestant churches come from all across the social spectrum, available evidence indicates that poor people and (in ethnically divided areas such as Central America or the Andean countries) Indians are disaffiliating from Catholicism at a faster rate than the population as a whole. For further details, see Levine, "Protestants and Catholics."

31. C. Smith, *Emergence;* Levine, *Popular Voices;* and Luis Pásara, Nena Delpino, Rocío Valdeavellano, and Alonso Zarzar, eds., *La Otra Cara de la Luna: Nuevos Actors Sociales en el Perú* (Lima: CEDYS, 1991).

32. This view of civil society and of how ethos and habits spill over from one arena to another echoes Tocqueville's arguments about the relation between associational life and democracy. It also recalls Weber's argument for the link between congregational religion, an individual's sense of social responsibility, and the capacity for participating in collective governance. For a detailed statement, see Levine, *Popular Voices,* and Levine, *Constructing Culture and Power,* chapter 1.

33. Putnam, *Making Democracy Work,* 183.

34. Ibid., 177.

35. See Levine, *Popular Voices,* and Levine, "Protestants and Catholics," for a discussion of the issues and an extensive bibliography. On specific issues like liberation theology or base communities, see Berryman, *Religious Roots;* Berryman, *Stubborn Hope;* and Dodson and O'Shaughnessy, *Nicaragua's Other Revolution.* On Protestantism, see Martin, *Tongues of Fire;* Stoll, *Is Latin America Turning Protestant?;* Stoll and Burnett, *Rethinking Protestantism;* and Levine, "Protestants and Catholics."

36. Examples from other times and places include the role of religious groups in the competition for popular organization in colonial Vietnam, the activities of religious groups in colonial and contemporary Africa, and the well-documented relation of religion to revolution in sixteenth-century England. For a full discussion, see Daniel Levine, "Religion and Politics in Comparative and Historical Perspective," *Comparative Politics* 19 (1) (October 1986):95–122.

37. Stoll notes that, "In a sense, charismatic renewal and liberation theology only brought Protestantism within the walls, where a series of dilemmas continued to drive Catholics into evangelical churches." *Is Latin America Turning Protestant?,* 36.

38. C. Smith, *Emergence;* Levine, *Popular Voices,* chapter 2.

39. Edward Cleary stresses similarities between the two, stating that both "Protestantism of a particular kind and a Catholicism fostered by Vatican II and interpreted by clerical and lay leaders in Guatemala offered forms of religion suitable to changing social and economic conditions in which traditional Indian religion (with its strong economic implications) was breaking up. In effect, Pentecostalism and reform Catholicism offer bridges for the socioeconomic and political changes taking place in the country." Edward Cleary, "Evangelicals and Competition in Guatemala," in *Conflict and Competition: The Latin American Church in a Changing Environment,* edited by Edward Cleary and Hannah Stewart-Gambino (Boulder: Lynne Rienner Publishers, 1992), 185.

40. See Levine, *Popular Voices,* chapter 2, for a review of the pattern of change.

41. Hewitt's careful study of groups in Sao Paulo, Brazil, *Base Christian Communities,* affirms the decisive role that agents and mediators play in setting the orientation and character of grassroots groups. Similarly detailed research on how media-

tions work on a regional scale is scanty, but available studies provide a mixed and often ambiguous image. There is clearly conflict and competition among competing networks: At the continental level, networks such as CLAR (the regional federation of religious orders) or ISAL (a progressive Protestant federation) promote autonomous communities, whereas CELAM (the continental bishops' group) works steadily to rein them in. At the same time, regional and subregional alliances of evangelical Protestants with strong ties to the United States encourage autonomy along with greater acceptance of political authority.

42. Alberto Micheo, "Una Experiencia Campesina," *SIC* (Caracas), no. 417, November 1983.

43. The experiences of this period aroused considerable enthusiasm and interest in making sense of these new patterns of social, cultural, and political change. See, for example, Carlos Ivan De Gregori, Nicolas Lynch, and Cecilia Blondet, *Conquistadores, de un Nuevo Mundo de Invasores a Ciudadanos en San Martin de Porres* (Lima: Instituto de Estudios Peruanos, 1986); Jose Matos Mar, *Desborde Popular y Crisis del Estado en el Perú* (Lima: Concytec, 1988); and Susan Stokes, *Cultures in Conflict* (Berkeley: University of California Press, 1995).

44. Key groups included: UNEC (Unión Nacional de Estudiantes Católicos, a national organization of university students), JEC (Juventud Estudiantil Católica, a similar group for secondary students), JOC (Juventud Obrera Católica, Young Catholic Workers), MTC (Movimiento de Trabajadores Cristianes, Movement of Christian Workers), MPC (Movimiento de Profesionales Católicos, Movement of Catholic Professionals), and ONIS (Oficina Nacional de Información Social, National Office for Social Information, a national priests' organization). ONIS was one of many groups of progressive clergy that sprang up all around Latin America in these years. Others include Colombia's Grupo Colconda, Argentina's Movement of Third World Priests, and a group known as "The Eighty" in Chile. These and others participated in a well-known meeting held in Chile in 1972 of "Christians and Marxists United for Socialism" that marked an early high point of enthusiasm for the political-religious left in Latin America. Christian Smith traces the history of these priests' associations in *Emergence*.

Many of these efforts were knit together by the influence of Gustavo Gutiérrez, whose collaborators and former students played important roles in all of these groups and in building the popular movement of the late 1970s and early 1980s. For details, see Catalina Romero, "The Peruvian Church: Change and Continuity," in *The Progressive Church in Latin America*, edited by S. Mainwaring and A. Wilde, 253–275 (Notre Dame, IN: University of Notre Dame Press, 1989); Luis Pásara, "Peru: The Leftist Angels," in *The Progressive Church*, edited by Mainwaring and Wilde, 276–327; or Jeffrey Klaiber, "The Church in Peru: Between Terrorism and Conservative Restraints," in *Conflict and Competition,* edited by Cleary and Stewart-Gambino, 87–104. On the popular movement, see Teresa Tovar, *Velasquismo y Movimiento Popular: Otra Historia Prohibida* (Lima: DESCO, 1985). Support from key elements of Peru's Catholic hierarchy (especially the Cardinal Archbishop of Lima) provided ecclesiastical and political cover along with access to key resources well into the late 1980s.

45. Julio Cotler, *Clases, Estado, y Nación en el Perú* (Lima: Instituto de Estudios Peruanos, 1968).

46. These courses are formally sponsored by the Department of Theology of the Catholic University in collaboration with the Institute. On the experience of popular involvement in theological reflection, see Romero, "The Peruvian Church," and McGovern, *Liberation Theology*. On the summer schools, see Klaiber, "The Church in Peru," 92ff.

47. Luis Pásara, "Peru," 291–301 and passim.

48. Jurgen Moltmann, cited in Pásara, "Peru," 298–299.

49. Pásara et al., *La Otra Cara*. See also Michael Smith, *Entre Dos Fuegos: ONG, Desarrollo Rural, y Violencia Política* (Lima: Instituto de Estudios Peruanos, 1992).

50. See Abraham Lowenthal and Cynthia McClintock, eds., *The Peruvian Experiment Reconsidered* (Princeton: Princeton University Press, 1983).

51. See Teresa Tovar, "La Ciudad Mestiza: Vecinos y Pobladores en el 90," in *Movimientos Sociales: Elementos Para una Relectura*, edited by R. Balbi, E. Ballón, et al. (Lima: DESCO, 1990).

52. Ralph Della Cava outlines the bases and consequences of Vatican policy in "Thinking About Current Vatican Policy"; in "Vatican Policy 1978–90"; and in "Financing the Faith: The Case of Roman Catholicism," *Journal of Church and State* 35 (1) (Winter 1993):1101–1122. Klaiber's *The Church in Peru* shows how recent changes in Peru's Catholic hierarchy undermine popular groups, which he describes as "in retreat but undaunted" (90). Citing a well-known incident, Romero states: "In a certain fashion, it was the Peruvian church's own recent history that was being questioned by Rome when the bishops were convoked to the Holy See and asked to make a declaration on theological developments in their jurisdiction. Egged on by members of *Opus Dei* and by a new organization which also has international ties, *Sodalitium Christiane Vitae*—with integralist and totalitarian traits and a liberal pro-capitalist ideology—the media have heated up the debate around liberation theology, singling out bishops and accusing priests of various errors, with the objective of achieving a clear condemnation of liberation theology" ("The Peruvian Church," 260). For a detailed account of the emergence and role of *Sodalitium Christiane Vitae* and its relation to liberation theology, see Milagros Peña, *Theologies and Liberation in Peru: The Role of Ideas in Social Movements* (Philadelphia: Temple University Press, 1995).

53. The neoliberal cast of economic and public policy in the Fujimori government has made resources scarce in the best of circumstances.

54. Peasant organizations and self-defense groups (*rondas campesinas* or peasant patrols) have often been decisive. See Klaiber, "The Church in Peru," for cases.

55. On the situation of terror in city and countryside, see America's Watch, *Peru Under Fire: Human Rights Since the Return to Democracy* (New Haven: Yale University Press, 1992), or Deborah Poole and Gerardo Renique, *Peru: Time of Fear* (London: Latin America Bureau, 1992). For detailed statistics on the toll of violence, see Desco, *Violencia Política*. Klaiber discusses the pattern of Shining Path attacks on Church projects and groups ("The Church in Peru," 97ff). For details on the situation of schools (teachers and students are favorite targets of Shining Path), see Juan Asión, Daniel Del Castillo, Manuel Piqueras, and Isaura Zegarra, *La Escuela en Tiempos de Guerra: Una Mirada a la Educación desde la Crisis y la Violencia* (Lima: Instituto Peruano de Educacion en Derechos Humanos, 1992). The situation of the Church in the countryside is discussed at length in a recent report

prepared by the Peasant Department of the Episcopal Commission for Social Action. "Rural pastoral work," the report states, "has had to confront many problems in the defense of the lives of the poor in the countryside. The effort to accompany these families has brought a state of permanent hostility to pastoral teams. Local power groups and many authorities have used classic accusations of agitators, communists, and subversives to frighten bishops, religious, and lay leaders and to make them pull back. Living this decade at the side of the people has meant a whole new way of living for pastoral agents. Frightened many times, questioned others, but firm in their commitment, these agents have not abandoned their positions. In cases where they have been forced to withdraw, they have moved to other, equally difficult areas." CEAS [Comisión Episcopal de Acción Social], *La Iglesia Católica en el Campo Peruano en la Década del 80: Elementos Para una Evaluación* (Lima: CEAS, Departamento Campesino, 1990), 16.

56. Tovar states: "In the 1970s, when popular groups that never before had a clear social presence made themselves more visible and flourished in a social context that made a place for them as (collective) actors, the idea of a popular movement came to stand for a totalizing subject—an uncomplicated and seemingly automatic gateway to a new future. In contrast, in the 1990s, popular social practices are widely viewed as leading to irrational disorder. If popular subjects once marched inexorably towards a socialist future, now they march towards disorder and barbarism." Teresa Tovar, "El Discreto Desencanto Frente a los Actores," *Páginas* (Lima) 111 (October 1991):27. Stokes, in *Cultures in Conflict*, provides an insightful discussion of transformations in urban popular culture in Peru.

57. Tovar, "El Discreto Desencanto," p. 31. Tovar provides further details, with a specific focus on Peru, in "La Ciudad Mestiza." For a general discussion, see Levine, *Constructing Culture and Power.*

58. Cited in Daniel Levine, "Perú, El Derecho a Pensar en Situación de Fin de Mundo" *SIC,* no. 548, September-October 1992. For a full account of this meeting, see the special number of *Páginas* (Lima) 118 (18) (November 1992), entitled "Desarrollo y Liberación en América Latina: Nuevos Horizontes," and Catalina Romero and Ismael Muñoz, eds., *Liberación y Desarrollo en América Latina: Perspectivas* (Lima: CEP, 1993).

59. Levine, "Perú: El Derecho."

60. Susan Stokes, "Hegemony, Consciousness, and Political Change in Peru," *Politics and Society* 19 (3) (1991):265–290.

61. A case in point often cited is the experience of Villa El Salvador, now a self-governing municipality within Greater Lima. Villa El Salvador began as a resettlement project for squatter settlement invaders elsewhere in Lima. Over the years Villa El Salvador has acquired a dense and interlocking network of economic, social, cultural, and political institutions founded on basic notions of popular participation and self-governance. Not surprisingly, leaders in Villa El Salvador have been a prime target for Shining Path. Some, such as María Elena Moyano, were brutally assassinated, while others, such as Michel Azcueta, barely escaped death. One useful account of the history and organization of Villa El Salvador is Gustavo Riofrío, Eduardo Zeballos, and Romero Grompone, *Lima ¿Para Vivir Mañana?* (Lima: CIDIAG/FOVIDA, 1992), Part II, "Estudio de Casos. Villa El Salvador: Tiempos de Lucha y Organización."

62. Some of this effort is under way. In the summer of 1993, for example, one of the authors (Levine) participated in a workshop held in Lima for grassroots leaders. This workshop was centered on the idea that group survival, and with it any hope for building a new kind of politics and civil society in Peru, depended on finding ways to work more effectively within the old politics. For details, see Levine, "Perú, El Derecho," and Romero and Muñoz, *Liberación y Desarrollo.*

63. Jon Sobrino argues that this is precisely what characterized the murdered Archbishop Oscar Romero's option for the poor in El Salvador. Jon Sobrino, "A Theologian's View of Oscar Romero," in *Voice of the Voiceless: The Four Pastoral Letters and Other Statements,* edited by Oscar Romero (Maryknoll, NY: Orbis Books, 1985).

64. Cf. Marjorie Becker, "Black and White in Color: *Cardinismo* and the Search for a Campesino Ideology," *Comparative Studies in Society and History* 29 (3) (July 1987):463–465, and for general comments, Levine, *Constructing Culture and Power.*

65. Ross Rohde, "Un Análisis Misionológico de la Iglesia Evangélica de Guatemala" (four-page typescript, n.d. [c. 1992]).

66. Kenneth Coleman, Edwin Eloy Aguilar, José Miguel Sandoval, and Timothy Steiginga, "Protestantism in El Salvador: Conventional Wisdom Versus the Survey Evidence," in *Rethinking Protestantism,* edited by Stoll and Burnett, 111–142; John Burdick found that Pentecostals in the shantytowns of Rio de Janeiro were joining a wide array of groups. He argues that misleading stereotypes of evangelicals stem from the fact that local political structures are controlled by Catholics. Evangelicals joined up where Catholic control had been disrupted. John Burdick, "Struggling Against the Devil: Pentecostalism and Social Movements in Urban Brazil," in *Rethinking Protestantism,* edited by Stoll and Burnett, 20–44. At the University of Pittsburgh, Mitchell Seligson has produced similar survey data for Guatemalan evangelicals. Mitchell Seligson, personal communication based on "Guatemalan Values and the Prospects for Democratic Development" (unpublished report).

67. Evangelicals have become more involved in several countries, including Brazil, Peru, Venezuela, and Guatemala. On Brazil, see Paul Freston, "Brother Votes for Brother: The New Politics of Protestantism in Brazil," in *Rethinking Protestantism,* edited by Stoll and Burnett, 66–110. For greater detail on Guatemala as of 1991, see David Stoll, "'Jesus Is Lord of Guatemala': The Prospects for Evangelical Reform in a Death Squad State," in *Accounting for Fundamentalisms,* edited by Martin E. Marty and R. Scott Appleby (Chicago: University of Chicago Press, 1994).

68. Elizabeth Brusco, "The Reformation of Machismo: Asceticism and Masculinity Among Colombian Evangelicals," in *Rethinking Protestantism,* edited by Stoll and Burnett, 143–158.

69. For a Brazilian case, see John Burdick, "Rethinking the Study of Social Movements: The Case of Christian Base Communities in Urban Brazil," in *New Social Movements in Latin America,* edited by Sonia Alvarez and Arturo Escobar (Boulder: Westview Press, 1992), 171–184.

70. See, among others, Douglas Brintnall, *Revolt Against the Dead: The Modernization of a Mayan Community in the Highlands of Guatemala* (New York: Gordon and Breach, 1979).

71. Levine, "Protestants and Catholics."

72. For further details on the Ixils, see Stoll, *Between Two Armies.*

73. See Teresa Caldeira, "Electoral Struggles in a Neighborhood on the Periphery of Sao Paulo," *Politics and Society* 15 (1) (1986–1987):43–66, and idem, *A Política dos Outros: O Cotidiano dos Moradores de Periferia e o que Pensam do Poder e dos Poderoso* (Sao Paulo: Brasilense, 1984).

74. The abundance of reverses indicates that caution is required in drawing conclusions about whether religious change is generating significant amounts of social capital in Latin America. Stretching the metaphor a bit, one might suggest that what is happening is less the accumulation and reinvestment of social capital than primitive accumulation (something like an initial stockpile of resources, painfully amassed, and only occasionally put to the uses to which it was intended). Latin Americans are making initial deposits of social capital whose returns lie sometime in the future. They are creating possibilities, not building on established foundations. This early accumulation of social capital is vulnerable and can easily be exhausted in experimentation with how energies and ideals can be deployed without provoking fatal levels of repression.

75. This is the case of many grassroots groups in Colombia. See Levine, *Popular Voices.*

76. See Della Cava, "Financing the Faith," "Thinking About Current Vatican Policy," and "Vatican Policy, 1978–90."

77. Vulnerabilities of this kind are of course not unique to religious groups, nor to Latin America. Poor people's movements everywhere lack resources and need allies; finding and securing allies often means putting the group's independence at risk. See Frances Fox Piven and Richard Cloward, *Poor People's Movements: Why They Succeed, How They Fail* (New York: Pantheon, 1977), and the broader debate about social movements visible, for example, in Susan Eckstein, ed., *Power and Popular Protest*; Aldon Morris and Carol M. Mueller, eds., *Frontiers of Social Movement Theory* (New Haven: Yale University Press, 1992); or Sidney Tarrow, *Power in Movement* (New York: Cambridge University Press, 1995).

78. Susanne Rudolph, personal communication.

79. See James Scott, *Weapons of the Weak: Everyday Forms of Peasant Resistance* (New Haven: Yale University Press, 1985), and *Domination and the Arts of Resistance: Hidden Transcripts* (New Haven: Yale University Press, 1990).

FOUR

Faces of Catholic Transnationalism: In and Beyond France

DANIÈLE HERVIEU-LÉGER

translated by Roger Greaves

Cultural Homogenization and Communitarian Pluralization

"Transnational religion" refers to any religious system whose organization transcends frontiers and weaves over and above national political and cultural specificities a network of ideologically unified communities linked to a single seat of government. Roman Catholicism represents just such a "religious International" with a capacity for rivaling the power structures of states. Most of the highly centralized "Roman model" was constituted during the Counter Reformation. It constantly reinforced itself throughout the nineteenth century and during the first half of the twentieth century by gradually curbing the local churches' appetite for autonomy and by laying down the limits of the political and cultural compromise that each was empowered to contract with its immediate environment. The long-term, gradual reinforcement of Roman centralization has been abundantly investigated by historians, and some aspects of it are explored in this volume by José Casanova and Ralph Della Cava.

Vatican II constituted a turning point in the process of centralization and produced a number of paradoxical results. On the one hand, the Council, by recognizing the new demographic reality of Catholicism (whose center of gravity is no longer in Europe or North America but in Asia, Africa, or Latin America) opened the way for an acknowledgment of the plurality of Catholicisms at the same time as it made possible, through a fresh approach to ecclesiology, the legitimate expression of their diversities. On the other hand, the workings of the Council, insofar as it initiated an overall theological renewal and a series of liturgical and other reforms applicable throughout Catholic Christendom, favored a process of rehomogenization of Catholicism reinforcing certain tendencies toward the bureaucratization of the Roman system itself. The "monarchical" structure of the Catholic Church was challenged, at least partly, by the Council's willingness to open the fold to diversity. The important role that was conferred on the national Episcopal conferences for the management of the Catholic world is the first sign of this. At the same time, however, the workings of the Roman offices and committees have gradually revealed that the ecclesiastical apparatus has been brought into line, to some extent at least, with the logistics of the large nongovernmental organizations (NGOs), which are essentially transnational.

This twofold contradictory development—receptiveness to the diversity of the local churches and increased central bureaucracy—has profoundly modified the Catholic landscape since the mid-1960s, despite the limits placed on the Council's reforms under the pontificate of Pope John Paul II. However, this is only one aspect of the changes that affected the very logic of the Catholic system during this period. The system, as constituted after the Council of Trent and formalized in its most rigorous form at Vatican I, operated without change up to the end of the pontificate of Pius XII. It was characterized by a powerful hierarchical structure that ensured both the organizational centralization of the institution and the ideological regulation of the Catholic communities. At the same time, however, the fact that Catholicism was rooted in national cultures that remained profoundly marked by specific religious traditions made possible the development of wide-ranging diversity within Catholicism. The "French tradition," the "American tradition," or the "Italian tradition" of Catholicism, all equally steeped in Roman antimodern intransigence, nonetheless each corresponded to very different cultural and mental worlds within the centrally regulated system based in Rome.

At Vatican II, the Catholic institution responded to the demand for autonomy, which appears to be an aspect of cultural modernity by abandoning its insistence on a directly institutional interpretation of the theological notion of "unity." It did so notably by recognizing the diversity of Catholic cultures and by promoting all legitimate forms of expression of this diversity. However, this recognition and promotion of diversity happened just as the worldwide distribution of a homogenized modern culture by means of the mass media was leading to the decline of the national cultural specificities in which the diversified Catholic cultures were rooted. Hence the development toward diversification and concentration is doubly paradoxical. It is not solely due to the contradiction between the bureaucratic rationalization of the Roman system and the internal affirmation of a "tempered pluralism"—a contradiction which is itself a significant indication of the influence exerted by modernity within the Catholic universe. It is also due to the more fundamental contradiction between the historical reality of this kind of plurality and the move toward a cultural homogenization of the planet which is tending to drain local cultures of their content.

The aim of this chapter is to bring out the major shift that has occurred, in this context, from one transnational religious regime to another, from the regulated transnationalism of the older Church to the deregulated transnationalism of communitarian movements within the Church. Despite the present pope's efforts to promote a "New Evangelization" and reunify the Catholic world around its Roman center, the centralized regime regulated from the Vatican—even in its modernized form dating from the latest Council—is suffering from dislocation. Its fate is ineluctably affected by the cultural disqualification of all traditions bearing a unified code of meaning, in a world committed to rapid change and extreme pluralization. This situation of generalized institutional deregulation is affecting all of the great universal religions, not just Catholicism. It favors both the standardization of religious culture in general within the modern culture of the individual and the rise in communitarian expectations that express the identification needs of human groups. The new transnational regime of Catholicism is taking form at the intersection of these two trends: a generalized do-it-yourself approach to belief and the multiplication of mobile affinity networks embodying the communitarian choices of individuals. In this context, the capital of symbols and Christian references has become available for extremely diverse individual and collective appropriations which are renewing the internal pluralization of the Catholic universe.

Today this pluralization is centered less on the affirmation of the historical particularities of national Catholicisms than on the development of new Catholic affinity networks with very diverse orientations—charismatic networks, fundamentalist networks, ecumenical networks, and so on. The cultural homogenization of today's world is ensuring the worldwide distribution of these new forms of religiosity. They are marked by subjectivity and the primacy given to individual experience, by the quest for a "wholly Christian" way of life in a secularized modern universe, and by the wish to confer a "new visibility" on this or that orientation as distinct from official Church structures such as parishes or volunteer movements. The widespread dissemination of some of the new forms of Catholicism shows that they are capable of organizing themselves into international networks with a considerable degree of independence from the hierarchical institution: This has been the case for several charismatic movements founded in America or France; the Comunione e Liberazione and Focolari movements founded in Italy; the Neo-Catechumenal Movement; and Opus Dei, which has spread from Spain to all parts of the world. It is possible to advance the hypothesis that this expanding tissue of extremely diverse worldwide networks constitutes, as such, a new model for a transnational Catholic regime at the intersection of the contradictory processes of cultural homogenization and communitarian pluralization that characterize modernity.

To determine whether this hypothesis has any substance, its validity must be tested in the field. The case chosen for this demonstration is that of French Catholicism, which seems to provide a good example of the type of contradictory changes mentioned above.

Case Study: French Catholicism Between Two Worlds

Until 1986 at least, opinion surveys including questions bearing on declared religious membership reveal with remarkable regularity that 82 percent of all French people declare themselves to be Catholics—despite the fact that the latest church attendance figures show that regular Sunday churchgoing has dropped to below 10 percent in every region. Further, the same opinion surveys reveal that only a tiny proportion of regular churchgoers (7 percent) feel any commitment to the Church's rulings on sexual morality. Does this mean that, at the close of the twentieth century, the country that was once known as *la fille aînée de l'Église* (the Church's eldest daughter) has declared that religious membership henceforth only marginally predicts specific group and individual behavior? This is not a conclusion that specialists in the political sociology of France will hasten to confirm. Election analysis has in fact shown that despite a slight shift to the left in the early 1980s—a shift that largely contributed to the election of François Mitterrand as president in 1981—the Catholic vote is characterized by its middle-of-the-road conservatism. More significant still, it has been possible to demonstrate the homogeneity of regular Catholic churchgoers' opinions on social and political issues such as money, speculation on the stock exchange, state involvement in the economy, the police, multiracial society, disarmament, family policy, schools, and so on.[1]

These contradictory survey findings present the paradox of French Catholicism in a nutshell. On the one hand, it is clear that Catholicism has ceased to be a driving force in the constitution of individual and group identities. On the other hand, it remains true that reference to religion is still a de facto and almost invisible dividing line within a society that in other respects has long since been secularized. The observations that follow set out to throw light, from a sociological point of view, on a few aspects of this configuration in order to reach a better appreciation of the significance of some current manifestations of what is said to be a religious "renewal."

The End of the Parish Civilization

The idea that religion inevitably declines as a society modernizes itself is one of the basic themes relating to secularization. In France, it has received long-unchallenged confirmation from the empirical studies of Catholicism that, up to the late 1960s, dominated work on the sociology of religion. Initiated in the period between the two world wars by Gabriel Le Bras, dean of the Law School at the University of Paris, surveys of churchgoing became particularly numerous after 1950. In spite of the limitations imposed by purely statistical methods, inasmuch as they set out to assess the vitality of religious practice in France, these surveys provided an overall picture of the religious landscape that was extremely useful for research.[2] They drew attention both to the very widespread low levels of regular churchgoing and to the large regional disparities in this respect. Boulard and Rémy showed the influence of ministration history on these disparities and stressed the need for nuancing the widespread belief that the map of urbanization and industrialization was coextensive with the map of religious disbelief.[3] Even when enriched in this way, the analyses persistently illustrated, on a massive scale, the fact that the modern world—the world of industry, technology, urbanization, and communication—is a world in which the Catholic Church is silent, or increasingly so. Recent work confirms that these tendencies are still in existence and are intensifying.[4]

This demonstration of the decline of religious observance in contemporary France was accompanied by a further discovery: the dramatic slump in the recruitment of priests and church members, particularly after 1945. Although the spectacular collapse of the number of callings has a number of remote causes, it is particularly meaningful in the contemporary period, insofar as the Church has ceased over the same period to play a central role in public life. The figures are sufficiently enlightening in themselves: In 1948, there were 42,650 priests in France; in 1960, there were 41,600; by 1975, only 35,000 were left, and since 1987 the number is fewer than 28,000. The annual ordination figure, which stood at 1,000 in 1950, has not risen above 100 since 1975, and since 1959 has remained constantly lower than the number of deaths. The result is a considerable aging of the clerical population: At present, one priest in ten is under forty years of age, and one in three is over sixty-five.[5]

Nevertheless, these downward trends in churchgoing and ordinations are merely indicators. They are truly meaningful only in relation to the type of religious society whose collapse they betoken. If the issues of attendance at Sunday mass and the number of priests are as important as they are for a sociology of French Catholicism, it is not only on account of the central character of church attendance in the Catholic tradition, it is also because they are bound up with the very foundations of the *parish civilization* that dominated France for centuries. In this parish civilization, of which the *clocher*, the local church bell tower, is both the landmark and the symbol in the French countryside, three elements come into play.

- The first is the system of extensive territorial control that makes every inhabitant, potentially at least, a member of a parish.
- The second is the system of total time control in the form of regular liturgical cycles and feast days.
- The third is the system of socioreligious power embodied in the typical figure of the *curé*, the parish priest. The authority of the *curé*, "priest first and foremost," set apart and specially trained for the monopolistic production and distribution of salvation goods, extends from his exclusive entitlement to religious power into every area of public and private life. Opposite the typical *curé* figure is the typical churchgoer figure, radically deprived of religious power and subject to having his commitment to Catholicism assessed from the frequency of his church attendance.

The type of ecclesiastical organization turning on this specific mode of division of religious responsibilities came into being throughout the Catholic world after the Council of Trent (1545–1564) as a reaction to the rise of religious individualism initiated by the Reformation. In order to situate our discussion within the perspective of this conference, it may be said that it was this type of organization that determined the *transnational regime of Roman Catholicism* up to the late 1960s. In France, in the aftermath of the Revolution, it was a springboard for the mobilizing utopia of a Church dreaming of reconquering its total hold on society. The years 1830–1850, during which French Catholicism seemed to be experiencing a rebirth after the trauma of the Revolution, were the golden age of the parish civilization: This period, marked by institutional reconstruction, vocational recovery, and intellectual and devotional renewal, expressed the utopia of a Church actually changing society. However, this balmy period was short-lived. The Church, which had made such a vigorous show of its dynamism in the first half of the nineteenth century, soon found itself in the position of a "besieged citadel," powerless to respond to the political, economic, social, and cultural challenges of modernity.[6] In the phase of ultramontane withdrawal and antimodern aggressiveness that characterized French Catholicism during the second half of the nineteenth century, the parish civilization continued to embody the vision—increasingly alien to the everyday reality of a religious society undermined by the development of industrialization, urbanization, and social mobility—of a total coextensivity of the Church and society.

Even the missionary perspective, which, in the 1930s, led to the founding of the Action Catholique movements whose dynamism characterized French Catholicism up to the late 1960s, was still rooted, to begin with at least, in the dream of a "parish society." It was this dream that for many years inspired mental representations of the reconquest in which Action Catholique militants were enjoined to take part. As Jeunesse Étudiante Chrétienne militants sang in the early 1930s: "We shall make our brothers Christians again." This grand scheme was first mooted in circles descended from the social Catholicism that, since Pope Leo XIII, had reoriented out-and-out rejection of modernity toward an active search for a Christian alternative to free enterprise and socialism, both products of the Reformation and the French Revolution.[7] However, to the minds of the founders of Action Catholique, the ultimate aim of missionary work was necessarily to lead the "new pagans" of the cities, the factories, and the universities back to religious observance under the control of the priests and the hierarchy. The founding of the Action Catholique movements,[8] which became the spearhead of a militant form of Catholicism particularly combative in France, was a forceful response to the religious desertification of France. It was still marked, at the outset at least, by the desire to transform, or re-transform, French society into a society of churchgoers.

In the postwar era, the practical effects of modernization have done more to undermine the parish civilization than the ideological offensives of secularization have done. They have eroded, along with an historical mode of religious organization and sociability, an ideal model of the social presence of the church institution. This ideal, despite being imperfectly inscribed in the reality of the cities and regions, constituted the chief point of reference for the identity of French Catholicism, its ethos, and its mobilizing horizon. Today, many country churches have been deconsecrated or are no longer used. French priests have ceased to be notables. They have joined the ever-growing ranks of the "proletaroid intellectuals" (to use Max Weber's term)—the cultural intermediaries, teachers, social workers, cultural organizers, and so on—who are confronted with a widening gap between the cultural capital that they possess and the precariousness of their socioeconomic status. More profoundly, however, from the viewpoint of the evolution of Catholicism as a system of beliefs, there has been a definitive shift in mentalities: Yves Lambert's study of the transformations of day-to-day Catholicism in Limerzel since the start of the century shows that even in the heartland of Brittany, with its traditionally very high church attendance, the institutionally regulated pursuit of otherworldly salvation has gradually been ousted by an imprecise private religiosity oriented toward this-worldly realities and the psychological fulfillment of the individual.[9] Henceforth, modernity must necessarily be taken into account by French Catholicism—no longer as a rival cultural universe in relation to which it might still contrive to position itself but as a matrix in which it paradoxically constitutes and reconstitutes itself.

A New Configuration of Religion in Modernity

Up to the late 1960s, study of the evolution of Catholicism provided French sociology of religion with good grounds for concentrating on the conjunction between the social decline of religion and the attainment of the autonomies that are specific to Western modernity. The case of French Catholicism made it possible to give substance to a theory of secularization based on three main propositions.

- The first was that the hegemony of technico-scientific rationality that characterizes all Western modern societies is the prime cause for the decline of religious belief (which the decrease in churchgoing is assumed to reflect).
- The second was that the contraction of the religious domain within the social domain is the hallmark of societies that have attained a very high level of institutional differentiation.
- The third was that, in the differentiated and rational societies that Western modern societies are, the nature of religious experience can no longer be anything but optional and private, and, this being so, the experience itself has become inessential to the formation of group identities.

It is only fair to say that, by the late 1960s, this rather sketchy outline had already been enriched and nuanced by a corpus of observations and analyses that obliged sociologists to reconsider the current diagnosis of an inevitable decline of religion in the modern world. Work done by historians questioned the validity of the notion of "de-Christianization" as it applied to modern transformations in religious life. Study of the religious innovations generated by the modernization process itself resulted in the emergence of a more complex dialectic at the conjunction of religion and modernity. It was discovered in the meantime that "popular religion," which had for many years been regarded as the residual trace of a premodern universe doomed to disappear, presented a remarkable degree of vitality and even an unexpected capacity for renewal extending well beyond the deprived sections of modern society.[10] Finally, it was pointed out that the religious institutions themselves, via a phenomenon of internal secularization,[11] were capable of discovering new ways of compromising with modernity, which, after all, they had historically helped to foster.

Nevertheless, the real turning point—from the viewpoint of the analysis of secularization—came a few years later, in the 1970s, when it became obvious in France, as in all Western countries, that the very places that claimed the most advanced forms of rational culture were becoming prone to what was called a "new spiritual culture" or a "new religious awareness." This new type of religious trend gave rise—well beyond the social levels where it originated—to a host of new religious movements outside, alongside, and even inside the main institutional religions. Particular attention was paid to these manifestations of "religious renewal" because they came at a time when, in the West and elsewhere, on both sides of the iron curtain, complex reorganizations of the relationships between religion and politics disproved classical views concerning the expulsion of religion from the public sphere. In the process, the assumed "return of religion," which was originally associated with the soul-searching found among members of the intellectual middle classes destabilized by the recession, took on the dimension of a political "retaliation" ordained by God.[12]

There may be no room today either for the simplistic old paradigm of decline or for celebration or denunciation of the "return of religion." But how is it possible then to think about the complex reality of a religious landscape in which the recomposition of the beliefs, practices, and modalities of religious sociability is based on the continuing decomposition of the traditional forms of institutional religion?

Without entering into a detailed consideration of this problem, I shall outline some of the structural features of the decomposition and recomposition process that make religious modernity an essentially mobile reality. While continuing to draw on the case of contemporary French Catholicism, I shall bear in mind—having taken part in several European and American comparative research networks—that similar trends are attested with varying degrees of likeness in other Western countries. I shall discuss five of these ideal-typical tendencies, the actual development of which can be followed in the field.

1. The first tendency is *the large-scale emergence of a religiosity that is increasingly in tune with the modern culture of the individual.* This tendency manifests itself, among Catholics, in the form of a growing atomization of testimony, as an indefinite number of believers' "personal accounts" refer increasingly loosely to the institutionally guaranteed "main account" provided by the Catholic tradition. In this movement, personal experience and the individual's spiritual quest are enhanced to the point where they become their own justification and yardstick. It is the "authenticity" of the personal quest that is considered important rather than the passive repetition of orthodox truths: "It's not what the Church says that counts, it's my own experience, my own spiritual progress." This insistence on the specificity of individual religious journeys, on the value of personal experience,

and on the subject's emotional involvement in that experience, is particularly apparent in the Catholic charismatic renewal.[13] It first appeared in France in the early 1970s and now comprises 1,800 to 2,000 prayer groups, often affiliated to one of the major communities such as L'Emmanuel, Le Lion de Juda, or Le Chemin Neuf. Having shed its early institutional marginality, the movement is now one of the major components of the present-day French Catholic landscape.[14] Further, the highly subjectivized and emotionalized style of religiosity that is gaining ground with the Catholic charismatic movement is also at work more diffusely in parishes, youth movements, seminaries, colleges of theology, and so on, where community fellowship—the warmth and intensity of interaction within the nucleus of believers—is pursued as the ideal condition and means of attaining personal illumination. In the perturbed circles of French Catholicism, this religiosity corresponds to a "religion of emotional communities" that is primarily a religion of voluntary groups.[15]

2. A second tendency is *the diffusion across national boundaries of the religious sociability of emotional communities*. Such diffusion is taking place on a European scale at the present time, due to the uncommon mobility of movements not restrained by the older parish structure. This sociability is the result, among other things, of the expansion of the major charismatic communities outside France and the intensification of their international networks. The main French charismatic communities are now established in eastern central Europe as well as in the French-speaking European countries. In more general terms, this emotional sociability manifests itself in the expansion of a *festive religiosity* marked by the dual aspects of intensity and mobility in the form of large public rallies. This sociability of the "powerful experience" and the "inspiring site" is well illustrated by the international youth rallies organized each year by the ecumenic community at Taizé and, above all, by the World Youth Days, particularly those held at Santiago de Compostela (1989) and Czestochowa (1991) when 500,000 and 1,500,000 young people, respectively, gathered to meet the pope. They parallel and link up with similar gatherings on the other side of the Atlantic, such as the Youth Rally at Denver, Colorado ("Popestock"), in August 1994. These rallies played an active role in the growth (and the institutional integration) of this expanding emotional Catholic sociability. Twenty-five thousand young people from France took part in the Czestochowa rally after a pilgrimage across Europe that lasted for several days. The Denver World Youth Day attracted 400,000.[16]

3. This tendency toward the emotionalization and subjectivization of religious expression is to some extent combined with a second, broader tendency that can be characterized as *a process of institutional deregulation of religious belief*. The primary expression of this tendency in Catholic circles is the gradual replacement of an authorized relationship with the articles of

the Christian faith, as guaranteed by the ministry, by a pragmatic relationship with the available stock of Christian meanings. In communities of the emotional type, this pragmatism can be seen in the spontaneous way in which the tradition is skimmed for those elements (texts, rites, symbols, and so on) that work best from the point of view of the intensification of the expressive and emotional life of the group and from the point of view of the personal fulfillment of the individuals. This possibility of using the Christian tradition as a "symbolic toolbox" that is accessible without the mediation of a regulating institution favors the development of syncretic homemade beliefs. For example, 25 percent of French people declare that they believe in universal reincarnation, while most of them also declare that they are Catholics.

At the same time, it must be noted that the "availability" of the Christian tradition, though favoring the proliferation of individual "religious entrepreneurs," also facilitates the development of identity-seeking appeals to tradition that are not necessarily linked with an experience of belief. The symbols of Christianity are socially available for reuse in other contexts—political, artistic, cultural, and so on—that are both very diverse and very diversely oriented. The figure of Joan of Arc is pressed into service by the far-right leader Jean-Marie Le Pen; the life of Christ is used as a scenario for pop musicals such as Robert Hossein's *Jésus était son nom;* and, of course, allusions to Christianity are used in advertising. Christian symbols can also be used for ideologico-political operations concerned more fundamentally with the delimitation of the frontiers of the national community faced with the rise, throughout Europe, of forms of multiculturalism resulting from large-scale immigration. Hence, the issue of the "Catholic roots" of France occupies a strategic position in the current public debate concerning the need to make (or refuse) room for Islam in the national community. France currently has over 2 million Muslim residents, and the council of bishops has spoken out very firmly in favor of the assimilation of the immigrant populations and the recognition of their religious rights.

4. A third significant tendency that must be underlined is the tendency toward *the axiological homogenization of French Catholicism,* a tendency that combines with the tendency toward dissemination discussed earlier. At the same time as religious and nonreligious appropriations of the Christian tradition become more individualized and more differentiated, there is a move toward the eradication of the "traditions within the tradition" that for centuries shaped the religious landscape of France. Contrary to a common assumption, France never constituted a homogeneous Catholic bloc. Historical and sociological research has long since shown that the different religious and local cultures that constituted the multiple image of Catholicism in France were extremely diverse. The post-Tridentine Church gradually contrived, not without great difficulty, to fold those diversities together

in the mold of the parish civilization. In a massively secularized society, the cultural dissemination of Christianity goes hand in hand, paradoxically enough, with the erasure of the visible traces of this complex history. Coincidentally with the dissolution of an integrated Catholic culture embodied in what Emile Poulat describes as "a holy history, a holy calendar, a holy geography, an onomasticon, a code of gestures, an ethics, a hermeneutics, a politics and an encyclopedia,"[17] French Catholicism is tending to emerge as a homogeneous ethico-affective milieu. While failing to develop more appealing social orientations, it draws a minimum amount of unity from proposing shared involvement in a number of values such as tolerance, care for the deprived, concern about interpersonal relationships, and the like.

5. It is against this withdrawal into ethics of Catholic social action, as much as against the atomization of Christian memory that makes it available for highly diverse cultural and social reutilizations, that a fifth tendency is developing today both within and outside the Catholic institution, namely *the rise of religious integralism*. Though diversely expressed, its inherent nature is to reject both the modern logic of the differentiation of social fields and the privatization of religious choices to which that differentiation leads. The most violent and most retrogressive form of integralism is that displayed by the fundamentalist groups founded by the schismatic bishop Marcel Lefebvre. Their aim to rebuild Christendom in line with a tradition that they identify with the antimodernist creed of the nineteenth century has led them to clash directly, indeed violently, with "modern perversions" such as freedom of conscience, freedom of expression, democracy, moral "permissivism," and so on. The break with Rome considerably slowed down recruitment—the Vatican's minimalist estimate puts the figure around 100,000 laymen worldwide. However, this movement's influence perdures owing to the mediation of publishing firms, journals, associations, and above all those who have not wished to break with Rome but who continue to disseminate the fundamentalists' views within official Catholicism.[18] Alongside this militant fundamentalism, another type of integralism, much more subtle than the former type, is developing today throughout Catholicism. In France, the leader of this renovated integralism—which is very close to the thinking of the present pope—is the cardinal archbishop of Paris, Jean-Marie Lustiger.[19] Unlike fundamentalism, this trend does not attack modernity head-on. Instead of refuting its ideals, it places a high negative value on them by pointing out that modernity itself has proved to be incapable of achieving them. It endorses the modern promises that the Western world fails to keep or only partly fulfills—solidarity, human rights, justice, and so on—in order to turn the tables on modernity. This integralism comes not to bury, but to praise, the illusory grandeur of the modern ideal of freedom, in order to reaffirm the inevitable subordination of that ideal to the liberation that comes from God alone,

but which the Church (i.e., the legitimate wielders of religious power and knowledge) alone knows how to attain. In a cultural context that is producing a dispersion of the systems of meaning and an individual homemade approach to the concoction of beliefs, the Church is attempting to present itself as the recourse institution. It offers itself as a rampart against the uncertainties of the modern world. It advertises itself as possessing a truth that the individual is unable to produce or discover on his own and that he must therefore, by renouncing the illusion of autonomy, receive from an authority exterior to himself.[20]

In between these two versions of Catholic integralism come a number of groups and movements of the "restitutionist" type. Some of them have been around for some time, others are more recent. Generally affiliated to strongly constituted international networks and acting with the aim of reconquering for the Catholic institution the "public visibility" (and the capacity for social control) that it was assumed to have in the past, these restitutionist groups—such as the powerful Opus Dei or the Comunione e Liberazione movement founded and widely established in Italy[21]—are present in France, but their development is hampered by the French secular tradition of spiritual and temporal separation, a tradition that is largely accepted today by middle-of-the-road French Catholic culture itself.

Conclusion

This account has focused on the shift from one transnational regime to another, from the regulated Catholicism of a bureaucratized Church to a deregulated Catholicism resting on the diffusion of emotional communities and affinity groups. The older religiosity rooted in parish, priest, and *clocher* has yielded to an expanded Catholic sociability that is spreading into domestic and transnational spaces. It is accompanied by the ethico-affective homogenization of Catholicism, which appears socially as a tendency toward the conversion of religious commitment into humanitarian commitment, particularly among young people. This homogenization not only displaces the "traditions within tradition" that characterized the now receding pattern of religiosity but also makes the new Catholicism more portable across national boundaries. These tendencies are to an extent countered by the marked reinforcement of various integralisms that are attempting to circumvent the atomization and banalization of Catholic culture in a country that has become massively indifferent to religion. It is not impossible that the recomposition of the *transnational regime* of Catholicism may partly be situated at the intersection of these tendencies, described here in terms of the specific characteristics of their development in France.

NOTES

1. G. Michelat and M. Simon, "Les catholiques et l'élection: À droite toujours, mais pas aux extrêmes," in *L'élection présidentielle de 1988*, in Dossiers et Documents, *Le Monde*, Paris, 1988.

2. F. Isambert and J. P. Terrenoire, *Atlas de la pratique religieuse des catholiques en France* (Paris: CNRS/FNSP, 1980).

3. F. Boulard and J. Rémy, *Pratique religieuse et régions culturelles* (Paris: Éditions Ouvrières, 1968).

4. G. Michelat, J. Potel, J. Sutter, and J. Maitre, *Les Français sont-ils encore catholiques?* (Paris: Cerf, 1991).

5. J. Potel, *Les prêtres séculiers en France* (Paris: Centurion, 1977); idem, "Crise du clergé catholique ou nouvelle race de prêtres?" *L'Année sociologique* 38 (1988): 63–78.

6. C. Langlois, "Permanence, renouveaux, et affrontements (1830–1880)," in *Histoire des catholiques en France*, edited by F. Lebrun (Toulouse: Privat, 1980).

7. Emile Poulat, *Église contre bourgeoisie* (Paris: Casterman, 1977); idem, *L'Église, c'est un monde* (Paris: Cerf, 1986).

8. A. Latreille and R. Rémond, *Histoire du catholicisme en France* (Paris: Spes, 1962); and Emile Poulat, *Naissance des prêtres-ouvriers* (Paris: Casterman, 1965).

9. Y. Lambert, *Dieu change en Bretagne: La religion à Limerzel, de 1900 à nos jours* (Paris: Cerf, 1985).

10. F. Isambert, *Le sens du sacré: Fête et religion populaire* (Paris: Minuit, 1982).

11. F. Isambert, "La sécularisation interne du christianisme," *Revue française de sociologie* 17 (1976):573–589.

12. Gilles Kepel, *La revanche de Dieu* (Paris: Seuil, 1991).

13. M. Hébrard, *Les nouveaux disciples: Voyage à travers les communautés charismatiques* (Paris: Centurion, 1979); idem, *Les nouveaux disciples, dix ans après* (Paris: Centurion, 1988); M. Cohen, "Figures de l'individualisme moderne: Essai sur deux communautés charismatiques," *Esprit*, April 1986, 47–68; idem, "Le renouveau charismatique en France ou l'affirmation des catholicismes," *Christus* 131 (July 1986):261–279; and idem, "Vers de nouveaux rapports avec l'institution ecclésiastique: L'exemple du renouveau charismatique en France," *Archives de sciences sociales des religions* 62 (1) (July-December 1986):61–79.

14. D. Hervieu-Léger, "Charismatisme catholique et institution," in *Le retour des certitudes: Evènements et orthodoxie depuis Vatican II*, edited by P. Ladrière and R. Luneau (Paris: Centurion, 1986).

15. D. Hervieu-Léger, *Vers un Nouveau Christianisme? Introduction à la sociologie du christianisme contemporain* (Paris: Cerf, 1986); idem, "Present Day Emotional Renewals: The End of Secularization or the End of Religion?" in *A Future for Religion? New Paradigms for Social Analysis*, edited by W. H. Swatos (Newbury Park, CA, and London: Sage, 1993); and F. Champion and D. Hervieu-Léger, eds., *De l'émotion en religion* (Paris: Centurion, 1989).

16. "For Young Catholics, Two Days of Faith and Music," *New York Times*, August 15, 1994.

17. Emile Poulat, "Le Catholicisme comme culture," in *Modernistica* (Paris: Éditions Latines, 1982).

18. L. Perrin, *L'affaire Lefebvre* (Paris: Cerf, 1989).

19. D. Wolton and J. L. Missika, *Le choix de Dieu: Entretiens avec le cardinal Lustiger* (Paris: Éditions de Fallois, 1987).

20. D. Hervieu-Léger, "Jean-Paul II: La stratégie de concentration catholique," *L'Année sociologique* 38 (1988):213–231.

21. S. Abbruzzese, *Comunione e Liberazione: Identité catholique et disqualification du monde* (Paris: Cerf, 1990).

PART TWO

Hierarchy: From a Center and from Above

FIVE

Globalizing Catholicism and the Return to a "Universal" Church

JOSÉ CASANOVA

As a religious regime, Catholicism preceded and is likely to outlast the modern world system of nation-states. The transnational character of Catholicism can almost be taken for granted, but historically the nature and manifestations of that transnationalism have changed radically along with changes in the worldly regimes in which Catholicism has been embedded.[1] The very attribute *transnational* only makes sense in relation to the system of sovereign nation-states that emerged in early modernity and eventually replaced the system of medieval Christendom, a system that had been centered on the conflictive interdependent relation between the Roman papacy, or "the political system of the popes," and the Holy Roman Empire.[2] The dynamic synergy of the new world system of sovereign states was such that one after another all the emerging national churches fell under the control of caesaro-papist rulers and the Roman papacy itself became just another, rather marginal and insecure, sovereign territorial state. It is precisely at the point when the Papal States were incorporated into the Kingdom of Italy and the papacy was finally forced to renounce its claims to territorial sovereignty, that the papacy could be reconstituted as the core of a transnational religious regime, this time on a truly Catholic, that is, ecumenical basis.

Ongoing processes of globalization offer a transnational religious regime like Catholicism, which never felt fully at home in a system of sovereign territorial nation-states, unique opportunities to expand, to adapt rapidly to the newly emerging global system, and perhaps even to assume a proactive role in shaping some aspects of the new system. Conversely, an analysis of the contemporary transformation of Catholicism may offer some clues as to the direction of contemporary processes of globalization.[3]

Progressively, from the middle of the nineteenth century to the present, one can trace the reconstruction, reemergence, or reinforcement of all those transnational characteristics of medieval Christendom that had nearly disappeared or been significantly weakened in the early modern era: papal supremacy and the centralization and internationalization of the Church's government; the convocation of ecumenical councils; transnational religious cadres; missionary activity; transnational schools, centers of learning, and intellectual networks; shrines as centers of pilgrimage and international encounters; transnational religious movements.[4]

This chapter explores changes in the character of the papacy as the transnational core of Catholicism, particularly in terms of the papacy's relation to three different types of worldly regimes—namely, to the medieval system of Christendom of which the papacy was one of the core institutions; to the modern system of sovereign nation-states to which the papacy became rather marginal; and to a newly emerging and still undefined global system within which the papacy is attaining once again a central structural role.

Papal Supremacy and the Globalization of the Papacy

The most telling indicator of the modern reestablishment of papal supremacy was the proclamation of the dogma of papal infallibility by the First Vatican Council in 1870. It was only in the course of the fifth century, once the Christianization of Rome was completed and the bishop of Rome had established its spiritual and temporal hegemony in the city, that the most significant elements of what would become the doctrine of papal supremacy were developed:

- The cult of Peter and Paul and Roman law served to legitimate the *cathedra petri*, making the bishop of Rome the rightful heir of the Apostolic See.
- The latinization of the Roman liturgy and the standardization of the cult of Roman martyrs established the foundation of the Latin Mass and the Roman Rite.
- The doctrine of "the two powers" rejecting the right of the state to interfere in church affairs served to emancipate the Roman Church from Byzantine caesaro-papism.

- The *Sylvester legend,* later elaborated into the *Donation of Constantine,* shows that by the end of the fifth century, after the fall of the Western Roman empire, the Roman bishops already claimed a position equal to that of the emperor and thus the right to the title of *Pontifex Maximus.*[5]

These Roman claims were never fully recognized by the Eastern churches that acknowledged the direct apostolic succession of the Roman bishops from Peter, and thus the claim to higher apostolic rank but not the claims to higher authority in doctrine or dogma. At first, the papal claims were no more successful in the West, but the preservation of papal letters in Rome, Spain, and Gaul and their later compilation into decretals with the addition of notorious forgeries served as the foundation for the eventual invention of a tradition of historical precedent and for the triumph of the doctrine of papal supremacy in the eleventh and twelfth centuries. The growth of papal government and the establishment of the medieval papacy as a central political institution of Western Christendom were determined primarily by three political developments that were to shape indelibly the self-identity and the geopolitical strategies of the papacy well into the twentieth century.

The Lombard conquest of northern Italy and threats to the Byzantine empire from the east in the second half of the sixth century first created the geopolitical conditions for the development of papal sovereignty over Byzantine Italy, that is, central and southern Italy and Sicily. This meant that, as put most succinctly by Bernhard Schimmelpfennig, "the papacy had power where it had territory."[6] Thereafter, the papacy would always insist on the need to maintain territorial sovereignty over the Papal States in order to preserve its spiritual autonomy. But the maintenance of papal territorial sovereignty always proved precarious.

The alliance of the Roman bishops and the Carolingian dynasty in the second half of the eighth century made possible the emancipation of the papacy from the Byzantine empire, the liberation from the Lombard threat, and the expansion of papal supremacy into northern Italy and Transalpine Europe. As *patricius Romanorum,* however, it was now the turn of the Carolingian emperor to assume the protection of the papacy. From now on, papal sovereignty over its territories always required the protection of a powerful political overlord.

The Romanization of Western Christendom and the partial triumph of papal supremacy during the Investitures conflicts of the eleventh and twelfth centuries was in many respects tied to monasticism. Along with the spiritual reform of ecclesiastical structures the monastic reform movement brought to Rome greater centralization and the internationalization of papal government. But from now on the disparate tasks of maintaining spiritual power over all of Christendom, political control over the papal territories, and the right geopolitical balance in foreign policy proved impossible to reconcile. The concentration of the Renaissance popes upon the consolidation of princely power over central Italy, following the negative experience of the Avignon captivity and the ensuing schisms, led to the loss of spiritual supremacy over most of Christendom and to the geopolitical marginality of the papacy within the emerging system of nation-states.

Even before the triumph of Erastian principles in Protestant countries, Spain's Catholic kings had been able to obtain from the papacy the series of royal privileges known as *Patronato Real* that allowed them to transform the Catholic Church in Spain and its colonies into an organ of state administration.[7] Everywhere, the alliance of national hierarchy and national ruler had the same effect. Cardinal Richelieu's role in enforcing Gallicanism was only the most notorious example. But the special liberties of the Gallic Church had been recognized by the pope already in the Concordat of 1515. Again and again, the papacy exchanged its transnational spiritual claims for the protection of its temporal sovereignty at home. As long as the sovereign rulers maintained officially their Catholic confession, an impaired papacy absorbed with the internal and external affairs of its own territories acquiesced.

Pius VI's belated but eventually firm condemnation of the 1790 Civil Constitution of the Clergy, after the majority of the Gallic Church had expressed its refusal to take the public oath, marks a turning point in the papacy's attempt to reclaim its supremacy over national bishops and clergy.[8] After the Spanish American colonies won their independence, the papacy refused to extend to the new republics the privileges of the old royal patronage, preferring to withdraw diplomatic recognition of the new states and to leave episcopal sees vacant.[9] When in the conflicts over "trusteeism" in American parishes the laity invoked the *jus patronatum*, arguing that the right of patronage, traditionally vested on the lay prince, now ought to be vested on the new sovereign, "the people," Rome consistently replied that patronage had never been a right but a privilege that it had conceded only under special circumstances.[10]

Ironically, it was the 1804 Concordat with Napoleon that served as blueprint for the successive concordats with conservative governments throughout Europe through which the Church established a modus vivendi with the new secular states that allowed the papacy to regain control of the national hierarchies. In the course of the nineteenth century, however, as conflicts with the liberal state became endemic throughout continental Europe and Latin America, it became increasingly evident that it was easier to safeguard papal rights in Anglo-Saxon countries that had institutionalized freedom of religion than in Latin Catholic countries even when Catholicism was officially protected as the state religion. Indeed, Anglo-Saxon and Protestant countries such as Holland or Germany, where Catholics constituted a sizable minority, became strongholds of modern Romanization and of a new liberal form of Catholic ultramontanism distinct from the integralist ultramontanism that was tied to the restoration of European monarchies.[11]

In recent times, the pope's control over the process of nomination of bishops through the nuncios has proven to be perhaps the single most important factor in papal control of the transnational Catholic Church. To this day, disputes over the rights to episcopal nomination have remained one of the most important issues of contention between the Vatican and authoritarian regimes.[12]

In 1870 the papacy lost its last remnant of temporal sovereignty, the province of Rome, at the very moment when the First Vatican Council issued its twin proclamation of papal primacy and infallibility.[13] Pius IX's refusal to accept the 1871 Law of Papal Guarantee offered by the Italian government and the unresolved "Roman question" made him and his successors virtual prisoners at the Vatican until the signing of the Lateran Treaty with Mussolini in 1929. Nevertheless, from their position of seeming captivity Pius IX's successors began to renew the papal tradition of speaking ever more frequently *urbi et orbi*, thus setting the basis for the process of globalization of the modern papacy, a process that has accelerated since the 1960s.[14]

This process of globalization finds expression primarily in three new directions: in the ever wider publication of papal encyclicals dealing not only with matters of Catholic faith, morality, and discipline but also with issues of the secular age and of the secular world affecting all of humanity; in the increasingly active and vocal role of the papacy in international conflicts and in issues dealing with world peace, world order, and world politics; and in the public visibility of the person of the pope as the high priest of a new universal civil religion of humanity and as the first citizen of a global civil society.

Papal Encyclicals

Leo XIII's *Rerum Novarum* (1891) inaugurated an impressive tradition of modern Catholic social teaching that has been constantly enriched and reformulated by later encyclicals—Pius XI's *Quadragesimo Anno* (1931), John XXIII's *Mater et Magistra* (1961) and *Pacem in Terris* (1963), Paul VI's *Populorum Progressio* (1967) and *Octogesima Adveniens* (1971), and John Paul II's *Laborem Exercens* (1981) and *Centesimum Annum* (1991). Surely the early teachings were permeated by a paternalistic view of social relations of production and by Catholic affinity for premodern hierarchical, corporatist social and political arrangements. The mirage of a Catholic "third way" between capitalism and socialism served to obscure the complexity of impersonal markets and modern differentiated societies. But in retrospect, the tradition appears as one of the most systematic, comprehensive, and consistent attempts to face the problems of modern industrial societies.[15]

Critics on the left often disdained the exercise, at best, as impotent moralizing palliatives of the inevitable class struggle between capital and labor, and, at worst, as antisocialist propaganda barely veiled under a supposedly evenhanded critique of capitalism and socialism. But considering the post–World War II institutionalization of the welfare state on the basis of a compromise between capital and labor and the crisis of socialism as a viable solution to the modern "social question," it would seem that Catholic social teachings have been closer to the historical mark than critics on the left wanted to acknowledge. Indeed, today those critics often welcome the papal encyclicals as one of the few public voices left criticizing the unjust division of labor and the dehumanizing effects of capitalism, while radical free market advocates on the right just as often dismiss the papal letters as rehashed Marxism.[16]

The most important reformulation of Catholic social teaching was connected with John XXIII's appropriation of the modern doctrine of human rights and the broadening of the papal vision to embrace also East-West and North-South conflictive relations. Paul VI and John Paul II have continued and furthered this tradition. Papal pronouncements have consistently presented the protection of the human rights of every person as the moral foundation of a just social and political order, the substitution of dialogue and peaceful negotiation for violent confrontation as the means of resolving conflicts and just grievances between peoples and states, and universal human solidarity as the foundation for the construction of a just and fair national as well as international division of labor and a just and legitimate world order.[17] Furthermore, while earlier encyclicals were usually addressed to the Catholic faithful, beginning with *Pacem in Terris* in 1963 the popes have tended to address their pronouncements to the entire world and to all people.

Public Role of the Papacy in World Affairs

Besides its power to consecrate rulers and thus to confer or withdraw legitimacy, to arbitrate between power disputants, and ultimately to excommunicate rulers, thus releasing their subjects from their oaths of fidelity, the medieval papacy also played the historical function of an international court of arbitration and appeal, guarantor of international conflicts, and peacemaker. Indeed, canon law and papal rulings served as the solely recognized authority in medieval international relations.

Naturally, the papacy could only play this role effectively as long as it was not a party to the conflicts and showed some impartiality. The theocratic claims of the pope, however, and the dual role of the papacy as spiritual and temporal ruler made the task difficult. The frequent abuses of spiritual power to advance temporal goals added to the general discredit of the papacy from the fourteenth to the sixteenth century.[18]

At a time when temporal rulers were singularly bent on the expansion, consolidation, and centralization of internal and external state power, two claims of the Church sounded particularly obnoxious: the power to bestow on the people the right of resistance to illegitimate rule and the *novit ille*, or the claim of the pope to have the right to annul international treaties or to free one of the parties from their sacred oath to honor the treaty. At the Congress of Westphalia (1648), the Catholic and Protestant princes of all of Europe (with the exclusion of Spain) agreed not only to exclude the papacy from being a party to the treaty but also to disregard all papal protests against the treaties of Münster, Osnabrück, and Westphalia. This concerted effort of secular rulers successfully shut out the papacy from European international affairs.[19]

At the Lateran Treaty (1929) Mussolini extracted from the papacy the acceptance of the definitive loss of temporal sovereignty and the promise that it would not lead an independent papal foreign policy nor interfere with Italy's foreign policy. Article 24 states, however, that the Holy See "reserves the right in every case to exercise its moral and spiritual power."[20]

The first modern pope who tried to exercise such a power was Benedict XV. Elected shortly after the outbreak of World War I, at a time when people, intellectuals, political leaders, and the clergy throughout Europe were caught up in war euphoria and jingoistic frenzy, the pope became one of the most eloquent spokespersons for peace.[21]

But the pope's interventions fell on deaf ears. Both sides viewed them as irritant siren songs interfering with their sacred national interests and their aims of military victory. He was accused by both sides of aiding the enemy and of trying to sap national resolve. His reply that he was supporting the cause of mankind rather than that of the belligerent parties was not appreciated. Ultimately, like transnational proletarian solidarity, Catholic or human solidarity proved much weaker than national solidarity or blind devotion and obedience to the state.[22]

Despite the apparent lack of immediate success, Benedict XV's interventions form the basis for the growth in international prestige and, ironically, diplomatic recognition of the papacy in the twentieth century. The role of Benedict XV's successors, Pius XI and Pius XII, in the rise to power of fascism in Italy and Nazism in Germany, as well as during World War II, is much more controversial. At least a posteriori, the papal interventions and, more damaging, the failure of the papacy to stand up to the dictators and to condemn publicly in the most unambiguous terms the Nazi Holocaust, reveal themselves as grave moral failures. This is so from the perspective of the ethical principles that have gained global acceptance after World War II, namely universal human rights and the defense of the sacred dignity of the human person, principles that the papacy itself has increasingly made its own.[23]

One can offer numerous explanations for the course of papal action:

- The clerical suspicion against autonomous lay movements and Catholic parties that were not under the direct supervision and control of the hierarchy; thus, the mandated dissolution of Don Luigi Sturzo's Popular Party and the lack of support and interest in the survival of the German Center Party. Both parties were the key to any viable organized effort to block the rise to power of Mussolini and Hitler.[24]
- The view of socialism at home and bolshevism abroad as the greater evil; thus, the adamant opposition to any Catholic-Socialist alliance or the view of Hitler as a shield against bolshevism. The 1933 Concordat with the Third Reich included secret clauses dealing with a common front against Russia.[25]
- The elective affinities between Catholic social teachings and fascist corporatism, of which Pius XI's *Quadragesimo Anno* is the paradigmatic expression. Generally, Italian Catholics supported fascism and various types of authoritarian corporatist regimes were established throughout the Catholic Iberian world.[26]
- Eugenio Pacelli's personal bias and professional preference for private diplomatic negotiations between elites over public prophetic condemnations.[27] The same professional diplomatic bias was noticeable in the Vatican's assumption of a policy of appeasement and its anxious and fastidious neutrality, more typical of a small neutral power caught in the middle of a struggle between superpowers than of the head of the universal church.

But above all, the course of action taken by the papacy can best be explained by reference to its traditional guiding principle, namely the protection of *libertas ecclesiae*. After the French Revolution and the global expansion of the modern secular state, the Vatican transnational policy initiated with the 1804 Concordat with Napoleon and followed thereafter consistently has been, at least until very recently, to extract from each and every state through the signing of concordats the most favorable conditions possible to protect the freedom of the Church. The Vatican assumed correctly that it would be possible to extract from Mussolini a concordat more favorable to the Church than any attainable with a liberal state. The 1929 Lateran Treaty comprised both an international treaty between the Kingdom of Italy and the State of Vatican City that settled definitively "the

Roman question" and a concordat between the Catholic Church and the Italian state.

Mussolini conceded practically everything the Church wanted: the confessionality of the state, the primacy of canon law on issues dealing with religion and marriage, compulsory religious education in all schools and state recognition of religious schools and universities, the payment of state salaries to bishops and priests, abolition of legislation against religious orders and legal recognition of religious congregations, the recognition of religious holidays as state holidays, the freedom to appoint bishops and free communication between the pope and bishops all over the world, and the promise of privileged treatment and freedom for all nonpolitical activities of Catholic Action.[28]

Similar considerations marked Vatican relations with Hitler's regime. Generally, the Nazis had not been very successful in winning Catholic votes from the Center Party. German Catholic bishops had repeatedly condemned Nazi pagan ideology and forbidden the faithful to vote for the Nazis. But by March 1933, under apparent pressure from Rome, as negotiations for a concordat started, there was an about-face. The bishops lifted the prohibition for Catholics to join the Nazi Party and allowed the Center Party and the Bavarian People's Party to vote for Hitler, giving him the two-thirds majority needed to accomplish the revolution legally. Once the concordat was signed, the Center Party and the Bavarian People's Party agreed to dissolve themselves as a sign of goodwill toward the new regime.

It is true that the Church eventually condemned the "statolatry" and the "pagan worship of the state" propagated by fascism and in the process developed a consistent critique of modern totalitarianism. But the public condemnations only came after it had become evident that those regimes were abridging the freedom of the Church and the privileged rights for Catholics that the Church had laboriously negotiated. *Non abiamo bisogno* (1931), the encyclical directed at fascism, came after the Fascists had begun to repress Catholic Action and youth organizations. *Mit brennender Sorge* (1937), written after a petition from the German bishops, was more a critique of the anti-Catholic policies of the Nazi regime than an outright condemnation of Nazism.[29]

Within days of the publication of *Mit brennender Sorge*, Pius XI also published his condemnations of communism, *Divini Redemptoris*, and of the Mexican regime, *Nos es muy*. It would seem that paramount in the mind of the pope was not so much an evenhanded critique of communist and fascist totalitarianism, as apologists tend to argue, but rather a joint critique of the anti-Catholic policies of those militantly atheist regimes. Only from the perspective of the lack of freedom of the Church and the abridgment of the rights of Catholics could the Mexican regime be placed on a par with the Nazi and Stalinist regimes.

There is an even more telling and reprehensible indicator that the Church viewed as its task the protection of the particular rights of Catholics and not the defense of universal human rights. While negotiating the Concordat with the Third Reich, Secretary of State Cardinal Eugenio Pacelli tried to inscribe a clause guaranteeing for baptized Jews the same status as that negotiated for German Catholics. But Cardinal Pacelli was able to obtain only a verbal promise that baptized Jews would be treated as Christians and not victimized as Jews.

The definitive assumption by the Church during the papacy of John XXIII of the modern doctrine of universal human rights has altered radically the traditional dynamic of Church-state relations and the role of the Church both nationally and transnationally. It has opened the way for a realignment in the relations between religious and worldly regimes. The cornerstone of the process is the Vatican II Declaration on Religious Freedom, *Dignitatis Humanae*. Significantly, the most eloquent voices in the crucial debate at the floor during the Council came from opposite blocs: from the American bishops, who unanimously defended religious freedom not only on grounds of practical expediency but also on theological grounds provided to them by their *peritus*, the great American theologian John Courtney Murray, and from Cardinal Karol Wojtyla from Kraków, who had learned from the experience of trying to defend the freedom of the Church under communism that the best line of defense, both theoretically and practically, was the defense of the inalienable right of the human person to freedom of conscience. Theologically, this entailed the transference of the principle of *libertas ecclesiae* that the Church had guarded so zealously through the ages to the individual human person—to *libertas personae*.[30]

From now on, the most effective way for the papacy to protect the freedom of the Church worldwide would no longer be to enter into concordats with individual states trying to extract from both friendly and unfriendly regimes the most favorable conditions possible for Catholic subjects but rather to proclaim *urbi et orbi* the sacred right of each and every person to freedom of religion and to remind every government not through discreet diplomatic channels but publicly of their duty to protect this sacred human right. In the process, the pope could be transformed from being the Holy Father of all Catholics to becoming the common father of God's children and the self-appointed spokesman of humanity, the *defensor hominis*. At long last, the papacy could free itself from the postmedieval trappings of territorial sovereignty that historically had hampered so much its freedom of movement. What the papacy and the national churches needed to carry out their spiritual mission was not the protective rule of political overlords who always ended up restricting the Church's freedom of movement but rather a free global civil society.

First Citizen of the Emerging Global Civil Society

Naturally, the pope's voice could only have its effect if three conditions were met: if the voice could infiltrate and cross state boundaries and be heard everywhere; if the papacy could use its transnational resources and the local churches to amplify its voice; and if the pope's voice could actually join and add volume and prestige to the already existing choruses of voices everywhere, until state walls came falling down. The globalization of mass media and the extremely effective use by the papacy of these media have met the first condition. The centralization and homogenization of Catholicism achieved by the Second Vatican Council and by the general process of *aggiornamento* to modernity have met the second condition. The third condition was also met, for, in questioning the principles of state sovereignty and *raison d'état,* the two cornerstones of the modern system of nation-states, the Church was only joining a whole array of local social forces and transnational institutions, organizations, and social movements, working toward the establishment of autonomous civil societies and toward the constitution of one free global civil society.[31]

Particularly in those societies in which the voice of the papacy carried a special weight, this concerted civil effort had dramatic effects. Suddenly, human rights doctrines could be used to put into question simultaneously the national-Catholicism of the Franco regime, the national security doctrines of bureaucratic-authoritarian regimes throughout Latin America, the corrupt oligarchic dictatorship of a cold war caudillo like Ferdinand Marcos, and the official lies of people's democracies in Poland and elsewhere.[32] Those who took the voice of the pope most seriously—priests and nuns, pastoral agents, and engaged laity—were at the forefront of a new worldwide democratic revolution.

Ironically, the diplomatic power of the papacy has also increased as the size of the Vatican state has shrunk and as the Holy See agreed to "remain extraneous to all temporal disputes between nations and to international congresses." The number of countries that have established diplomatic relations with the Vatican has increased continuously: It was four in 1878 at the time of Pius IX's death, fourteen in 1914 when Benedict XV began his papal reign and twenty-five in 1922 at the time of his death; by 1939, on the eve of World War II, the number was thirty-eight, and it reached seventy by 1973. At long last in 1984, overcoming its anti-popish bias, the 1867 U.S. congressional ban on diplomatic relations with the Vatican was lifted and the Reagan administration established full diplomatic relations with the Vatican. The collapse of the Soviet system of states and the disintegration of the Soviet Union have added a significant number of countries to the diplomatic corps at the Vatican. By 1993, 144 countries had established diplomatic relations with the Vatican.[33]

The reason for the growing diplomatic relevance of the Vatican is clearly not that Vatican City is such a powerful sovereign state. Rather, the Catholic Church has become such an important transnational organization in the emerging world system that no state can afford to ignore it. In the open public field of a global civil society the pope's divisions and their allies have appeared to be more effective and to have greater freedom of movement than the riot control units and the mechanized tank divisions amassed by Machiavellian princes and statesmen following the outmoded rules of engagement of realpolitik. In today's world, power does not come solely or even primarily from the barrel of a gun, particularly when states holding onto the monopoly of the means of violence have no legitimacy in civil society and do not have the moral or political resolve to use those guns against unarmed civilians.

The striking image of a penitent emperor at Canossa, submitting to the higher spiritual authority of a pope in order to regain his legitimacy and his temporal power, has always served as the paradigmatic symbolic expression of medieval papal authority. In recent decades, images of apparently powerful rulers surrendering their power without resistance to higher forms of authority, to "people's power," or to "the power of the powerless" have repeated themselves ever more frequently. When human rights and the internal affairs of sovereign states become everybody's business, being constantly monitored by governments, by the mass media, and by governmental and nongovernmental transnational organizations, and when global public opinion and the United Nations no longer respect the principle of noninterference in the internal affairs of sovereign states, it becomes ever more difficult for sovereign absolutist rulers to erect Berlin Walls or to protect their frontiers from an ever expanding civil society.

To a large extent this process of globalization and the ability of the papacy to exploit the opportunities created by this process, thereby enhancing its role and prestige in the emerging world system, have their origins in World War II and its aftermath. The cold war and the policy of containment of communism offered the Catholic Church, Catholic countries, and Catholic minorities within Protestant countries the possibility to realign themselves and to join the center of the North Atlantic Protestant capitalist system from which they had been alienated or marginalized since the Counter Reformation. The Washington-Rome alliance became one of the key axes in the policy of containment of communism.[34] Catholics became full partners of a Christian Democratic West and of the North Atlantic alliance. Catholics and Christian Democracy led the process of integration of the European Community. The Second Vatican Council had to be called precisely in order to ratify officially the process of *aggiornamento* to modernity that was already well under way in Catholic Western Europe. Once convened, however, the Council created a totally unforeseen dynamic of Catholic transformation and globalization.

The centrality of the papacy in the new global system was even recognized by the Soviets when Nikita Khrushchev welcomed John XXIII's mediation during the Cuban missile crisis and solicited that this mediation for the cause of peace and the sacred values of human life should not be limited to moments of crisis. When the superpowers and the entire world saw themselves at the brink of nuclear war, a higher principle of mediation had to be found. Once it could no longer be taken for granted, the survival of the species had to become a conscious and concerted effort of all of humanity. The security of humanity and of the planet had to have precedence over national and state security. Thereafter, the Vatican's *Ostpolitik* and the United States policy of détente took parallel tracks.[35] Yet the Vatican was careful to cultivate an image of mediation above the superpowers. Indeed, it claims to represent the interests of the international system as a whole. Since Benedict XV's enthusiastic support for the League of Nations, the popes have been consistent advocates of worldwide international bodies, from the World Court to the United Nations, which would limit absolutist state sovereignty, arbitrate international disputes, and represent the interests of the entire family of nations.[36]

The papacy has also assumed eagerly the vacant role of spokesperson for humanity, for the sacred dignity of the human person, for world peace, and for a more fair division of labor and power in the world system. The role comes naturally to the papacy since it is fully in accordance with its traditional claims of universal authority. In a sense the papacy has been trying to re-create the universalistic system of medieval Christendom, but now on a truly global scale. The fundamental difference, however, is that the spiritual sword can no longer seek the protection of the temporal sword to buttress its authority against competing religious regimes in order to gain monopoly of the means of salvation. The official recognition of the principle of religious freedom means that the Church has accepted the challenge to compete in a relatively open global system of religious regimes. Given its highly centralized structure and its imposing transnational network of human, institutional, and material resources, the Church can reasonably assume that it has a competitive advantage.

Considering the fact that for centuries, practically since the early modern era, the papacy has been physically tied to the Vatican and symbolically to Rome, it is striking how eagerly recent popes have tried to globalize their image and become world travelers. Modern mass media and means of communication have given the papacy the opportunity to communicate directly with Catholics, as well as with non-Catholics, all over the world. Particularly, John Paul II has deployed this direct contact with the masses of faithful extremely effectively as a kind of popular plebiscitarian support for his authority and his policies, using it whenever necessary to impress secular leaders, to bypass national hierarchies, or to check dissenting tendencies from Catholic elites.

Even though the Catholic Church has its own network of national and transnational mass media, the impact of the papacy on world public opinion does not derive primarily from Catholic mass media but rather from the prominent and extensive coverage that the pope's words and deeds receive in Western media.[37] Considering that since the late Middle Ages the image of the papacy had been associated, at least in modern hegemonic Protestant cultural areas, with strongly negative symbols, the fact that the very person of the pope has become today a positive media event is in itself an impressive achievement, indicative of the level of prestige and influence reached by the modern papacy. Without discounting the relevance of John Paul II's repeatedly manifest personal charisma, nor the role of a well-orchestrated job of charismatic image management by the Vatican staff, it would seem that the papacy has found a fitting role that meets the expectations of a much wider audience than the Catholic faithful. The pope has learned to play, perhaps more effectively than any competitor, the role of first citizen of a catholic, that is, a global and universal, human society. It just happens that this role is often in tension with his other official role as infallible head and supreme guardian of the particular doctrines, laws, rituals, and traditions of the *Una, Sancta, Catholica,* and *Apostolica* Roman Church.

The Globalization of Catholicism

In order to validate its claims to catholicity, or universality, the Roman Catholic Church and its supreme pontiff have to resolve two sets of tensions. There are tensions between the Roman, the national, and the increasingly global character of the ecclesiastical institution. There is further tension between the particularity and the claimed universality of Catholic doctrinal principles and moral norms. Both sets of tensions are closely related with ongoing processes of globalization.

Looking at Catholicism globally throughout the twentieth century and particularly since the 1960s, one can observe three interrelated processes in dynamic tension with one another. There is first the strengthening of papal supremacy, Vatican administrative centralization, and the Romanization of Catholicism throughout the world. Among signposts in this process one could mention: the convocation of the First Vatican Council and the proclamation of papal infallibility, the papal control of the selection of bishops, the uncontested condemnation of the Americanist and modernist heresies, the promulgation of the 1918 Universal Code of Canon Law and of a new Code of Canon Law in 1983, the continuous expansion of the Roman Curia and of the Vatican diplomatic corps, the prominent role of papal nuncios in the internal affairs of national churches, and the preponderant role of Roman universities, collegia, and institutes in the education and socialization of the prospective hierarchy and of national and transnational clerical elites.[38] Most of all, the Second Vatican Council and the ensuing general *aggiornamento* produced not only administrative and doctrinal centralization but also the homogenization and globalization of Catholic culture, at least among the elites, throughout the Catholic world.

Simultaneously with this process of Vatican centralization and Romanization of Catholicism, however, there has taken place a parallel process of internationalization of the Roman administrative structures and of globalization of Catholicism as a religious regime. The Roman Catholic Church has ceased being a predominantly Roman and European institution. Along with the demographic increase in Catholic population from 100 million in 1900 to 600 million in 1960 and to close to one billion in 1990, there has been a notable displacement of the Catholic population from the Old to the New World and from North to South. The episcopal and administrative cadres of the Church have changed accordingly. The First Vatican Council was still a predominantly European event, even though the forty-nine prelates from the United States comprised already one-tenth of the gathered bishops. The Second Vatican Council, by contrast, was the first truly ecumenical council. The 2,500 Fathers in attendance came from practically all parts of the world. Europeans no longer formed a majority. The U.S. delegation, with over 200 bishops, was the second largest, though it was already smaller than the combined number of 228 indigenous Asian and African bishops at the end of the Council. The number is significant considering that only under the papacy of Benedict XV did the Vatican begin to promote the recruitment of indigenous clergy and the formation of native hierarchies, thus abandoning the European colonial legacy of considering missions as religious colonies. Even more significant has been the internationalization of the College of Cardinals and, though more slowly, the internationalization of the Curia. Since the time of Julius II (1503) not only the popes but also most of the curials had been Italian. In 1946, Italians still constituted almost two-thirds of all cardinals. That year Pius XII created thirty-two new cardinals, only four of whom were Italians and thirteen were non-European. The College of Cardinals that voted for a non-Italian pope in 1978 already had a much more international and representative composition: 27 Italians, 29 from the rest of Europe, 12 Africans, 13 Asians, 19 Latin Americans, 11 North Americans.[39] The contemporary process of internationalization of Catholicism, moreover, does not have only a radial structure centered in Rome. In the last decades there has been a remarkable increase in transnational Catholic networks and exchanges of all kinds that crisscross nations and world regions, often bypassing Rome.[40]

Interrelated with, yet in tension with this dual process of Romanization of world Catholicism and internationalization of Rome, there has also taken place a process of "nationalization," that is, of centralization of the

Catholic churches at the national level. The institutionalization of national conferences of bishops following Vatican II reinforced the dynamics of the process of nationalization that had been carried primarily by different forms of Catholic Action with their shared strategy of mobilization of the Catholic laity to defend and promote the interests of the Catholic Church in what was perceived as a hostile modern secular environment. This political mobilization of Catholicism had been oriented toward the state, its aim being either to resist disestablishment or to counteract state-oriented secularist movements and parties. The final Catholic recognition of the principle of religious freedom, together with the Church's change of attitude toward the modern secular environment, has led to a fundamental transformation of the national Catholic churches. They have ceased being or aspiring to become state compulsory institutions and have become free religious institutions of civil society. In the process, Catholic churches throughout the world have dissociated themselves from and entered into conflict with authoritarian regimes that were predominant in many Catholic countries. This voluntary "disestablishment" of Catholicism has permitted the Church to play a key role in recent transitions to democracy throughout the Catholic world.[41]

The traditional position and attitude of the Catholic Church toward modern political regimes had been that of neutrality toward all "forms" of government. So long as the policies of those governments did not infringe systematically upon the corporate rights of the Church to religious freedom, *libertas ecclesiae*, and to the exercise of its functions as *mater et magistra*, the Church would not question their legitimacy. The assumption of the modern doctrine of human rights entails, however, more than the acceptance of democracy as a legitimate "form" of government. It implies the recognition that modern democracy is not only a form of government but a type of polity based normatively on the universalist principles of individual freedom and individual rights. As national churches transfer the defense of their particularistic privileges to the human person, Catholicism becomes mobilized again, this time to defend the institutionalization of modern universal rights and the very right of a democratic civil society to exist.

As national conferences of bishops take an active role in defining national issues, there emerges a dynamic tension between Roman and national centralization. Such a tension accounts for both the globalization of a Catholic position on many issues as well as the particular reflections that the general Catholic position assumes in any given national context. As the conference of bishops take a "Catholic" position, however, a tension between Roman Catholic particularity and catholic universality often becomes evident. Striking in recent papal and episcopal pronouncements, particularly in those dealing with issues of public morality, is the fact that they are not addressed to Catholics as faithful members of the Church, obliged to follow specific particular rules of the Catholic moral tradition, but rather to every individual qua member of humanity, obliged to follow universal human norms, which are derived from the universal human values of life and freedom. The fact that those allegedly universal norms and values are tied to a particular religious tradition is certainly bound to affect the reception of these universalistic claims by non-Catholics. But at the same time, in places where this particular religious tradition is alive, it will probably serve to sanctify and legitimate modern norms and values as Christian ones.

But given modern structural conditions, if the Catholic Church wants to maintain its universalistic claims, it will have to learn to live with social and cultural pluralism both outside and, especially, inside the Church. In order to maintain its effectiveness as a public religion in modern civil societies its public interventions will have to be and appear nonpartisan and nondenominational; that is, they will have to be framed in a universalistic language. This by no means precludes a "preferential option for the poor" or a continuation of the traditional Catholic opposition to abortion. Indeed, the Catholic Church today is presenting its public interventions not as the defense of a particular group or a particular moral tradition but on the basis of its moral obligation as a universal church to protect human life and the sacred dignity of the human person and to demand universal access to discourse, justice, and welfare. This means that, whichever position or option it takes, the Church will have to justify it through open, public, rational discourse in the public sphere of civil society. The lesson of the public interventions of the American bishops indicates, moreover, that the Church will have to learn to let all the faithful participate in the constant elaboration and reformulation of its normative teachings and allow for different practical judgments as to how to interpret those normative teachings in concrete circumstances.[42]

Roland Robertson has convincingly argued the dual nature of the ongoing processes of globalization, the emergence of global humankind, and the emergence of a global system of societies. These entail the relativization of the personal identity of the self in reference to humankind as a whole, the relativization of membership in any particular society by reference to global humankind, and the relativization of particular national societies from the perspective of the world system of societies.[43]

The combination of globalization, nationalization, secular involvement, and voluntary disestablishment has led the Catholic Church to a significant change of orientation from nation-state to civil society. National churches ceased viewing themselves as integrative community cults of the nation-state and adopted a new transnational global identity that permitted them to confront prophetically the state and the given social order. Among the most significant developments of recent decades has been the crisis of absolute principles of state sovereignty and *raison d'état* and the emergence of global dynamics of democratization. The collapse of the system of socialist states, the global defeat of national security doctrines, the crisis of the established principle of noninterference in the internal affairs of nation-states, the crisis of state-led models of economic development and modernization are all related with new dynamics of civil society formation both intrasocietally and globally. Transnational religious regimes are reacting to the new challenges and are playing a crucial role both in the revitalization of particular civil societies and in the emergence of a global civil society. Particularly, the Catholic Church, which resisted so long and ineffectively the emergence of the modern system of nation-states, is now responding successfully to the opportunities offered by the crisis of territorial state sovereignty and by the expansion of a global civil society.[44]

NOTES

This chapter was originally presented at the annual meeting of the American Political Association at the New York Hilton, September 1, 1994.

1. Ivan Vallier, "The Roman Catholic Church: A Transnational Actor," in *Transnational Relations and World Politics*, edited by Robert O. Keohane and Joseph Nye (Cambridge, MA: Harvard University Press, 1972). Mart Bax has pointed out that the dynamics of religious regimes spring from three sources, namely: "the relationship between the religious regime and the worldly regime with which it is linked; its confrontations with other religious regimes; and internal tensions and polarities between what may be called the 'dominant religious regime' and the 'dominated regime.'" Mart Bax, "Religious Regimes and State-Formation: Toward a Research Perspective," in *Religious Regimes and State-Formation*, edited by Eric R. Wolf (Albany: State University of New York Press, 1991), 11. The present essay only addresses the first source of Catholic dynamics, and thus focuses on the papacy as the institutional core of Catholic transnationalism and its relations to the external worldly regime. If one wanted to address the other two sources of Catholic dynamics, then one would have to focus more systematically on the changing relations among papacy, episcopacy, religious orders, and laity and to focus, above all, on Church councils. Throughout its history, it is primarily through local, regional, and ecumenical councils that the Catholic Church has defined its "official" hegemonic doctrines and anathematized "error" while reacting to internal "schismatic" and "heretic" challenges and to external competition from "infidels" and "pagans." Traditionally, these four categories—"schism," "heresy," "infidelity," and "paganism"—have served to mark the internal and external boundaries of Catholicism as a religious regime.

2. Lord Acton, "The Political System of the Popes," in *Essays on Church and State* (New York: Thomas Y. Crowell, 1968).

3. On globalization, see Roland Robertson, "Mapping the Global Condition: Globalization as a Central Concept," in *Global Culture*, edited by Mike Featherstone (London: Sage, 1991), and Roland Robertson and JoAnn Chirico, "Human-

ity, Globalization, and Worldwide Religious Resurgence: A Theoretical Explanation," *Sociological Analysis* 46 (3) (1985):219–242.

4. The outburst of missionary activity that accompanied the early modern overseas colonization by Western European states and the establishment of the Jesuits as a militant ultramontanist order at the service of the papacy to counter the Reformation as well as the emerging system of nation-states are two significant exceptions. However, colonial Catholicism soon fell even to a larger extent than the territorial national churches into the caesaro-papist control of secular state rulers who severed any direct link of the colonial churches with the Vatican. The expulsion of the Jesuits from all Roman Catholic dominions during the second half of the eighteenth century and the final suppression of the order by papal decree in 1773 mark the high points of Catholic caesaro-papism and of papal accommodation to absolutist state sovereignty. See C. R. Boxer, *The Church Militant and Iberian Expansion, 1440–1770* (Baltimore: Johns Hopkins University Press, 1978); Christopher Hollis, *The Jesuits: A History* (New York: Macmillan, 1968); and William J. Callahan and David Higgs, eds., *Church and Society in Catholic Europe of the Eighteenth Century* (New York: Cambridge University Press, 1979).

5. I have based my reconstruction of the growth of the papacy in late antiquity and the Middle Ages primarily on Bernhard Schimmelpfennig, *The Papacy* (New York: Columbia University Press, 1992). See also Walter Ullmann, *The Growth of Papal Government in the Middle Ages* (London: Methuen, 1962), and Geoffrey Barraclough, *The Medieval Papacy* (London: Thames and Hudson, 1974).

6. Schimmelpfennig, *Papacy*, 71.

7. W. Eugen Shiels, SJ, *King and Church: The Rise and Fall of the Patronato Real* (Chicago: Loyola University Press, 1961).

8. See E.E.Y. Hales, *Revolution and Papacy, 1769–1846* (London: Eyre & Spottiswoode, 1960), and Owen Chadwick, *The Popes and European Revolution* (Oxford: Clarendon Press, 1981).

9. Lloyd M. Mecham, *Church and State in Latin America* (Chapel Hill: University of North Carolina Press, 1966).

10. Patrick W. Carey, *People, Priests, and Prelates: Ecclesiastical Democracy and the Tensions of Trusteeism* (Notre Dame, IN: University of Notre Dame Press, 1987).

11. See Lord Acton, "Ultramontanism," in *Essays on Church and State*; J. Derek Holmes, *More Roman Than Rome: English Catholicism in the Nineteenth Century* (London: Burns and Oates, 1978); John Henry White, *Catholics in Western Democracies* (New York: St. Martin's Press, 1981); John A. Coleman, *The Evolution of Dutch Catholicism, 1958–1974* (Berkeley: University of California Press, 1978); Frances Lannon, *Privilege, Persecution, and Prophecy: The Catholic Church in Spain, 1875–1975* (Oxford: Clarendon Press, 1987).

12. See José Casanova, *Public Religions in the Modern World* (Chicago: University of Chicago Press, 1994), and Eric O. Hanson, *The Catholic Church in World Politics* (Princeton: Princeton University Press, 1987).

13. Ironically, the foundations for the doctrine of papal infallibility had been first laid toward the end of the thirteenth century, at the height of papal power, by Franciscans who were critical of Pope Boniface VIII. According to Schimmelpfennig, it was "an attempt to limit the pope's jurisdictional competence by binding him to the

decrees of his predecessors." Schimmelpfennig, *Papacy*, 194. The modern formulation of papal infallibility, by contrast, was an attempt to buttress the personal authority of the pope and his official right to speak *ex cathedra*, at a time when the papacy as an institution and the Catholic tradition appeared everywhere under siege. See James Hennesey, SJ, *The First Council of the Vatican: The American Experience* (New York: Herder and Herder, 1963).

14. J. Derek Holmes, *The Papacy in the Modern World, 1914–1978* (New York: Crossroad, 1981).

15. See Jean-Yves Calvez and Jacques Perrin, *The Church and Social Justice* (Chicago: Regnery, 1961); Joseph N. Moody, *Church and Society: Catholic Social and Political Thoughts and Movements, 1789–1950* (New York: Arts Inc., 1953); Richard L. Camp, *The Papal Ideology of Social Reform* (Leiden: Brill, 1969); and John A. Coleman, ed., *One Hundred Years of Catholic Social Thought* (Maryknoll, NY: Orbis, 1991).

16. For an illustrative sample of some of these debates, see George E. McCarthy and Royal W. Rhodes, *Eclipse of Justice: Ethics, Economics, and the Lost Tradition of American Catholicism* (Maryknoll, NY: Orbis, 1991).

17. See Peter Hebblethwaite, *Pope John XXIII: Shepherd of the Modern World* (New York: Doubleday, 1985); David Hollenbach, *Claims in Conflict: Retrieving and Renewing the Catholic Human Rights Tradition* (New York: Paulist Press, 1979); David Hollenbach, ed., *Human Rights in the Americas: The Struggle for Consensus* (Washington, DC: Woodstock Theological Center, 1981).

18. See Brian Tierney, *The Crisis of Church and State, 1050–1300* (Englewood Cliffs, NJ: Prentice-Hall, 1964), and John A.F. Thomson, *Popes and Princes: Politics and Polity in the Late Medieval Church* (London: Allen and Unwin, 1980).

19. Carl Conrad Eckhardt, *The Papacy and World Affairs* (Chicago: The University of Chicago Press, 1937).

20. In Eckhardt, *The Papacy*, 244.

21. While seventy-six prominent German Catholics described the war as "the new springtime of religion," the pope more soberly viewed it as "the darkest tragedy of human hatred and human madness," telling the German bishops that he was "supremely bound in conscience to counsel, suggest, inculcate nothing else but peace." Tirelessly, he denounced the war as a "scourge," a "horrible and useless slaughter" that was turning the world into "a hospital and a charnel house," the "suicide of civilized Europe"; he organized all types of humanitarian aid on a large scale, generously depleting his own and Vatican financial resources; he demanded repeatedly peace negotiations, worked practically as an intermediary seeking negotiations, and appealed to the nations to establish a just peace and not one imposed on the defeated. See Holmes, *Papacy*, 1–19.

22. Catholic priests answered enthusiastically the patriotic call to arms everywhere. In France alone, despite the long history of religious-secular cleavages, anticlericalism, and deep-seated suspicions of disloyalty, 45,000 priests rallied to the defense of *la patrie*. Their military deportment, moreover, was exemplary. Over 5,000 priests died in the war, 9,000 received the *croix de guerre*, and almost 900 received the *Légion d'honneur*. Most significantly, members of transnational religious orders who had been expelled from many countries by anticlerical legislation returned to fight for their national causes. Even the Jesuits, the most transnational of all

Catholic orders, proved unable to side with the pope and resist nationalism. Over 850 French Jesuits and 534 German Jesuits returned from exile to take part in the war as combatants (a majority), military chaplains, or auxiliaries. See Holmes, *Papacy*, 20, and Hollis, *Jesuits*, 247. See also Christine Alix, *Le Saint-Siège et les nationalismes en Europe, 1870–1960* (Paris: Sirey, 1962).

23. Guenther Lewy, *The Catholic Church and Nazi Germany* (New York: Mc-Graw-Hill, 1964); Anthony Rhodes, *The Vatican in the Age of the Dictators, 1922–1945* (London: Hodder and Stroughton, 1973).

24. See Jean-Guy Vaillancourt, *Papal Power: A Study of Vatican Control over Catholic Lay Groups* (Berkeley: University of California Press, 1980); Ellen Lowell Evans, *The German Center Party, 1870–1933* (Carbondale: Southern Illinois University Press, 1974); John N. Molony, *The Emergence of Political Catholicism in Italy: Partito Populare, 1919–1926* (Totowa, NJ: Rowman and Littlefield, 1977); and Gianfranco Poggi, *Catholic Action in Italy* (Stanford: Stanford University Press, 1967).

25. Hansjakob Stehle, *Eastern Politics of the Vatican 1917–1979* (Athens: Ohio University Press, 1981).

26. Fredrick B. Pike and Thomas Stritch, eds., *The New Corporatism: Social-Political Structures in the Iberian World* (Notre Dame, IN: University of Notre Dame Press, 1974); Norman Cooper, *Catholicism and the Franco Regime* (Beverly Hills, CA: Sage, 1975); Guy Hermet, *Les catholiques dans l'Espagne Franquiste,* 2 volumes (Paris: Presses de la Fondation Nationale des Sciences Politiques, 1980).

27. In self-defense against the accusations of callousness toward the fate of European Jewry, the Vatican has replied that, under the circumstances, discreet diplomatic initiatives and the personal humanitarian efforts of the pope to help rescue and give shelter to as many individual Jews as possible was to prove more effective than public condemnations of Nazism that were likely to jeopardize the success of the humanitarian initiatives. See Holmes, *Papacy*, 152–168.

28. Pius XI expressed effusively his satisfaction with the Concordat: "[I]f not the best that could possibly be made, [it] is certainly among the best that have so far been devised . . . through it We have given back God to Italy and Italy to God." In Holmes, *Papacy*, 56.

29. The mode of publication of both encyclicals shows how effectively the Church could use its transnational resources when it wanted. Both were written in the vernacular rather than in the customary Latin. To bypass state censorship and the totalitarian control of the media, *Non abiamo bisogno* was first distributed abroad, and *Mit brennender Sorge* was distributed secretly and read throughout Germany from Catholic pulpits on Palm Sunday.

30. See John Courtney Murray, "The Problem of Religious Freedom," *Theological Studies* 25 (1964):503–575; George Weigel, *The Final Revolution: The Resistance Church and the Collapse of Communism* (New York: Oxford University Press, 1992), 70–74.

31. On the concept and the contemporary transformation of civil society, East and West, North and South, see Jean Cohen and Andrew Arato, *Civil Society and Political Theory* (Cambridge, MA: MIT Press, 1992). On global civil society, see Ronnie D. Lipschutz, "Reconstructing World Politics: The Emergence of Global Civil Society," *Millennium: Journal of International Studies* 21 (3) (1992):389–420.

On the human rights revolution, see Robert F. Drinan, SJ, *Cry of the Oppressed: The History and Hope of the Human Rights Revolution* (San Francisco: Harper & Row, 1987).

32. For an analysis of the role of the Catholic Church in transitions to democracy in Spain, Poland, and Brazil, see Casanova, *Public Religions*. On the role of the Church in the struggle for human rights in Latin America, see Penny Lernoux, *Cry of the People* (New York: Penguin, 1982), and Brian Smith, "Churches and Human Rights in Latin America," *Journal of InterAmerican Studies and World Affairs* 21 (February 1979):89–127.

33. *Catholic Almanac, 1993* (Huntington, IN: Our Sunday's Visitor Publications, 1993).

34. See Hanson, *Catholic Church*.

35. Dennis Dunn, *Detente and Papal-Communist Relations, 1962–1978* (Boulder: Westview Press, 1979), and Stehle, *Eastern Politics*.

36. A survey of lay Catholic elites from 103 different countries taking part in the Third World Congress for Lay Apostolate in Rome in 1967 shows positive attitudes toward "internationalism": 69 percent favored the development of the United Nations into a world government; 84 percent agreed that individual countries should give up some power so that the United Nations could do a better job; 67 percent considered immigration quotas immoral, thinking that anyone should be able to immigrate freely into another country; and 90 percent asserted that Catholic organizations should be active in peace movements. The survey's classification of the geocultural origin of the delegates to the lay congress was the following: African, 11 percent; Asian, 11 percent; Latin American, 19 percent; English-speaking outside Asia and Africa, 18 percent; Western European, 26 percent; Eastern and Southern European, 15 percent. The survey evinces relative homogeneity and few significant differences of opinion among the geocultural groups, and even between the Third World delegates and others, on these or on most other issues. See Vaillancourt, *Papal Power*, 134–167.

37. Vatican Radio was used first by Pius XI in the 1930s as a symbol of the independence of the Holy See. Pius XII used it more extensively to communicate with Catholics throughout the world. The Vatican foreign radio service, which broadcasts over 200 hours of programming per week in thirty-five languages, has been particularly relevant for persecuted Catholics.

38. Other transnational centers of Catholic learning, such as Louvain, Paris, Lyons, Freiburg, Innsbruck, and so on have played a similar role in the process of cultural homogenization of Catholicism and, at times, in the socialization of more liberal transnational Catholic counter-elites. Theologians from such centers played a crucial role as *periti* at the Second Vatican Council.

39. The data are from Holmes, *Papacy*, 23–24, 187, 233.

40. See Penny Lernoux, *People of God: The Struggle for World Catholicism* (New York: Viking, 1989); Brian H. Smith, *More Than Altruism: The Politics of Private Foreign Aid* (Princeton: Princeton University Press, 1990); Hanson, *Catholic Church*; Ralph Della Cava, "Vatican Policy, 1978–90: An Updated Overview," *Social Research* 59 (1) (Spring 1992):169–199; and Ralph Della Cava, "Financing the Faith: The Case of Roman Catholicism," *Journal of Church and State* 35 (1) (Winter 1993):1101–1122.

41. See José Casanova, "Church, State, Nation, and Civil Society in Spain and Poland," in *The Political Dimensions of Religion*, edited by Said Amir Arjomand (Albany: State University of New York Press, 1993), and Casanova, *Public Religions*.

42. See my discussion of the public interventions of the American bishops on nuclear policies, the economy, and abortion in *Public Religions*, 184–207.

43. Robertson and Chirico, "Humanity, Globalization, and Worldwide Religious Resurgence," 242.

44. All significant differences notwithstanding, the current situation of Islam is similar in this respect.

SIX

World Religions and National States: Competing Claims in East Asia

DON BAKER

Historians have long been aware that the arrival of European and American gunboats and businessmen off the shores of China, Japan, and Korea in the nineteenth century changed East Asia dramatically and permanently. When Western weapons and merchants arrived on East Asian soil, they brought Western political and economic concepts with them. These new concepts undermined traditional East Asian approaches to waging war and trading goods, challenging and changing the ways that the Chinese, Japanese, and Korean states had related to other states and how they had related, politically and economically, to people both within and beyond their borders.

That encounter with the West changed not only the way East Asian states behaved but also the way they defined themselves. After their encounter with the West, China, Japan, and Korea could no longer remain kingdoms operating within the isolation of the Sino-centric world. In order to survive in a geopolitical environment not only very different from but also much larger than that to which they had been accustomed, they had to embark on a rapid and traumatic transformation into modern nation-states. Historians have frequently noted that this change in political and economic behavior and thought constituted a revolution in the prevailing weltanschauung of East Asia. Few have noted, however, that as part of this change in the dominant worldview, traditional attitudes toward religion, and the relationship of religious communities to the state, were changed as well.

A major driving force behind this transformation of traditional East Asia has been the invention and promotion of nationalism by political elites determined to create strong nation-states with a greater sense of national unity and national identity than had ever before existed in that part of the world. These nationalist modernizers were convinced that if they did not respond quickly to the challenge of the modern world, with its Darwinian struggles between competing national political entities, they and their fellow countrymen would be swallowed up by stronger, alien political powers. They believed that their only hope for such a rapid response lay in harnessing the energies of their people toward one end and one end only—the construction of a powerful and wealthy nation. This could only be done by replacing the centrifugal loyalties to clan and neighbors of the past with centripetal loyalty to the state of the future.

One barrier to this redirection and unification of loyalty arose from an unexpected direction. The West, which had supplied the blueprint for the modern nation-state, also supplied a new paradigm for conceptualizing religion and managing church-state relations. This imported Western approach granted religious communities more autonomy than they had traditionally enjoyed in East Asia. Such autonomy appeared to threaten the national unity that these nation-building governments so desperately needed.

This threat to emerging national unity was heightened by the fact that representatives of transnational religious regimes living in East Asia were able, for the first time in history, to call on international support to defend their autonomy and to enhance their power. That meant the government of a nascent modern East Asian nation could not avoid at least the appearance of permitting freedom of religion if it wanted to win acceptance as a respectable member of the international community. The stage was thus set for a conflict in the religious arena between the demands of nationalism and the need for international acceptability, fought within a framework in which tradition still provided much of the scaffolding but imported elements provided many of the bricks. The governments of modern East Asia—totalitarian, authoritarian, and democratic—have all sought to resolve this struggle in strikingly similar ways.

Though China, Japan, and Korea differ from one another as much as England, Spain, and Germany, they share quite a few common cultural traits and similar historical memories. China, as the oldest and the largest civilization in East Asia, established many of the patterns of governance that the other two also followed for centuries. One such pattern made religious communities and organizations subordinate to, and supportive of, the state.

In traditional East Asia, there was no word for religion as a separate and distinct sphere of life. There were religions, of course, but Buddhism, Taoism, Shinto, Confucianism, and folk beliefs and traditions were not brought together under one umbrella term or seen as inherently different from other forms of communal activity. Religious groups were granted no privileges that political, economic, or social groups did not share. All were treated as a part of society rather than as apart from society and were expected to recognize that the locus of ultimate authority was the state. The little autonomy religious communities did enjoy, they enjoyed only because of neglect or indifference by the state, and this autonomy could be violated by the state at any time the state chose to do so.

Religious communities and organizations were even denied the moral autonomy and authority that was the core of their power and independence in the West. For most of East Asian history, religious pluralism prevailed alongside moral orthodoxy. The political community normally included a number of religious groups with varying beliefs about the nature of the supernatural realm and man's relationship to it. These religious groups were usually overlapping, with believers feeling no need to adhere to only one religion to the exclusion of all others. Nor did the political community feel compelled to favor one group exclusively at the expense of the others. However, all of these religious groups had to operate as subgroups of the larger political community.

The larger political community, in the form of the state, imposed on all religious communities a moral orthodoxy of certain ethical and ritual standards as well as obligations. Chinese, Japanese, and Korean people were usually free to believe whatever they wanted to believe as long as they remained loyal to the state and dutiful to their parents and did not challenge or appropriate for themselves the rituals that the state used to legitimize its own authority and preserve social order and harmony. Only those religious organizations that seemed to threaten the state by denying its legitimacy or to threaten society by encouraging its members to act in ways contrary to accepted moral norms came under attack by the state.[1]

Religious communities, in other words, were compelled to accept the supremacy of the state on basic moral issues. The ethical teachings of religious bodies were not allowed to override the behavioral demands of the political community. Rather than serving as a primary or even an alternative source of moral guidance, as it had in the West, religion in traditional East Asia accepted the subordinate role of lending support to the state's moral code.

The history of Buddhism in East Asia provides a paradigmatic example of the traditional relationship between the state and religious communities. Buddhism was the first organized religion with international ties to penetrate East Asia, reaching China in the first century from India via Central

Asia. Buddhism first took root in China not as a challenge to the government but as a servant of the state. Aspirants for hegemony at a time of warfare among competing kingdoms imported Buddhist monks and patronized Buddhist temples in order to enhance the prestige of their courts over those of their rivals, as well as out of the hope that the Buddha's power would be used to support those rulers who supported him.

However, once the centuries of civil war were over and Buddhism no longer needed to be courted to ensure that disgruntled monks would not flee to the court of a rival, the state acted quickly to assert its supremacy. In 845, the government of T'ang China closed 4,600 temples and laicized roughly 250,000 monks and nuns, dealing Buddhist autonomy a blow from which it never recovered. Buddhism per se was not persecuted. Not all temples were closed, nor were all monks and nuns forcibly returned to secular life. There were no Chinese inquisitions to ferret out believers, and public Buddhist rituals and Buddhist publications were not banned. The state acted to weaken Buddhism so that it could not pose a serious challenge to state authority. It did not try to eliminate it.

One reason that Chinese Buddhists were unable to resist this assertion of state authority was that Buddhism in China was answerable only to Chinese authorities, as it maintained no formal institutional links to Buddhist institutions outside of China. Chinese Buddhism was not linked to any transnational religious regime and hence was unable to use transnational support as leverage against the state. The same was true of Buddhism in Japan and Korea. Buddhist monks in both of these countries often relied on Chinese texts and imitated Chinese sectarian divisions. Nonetheless, there was no transnational network that bound Japan or Korea to China in terms of personnel, organizational hierarchy, or financial support.

In Korea the Korean state rather than any Buddhist body outside of Korea determined who was a legitimate monk. The Koryeo dynasty (918–1392), for example, required those who wished to be monks to pass government-administered examinations. Koryeo officials also named the abbots of major monasteries. The dynasty that followed, the Choseon dynasty (1392–1910), asserted its authority by barring Buddhist monks from public life, from even appearing on the streets of the capital city, and from building temples within city walls.[2] In Tokugawa Japan (1600–1868), the state did not assert such overt control over Buddhist monks and institutions, but that may have been because Japanese Buddhism had become so domesticated that its priests and temples were often almost indistinguishable from those associated with the native worship of local Shinto deities.

Only in the past few centuries, as the political communities in these three East Asian neighbors have been penetrated by foreign religious communities with strong external military and economic backing, have China, Korea, and Japan had to rethink not only how they conceived the relationship between political and religious communities within their borders but also how they defined religion itself. They have been forced to draw sharper lines between religious and political spheres than they ever had to draw before and, in the process, have had to wrestle with transnational religious communities over the definition of religion, the status of religious organizations, and the legitimate functions of both religious followers and their organizations in such disparate fields as education, medical care, social welfare, communication, politics, and moral discourse. The debate has even extended to some indigenous religious communities that have tried to benefit from imported notions of autonomy for religious communities.

More important, since the early nineteenth century the political communities of East Asia have fought with religious communities, both international and internal, over priorities of identity—what comes first, membership in a political community or membership in a religious community? In other words, is a Chinese Catholic Chinese first or Catholic first? Where do the primary loyalties lie?

This battle has not been so unequal that one side has been able to impose its position on the other—not for long anyway. The history of the interaction between the political and the religious communities of East Asia over the past two centuries is a story of compromises, of retreats and regroupings, as attempts were made to create institutional and ideological frameworks in which both sides could feel they had sufficient autonomy to operate according to their own principles and values in what they saw as their rightful respective spheres of influence.

Aware of the threat to national unity that a traditional religious pluralism could pose when coupled with the imported Western notion of religions as alternative sources of moral authority and legitimacy, the governments of China, Japan, and Korea nonetheless were forced by international pressure to grant some degree of autonomy to religious communities within their borders, especially to those communities with international connections. The struggle has been over how much autonomy to grant, not whether autonomy should be granted at all.

The initial concession that religious communities are not totally subject to the dictates of the state was made reluctantly and with reservations. All three East Asian nations have historical memories of confrontations in the not-too-distant past in which followers of religions with either real or perceived transnational ties posed a serious military threat to established political authority. Over the centuries, several religious leaders and religious organizations have rejected the traditional subordinate role assigned to them by the state. The more dangerous challenges in recent centuries have come from religious communities with links to foreign ideas or institutions.

In the second half of the nineteenth century, for example, the Qing dynasty of China (1644–1911) almost disintegrated when it came under attack along its borders from Muslim separatists at the same time as a pseudo-Christian sect was seizing control over a sizable portion of Central China. The Taiping Rebellion (1850–1864) was inspired by a religious ideology that borrowed much from Christianity; the Taiping claimed that the founder of their religion of "Great Peace" was the younger brother of Jesus Christ. At their height, the Taiping ranged over sixteen provinces of China from the Yangtse River to the south to the Yellow River in the north. Before their drive to overthrow the Qing was crushed, millions, possibly tens of millions, had died.[3] Though Western nations aided the Qing dynasty against the Taiping rebels, Christian elements in Taiping ideology convinced many Chinese officials and intellectuals that Western religion was a serious threat to the Chinese state.

Chinese officials were equally suspicious of Islam. When Muslims along China's southwestern border rebelled in 1856 and attempted to establish an independent Muslim kingdom, Qing armies spent seventeen years regaining control. It took the Qing almost as long to suppress a separate rebellion by Muslims in the northwestern provinces. From 1862 until 1873, Qing troops fought against fervent followers of a "new Teachings" sect of Islam over the cities and towns of Shaanxi and Gansu provinces, and they continued to battle with other Muslim rebels further west in Xinjiang province until 1877.[4] Though none of these Muslim rebellions had foreign support, the fact that they were religious rebellions confirmed official Chinese fears of divided loyalties among religious communities.

Korea faced a similar crisis, though on a much smaller scale, in the late nineteenth century. The Tonghak rebellion of 1894 was sparked by followers of a new Korean religion created mostly out of a mélange of traditional elements, but which borrowed some of its theological language and its organizational structure from the Roman Catholic Church, which had penetrated Korea's borders a century earlier. Though that uprising was suppressed after only a few months, its memory remained as a reminder that religious organizations, especially those influenced by alien ideas, could pose a subversive threat.[5]

Korea prevented a potentially more serious religious challenge to its sovereignty in 1801 when it intercepted a letter from a persecuted Korean Catholic asking the bishop of Beijing to send the French fleet to Korea to protect Korea's young and beleaguered Catholic community.[6] Japan, almost two centuries earlier, had been less successful in preventing an armed Catholic reaction to official persecution. In 1637, less than four decades after the Tokugawa shogunate had established peace among Japan's warring fiefdoms, Catholics in the southwestern region of Shimabara rose up against their feudal overlords. They were crushed and forced underground, not to resurface until after the fall of the Tokugawa more than two hundred years later.[7] However, their violent rejection of non-Catholic political authority entered the institutional memory of the Japanese government and served as a warning that religious affiliations, particularly those with alien overtones, can be divisive and subversive.

China, Korea, and Japan thus entered the twentieth century with historical grounds for concern over the impact that religious communities could have on national unity. Compounding their concern was the fact that the traditional tools they had used to minimize such concern had been taken from them by clauses in treaties that they had been forced to sign with more powerful Western nations.

The Unequal Treaties

China, which had led the way in establishing state authority over religious organizations and communities, was also the first to be forced to cede that authority. At the same time that the Qing armies were quelling the Taiping and Muslim rebellions, a series of defeats in military encounters with European forces forced the Qing court to grant privileges to representatives of transnational religious regimes that China had never previously had to grant. After its defeat in the Opium War with Britain in 1842, China signed treaties with the British, Americans, and French that granted foreigners permission to build churches in certain designated treaty ports.

That was just an opening wedge. After another defeat at the hands of the British in 1856, China was forced to revise those treaties to open more treaty ports and to guarantee religious freedom for Christians—Chinese and non-Chinese alike—throughout China. Treaties signed at that time with the British, French, Americans, and Russians contained clauses that read, "persons teaching it [i.e., Christianity] or professing it, therefore, shall alike be entitled to the protection of the Chinese authorities; nor shall any such, peaceably pursuing their calling, and not offending against the laws, be persecuted or interfered with."[8]

These treaties placed Chinese Christians under the protection of foreign powers, since whenever they faced Chinese justice they would claim religious persecution. This meant that the Chinese political community was forced to accept rents in its fabric as the transnational Christian religious community, with support from Western governments, began to carve out zones of autonomy for its Chinese members. This was an unprecedented challenge to the traditional subordination of religion to the state. Never before had China been forced to offer privileged status to a religious community. Never before had religious affiliation been grounds for demanding a privileged position within the political community.

These unequal treaties—so called because all the concessions were made by one side (China) and all the successful demands by the other (the West)—provided a precedent for early Western diplomatic relations with

Japan and Korea. The Tokugawa government in Japan, which had defeated the Christians in 1637, was compelled by unequal treaties that it was forced to sign with Western nations in the 1850s to accept the presence of Europeans and Americans on its soil. When the Tokugawa fell in 1868, overthrown partially because it had humiliated Japan by signing such unequal treaties, it was replaced by a new government intent on building a strong and wealthy country respected by the rest of the world. Japan soon learned that to win the respect of the West, and to win the revision of those unequal treaties, it had to allow religious freedom. It is for that reason that Christianity was legalized in Japan in 1873.[9]

Mere legalization, Japan soon learned, was not enough. The modern nations of the West demanded constitutional protection for the representatives of transnational religious communities in Japan. Under pressure from foreign governments and under the urging of German constitutional scholars who helped draft Japan's first constitution, which was promulgated in 1889, Japan took a step that China had yet to take. Japan included the line "Japanese subjects have freedom of religious belief, within limits not prejudicial to peace and order and not antagonistic to their duties as subjects" as Article 28 of East Asia's first formal constitution.[10] However, Japanese authorities interpreted the clause in the light of Japanese tradition. As Ito Hirobumi (1841–1909), one of the prime authors of the constitution, stated:

> The freedom of religion expressed in Article 28 is not an unqualified freedom, but a limited one. To list some of the limits, the people must not disregard their duties, and exercise of this freedom should not disturb social order, or interfere with freedom of individual beliefs. According to this Constitution, Japanese subjects have freedom of belief as long as they do not overstep these limits.[11]

Japan may have been forced by Western pressure to recognize some right to religious freedom, but those rights were still circumscribed by the traditional East Asian belief that even religious communities had to accept the ultimate authority of the state.

Korea, tucked away in the northeast corner of Asia and far from major East-West sea routes, was the last East Asian state to accept some restrictions on its traditional authority and legalize Christianity. In the early 1880s the king of Korea began signing treaties with Western powers in the hope that such diplomatic ties would serve as a counterbalance to growing pressure on Korea from Japan, which had forced its own unequal treaty on Korea in 1876. As the price of such ties, the French forced the king to agree to tolerate Catholics, including French missionaries, on Korean soil. Other Western powers soon demanded similar protection for their missionaries and their missionaries' converts. By 1898 Korea had succumbed to these demands, eliminating the last major legal barriers to the practice and proselytizing of Christianity in East Asia.[12]

Unequal treaties may have forced Korea, Japan, and China to accept, however reluctantly, the Western notion of special privileges for certain religious communities and their representatives, but none of these nations was willing to abandon totally the notion that the state retains final authority over every phase of its subjects' lives, including their religious lives. This notion remains embodied in the government agencies that have been established in all East Asian nations to supervise and regulate religious activities, religious organizations, and religious communities.

Bureaus of Religious Affairs

If China provided the paradigm for relations between states and religious communities in traditional East Asia, Japan has provided the paradigm for the twentieth century. It was Japan that first promulgated a constitution, and it inserted into its constitution a clause guaranteeing religious freedom, a precedent all other states in East Asia have subsequently followed. Japan was also the first to establish a government agency responsible for dealing with religious bodies and religious believers.

In Japan today, religious organizations operating nationwide register with an office of the Agency for Cultural Affairs within the Ministry of Education. Though today such registration is necessary only to receive the tax exemptions to which religious organizations are entitled, before 1945 such registration was used by the government to define what was a legitimate religious organization deserving of some measure of autonomy, and what was not. The Bureau of Religious Affairs also had authority to define what was and was not legitimate religious activity.

In the past, this authority has meant that the state could, and did on occasion, interfere even in matters of doctrine or denominational boundaries if the officials felt that such matters threatened the supremacy of the state. In 1941, for example, all Protestant denominations in Japan—Presbyterian, Congregational, Methodist, Lutheran, and Baptist—were forced to suppress their differences and merge into a United Church of Christ in Japan. Jehovah's Witnesses were suppressed altogether.[13]

Local representatives of transnational religious groups, though an object of special concern when Japan was at war with China and the West, were not the only ones to suffer from the state's assumption of ultimate authority. In fact, those religious communities rooted in the new religions of Japan, lacking the support of a transnational network, were even more vulnerable. One example is Tenrikyo, a religion with around 2 million adherents in Japan.

In 1880, Tenrikyo, which was founded in 1848, put itself under the administration of a Buddhist temple in order to have official recognition and protection. Five years later, however, Tenrikyo abandoned its Buddhist disguise and moved under the protective umbrella of the state-sponsored religion of Shinto as a separate Shinto sect, changing the name of its supreme deity in the process. Despite that protection, in 1940 the military government of Japan forced Tenrikyo to rewrite its catechism completely so that there would be no suggestion that the God of Tenrikyo might be superior to Amaterasu Omikami, the emperor's divine ancestor. Only in 1949 were the original catechism and its doctrines restored, and only in 1970 was Tenrikyo able finally to present itself formally as a totally independent religion, neither Buddhist nor Shinto.[14] As Tenrikyo authorities explain in official church histories, before 1945 "it was not possible openly to acknowledge and publish the original teachings as they had been received."[15] Nor was Tenrikyo the only indigenous religion in Japan to suffer from state interference even in such intimate matters as what name to call its deity. In 1939 the Diet passed a bill giving the government the legal authority to disband any religious organization whose teachings or rituals detracted from undivided devotion to the emperor, though such a bill hardly seemed necessary, since the government had by then already dissolved a couple of Japan's new religions, Omotokyo and Hitonomich Kyodan (now known as the Church of Perfect Liberty), under the Peace Preservation written originally to curb leftist political activity.[16] Though the new law was used against Christian and Buddhist groups to force them to merge into more manageable state-regulated organizations, the new religions, rooted in Japan's native religious traditions and lacking any transnational network of supporters, fared much worse and were often forced underground until 1945.

The religious affairs bureaus of Japan's neighbors have shown a similar inclination to grant indigenous religions less respect than local representatives of transnational religious movements. In the Republic of China (ROC), for example, Article 13 of the constitution states that "the people shall have freedom of Religion." However, until 1987, whenever I-Kuan Tao, an organized religious body that grew out of China's folk religious traditions, attempted to register with the Religion and Temples section of the Civil Affairs Department of the Ministry of the Interior—which all religious organizations that wish to operate legally must do—it was denied registration.[17]

By the time it won legal recognition, I-Kuan Tao claimed the allegiance of 9 percent of the population of Taiwan, making it the second largest religious community in Taiwan, with substantially more adherents than some of the Christian denominations that had won legal recognition much earlier.[18] It is probably no coincidence that I-Kuan Tao was legalized in Taiwan only after two North American scholars published a book through a respected university press that discusses I-Kuan Tao as a serious religious movement, conferring on it a legitimacy that the ROC government had tried to deny.[19]

By whatever name they are called, religious affairs bureaus reveal through their decisions on which religious organizations will enjoy the benefits of religious autonomy that one of the reasons they were established was to satisfy the demands of representatives of transnational religious regimes—which in turn would secure respectability for their government in international circles. These bureaus are responsible for ensuring that the religious freedom that the international community demands is respected, but also that the centrifugal push of religious loyalties that transnational religious regimes foster does not grow strong enough to overcome the centripetal pull toward national unity that the state must nurture. This is the reason that the more visible a religious organization is internationally, the more likely it is to be granted whatever freedom and privileges the state grants to religious communities.

The reverse, of course, is that the more invisible a religious community is, the fewer international connections it has, the less likely it is to be granted official recognition as a legitimate religious community deserving of all the privileges such recognition brings. The states of East Asia have preferred to grant no more autonomy to religious bodies than they have had to, and they have preferred to grant even limited religious freedom to no more organizations than they have had to. Notice, however, that local indigenous religious activity that is not linked to a national organization that can threaten the state is tolerated, though usually denied legal recognition as religious. Thus there are massive temples and shrines to folk deities throughout Taiwan that are tolerated by the government as long as they remain locally run and do not join together to form a national religious organization such as the Buddhists and the Christians have formed.[20]

In South Korea, for example, all religious organizations are required to register with the appropriate bureau in the Ministry of Culture and Sport. However, the practitioners of Korea's indigenous popular religion are denied such recognition. The largest association of shamans in South Korea, the Korean Association for Piety and Victory over Communism, is permitted to register only as a social organization, not a religious organization, and thus shamans are denied the status, privileges, and autonomy enjoyed by monks, priests, and nuns of recognized religious communities.[21] Most of these monks, priests, and nuns belong to the many separate Christian and Buddhist organizations that are registered with the Ministry of Culture and Sport in South Korea, and a few come from some of South Korea's new religions, which have adopted some of the organizational structure and doctrinal format of Christian denominations and have thus been granted legal status. North Korea grants the same legal recognition, though somewhat more limited, to Christianity, Buddhism, and one indigenous religion, for the same reason that South Korea does: the need to win friends and appear respectable in the international community.

The current constitution of North Korea states, in Article 54, that "All citizens are free either to hold religious beliefs or to propagandize against religion."[22] There are now four small but active and officially recognized religious organizations in North Korea: a Christian Federation, a Catholic Federation, a Buddhist Federation, and a Ch'eondogyo Central Committee.[23]

A look at the activities in which these organizations have engaged over the last few years makes it clear that their primary purpose is to establish friendly contacts with fellow believers in foreign countries. Of the four, only Ch'eondogyo is an indigenous Korean religion, and it has been the least active and the least visible of the four. It was probably established because of the revolutionary history of this religion, founded in the nineteenth century and identified with Korea's first large-scale peasant rebellions, and because there is a substantial Ch'eondogyo community in South Korea. The Protestants and the Buddhists have been dispatching delegates to international religious conferences since the mid-1980s. The Catholics, a much smaller group, have been less active outside of Korea, but they have built a church in the North Korean capital, Pyongyang, and have invited both foreign and expatriate Korean priests to come to Pyongyang and say mass.

The only religious community not heard from are the shamans and their clients. North Korean officials claim that there are no more practicing shamans in North Korea. Nor are there any associations of shamans listed among the various officially sanctioned religious organizations in the Democratic People's Republic of Korea.[24] Apparently, the lack of support from a transnational religious network and the failure to resemble in doctrine or structure transnational religious movements have rendered the shamans of North Korea's villages officially invisible.

In the People's Republic of China (PRC), there is similar discrimination against religions with neither strong transnational ties nor a strong domestic organization. I-Kuan Tao, though recently legalized in Taiwan, remains banned on the Chinese mainland.[25] And the Religious Affairs Bureau, established in 1951 directly under the State Council of the National People's Congress, also denies legality to the informal folk religion so prevalent in the villages of China, partially because the folk religion has no organized international network able to speak out on its behalf. In fact, the Chinese government has stated explicitly that only those religions that contain an international component may enjoy religious freedom in China.

For example, in 1979 the official newspaper of China, the *Renmin Ribao*, declared that "by religion, we chiefly mean worldwide religions, such as Christianity, Islam, Buddhism, and the like. They have scriptures, creeds, religious ceremonies, organizations, and so on. . . . Religious freedom, first of all, refers to those religions."[26] The *Renmin Ribao* went on to distinguish legal religions from folk religion, which it defined as superstition, "activities conducted by shamans and sorcerers, such as magic medicine, magic water, divination, fortune telling, . . . praying for rain, praying for pregnancy, exorcising demons," and so on.[27]

Chinese officials frequently cite specific criteria for distinguishing which religions must be granted some degree of religious freedom. Legitimate religion is differentiated from illegitimate superstition by its possession of five identifying characteristics: "it is complex, mass-based, long-lasting, and has implications for relations with both ethnic nationalities and the nations of the world."[28] Just as does the *Renmin Ribao*'s definition, these five characteristics favor transnational over indigenous religious communities. As a result, the freelance ritual specialists who inhabit many of China's villages stand condemned as practitioners of "feudal superstition," and if they accept donations for their services, they may find themselves arrested for selling a "fraudulent commodity," that is, their claim to influence over spiritual forces.[29]

Obviously, one major reason for granting religions with transnational connections a status that the indigenous folk religion does not have is that China recognizes the role that Chinese representatives of transnational religious communities can play in enhancing China's image overseas and in gaining support for China from abroad. After all, it is primarily its relationships with the world beyond East Asia over the past century and a half that have forced not only China but Japan and Korea as well to recognize religion as a separate and distinct sphere of life and to grant at least the appearance of religious freedom.

National Security and the Definition of Religion

Religious affairs bureaus have provided powerful administrative tools for East Asian governments to deal with the demands their relationship with the rest of the world has placed on their policy toward religious believers among their own citizens. In effect, they are national security organs, working to minimize the divisive impact religious loyalties could have on national unity while at the same time maximizing the image of those governments as conforming to the norms expected of a civilized nation and thus meriting the respect of other nations. One set of practices they have adopted to pursue these twin imperatives is to fashion definitions of religions that allow more freedom to religious organizations the more they are visible overseas, and to permit a more public role for religious organizations that are hierarchically organized and thus more susceptible to centralized control. The definitions of religion employed are primarily Western in origin because Western religious organizations were, at first, the most visible internationally as well as the most hierarchical. Consequently, in defining religion in such a way as to promote their own national security, East Asian governments have favored Western and other transnational religious regimes at the expense of less visible and less organized domestic expressions of religiosity.

Ironically, this is the opposite of the effect that Japan—which first coined the Chinese character translation for the word "religion" that is now used throughout East Asia—originally intended. The builders of modern Japan looked at the West in the last quarter of the nineteenth century and saw shared faith in Christianity as supplying the cohesion that could undergird its power. They therefore decided to create a similar religious basis for Japanese power. Japan did not have a clearly definable Japanese religion, however, and so the builders of modern Japan decided to create one. They elevated the worship of local deities into a new national cult they called Shinto ("The Way of the Gods") and then proceeded to establish a nationwide network of priests both to perform the rituals and to promulgate a creed that they hoped would inculcate in the Japanese people a love of Japan and a love of the Japanese emperor. They were aware, however, that Westerners would frown on their attempt to create a state religion, and they sought a way around that by adopting a definition of religion that would allow them to promote Shinto while still denying that it was a religion.

The definition Japan adopted in the last quarter of the nineteenth century claimed that a legitimate religion had to have a doctrinal and scriptural base, had to be limited (i.e., sectarian) rather than all-encompassing in its membership, and had to extend beyond the boundaries of one nation. These were characteristics shared by the Christian communities that the West wanted to protect, but they were also characteristics that Shinto did not have. This denial by definition of Shinto's religious character allowed Japan's leaders, or so they believed, to promise freedom of religion in its 1899 constitution while insisting that all Japanese citizens, no matter what their religious affiliation, affirm certain propositions about the special status of the Japanese emperor and the Japanese nation.

There were two unexpected consequences to the Japanese adoption of the Western definition of religion, one almost immediate and the other not apparent until much later. The first was the use of this definition by Japanese Buddhists to change government policy toward Buddhism. The Japanese Buddhist community found itself under attack by a modernizing state trying to forge national unity through a forced shift in religious loyalties from Buddhism, identified with the old regime, to Shinto. At first bereft of transnational support, Japan's Buddhists were not sure how to defend themselves. Then the World Parliament of Religion, held in Chicago in 1893, provided them with just the opportunity they needed. Five prominent Japanese Buddhists traveled to that meeting and were accorded recognition as representatives of one of the world's great religions. By gaining recognition abroad, the Buddhists of Japan forced their own government as well to recognize them as leaders of a respectable and legitimate religious community. They also convinced their government that Buddhism's international connections could prove to be useful in Japan's drive to create what came to be called the "Greater East Asia Co-Prosperity Sphere."[30]

The second unexpected consequence did not appear until after 1945 when the American occupation government insisted that Shinto was a religion after all and was thus sectarian, according to the definition Japan itself had adopted earlier, and could claim no more universal support and government patronage than any other religion. This has created a cloud of ambiguity over the Shinto shrines that remain in Japan. Are they now merely historical monuments that government officials may visit in their official capacity with no implications of support for one religious organization at the expense of others? Or do they maintain their religious character and hence prevent government officials, as public officials, from performing or participating in any ceremonies that take place on their grounds?

The Yasukuni shrine in Tokyo has been the focal point for this debate. This Shinto shrine was established by the first post-Tokugawa government to honor the spirits of the military heroes who gave their lives for the Japanese nation. In recent years cabinet ministers and even prime ministers have visited the Yasukuni shrine annually to pay their respects. However, they usually declare, when they bow before the altar or present an offering, that they do so as private individuals, not as government officials, though they may have traveled to the shrine in an official caravan.[31] This legal fiction continues to arouse the ire of some Christians, Buddhists, and followers of new religions who want the religious freedom clause of their post-1945 American-authored constitution interpreted strictly in order to ensure that Shinto will never again hold the privileged status that it enjoyed before 1945.[32]

Unlike what transpired in Japan, the encounter with the modern world in China and Korea did not lead to the temporary elevation of any indigenous deities or rituals above those of religions with foreign origins. On the contrary, indigenous expressions of religiosity were delegitimized in favor of a religiosity expressed through organizations with a clear doctrinal or scriptural base, a limited membership, and a hierarchical clerical structure—criteria that clearly favored transnational religious regimes. The only native-born religious communities able to share in the privileges of those with alien origins were those that developed international connections or obtained international recognition as a legitimate religion by emphasizing their sectarian character, their scriptural base, or their clerical hierarchy.

In the People's Republic of China, for example, the Religious Affairs Bureau has sections for dealing with only four religions: Catholicism, Protestantism, Buddhism, and Taoism. A fifth, Islam, is dealt with separately in offices responsible for minority affairs.[33] The PRC government recognizes only those five religions, only one of which, Taoism, is native-born. Taoism is awarded official recognition primarily because it plays an important role in many overseas Chinese communities, and Taoist temples in China earn foreign exchange through donations from Chinese abroad. Taoism also qualified as a legitimate religion under the standard imported definition because, like Christianity, Buddhism, and Islam, it has a textual base, a hierarchical institutional structure, and clearly articulated doctrines.

Even that is not enough to win Taoism legitimacy in the more Western-influenced atmosphere of Taiwan. Though Taoist temples operate legally in Taiwan, only Buddhism, Islam, and Christianity are treated unequivocally as religions in the textbooks supplied by the ROC government to all of Taiwan's schools. Taoism is treated more as superstition than religion, unlike its imported competitors.[34] And the folk religion of Taiwan, with no international ties or domestic organizational support, is not recognized as religious at all. In fact, the government of the ROC has mounted propaganda campaigns against the large-scale rituals that are the main expressions of popular religiosity in rural villages.[35]

As already noted, the situation in Korea is not very different. Both North and South Korea deny legitimacy to shamanism and other manifestations of informal popular religiosity. Only Ch'eondogyo and, in the South, other native religious organizations, such as the Unification Church, which have adopted a sectarian identity, a scriptural base, a standardized liturgy, and an identifiable leadership hierarchy, are recognized as legitimate religions. Even they have encountered more difficulty in winning such recognition than the transnational religious communities have had in trying to establish an outpost in South Korea. Often these new, native-born religions must endure years of denigration as "pseudoreligions" before they can enjoy the same privileges as religious organizations with roots overseas.

Despite or perhaps because of this tilt in favor of religious organizations with transnational backing, China, Japan, and Korea have been generally successful in meeting the sometimes conflicting demands of both national unity and international respectability. Two of these nations have been split in two by rival claimants to national hegemony, and the third lost a world war in 1945. But in none of these instances were the divided loyalties of religious communities a factor. Nor have any of these nations become international pariahs because of accusations of mistreatment of communities of believers.

Yet areas of tension between the state and religious communities remain, particularly in China.

Unresolved Conflicts

The People's Republic of China, more ethnically and culturally diverse and thus more sensitive to the centrifugal pull of religious affiliation upon its citizens than its neighbors, has had the most difficulty in meeting international expectations while maintaining its own standards of domestic unity and national autonomy. With suspicions of the West fueled by historical memories of close connections between Western imperialism and Western missionaries, the PRC has acted more firmly than any other East Asian state, even North Korea, to minimize the transnational character of Christian communities.

The post–Cultural Revolution constitution of 1982 states explicitly, alongside the clause guaranteeing religious freedom, that "religion is not subject to the control of foreign countries."[36] This has been interpreted as forbidding religious organizations from openly accepting money that foreign organizations offer to donate for religious purposes (though they may accept donations from individual foreigners).[37] Long before 1982, in the early 1950s, this insistence on financial, and therefore institutional, independence from transnational religious regimes led to a reorganization of Chinese Protestantism and Catholicism. In 1951, Protestant churches were forced to cut off all ties to foreign mission boards. They were also forced to abandon their denominational affiliations, which tied them to religious organizations outside China, and join as one in the Chinese Christian Council.

Since Protestants could sever ties to foreign mission boards without damage to their faith, most of China's Protestant leaders went along with these demands. Catholics, however, could not sever ties to the Vatican without seriously compromising their Catholicism. At least this is what many Chinese Catholics believe, and this is why it took so long for the Chinese to organize the Catholic counterpart to the China Christian Council. It was not until 1957 that enough priests and laypeople who were willing to break with Rome could be found for the Chinese Catholic Patriotic Association to be formally established. One year later, in 1958, Chinese Catholics began electing and consecrating their own bishops—consecrations Rome considers valid but illicit since they were done without papal approval.

There are, of course, Christians who refuse to accept the Communist demand for a church free of all foreign strings. In the Protestant camp, they hold "home meetings" where they pray and read the Bible together without the presence or assistance of officially recognized clergy. These meetings are technically illegal, as are the activities of the underground Catholic Church, which continues to meet in unsanctioned locations.[38]

Despite the embarrassment of having some of its own citizens reject its attempts to create purely national religious organizations, China has, by and large, been successful since the end of the Cultural Revolution in meeting the twin demands of nationalism and internationalism by minimizing foreign influence on believers within China while maximizing China's visibility in international religious circles. As one recent officially sponsored study of religion in the PRC noted:

China's religions, while holding to the principle of independence and self-government since the founding of the New China, have made contacts with religious circles abroad, carrying on religious activities and academic studies together, strengthening friendship between Chinese and people of other countries, helping the cause of world peace.[39]

This does not mean that China has totally resolved the tension between its need for national unity and the requirements of international respectability. It continues to have problems with Roman Catholics, both in China and around the world. Catholic clergy and laypeople who remain loyal to the pope have maintained, despite a series of arrests, an illegal clerical hierarchy that is independent of the official Chinese Catholic Patriotic Association.[40] As long as bishops and priests remain in confinement or in prison for refusing to support the Chinese Catholic Patriotic Association's rejection of papal authority, the Vatican and those who follow its lead will continue to condemn China for its violations of religious freedom, damaging China's reputation in the international community.[41]

Of particular concern are the more than 270,000 Chinese Catholics living in Hong Kong. What will happen to them in 1997, when control of the British crown colony reverts to the Chinese government? Will Hong Kong's Catholics be forced to renounce their allegiance to the pope? Will their bishops and priests be jailed if they do not betray the Vatican?[42] This is only one of many difficult issues China will have to deal with when it absorbs that capitalist outpost into its Communist bosom, but it will be a particularly intractable issue because of China's stubborn insistence that religious bodies be free of any non-Chinese control and Catholic religious conviction that the authority of the Vatican must be respected.

China may also face significant problems in the near future with its large Muslim community. There are nearly 20 million Muslims of varying ethnic backgrounds in the PRC.[43] Many of them are indistinguishable from their Chinese neighbors, except for their aversion to pork. Others, especially those in the once rebellious northwest, are members of distinctive ethnic minorities, closer culturally in some respects to their Muslim neighbors in the new republics that have appeared in Central Asia since the fall of the Soviet Union than they are to their fellow Chinese citizens in Beijing and Shanghai.

These various Muslim peoples of China have been brought closer together by a government policy that labels all of them as Muslims, whether Islam is their religious or ethnic identity. Thanks to another government policy that uses Chinese Muslims to promote friendly relations with Muslim nations, they have also grown more conscious of their membership in an international Muslim community. The result, contrary to what the PRC had hoped for, is a strengthened sense of Muslim identity.[44] China's Muslims have grown increasingly proud of their common religious heritage, creating what one scholar identifies as a rising tide of ethnic nationalism among those the Chinese government officially identifies as members of the Muslim ethnoreligious community.[45]

That became clear to the citizens in Beijing in the spring of 1989, when over 3,000 Chinese Muslims protested in the streets of the Chinese capital against the publication of a book on sexual customs that claimed, among other slanders, that the minarets from which the call to prayer is heard were actually phallic symbols and, even worse, that Muslim pilgrims to Mecca often engaged in sexual orgies there, even going so far as to sexually engage the camels of the Saudi desert. Unlike the pro-democracy demonstrations in Tiananmen Square at the time, the Muslim protest was resolved peacefully, and the government confiscated all copies of the offensive book and jailed its authors.[46]

Not all disputes between Chinese Muslims and the government have ended so peacefully. Several times since 1949, there have been credible reports of clashes between groups of Muslims and Chinese government forces, though not on as grand a scale as the uprisings in southwestern and northwestern China in the nineteenth century. There was a major incident in 1975 near the border with Vietnam, and a separatist riot broke out in 1990 in a city not far from China's border with Kyrgystan (when it was still the Kirghiz Soviet Socialist Republic), costing at least twenty-two lives.[47] As recently as October 7, 1993, Chinese troops had to be used to suppress a Muslim demonstration in the capital of the largely Muslim province of Qinghai at a cost of at least nine lives.[48]

Obviously, for a central government determined to maintain national unity, Muslim separatism must be a matter of grave concern. However, Beijing cannot afford to reverse the policy it has followed for over half a century of recognizing Islam as a legitimate religion and Muslims as a distinct people. Such a reversal might provoke China's Muslims into further resisting central government authority as well as antagonize Muslim states, such as Indonesia and the nations of the Middle East with which China needs to maintain friendly relations. The need to foster national unity as well as to cultivate international friendship continues to limit what steps the PRC state can take toward religious communities within its borders.

Relations between the political and the religious realms are much less tense in the other nations of East Asia. Blessed with more homogeneous populations and, except in the case of North Korea, more democratic governments, Taiwan, North and South Korea, and Japan have had neither major confrontations with transnational religious groups nor domestic religious unrest in recent decades.

One factor that surely helped North Korea to maintain domestic tranquillity is that it is ruled by a remarkably efficient repressive regime. If any North Koreans feel any conflict between the demands of their faith and the demands of their government, they are not allowed to say so publicly. The Buddhist and Christian leaders who are North Korea's links with believers overseas speak of their late Great Leader Kim Il Sung with the same reverence as when they speak of the Buddha or Jesus. In international conferences with fellow Buddhists or Christians, they never deviate from the official government line.

The followers of the one indigenous religion allowed to operate in North Korea, Ch'eondogyo, are so trusted by the government that since 1946 a Ch'eondogyo political party (the (Ch'eondogyo Young Friends Party) has been officially a junior partner in the united front that rules North Korea.[49] It does not appear to operate as a truly independent political force, however, and nor does the religion behind it appear to be thriving in North Korea, as no foreign visitors have reported seeing any evidence of Ch'eondogyo churches or public religious gatherings.

Democracy rather than repression is responsible for the lessening of tension between the Christian communities of South Korea and Taiwan and their respective political leaders. Before the democratization of recent years, Christian pastors and laypeople in both countries tended to be among the most vocal critics of their authoritarian governments. Both nations were heavily dependent economically and diplomatically on the United States and could not afford to alienate an American population that treasures religious freedom, especially freedom for Christians with ties to American denominations, seminaries, and mission boards. This provided some measure of protection for Christian leaders to speak out when others could not. Consequently, Christians tended to be overrepresented, in terms of the percentage of the Christian population, among the leadership of the democratization movements in these two countries.

As both Korea and Taiwan began to allow their citizens more freedom of speech in the late 1980s, however, more non-Christians joined Christians in voicing opposition, and now the Christian communities in both countries are simply seen as part of a much larger political community that can debate government policies without fear of repercussions. The protection Christians received as representatives of transnational religious regimes no longer gives them any special privileges.

Unlike North Korea, neither South Korea nor Taiwan has any political parties linked to a particular religious community. The only East Asian nation with a significant religious political party—North Korea's Ch'eondogyo Young Friends Party does not play a significant role in North Korean political life—is, surprisingly, the nation that was forced by U.S. occupation after World War II to erect a concrete barrier between church and state. In Japan's parliamentary elections of July 1993, four decades of uninterrupted Liberal Democratic Party rule over Japan ended as the Clean Government Party, or Komeito, won 52 seats in a Lower House of 511.[50] This made the

Komeito Japan's fourth largest political party and earned it its first cabinet posts. As part of the new ruling coalition, the Komeito held four seats in the cabinet that governed Japan from August of 1993 until the spring of 1994.[51] When that governing coalition dissolved in the summer of 1994, the Komeito joined with five other opposition parties in December 1994 to form the New Frontier Party, the Shinshinto. Former Komeito party members constitute the largest bloc in the new party, behind only party head Ozawa Ichiro's New Life Party (Shinseito), and are believed to have mobilized about half of the more than 12 million votes that Shinshinto garnered in the Upper House elections in July 1995, indicating that Komeito remains a potent political force.

The Komeito made its first formal appearance in Japan in 1964 as the political arm of the Sokagakkai ("Value-Creation Academic Society") and since 1967 has controlled slightly less than 10 percent of the seats in the Japanese Diet. Although in 1970 the Komeito severed all formal ties with Sokagakkai—officially a lay wing of Nichiren Shoshu, a Japanese Buddhist denomination, until 1991—it remains aware of its Buddhist roots and is deeply influenced by the Sokagakkai's Buddhist philosophy and values.[52] Some observers, remembering the role that state-sponsored Shinto played in supporting Japanese imperialism, feared that a rise to at least a share of national power by the political arm of a nationalistic Japanese religious movement might pose "a potential threat to democracy."[53] However, during those few months that it occupied a few cabinet posts, the Komeito did not act any differently from its secular partners in Japan's short-lived governing coalition.[54]

A more dangerous religious presence in Japan in the 1990s has been the Aum Shinrikyo. Founded in 1987 and given legal recognition as a religious corporation in 1989, Aum Shinrikyo tried to follow the example of the Sokagakkai and place some of its members in the Diet. When all twenty-five Aum Shinrikyo candidates lost their races for seats in Japan's House of Representatives in 1990, their leader, Asahara Shoko, began turning to violence against his critics and then against the general population, something no other religious leader had done in modern Japanese history. Apparently, he and his followers hoped that their gas attack on five Tokyo subway trains in March 1995 would hasten the Armageddon that would destroy all existing governments and allow Aum Shinrikyo to seize power.[55]

Only two days after that attack on Tokyo's subways, Aum Shinrikyo found itself under attack from the government it had sought to destroy. Police raided twenty-five Aum Shinrikyo centers across Japan—but this was just the beginning of the Japanese government counterattack against Aum Shinrikyo. Shocked by how much illegal activity the organization had been able to engage in under the cover of being a religious organization, the government has gone beyond simply dismantling Aum Shinrikyo to trying to change the relationship between the state and religious organizations that has held in Japan since the end of World War II.

The first step the government took was to revoke Aum Shinrikyo's legal status as a religious organization—the first time this has happened to a genuine religious organization since 1945. The Supreme Court of Japan ruled in January 1996 that the revocation of Aum Shinrikyo's right to public recognition as a religious organization did not violate Japan's constitutional guarantee of religious freedom, since Aum Shinrikyo followers were still free to continue their religious activities without the benefit of the tax exemptions that religious organizations normally enjoy. However, once Aum Shinrikyo was judged to be no longer a religious organization, the government decided that it could be the first organization in Japan to be disbanded under the provisions of the 1952 Antisubversive Activities Law. If this decision is upheld by Japan's courts, Aum Shinrikyo members would be banned from such religious activities as publishing the writings of their guru, trying to recruit new followers, or even engaging in religious rituals or religious training under the guidance of those few leaders of the group who might remain out of jail.

Moreover, in reaction to their discovery of how much illegal activity Aum Shinrikyo was able to engage in under the protective cover of religious freedom, the government has tightened its control over all religious corporations. For example, all recognized religious corporations now must annually submit a list to government authorities of all of their senior officials and of their assets. In addition, bureaucrats in the Education Ministry now have the right to investigate religious organizations if there is some suspicion that they are abusing their status as officially recognized religious organizations. This new law passed the Diet in December 1995 despite the objections of the Shinshinto, which fears that the law may be used to harass the Sokagakkai.

Despite these recent changes in the relationship between the government and religious organizations—the full impact of which is not yet known—Japan appears, since 1945, to have successfully adopted the imported model for relations between political and religious communities in which political communities exist alongside religious communities, with much overlapping but also with sharply delineated spheres of autonomy. One major difference between Japan and its neighbors, however, is that the beneficiaries have not been religions from the West, which still attract very few believers in Japan, but rather Japanese religious communities, such as Sokagakkai, which have a much stronger position vis-à-vis the state than they have ever had before.

In the Koreas, Taiwan, and China, in contrast, Christian and, to some extent, Buddhist organizations have gained more autonomy and protection from government interference than they ever had under traditional governments, but traditional forms of indigenous religiosity have been marginalized and forced to survive in the shadows of modern religious organizations with a greater international visibility. In East Asia overall, the modern era has clearly favored transnational religious communities.

Conclusion

What conclusions can we draw from this survey of government attempts to rein in the centrifugal pull of religious loyalties in modern East Asia? What does it tell us about the role that transnational religious regimes and their constituent communities played in redefining the relationship between religious and political communities in East Asia?

First of all, when Christianity forced its way into East Asia in the nineteenth century, supported by the superior technology and economic clout of the West, it forced China, Korea, and Japan to begin to admit the existence of a separate sphere of human existence called "religion" whose autonomy the political community must respect. Not only Christian communities but all religious communities that fit the imported Western definition of a religious community benefited. They have now all been granted some measure of autonomy. The battle is now fought over how to define that sphere, not over whether or not it exists, and that in itself is a victory for the Western concept of religion.

The current quarrel over where to draw the line limiting the reach of government into religious communities is being waged over competing definitions of what constitutes a true religious community, what constitutes the legitimate range of religious activities, and what is the relative hierarchy of religious and political obligations. Specific areas of combat not discussed in this chapter are the battles for control of education, property (e.g., worship halls), school buildings, communication media, medical facilities, and medical treatment, as well as of moral discourse.

The main issue behind these skirmishes is the same. The governments of East Asia have tried, and continue to try, to limit the autonomy of religious organizations and to enhance their own authority, whereas transnational religious regimes have tried, and continue to try, to enhance their own autonomy by limiting or restraining the authority that governments exercise over them. The most ardently fought battles are often for control of moral authority, as political communities attempt to limit the scope of moral pronouncements by leaders of religious communities, especially when they imply criticism or rejection of government policy, while religious leaders try to make their voices heard by a larger and larger audience on a greater and greater range of issues.

In this struggle, transnational religious communities have an advantage over indigenous religious communities. International connections often skew the outcome of the struggle in favor of the religious community. We have seen that in China and Korea the indigenous religion in its traditional form has not even been able to win official recognition as a legitimate expression of religiosity, though local representatives of transnational religious regimes have won at least official recognition of their existence and have gained some limited autonomy. The most successful indigenous religious communities have been those that have cloaked themselves in foreign organizational, doctrinal, and conceptual forms in order to share in the respectability that transnational religious regimes have earned for religion. Thus, the last century of East Asian history has seen a revolution not only in how religious and political communities relate to each other but also in how religion and religious communities are defined and conceived. This revolution is the direct product of the penetration of East Asia by transnational religious regimes.

This revolution has resulted not in the wholesale adoption of Western concepts and practices but in a compromise between the demands for international acceptability on the one hand and the need for national unity on the other. Trying to create strong national loyalties where nationalism had been weak before, the leaders of modernizing regimes in China, Japan, and Korea would have preferred that their respective governments monopolize the loyalty and obedience of their citizens. They feared that their still fragile nations might disintegrate if subjected to the centrifugal pull of another locus of authority, even if that competing claimant to loyalty and obedience was religious rather than political.

Transnational religious regimes offer alternative access to the international community as well as alternative standards and symbols of legitimacy. Such alternatives may challenge the dominion of the state. Yet states cannot ignore or shut down this alternative access to the international community without endangering their own channels to that same community. Thus compromise has been necessary.

The fragile states of emerging East Asia have needed both national unity and international goodwill to enhance their actual and perceived security. Religion plays a double role in this equation, serving both as a potentially divisive force internally while simultaneously providing international linkages. Since indigenous religions primarily play a divisive role, they are more likely to be suppressed. They usually fail to meet the standards of modernity set by the West in that they often represent the less structured, less textual, less standardized pre-literate culture of the past and have few, if any, links with the modern international community.

Religious communities with international backing or with international recognition could not be so easily suppressed. East Asian governments have instead often attempted to tame those religious communities by defining them as cultural phenomena that are to be supervised by an appropriate government ministry (e.g., the Ministry of Culture and Sport in South

Korea, the Ministry of Education in Japan). Moreover, the states of East Asia have all tried to keep representatives of transnational religious communities within their borders from engaging in organized political activities as religious communities. It is no accident that the only religious political parties in East Asia today, Komeito in Japan and the Ch'eondogyo Young Friends Party in North Korea, both represent native-born religious organizations.

Whether communist, fascist, or democratic, the leaders of the emerging states in East Asia have all been remarkably successful in balancing the need to unify their nation with the need to maintain friendly ties with the international community—including transnational religious groups with representatives within their borders. They have usually managed to keep the particular loyalties of religious bodies and communities within national borders from becoming so particularistic that they threaten the unity of the nation as a whole without forcing them to give up so much of their particular religious beliefs and practices that believers would become alienated from their nation and fellow believers beyond national borders would grow antagonistic.

Problems remain, particularly in China with its increasingly self-conscious Muslim population and its plans to absorb Hong Kong, which has a large Christian population and experience with religious freedom. North Korea, too, will face problems as it opens up its economy to more interaction with the outside world and, in the process, exposes its relationships with its religious communities to external scrutiny. But Taiwan, South Korea, and Japan have apparently made the transition successfully from the traditional dominance of religion by the state into the modern era of greater autonomy for religious communities. And they have done so while building even stronger governments than they had in the past.

The collision between the two worlds of Western concepts of religion and appropriate church-state relations on the one hand with the traditional East Asian understanding of religious organizations and their place in society on the other has resulted in a new East Asian model of church-state relations, one that reverses the predictions of modernization theory. Instead of religious communities becoming less autonomous and religious leaders becoming less powerful under the impact of, and sometimes with the support of, the West, religious communities in modern East Asia have become more organized and more independent of government intervention, and their leaders have become more powerful.[56] Perhaps world-system theory offers a better approach than modernization theory, since it emphasizes that relations among nations affect domestic as well as international developments. Most world-system theorists concentrate on political, economic, or social interaction among member states of the international community. Religious ties should be added to that list.

This survey suggests that over the past 150 years China, Japan, and Korea have been pulled into a global network of religious believers who interact across national boundaries. The penetration of East Asia by Christian transnational religious movements has changed more than the relationship between the governments of East Asia and their Christian citizens. It has also transformed the organization and activities of other religious communities as well and has permanently altered the way both East Asian governments and East Asian citizens view religion and its relationship to the state. Believers in East Asia no longer practice their faith in isolation. What they say and do, and what happens to them, can have global repercussions, just as what happens to fellow believers elsewhere on the globe can affect them. They are now part of the transnational religious community, with all the opportunities and uncertainties that this entails.

NOTES

1. This is the picture of premodern China presented in Kwang-Ching Liu, ed., *Orthodoxy in Late Imperial China* (Berkeley: University of California Press, 1990), but it would be equally valid for Japan and Korea, as can be seen in Masaharu Anesaki, *History of Japanese Religion* (Rutland, VT: C. E. Tuttle, 1963), and Don Baker, "A Different Thread: Catholic Koreans and the Redefinition of Orthodoxy," in a forthcoming volume tentatively entitled *Confucianism and Late Choseon Korea*.

2. For a brief discussion of the relationship between the premodern Korean state and the Korean Buddhist community, see Hee-Sung Kee, "Word and Wordlessness: The Spirit of Korean Buddhism," *Korea Journal* 33 (3) (Autumn 1993):12–15.

3. Franz Michael, *The Taiping Rebellion: History* (Seattle: University of Washington Press, 1972).

4. Mary C. Wright, *The Last Stand of Chinese Conservatism: The T'ung-Chih Restoration, 1862–1874* (Stanford: Stanford University Press, 1957), 96–124.

5. Benjamin B. Weems, *Reform, Rebellion, and the Heavenly Way* (Tucson: University of Arizona Press, 1964).

6. Suk-woo Choi, "Korean Catholicism Yesterday and Today," *Korea Journal* 24 (8) (August 1984):8.

7. George Elison, *Deus Destroyed: The Image of Christianity in Early Modern Japan* (Cambridge, MA: Harvard University Press, 1973).

8. Cited in Eric O. Hanson, "Political Aspects of Chinese Catholicism," in *China and Christianity: Historical and Future Encounters* (Notre Dame, IN: University of Notre Dame Press, 1979), 141.

9. Joseph M. Kitagawa, *Religion in Japanese History* (New York: Columbia University Press, 1966), 190.

10. Kyoko Inoue, *MacArthur's Japanese Constitution: A Linguistic and Cultural Study of Its Making* (Chicago: University of Chicago Press, 1991), 115, and Helen Hardacre, *Shintō and the State: 1868–1988* (Princeton: Princeton University Press, 1989), 114.

11. Inoue, *MacArthur's Japanese Constitution*, 116.

12. Chongko Choi (Ch'oe Chonggo), "State and Religion in Korea" (in English), in *Kukka wa Chonggyo* [State and Religion] (Seoul: Hyeundai Sasangsa, 1983), 291–301.

13. Agency for Cultural Affairs, ed., *Japanese Religion* (Tokyo: Kodansha, 1981), 218; Sheldon M. Garon, "State and Religion in Imperial Japan, 1912–1945," *Journal of Japanese Studies* 12 (2) (Summer 1986):274, 290.

14. Henry Van Straelen, *The Religion of Divine Wisdom* (Kyoto: Veritas Shoin, 1957); Agency for Cultural Affairs, *Japanese Religion*, 225–226.

15. The Tenrikyo Overseas Mission Department of the Tenrikyo Church Headquarters, ed., *Tenrikyo: Its History and Teachings* (Tenri, Japan: Tenri Jihosha, 1978), 265–266.

16. Garon, "State and Religion in Imperial Japan," 273–301. For more examples, see H. Neil McFarland, *The Rush Hour of the Gods* (New York: Macmillan, 1967), 62–64; Agency for Cultural Affairs, *Japanese Religion*, 184–186, 227–229.

17. Joseph Bosco, "Yiguan Dao: 'Heterodoxy' and Popular Religion in Taiwan," in *The Other Taiwan: 1945 to the Present,* ed. Murray A. Rubinstein (Armonk, NY: M. E. Sharpe, 1994), 422–444.

18. *Republic of China Yearbook, 1991–92* (Taipei: Kwanghua Publishing Co., 1992), 419–420. The figure of 9 percent of the population of Taiwan comes from the 1989 edition of the *Republic of China Yearbook*, 562.

19. The book is David K. Jordan and Daniel L. Overmyer's *The Flying Phoenix: Aspects of Chinese Sectarianism in Taiwan* (Princeton: Princeton University Press, 1986).

20. See, for example, Robert P. Wellers, "Capitalism, Community, and the Rise of Amoral Cults in Taiwan," in *Asian Visions of Authority: Religion and the Modern States of East and Southeast Asia,* edited by Charles Keyes, Laurel Kendall, and Helen Hardacre (Honolulu: University of Hawaii Press, 1994), 141–164.

21. T'aegon Kim, *Han'guk musok yeon'gyu* [Studies of Korean shamanism] (Seoul: Chimmundang, 1991), 458.

22. Iheum Yun, *Han'guk Chonggyo yeon'gyu* [Studies in Korean Religion], vol. 3 (Seoul: Chimmundang, 1991), 184.

23. Information on the Korean Christian Federation is available in "Report of the Canadian Council of Churches' Delegation to the Democratic People's Republic of Korea, 4–13 November 1988," *Currents* 10 (4) (January 1989):5. A Report on the Korean Catholic Federation appears in "The Korean Catholic Federation," *Inculturation* 6 (1) (Spring 1991):43–46. The Korean Buddhist Federation is discussed in Korean in Cheong T'aegyeok and Sin Peopt'a, *Pukhan eui cheol kwa pulgyo* [Buddhist temples and the Buddhist religion in North Korea] (Seoul: Minjoksa, 1990), 281–300.

24. Such a list is provided in Yun, *Han'guk Chonggyo yeon'gyu*, 205.

25. Asia Watch, *Freedom of Religion in China, January 1992* (New York: Human Rights Watch, 1992), 15.

26. Donald E. MacInnis, *Religion in China Today* (Maryknoll, NY: Orbis Books, 1989), 33.

27. Ibid., 34.

28. Ibid., 2.

29. Ann Anagnost, "The Politics of Ritual Displacement," in *Asian Visions of Authority,* edited by Keyes, Kendall, and Hardacre, 221–254.

30. James Edward Ketelaar's *Of Heretics and Martyrs in Meiji Japan* (Princeton: Princeton University Press, 1990) is a fascinating account of this persecution of Buddhism by a modernizing Japan and the Buddhist response.

31. In 1985 Prime Minister Nakansone visited the Yasukuni shrine in his official capacity. Prime Minister Ryutaro Hashimoto did the same in 1996 ("Japan Premier Visits Shrine to War Dead," *New York Times,* July 30, 1996, A3). Other prime ministers after 1985 adopted the less controversial stance of making officially private visits on August 15. See Karl van Wolferen, *The Enigma of Japanese Power* (New York: Random House, 1990), 321–322.

32. Article 20 of the 1947 MacArthur constitution states: "The state and its organs shall refrain from religious education or any other religious activity." See Kyoko Inoue, *MacArthur's Japanese Constitution,* 279. For more on the creation of Shinto and the repercussions of its creation, see Helen Hardacre, *Shintō and the State.*

33. Bob Whyte, *Unfinished Encounter* (Harrisburg, PA: Morehouse Publishing, 1988), 213.

34. Jeffrey Meyer, "The Image of Religion in Taiwan Textbooks," *Journal of Chinese Religion* 15 (Fall 1987):44–50.

35. Robert P. Weller, "The Politics of Ritual Disguise," *Modern China* 13 (1) (January 1987):32.

36. MacInnis, *Religion in China Today,* 35. Article 36 of the 1982 constitution states: "No state organ, public organization or individual may compel citizens to believe in, or not believe in, any religion; nor may they discriminate against citizens who believe in, or do not believe in, any religion." See Asia Watch, *Freedom of Religion in China,* 5.

37. MacInnis, *Religion in China Today,* 23–24. This interpretation was made explicit in early 1994 when the PRC government issued a series of decrees placing specific restrictions on the religious activities in which foreigners may engage or support while in China. Ari Goldman, "Religion Notes," *New York Times*, February 12, 1994.

38. Nicholas D. Kristof, "Christianity Is Booming in China Despite Rifts," *New York Times*, February 7, 1993, 10.

39. Luo Zhufeng, ed., *Religion Under Socialism in China*, translated by Donald E. MacInnis and Zheng Xi'an (Armonk, NY: M. E. Sharpe, 1991). This is a report prepared by a group of scholars at the Institute for Research on Religion of the Shanghai Academy of Social Sciences in 1987.

40. Asia Watch, *Freedom of Religion in China*, 16–25, and "Religious Repression in China Persists," *Asia Watch*, April 27, 1992.

41. Asia Watch, *Freedom of Religion in China*, 16–25, and "Religious Repression in China Persists."

42. See, for example, the concerns expressed by Beatrice Leung, a Chinese nun from Hong Kong, in her *Sino-Vatican Relations: Problems in Conflicting Authority* (Cambridge, England: Cambridge University Press, 1992), 238–287. For more on China's 3 million–strong Catholic Church, see Richard Madsen, "The Catholic Church in China: Cultural Contradictions, Institutional Survival, and Religious Re-

newal," in *Unofficial China: Popular Culture and Thought in the People's Republic,* edited by Perry Link, Richard Madsen, and Paul G. Pickowicz (Boulder: Westview Press, 1989), 103–120.

43. Dru Gladney, *Muslim Chinese: Ethnic Nationalism in the People's Republic* (Cambridge, MA: Harvard University Press, 1991).

44. Gladney, *Muslim Chinese,* 322.

45. Ibid., 612–663.

46. Dru C. Gladney, "Salman Rushdie in China: Religion, Ethnicity, and State Definition in the People's Republic," in *Asian Visions of Authority,* edited by Keyes, Kendall, and Hardacre, 225–278.

47. Ibid., 136–140; Leung, *Sino-Vatican Relations,* 310; Nicholas Kristof and Sheryl WuDunn, *China Wakes: The Struggle for the Soul of a Rising Power* (New York: Random House, 1994), 134–137.

48. "Regional Briefing," *Far East Economic Review,* November 11, 1993, 15.

49. Yun, *Han'guk Chonggyo yeon'gyu,* 200. On this political arm of the Ch'eon-dogyo, see Robert A. Scalapino and Chong-sik Lee, *Communism in Korea* (Berkeley: University of California Press, 1972), 696–698.

50. David Sanger, "Japanese Reject Old Guard but Splintered Vote Means a Struggle for Coalition," *New York Times,* July 19, 1993.

51. Charles White, "Tilting the Balance: Buddhist Group Supports Main Conservative Party," *Far Eastern Economic Review,* November 4, 1993, 23–24.

52. Ibid., 23–24.

53. Ibid., 24.

54. For more on the Komeito, see Ronald J. Hrebenar, "The Kōmeitō: Party of Buddhist Democracy," in *The Japanese Party System,* 2d edition, edited by Ronald J. Hrebenar (Boulder: Westview Press, 1992), 151–183. See also the cover story in November 20, 1995, issue of *Time International,* "The Power of Soka Gakkai," 20–26.

55. For more on Aum Shinrikyo, see Daniel A. Metraux, "Religious Terrorism in Japan: The Fatal Appeal of Aum Shinrikyo," *Asian Survey* 35 (12) (December 1995):1140–1154.

56. According to Robert Wuthnow, modernization theory predicts that the increasing secularization of society will lead to a concomitant loss of influence for religious leaders and a lowered profile in society for religious organizations. Robert Wuthnow, "Understanding Religion and Politics," *Daedalus,* Summer 1991, 2–5.

SEVEN

Religious Resource Networks: Roman Catholic Philanthropy in Central and East Europe

Ralph Della Cava

The issue at hand is how transnational religious regimes allocate resources across national frontiers and the world economy.[1] This chapter focuses on a specific contemporary case: the transfers of money and manpower between Roman and Uniate Catholics in the West and their confreres in Central and East Europe during the years immediately preceding and following the collapse of autocratic state rule in former communist nations. It situates in time some of the key institutions that have linked co-religionists across frontiers and suggests the role, importance, and significance that such institutions may have played in the maintenance and expansion of local communities of believers.

Three assumptions underlie this essay. The first takes as a given the universal and unchanging moral injunction of Catholicism to "love thy neighbor," to succor both body and soul of those in need. By contrast, however, the actual collection of material alms, the structures mounted to organize and distribute them, the very rationale for their need, and the selection of their beneficiaries follow more complex rules. Organized alms-giving and alms-getting frequently reflect, obey, and coincide with larger policy objectives whether of the particular ecclesiastical or religious bodies engaged in charitable deeds, or of the societies in which such bodies subsist. This chapter will allude to these dimensions as they arise.

The second assumption has to do with the manner of organizing religious structures in our times: It posits that individual communities of a common faith are not always coterminous with the institutional (i.e., ecclesiastical) expression of that same faith. Frequently, there is considerable tension between the two. It is the ever recurring task of the ecclesiastical institution to integrate or reintegrate individual believers or local or grassroots expressions of faith. This work goes by names imbued with pastoral and theological significance, such as "evangelization," "mission," and "pastoral care." Over the course of time there have been "heretics" and "schismatics" who have broken with existing ecclesiastical structures, or within the same faith, a great variety of "dissidents" and "deviations" (such as Latin America's liberation theologians and the ecclesial base communities, to mention only the most recent) that may exercise considerable pressure for change. Both types of resistance are almost always intertwined with the broader social fabric.

Meanwhile, within the Catholic world, the institution's success in containing or co-opting such diversity is borne out in part by the unending creation of new "sub-institutions"—from religious orders and congregations to lay movements and secular institutes that collectively correspond to nearly every niche and stratum of society. This intrinsically sociological process of constant adaptation and readaptation of ecclesiastical authority to the reality of its constituencies has long been recognized within Catholicism under the Latin rubric *ecclesia semper reformanda*.

The third assumption is that co-religionists located in the modern world's economically less developed regions might never have come into being and might not have continued to prevail today were it not for the institutional networks (ecclesiastical structures) of confreres "elsewhere." Not surprisingly, the latter operate through transnational structures that are almost always anchored in the economically developed areas.[2]

Admittedly, such a contention is controversial among students of religion, especially for those who contend that local communities of faith arise from truly autonomous initiatives and action. It could be argued, to the contrary, that the very origins of Christianity in Latin America are the direct historical outcome of religious institutions rooted from the start in the colonizing nations of the Iberian peninsula, and that the disappearance of most of the communities of Christian believers across North Africa in the wake of the advance of Islam might very well be attributed in part to the failure of the Christian institutions of Imperial Rome to persist independently of the empire's collapsing state and military networks. In short, religious origination and continuity in any specific territory or cultural region may never be taken for granted or assumed to be a "given," but ought rather to be appreciated as part and parcel of the historical process, ever subject to alteration.

Today, global church networks of material and religious support and of available qualified personnel influence significantly both the ability of and the terms on which so-called spontaneous or grassroots communities of faith survive and flourish. The latter's programs of social action and welfare (frequently ecumenical in character and increasingly in the form of voluntary civic associations, almost universally denominated today as nongovernmental organizations, or NGOs) appear to be on the increase not only in number and scope of activity, but also with regard to their dependence on external assistance.[3]

These observations implicitly challenge explanations that favor the "spontaneity and autonomy" of religious experience. But it is all too clear that more conclusive data—on both sides of the argument—still remain to be marshaled. In this respect, the focus of this chapter on a region of the world, Central and East Europe—which in regard to Catholicism has been the opposite of a colonial appendage or an outpost of empire, and where, even after nearly half a century of communist rule, the faith is anything but on the way to extinction—should provide still another prism through which to view the issue of autonomy.

The ensuing account attempts to reconstruct relevant aspects of recent Central and East European Catholic history and brings to bear on it the comparative predispositions about Church history that might be expected from a longtime observer of Brazilian Catholicism and Vatican policy in world affairs. In that context, the present essay strives to render an account of one of the most crucial aspects of modern religious organization, namely, its philanthropic role in the world order, the connection of this philanthropy to the expansion of the body of the religious, and its relations to the polities in which it is embedded.

* * *

Three time periods help to demarcate distinctive phases in the movement of organized Catholic resources from West to Central and East Europe. The first encompasses the entire post–World War II era up to the late 1970s; the second period embraces most of the decade of the 1980s; the third extends from the fall of the Berlin Wall in November 1989 until the mid-1990s. In the discussion that follows, the rationale for demarcating each of the periods is spelled out; at the same time, the politics and operations as well as the complexity and interrelationship of the principal structures of Roman Catholic philanthropy are set forth.

1947–1977

The first period coincides with the cold war when the rivalry between the Soviet Union and the United States was at its zenith and exchanges (in most forms) between the peoples on both sides of the iron curtain were no easy matter. But, contrary to the political discourse of the day, the curtain appears to have been far more porous than most people at the time were aware.[4] Two Roman Catholic institutions help to elucidate this point— Kirche in Not and the Europäischer Hilfsfonds. Premier in point of origin and size of enterprise among charitable agencies to engage in aiding confreres in the East is Kirche in Not (KIN), or as it later became known throughout the English-speaking world, Aid to the Church in Need. Perhaps also the first to penetrate the iron curtain, KIN today expends considerable sums annually in the region, even though its activities have eventually come to encompass the Church's needs around the world. Paradoxically, KIN originated in 1947 among Catholics of West Europe who, recently liberated by Allied armies and intent to put behind them memories of the Nazi occupation of their homelands, chose spontaneously and generously to come to the aid of millions of German Catholic refugees. Abandoning the eastern territories of Germany itself and the lands of Central and East Europe where many had resided for centuries as nationals of a "greater Germany" or as a major ethnic minority (second in numbers only to Jews, most of whom perished in the Holocaust), some 16 million civilians took flight before the advance of Soviet troops and the anticipated imposition of Communist Party rule in the soon-to-be-established people's democratic republics.

It was among these displaced Germans in West German camps that Kirche in Not initially worked out a set of priorities that has ever since continued to mark its philanthropy. First and foremost, priests, religious (male and female), and seminarians—in short, ministers to the spiritual and temporal needs of still greater numbers of believers—were armed with the wherewithal, from automobiles and altar vestments to printing presses and a monthly wage, to conduct their apostolate. So prominent was this initiative on behalf of clergy that the charity was called at the outset Ostpriesterhilfe, or Help to Priests from the East.[5] Next to be systematically secured was the physical presence of the faith itself: Bombed churches were rebuilt, temporary houses of worship erected, and mobile altars dispatched to the countryside; hospitals, orphanages, and parish halls rose anew. Lastly, but simultaneously with both preceding directions, humanitarian aid of all kinds was swiftly directed to the laity in need—from clothing, food, and medicine to hospital equipment, beds, and kitchens; school supplies and textbooks; catechisms, prayer books, and religious artifacts.

With the Hungarian Revolution of 1956, KIN's strategy of charity publicly "jumped over the curtain." Even after Soviet troops sealed the borders, convoys of provisions continued to roll across, while endless parcels of necessities defiantly pierced postal laws, trade regulations, and border security. Moreover, from the 1960s on, according to an authoritative KIN source, the penetration of the Eastern bloc had become irreversible, whether through continued clandestine operations, such as the shipment of donations "under foreign flags," or, within the decade, and unmistakably so by the 1970s, with the official permission of communist governments.[6]

Now, in retrospect, the latter development is not at all that surprising. Various circumstances make that plain. For one thing, not everywhere did persecution besiege the Church with the same intensity. Except for the Uniate hierarchies and faithful in Ukraine, Romania, and Slovakia[7] and Latin rite believers in Albania and the former Czechoslovakia (especially in Bohemia and Moravia, although less intensely in Slovakia), the state policy of systematic cruelty to religious believers and the policing of the hierarchy and its clergy had begun to abate perceptibly in several of the satellites soon after the 1956 Twentieth Congress of the Communist Party of the Soviet Union.[8]

For another, in three of the so-called people's democratic republics—Yugoslavia, Poland, and East Germany—party policy came around to court Church "cooperation" eagerly, the occasional and arbitrary application of harassments notwithstanding. A brief glance at each case reveals not only just how varied national contexts were—and hence the status of religion and the institutional church as well—but also how equally complex the emerging pan-European Catholic network had already become a full two decades before the collapse of autocratic state regimes.[9]

Particularly pertinent to the fate of religion in the East from the start of the new postwar order was the exit of the former Yugoslavia from the Soviet camp in 1948. This rupture might well be considered today the real starting point of "polycentrism," the term first employed in the 1960s to denote in the wake of the Sino-Soviet split the gradual but certain waning of Soviet hegemony within the so-called socialist bloc at the time.[10] As a consequence, the Yugoslav state proceeded independently with respect to its own varied ethnic populations to implement a domestic policy (distinctive from the USSR's "nationalities" practices), called "ethnic balancing." Each of the country's major religious unities—Orthodoxy, Catholicism, Islam, Judaism, and Uniatism—which usually corresponded to one or another specific ethnicity or territory or both, was permitted a wide margin of institutional self-government and autonomy in religious activities—provided that they were expressed behind closed doors and stayed clear of public life.[11]

With that proviso, the Church in Croatia and Slovenia, the two largest Roman Catholic regions, could, from the 1960s on, conduct its religious activities largely without interference, enjoy autonomy in the nomination of bishops, and promote closer ties between the respective episcopacies and the Holy See. Moreover, bishops of both regions participated in the Second Vatican Council (1962–1965), operated minor and major seminaries without restraint, steadily ordained new secular and religious clergy, staffed diocesan hospitals and orphanages with female religious orders, and, after the signing of the Protocol of 1969 between the Holy See and the Yugoslav State, won greater opportunities for religious to study and travel abroad.

More important for the operations of Kirche in Not throughout Central Europe at the time was the authorization granted the then Yugoslav Catholic Church to publish religious materials without prior censorship or government-imposed restrictions on the supply of paper. Bibles, magazines, catechisms, and theological and liturgical texts intended for some dozen or so ethnic, religious, and linguistic minorities within the country were uninterruptedly produced and distributed. Such materials also ended up—as a matter of local church policy—in Hungary, Bohemia, Slovakia, Poland, Ukraine, and even Russia, countries from among which the said minorities originally hailed and with which, insofar as it was possible, they maintained varying degrees of contact.[12]

The case of Poland was not dissimilar with respect to several of the foregoing conditions. That became especially true after the 1956 rise to power of Wladyslaw Gomulka. A communist reformer and Polish nationalist, he avidly pursued coexistence of Church and state while walking the tightrope of Polish-Soviet relations. But in one critical respect, Poland was unique: Unlike in Yugoslavia, Catholicism was by then the professed faith of nearly every Pole, and the Church was the only nationwide structure that effectively challenged the policies and principles of pro-Soviet communist rule just as it had the Nazi occupation.[13]

The Church's leverage, of course, was historically rooted in its oft-espoused millennial oneness with the Polish nation, especially during the repeated partitions of the nation, and its trump card in the postwar era lay partly in the role it could play in helping to secure eventual Vatican recognition of new Polish dioceses and hence the new Polish frontiers. The sees in question were in the former German territories in the west and north conceded to Poland after the war in compensation for the loss to the USSR of the formerly Polish-held parts of Lithuania, Byelorus, and western Ukraine (in all of which Polish cultural, religious, and ethnic influence nonetheless continues to remain substantial, or as in southeastern Poland, where from the end of the war on it proved indispensable to the clandestine survival of Ukrainian Uniates).

Another strong suit lay in the Church's continuing ties between the Polish hierarchy and the Holy See despite the former's frequent criticism of Rome's "*Ostpolitik*." Essentially, the Vatican adhered to a policy of diplomatic recognition of communist states, which reached its apogee during the 1970s.[14] As a consequence, Polish bishops took part in significant numbers at Vatican Council II and thereafter at all subsequent Synods of Bishops, convened every two years in Rome. Moreover and above all, they operated a vast pastoral and educational network (including, at Lublin, the only functioning Catholic university throughout the then communist world), one that the Church continually expanded for the purposes of training youth, educating religious, nurturing a Catholic lay intelligentsia, and, in its thousands of parish halls, defending and promoting workers and human rights.

Out of this symbiotic relationship between the Church and civil society, there eventually arose Solidarity, and in the person of Karol Cardinal Wojtyla, then archbishop of Kraków, there came to pass the election in 1978 of a Polish-born pope of Rome. After his accession to office as Pope John Paul II, the continuing underwriting by Catholic foundations in the West of so many of the projects just described became a priority of the Holy See itself.

For its part, the Diocese of Berlin—straddling as it did the four allied sectors of the city and the division of Germany itself[15]—provides a most unexpected insight into state-church relations under communist rule. It suggests that both the growing economic crisis of the people's democracies from the late 1950s on and the East German state's pursuit of legitimation through international conventions significantly contributed to extending the degree of religious freedom at home and the strengthening of ties of East Germany's Catholic minority to fellow Catholics throughout the Eastern bloc.[16]

Clerics who still reside in the former German Democratic Republic have remarked that the regime's need of hard currency accounted for no few "barter deals" between church and state.[17] In one instance, cash donations from Western charitable institutions for one or another church project were used by the government to purchase copper in the West. In turn, its value was meted out to Catholic churchmen in ostmarks at an official rate of exchange well below the black market price for whatever their intended activities (most usually the restoration or repair of churches and other ecclesiastical properties).[18]

In another instance, the state actively promoted congresses and conventions of pan-German and pan-European Catholic activities in Berlin and other East German cities. In addition to revenues earned by the state-controlled tourist industry (which ultimately held power over all such gatherings through the allocation of scarce hotel reservations), the country gained a measure of political legitimacy among Western institutions and governments. For churchmen from throughout the East, who were freer to travel to and from other socialist countries than to the West, face-to-face opportunities to keep abreast of Catholicism's course were thereby not entirely wanting.[19]

In one final respect, Berlin's importance to the Catholic world of Central Europe during communist rule should not be forgotten. As a diocese that encompassed the entire city and whose presiding bishop resided in West

Berlin, but whose chancery office was in the East, it enabled contacts within the whole of the German Church to remain unbroken. As a result, access to the West was more frequent for East Germany than for any other communist country.[20] Moreover, at no time was the bishop of Berlin excluded as a member of the German Bishops Conference, located in the historic see of Fulda (in West Germany), even though until the 1970s attendance by other East German bishops at the biannual assemblies was problematic (largely because of the pending resolution of territorial jurisdictions of prewar dioceses).[21]

Perhaps symbolic of the primacy of the principle of German unity over and above the postwar division was the appointment in December 1988— nearly a full year before the *Wende,* or great change—of the former bishop of Berlin as cardinal archbishop of Cologne, Germany's wealthiest see;[22] then, shortly after German unification, another easterner, the longtime priest-director of charitable works for East Germany, was elected president of German Caritas, one of the richest Catholic welfare agencies in the world.[23]

Indeed, the initial organization in November 1970 of the Europäischer Hilfsfonds (EHF), or European Aid Fund, the second of the two major pre-1989 Catholic agencies operating in the East, would have never been possible without the West German bishops—and, of course, without West Germany's "economic miracle." Catholics participated fully in the nation's postwar prosperity and for a variety of reasons generously shared their good fortune through a network of newly created church agencies with others at home and abroad.[24]

But more than wealth and generosity marked the German bishops' efforts; genuine enthusiasm and organizational talent were also deployed with consummate skill. The EHF was in reality their enterprise, even though it had first been suggested, then jointly established by, and finally cooperatively run with the episcopacy of neutral Austria (a crucial listening post on Central Europe during the cold war and a major refugee center in the aftermath of the Hungarian Revolution).

EHF's mission was to coordinate the continuation of aid, begun in the early 1960s, to the Church in East and southeast Europe.[25] But a profound political change as well as a quest for greater proximity and efficiency may also have been a compelling motive. As the Vatican's *Ostpolitik* began to gather momentum at the start of the 1970s, new opportunities for dialogue were arising in the East. At the same time, however, Catholic resistance to the Holy See's alleged "betrayal of martyrs" found resonance among several elements within the West European Church.

Kirche in Not was apparently in those ranks, as its founder bluntly criticized "those who believe that God's church can live in peace with communism." His protest was registered around the very same time that the Holy

See had entrusted the cardinal archbishop of Vienna with the delicate mission of negotiating a modus vivendi for the Church with the communist regime in Budapest.[26] It will be remembered that the ensuing three-way accord among the papacy, the U.S. government, and the Hungarian state led first to the 1974 release of the defiant prince-primate, Jozsef Cardinal Mindszenty, from his asylum in the U.S. Embassy in Budapest, and then to his immediate removal to Rome, where he was thereafter ordered "silenced"—ignominiously, in the opinion of many supporters—until his death in 1977. In this context, KIN allegedly refused to continue any further aid to Hungary. But Austrian and German bishops spared neither time nor effort to fill the vacuum and rush to the aid of co-religionists across the Danube.[27]

For German and Austrian Catholics, there may have also existed other compelling reasons that both antedated and were unrelated to the differences that had now arisen between KIN and the EHF. For Germans, there was the continuing postwar task of reestablishing ties to some of the surviving, historic ethnic German Catholic populations in Silesia, Pomerania, and Prussia (now part of Poland); in the Sudetenland (in the new Czech Republic); and even in distant Romania, where secular, German-speaking immigrant settlements still flourished.[28] For the Austrians, ties to the faithful in Hungary and other German-speaking regions of the former Austro-Hungarian empire seemed not only fitting but also opportune, as Austrian diplomatic and economic activities were themselves around the same time cautiously expanding southward and eastward.

Indeed, by January 1972, EHF structures had become firmly consolidated, and a permanent headquarters was located in Vienna and its direction assigned to a noted German cleric.[29] As to the finances, the standing joke had it that the new "European" entity was "Austrian in name and German in money"; but that was also the truth.[30]

For the next two decades, EHF aided the Catholic Church in Central Europe. Bishops en route to and from Rome habitually changed planes in Vienna, remaining just long enough to discuss their plight and plans. As had been the case with Kirche in Not—with which, despite differences, the EHF routinely consulted so as to avoid duplication of efforts—contacts were wide open with Croatia and Slovenia, ever more frequent with Poland and, after the Vatican protocols, with Hungary as well. Contacts with Romania and Bulgaria often took place under the surveillance of security forces, and until the fall of the Berlin Wall, those with Czechoslovakia remained extremely difficult, and with Albania almost nonexistent.[31]

As to the type and range of activities and projects, EHF's were not unlike KIN's. But in one respect, a fundamental difference now prevailed: With the papacy's appointment of scores of new bishops who were officially recognized by communist authorities—a direct result of the *Ostpolitik*—the EHF could now operate for the most part entirely in the open and in complete harmony with the Holy See's diplomatic strategy.[32]

1978–1988

In the decade preceding the fall of the Berlin Wall, two events—momentous and memorable in themselves—held particular significance for Catholic philanthropy in Central and East Europe: the 1978 election of Pope John Paul II and the legalization two years later of Solidarity, the first independent trade union in Poland and very first free, voluntary civic association to arise in any postwar state under communist rule.[33]

The election, of course, placed at the head of Catholicism's vast array of charitable institutions a pope who knew firsthand the needs and conditions of believers in the region. Moreover, the success of the Polish workers' movement triggered an unparalleled mobilization at home and abroad and the transfer of worldwide Church resources not only to Poland but also to neighboring states.

While the new pontificate and the rise of Solidarity followed in swift succession and are well documented,[34] the details of Church charities remain to be sorted out. Only the barest outline is currently available, but at least three undertakings are clearly discernible.

In Vienna, representatives of the U.S., West German, Austrian, and Polish episcopacies met sometime in 1981 or 1982.[35] Independently of the EHF, but apparently through its good offices and those of the National Office of Austrian Caritas, the country's largest Catholic philanthropy and part of a worldwide federation of like organizations, the prelates decided upon a strategy to aid the Polish Church, and in so doing, Solidarity as well. Under the direction of the Poles and at their request, the nation was divided up geographically: The Americans were to be responsible for northern Poland, including Gdansk and Warsaw; the Germans were assigned to central Poland; and the Austrians to southern Poland, including Kraków.

Precisely by and through which of the numerous Catholic agencies in each of the donor nations aid was to be raised and channeled is no easy matter to piece together. Nor have the recipient agencies in Poland yet been specifically identified, although it may be presumed that the Commission for Charities of the Polish Bishops Conference had likely played the central role in coordinating efforts inside the country.[36] Indeed, between 1981 and 1985, Poland received considerable support for three distinct types of need: food and clothing; agricultural machinery (likely earmarked for members of "Rural Solidarity," a notably Catholic structure founded on the heels of the industrial workers' initiative); and a variety of financial and material aid to Church social enterprises such as old age homes, day-care centers, orphanages, and the like.[37] With respect to this third category, one of the directions of Polish Catholicism since the 1970s had been the construction of imposing churches, buildings, and other facilities. These were often designed by some of the country's outstanding (but politically out-of-favor) architects, and stood as symbols of resistance to state rule, which for its part had erected around the country some of the most functional, drab, and inhumane edifices ever conceived by the human mind and committed to a drafting board. Much of the Church's building capital came from both parishioners at home and donors abroad.[38]

In West Germany, efforts were redoubled after the declaration of martial law in Poland in December 1981; the following year, the country's bishops took up a onetime special collection in all the nation's churches destined for the needy in Poland.[39] Of course, the German episcopacy had been central to the EHF for over a decade, as has already been mentioned. But donations to it depended largely on annual allocations sent by the Association of German Dioceses (to which all dioceses belonged) and whose own funding accrued in part from the voluntary "church tax" (*Kirchensteuer*) levied by the government for religious institutions.[40]

In addition to the eventual institution of an annual collection specifically earmarked for assistance to the East,[41] scores of local parish-to-parish initiatives whose value cannot be readily tallied had got under way in the 1980s across the German-Polish borders. Indeed, taken together these efforts might be considered an "index of commitment" of German Catholics for reconstructing the Church in the East.

The third and last enterprise involved Caritas Internationalis (CI) and several of its national affiliates. CI had been established under Vatican auspices in the early 1950s,[42] but national affiliates—several in West Europe as well as that in the United States, which is known as Catholic Relief Services—had existed ever since the turn of the century. They had been constituted and continue to be run by the Catholic laity, but always in close harmony with the wishes and priorities of national or diocesan episcopal authorities. It was in the aftermath of World War II, marked by refugee problems and poverty on a grand scale throughout Europe, that the need for the coordination of humanitarian efforts, for getting information out about them, and finally for some kind of representation of Catholic interests before newfound international structures such as the United Nations and its specialized agencies could no longer be postponed.

In the 1970s two developments proved especially noteworthy for the story at hand. On the international level, Caritas (or rather its national affiliates) started responding to emergency situations in several parts of Central and East Europe: earthquakes in Yugoslavia and, later in the decade, floods and earthquakes in Romania. Among such state regimes, Caritas soon won acceptance—as it had elsewhere in the world, even in regions where Catholics were a minority—as a reliable relief agency despite its Western origins and initial lack of institutional affiliates in most of the region.[43] Needless to say, its growing presence was not unrelated to the Vatican's expanding ties to local governments, thanks to the *Ostpolitik*.

On the national level, German Caritas and the U.S. Catholic Relief Service (CRS) increasingly undertook major programs on their own (as well as in conjunction with a variety of other Catholic aid agencies, as we saw earlier). By the 1980s, both disposed of substantial funds, garnered from believers as well as from various government ministries and agencies concerned with domestic social issues or international development and humanitarian programs. Caritas in Germany—with a staff of 300,000 employees—had become a virtual ministry of social welfare, operating hospitals and old-age homes, day-care centers, drug rehabilitation centers, home care services, and many other types of social programs.[44] In the United States, CRS functioned only overseas, and a separate agency, Catholic Charities, presided over domestic needs.

One final observation is in order. By the early 1970s the question of Church aid to people in need, particularly in the developing world, had already grown institutionally so complex, financially significant, and politically crucial that the Holy See sought still another instrument—but now at the highest level of ecclesiastical (rather than lay) administration—in order to measure needs and allocate resources more effectively. To that purpose, Cor Unum, or One Heart, was established in 1971 as a pontifical council within the Roman Curia. Within the decade, it had become a kind of papal clearinghouse and roundtable for both sponsors and recipients of world-wide Catholic relief.[45]

1989–1993

Despite the fall of the Berlin Wall, the utterly unexpected but boundless inspiration it fired in the human imagination, the jubilation and promise it released, the symbolism it projected of a cosmic conflict in which good had at last triumphed over evil,[46] the papacy turned without illusion to the structures that had been set in place decades before and counted on its own tested ability to forge still others, should new circumstances so demand.

Demand they did. After all, between November 1989 and November 1993, a succession of new governments came to power and new states into existence throughout all Central and East Europe, a story that is now being documented.[47] Relations with the Catholic Church altered too, and in most cases dramatically. Decades of cautious concessions negotiated under the *Ostpolitik* now seemed an antiquated exchange as, almost daily, new state laws boldly decreed freedom of religion, restored religious education (in some cases even in public schools), returned confiscated church properties, and subsidized a wide range of Catholic social enterprises, including the salary of clerics; that story too is now being pieced together.[48]

From the perspective of ecclesiastical history, "la chiesa del silenzio non c'è più," as the editor of *L'Osservatore Romano* remarked: It is the "Church of Silence" no longer.[49] To be sure, scores of new dioceses were instantly erected, bishops consecrated, and apostolic nuncios and administrators dispatched for the first time in centuries to distant republics and regions, including those of the former Soviet Union, as far as Siberia.[50] With the newly won freedom, young men flocked to seminaries, which, after decades of neglect or outright prohibition like those in Ukraine, Byelorus, and Romania, had to be improvised on the spot to meet the demand.

Material needs were just as urgent as the spiritual. An insatiable demand soared for everything from fax machines, photocopiers, and computer equipment to powerful radio transmitters, fully equipped broadcasting studios, and crash courses in a dozen languages in management skills and accounting. The modern age had arrived with the proverbial vengeance, and with it prayer rose on the wings of technology and technique.[51]

The need for information and coordination also rose commensurably. Responses came forth remarkably swiftly considering how rapidly the world order was changing. They did so, moreover, at every level of Church administration. It would be helpful, then, to review such responses in three distinct but interrelated arenas: first, within the Roman Curia; then among selected national conferences of bishops; and lastly among several religious orders and congregations and international lay movements. These three arenas might well be considered the key caretakers and managers of Catholicism's material patrimony and the authors of its disbursement in the form of philanthropy around the globe.

* * *

From within the Vatican, long-standing structures—particularly Cor Unum and Caritas Internationalis—invested fresh urgency into their rounds of biannual meetings, the former to consider overall policy, the latter to implement operations of emergency and humanitarian aid.[52] Thus, in February 1991, Cor Unum convened a meeting of all major West European Catholic agencies; in November 1992, still another was called to set an agenda for aid to Central and East Europe. In the interim, several national agencies met twice—independently and informally—in various European cities to discuss the situation of each country in the East. The upshot was a division of labor by which a West European or North American donor nation was paired to an East European recipient: among others, Germany was responsible for Russia and Hungary, Austria for the then Czechoslovakia, France for Poland, Italy for Albania.[53]

Similarly, Caritas Internationalis settled on a division of labor of its own. Its national affiliate in Austria had been for decades a window on Central

Europe. Its sources of information were unmatched. Now it would serve as a clearinghouse for projects that might possibly be implemented in the former Czechoslovakia and Yugoslavia, as well as in Hungary and Romania, the lands once embraced by the Austro-Hungarian empire. In addition, CI's international secretariat helped to promote the establishment of diocesan and national Caritas offices throughout Central and East Europe, and several West European affiliates and the U.S. Catholic Relief Services set up and continue to provide training on a permanent basis for the staffs of the fledgling national conferences of bishops.[54] In addition, informal courses in the art of diocesan administration for the new bishops themselves are not uncommon.

But it was the stunning and unthinkable dissolution of the former Soviet Union in 1991 that forced significant changes on Curia structures and set out still another new and obligatory avenue for Catholic philanthropy. It could not have been otherwise. The simultaneous end to both communism and empire seems to have closed for good the chapter on the twentieth-century war on religion, and it most certainly opened wide the gates of Moscow, even if only momentarily, to the advance of Latin or Western Christianity and, for that matter, a variety of other "new age" religions. Moreover, the new situation set before Rome and the spiritual heirs to Byzantium the unparalleled prospect of rapprochement after a millennial history of separation. That recent Western popes and some Eastern patriarchs of the Orthodox faith have expectantly entertained such a vision over recent decades—despite insurmountable difficulties that arise at every turn—should not be doubted for a moment.[55]

Not surprisingly, then, the turn of events in Russia directly affected two additional branches of the Roman Curia pertinent to this inquiry, one old, the other new. The old was the Pontifical Congregation for Eastern Churches, founded more than a century ago. One of the nine Vatican *dicasteri* (departments or, as they are formally named, "pontifical congregations") charged with the governing of the Universal Church, it might be more aptly thought of as a highly autonomous ministry for the care of nearly a score of non-Latin rite churches in communion with the See of Peter.[56]

Today these embrace the Ukrainian, Greek, Maronite, Chaldean, Armenian, Coptic, and more than a dozen other Catholic rites whose liturgies arose prior to or contemporaneously with the distinctively Latin liturgy celebrated throughout much of the realm of the former Roman Empire and "fixed" in form only by the Council of Trent. The "non-Latin" rites, which enjoy full freedom to celebrate in their own languages, are also variably referred to as the churches of Byzantine or Eastern rite; the Vatican refers to them collectively as "the Eastern churches" (*chiese orientali*) and geographically understands by the term those located in the Near, Middle, and Far East as well as those in Central and East Europe.

In this same vein, the term "Greek Catholic," which enjoys widespread use throughout Central Europe, does not refer to Catholics of Greek national origin or mother tongue. Rather, it applies to those Catholic believers primarily of Slavic and Hungarian origin who, in union with Rome, celebrate a liturgy similar to that of Greek, Russian, and other Slavic Orthodoxy. Often, the term "Greek Catholic" is used interchangeably with "Uniate," the latter term signifying the recognition by these Catholics of their spiritual unity with the See of Peter.[57]

Over all of these eastern churches united with Rome (i.e., over their dioceses, bishops, clergy, orders, laity, and liturgy—precisely the areas otherwise governed in the Latin rite by four distinct congregations), the Pontifical Congregation for Eastern Churches alone exercises full jurisdiction. Moreover, since Vatican Council II, it has also shared with the secretary of state and the Pontifical Council for the Promotion of Christian Unity a measure of responsibility for the ongoing dialogue with Orthodox Christians.

One of the Congregation's major tasks has been the administration of ROACO (the Italian acronym for Riunione Opere Aiuto Chiese Orientali, or the Meeting for Works of Aid to Eastern Churches), in effect, a modest, multimillion-dollar foundation, comparable in its operational aspects to Caritas Internationalis.[58] Twice a year since the 1970s, it brings together a dozen or more donors (German and American charitable institutions predominate) and an unspecified number of recipients.[59] The latter are mostly Uniates, among which the Ukrainian Church, with over 5 million members in the newly independent Republic of Ukraine alone, is the largest.[60] Understandably, it is also a major ROACO beneficiary. But the literal resurrection of the Ukrainian Uniate, or Greek Catholic, Church from clandestinity despite seven decades of persecution, arrest, and execution of their prelates and faithful has viscerally angered Orthodox patriarchs. They have disputed the Uniates' right to reclaim their properties (churches, seminaries, and schools that were forcibly subsumed in 1946 by the Orthodox Church) as well as their right and propriety to receive substantial material resources remitted by Western funding agencies and the countless, rather prosperous, communities of the Ukrainian diaspora in the Western Hemisphere.

Moreover, the Orthodox patriarch of Moscow as well as the leaders of the several Orthodox churches in Kyiv (in Russian, Kiev) have let it be known in Rome that they consider the Uniates a "parallel ecclesial structure" to their own and suspect it of being part of a broader policy of proselytization of their flocks by the Latin Church.[61] To underscore the point, Orthodox leaders had in late 1991 all but broken off an ecumenical dialogue with Rome that is of more than two decades' standing.[62]

A new branch of the Curia, designated the Permanent Inter-Dicasterial Commission for the Church in Eastern Europe (PIDCCEE) was inaugurated in January 1993 partly as a consequence of the breach just described.

It is, in effect, a supra-ministry charged with a triple task: first, to care for all Catholics who formerly lived under communist rule, whether in Central or East Europe; next, to conduct relations with both the Uniate and Orthodox churches in the region; and last, to coordinate all Catholic charitable and development agencies, principally those of Western Europe and North America, which have in recent decades aided the Church in the East. Alone among Curia structures, the PIDCCEE enjoys a monopoly of moral authority—and, above all, the pope's unbounded favor—to define, organize, and execute Vatican policy from the Danube and Oder-Neisse to the Sakhalin Peninsula and the Port of Vladivostok. To grasp the significance of this new branch, it would do well to reflect momentarily on the papacy's dilemma that the dissolution of the Soviet Union helped to accentuate.

On the one side, the papacy can in no way abandon the Uniates, who, severing ties to Orthodoxy, reunited themselves four centuries ago to Rome and then over the past four to seven decades repeatedly proved their steadfast fidelity to the See of Peter by enduring unspeakable adversities for the sake of their faith.[63] On the other, the Holy See cannot but act on its duty to attend to the more than 2 million, mostly Latin rite Catholics who have suddenly "emerged," scattered throughout Russia, especially east of the Urals into Siberia, and Kazakhstan. Almost all are former Soviet nationals of Polish, Lithuanian, Volga German, or Ukrainian origin or descent and had either been deported there during the Stalin era or shipped off in forced-labor gangs in the decades that followed.[64] True, Rome seeks only the best of relations with Orthodoxy, which it today repeatedly proclaims nothing less than a "sister" church, closer to Rome in theology and ecclesiology than is any Protestant denomination.[65] But it cannot fail to weigh and here too act upon the paradox by which the fateful dialectic of the "Gulag" has extended the Latin Church's presence across the entire expanse of the northern Eurasian mainland from which it had been historically excluded, first by Orthodoxy, then by communist rule.

Of course, finding common ground with the Orthodox Church has been a major thrust of the post-conciliar Catholic ecumenical dialogue. But its pursuit, particularly with the Russian Orthodox patriarchate of Moscow, has met with difficulty ever since the USSR dissolved into more than a dozen independent states. A general case in point was the special pan-European Synod of Bishops, convened by the papacy in late November and early December 1991. Conceived of by Rome as a demonstration of postcommunist Christian unity to which all Orthodox patriarchates and prelates were purposely invited, only two attended, and the one of greater rank did so pointedly to criticize papal advances.[66] Moreover, inside Russia, the risk of an anti-Western backlash led by an alliance of ecclesiastical advocates of close church-state relations, nationalists, and former communists is by no means insignificant. Indeed, with the support of the Moscow Patriarchate, bills were passed by the Russian congress in July and August 1993 to curb most "foreign religions" within Russia (though none has yet become law for want of a signature from President Boris Yeltsin).[67]

The charges that Catholicism intends "to lure Orthodox Russians" with its more plentiful material resources have been hotly denied. In June 1992 the papacy fully endorsed a major declaration that unequivocally eschewed "proselytism" and went so far as to propose cooperation with the Orthodox in pastoral matters, such as sharing places of worship, centers for theological study, and so on.[68] But at the same time the Holy See defended the right of the once clandestine Uniate communities to remain in union with Rome as well as every religion's right, for that matter, to preach its message beyond national frontiers (in contradistinction to the recently oft-reiterated Orthodox principle of "canonical territory," similar in significance to the post-Reformation principle of religious territorial exclusivity summed up in the Latin phrase, *"cuius regio, eius religio,"* or "whose realm, his religion").[69]

Differences over fundamentals, however, continued to persist; this partly explains "Europae Orientalis," the Apostolic Letter signed by Pope John Paul II on January 15, 1993, establishing the new PIDCCEE.[70] Of equally pointed political significance, the decree also extinguished the old Pontifical Commission for Russia (PCR). Founded shortly after the Bolshevik Revolution, the PCR was almost always perceived as a sort of papal vanguard dedicated to the overthrow of communism and the conversion of the orthodox. Its abolition is widely thought to have signaled Rome's reiteration of firmly abandoning any policy of proselytizing.[71] Whether this prefigures "collaboration" between Catholics and Orthodox at the highest levels of authority beyond that which now sporadically prevails at lower and less official levels is difficult to predict. But as one Curia official put it, off the record: "We go to the East today not, as the Conquistadors went to the New World, to impose our faith and Western culture, but rather as witnesses to God's love and as servants to a world in need. This is the 'new evangelization' announced by the Holy Father: one based on respect for the freedom of every person and every nation to embrace the faith of their choice."

Indicative of the new PIDCCEE's prestige is that its president is the current Vatican secretary of state, and its members represent the four other curial *dicasteri* that have or will have key responsibilities for the faith in the East. But it is far more than just another high-level administrative task force.[72] Surely its sweeping mandate would seem likely to raise suspicions, if not potential enmities in two quarters. For one, a minority of Ukrainian Uniates has already voiced fears, whether well-founded or not, that the papacy would sacrifice them on the altar of a Rome-Moscow accord.[73] For these groups, even the joint Catholic-Orthodox statement, hammered out at a high-level ecumenical conference convened in June 1993 in Balamand,

Lebanon, that declared Uniate communities to be canonically legitimate churches proved unsatisfactory. Far too questionable in their opinion was the meeting's further declaration that Uniatism was a method of union *of the past* that had resulted *in piecemeal unity*, while today a search for *"full communion"*—presumably between Rome and Moscow—must be found and pursued.[74]

For another, misgivings might also arise from among members of the old Congregation for Eastern Churches and ROACO. Despite their membership in the new Inter-Dicasterial Commission, it is said that they consider it a potential encroachment on their own authority and a competitor for funding. But in the latter case no such charge has so far even been raised; on the contrary, the new commission has apparently yet to respond to specific requests from some major donor agencies for guidance and direction.[75]

Whether or not any of these concerns comes to pass in the long run, the apparent increase of recent collaborative efforts between Catholics and Orthodox in several parts of the former Soviet Union cannot be minimized. Some are humanitarian in nature, such as the dispatch of food and medicines to Armenia, whose population is primarily orthodox. In Novosibirsk and Vladivostok and other cities of Siberia and the Russian Far East, individual American bishops are helping to build churches as well as to provide food and medicines. To the Volga-Germans in Ekaterinenburg (Russian, Sverdlovsk) and elsewhere, half of whom are likely to be Lutheran, German Catholics ship medical supplies. In Moscow, Caritas Internationalis has helped to found a local branch office for all of Western Russia that is open to Catholics and Orthodox alike.

*   *   *

In turning now to national episcopacies, it is appropriate to consider their role in philanthropy separately from the Curia's. Four national conferences of bishops are of particular importance, those of Germany, the United States, Poland, and Italy.

As Caritas's record makes clear, the German Church has had a long history of aid to Catholics around the world. To that specific end, seven new philanthropic agencies were created after the war; two—Adveniat and Misereor—are renowned for their contributions, respectively, to the ecclesiastical needs of Latin America and to social development projects throughout the Third World. In April 1993 an eighth agency was founded specifically for East and southeast Europe; named Renovabis, or "renewal," it aims at training the Catholic laity in the region.[76]

The implications of such a program are far-reaching, for this is the first major effort to focus almost exclusively on forming lay cadres and helping to build or rebuild a Catholic intelligentsia. As with Adveniat and Misereor, Renovabis will rely heavily on an annual collection (in May) in all German parishes, donations from individual Catholics, and most likely those government funds that are specifically earmarked for either German ethnic Catholic populations in the East and for nationwide development projects and technical assistance programs throughout the region.[77]

This initiative also poses not a few questions for the overall picture of Catholic funding in Germany and the rest of Europe. The possible competition for donations by the new agency with the Europäischer Hilfsfonds in Vienna, 90 percent of whose budget is contributed by Germany's bishops, was ruled out in principle by Renovabis founders.[78] Less clear is the new fund's stance toward Kirche in Not, which in the past has also raised much of its revenues directly from among German Catholics. Moreover, KIN's relative independence from the German episcopacy, and for that matter from most other Catholic philanthropies, despite (or because of) its "official" recognition by Rome, has until now never been seriously challenged, except by the establishment of the Europäischer Hilfsfonds in 1971.[79] Whether German generosity can sustain such a three-sided quest for support among Catholics—Renovabis, KIN, and EHF—remains to be seen, even though the "bottom line" may likely depend more on the country's economy than on the individual donor's personal preferences.[80]

Similarly critical is the very act of policymaking with respect to projects in the East. In one respect, it is especially sensitive: Wartime memories of Nazi occupation are by no means extinguished. Consequently, German prelates have from the start insisted that their confreres in the East fully participate in establishing priorities. The current archbishop of Cologne, formerly the bishop of Berlin and a native son of the former East Germany, personally took up Renovabis with Eastern confreres before its creation. As a result, the newly established national conferences of bishops throughout the region will likely become Renovabis's principal interlocutors. Indeed, *"Partnerschaft"* (partnership) has become Renovabis's byword and reflects its pledge to foster truly cooperative rather than unilaterally inspired ventures.

Furthermore, just as the German Republic dares not jeopardize its friendship with the nations of both West and East Europe, so too has the German Church—through acts of reconciliation and solidarity—cultivated especially close ties with the Catholics of France and Poland.[81] Now, however, the architects of Renovabis must balance German Catholicism's long-term, postwar policy of pan-European cooperation and coordination in West Europe with their growing interests in the East and their own political need at home to set up and maintain the new fund's administrative center inside Germany, where the money is raised.[82] The entire process will require masterful diplomacy in reestablishing the long-term centrality of Germany as a whole and of the German Church in particular to the new post–Cold War Europe. But, as the uncertainty of Maastricht's future—that is, the long-sought, but still to be achieved, political and economic unity of West

Europe—increasingly reveals, "Europe" as a "place and mentality" is very much in flux. Indeed, its geographical boundaries are hardly fixed and, as both the former Yugoslavia and Czechoslovakia make clear, they are in the throes of constant redefinition, and they will likely remain so for some time to come.[83]

In contrast, the American bishops foresee a fixed short-term financial commitment of four, and no more than five, years. Following their delegation's 1990 visit to East Europe, a special "Office to Aid the Catholic Church in Central and East Europe" was established within the U.S. Catholic Conference (USCC).[84] An annual November collection (one-third smaller in size than Germany's) was approved, an office was inaugurated in Washington, D.C., and a policy was adopted to support the training in loco of priests, religious, and catechists as well as, in a notable departure from Renovabis, professionals for the mass media.

With regard to media, the USCC was committed to furnishing a transmitter for Radio Resurrection in Lviv (Russian, Lvov), Ukraine (a project matched only by KIN's Radio Blagovest [Gospel News], beamed from the Philippines to all of Siberia). In addition, four studios for the training of personnel were to be outfitted in Latvia, Lithuania, Slovakia, and Ukraine. With these exceptions, excluded from the American charity agenda are all other building projects—churches, chapels, schools, seminaries (except in Grodno, Byelorus, and Lviv, Ukraine, "where they are desperately needed"), orphanages, hospitals, or, as if on cue from German Caritas, "anything that smacks of a bishop's 'edifice complex.'"

For the Americans, just as for the German bishops, the overall strategy is, first and foremost, to allow newly formed national conferences of bishops in the East to set their own priorities. "We're not going to second-guess the judgments of the bishops" is the maxim of U.S. prelates, who, after decades of aid to Latin America, are especially sensitive to charges of "interventionism." This policy, it now appears, has been endorsed (even if not initiated) by Rome. At issue is not only the strengthening of episcopacies (after all, a bishops conference with resources is likely to enjoy greater national political clout) but also the reinforcing of the papacy's apparent thrust to centralize within the Curia as much policymaking and resource allocation for the region as possible.

In contrast to the Germans and the Americans, the Polish Church's greatest resource is manpower, some of which is now being directed to the East, though with apparently mixed results. It is of course useful to remember that Poland is Central and East Europe's largest Catholic nation, that more than 90 percent of the country's 38 million inhabitants are professedly Roman Catholic, and that from this base, during decades of communist rule, vocations to the diocesan priesthood, to some forty male religious orders, and to more than a hundred female congregations, never ceased to grow (until the latter half of the 1980s).[85] Even before the end of autocratic state rule, the Polish Church had continuously sent clergy to all corners of the earth.

It comes as no surprise that toward the end of 1989, "the Primate of Poland established a 'Team for Ecclesiastical Aid to the East,' with head-quarters in the office of the Polish episcopate."[86] By Easter of the following year, it had sent a priest to Moscow.[87] Others followed. From the several dozen permitted at the outset of the 1990s as part of an agreement between the Polish episcopacy and the Council for Religious Matters of the then Supreme Soviet of the USSR, there are today well over a hundred.

Of course, the Polish clergy have three advantages for such a mission over other Europeans. First, they are culturally Slavs and their mother tongue makes them potentially intelligible to most neighboring peoples. Nevertheless, intensive, two-month courses in the Russian and Ukrainian languages have been offered at the Eastern Mission Institute, run by a religious order, as were other courses in comparative theology, Eastern canon law, and icons. Seminars with returning "missionaries" and visiting Orthodox clergymen are part of the curriculum. Secondly, the principal missionary target consists of the large Polish-speaking minorities in Russia, Byelorus, Lithuania, and Ukraine, parts of which lay under Polish jurisdiction between the wars. Thirdly, Polish Catholics have backed these efforts of their clergy with material support of one kind or another.

But criticism, some familiar, abounds among both Orthodox and Ukrainian Uniates. "The Catholic Church doesn't really spread the faith but instead buys new believers," claims an Orthodox cleric, aware of his own church's lack of resources. In the Ukraine, the Polish clergy is seen as part of a movement of Polish heritage and nationalism and "aggressive in this respect," according to an official of the Uniate curia in Lviv. In Byelorus, three priests had their tourist visas revoked for being too active among the Polish minority, for not preaching in the Byelorussian language, and for allegedly trying to act as intermediaries between the Holy See and the national government, which, a Byelorussian official declared, enjoy full diplomatic relations on their own.[88] Finally, concern is rather frequently voiced, more so in Western Europe, that Polish Catholicism still overly adheres to rural religious folk practices rather than the teachings of Vatican Council II. But while increasing numbers of foreign priests other than Poles now find themselves scattered throughout the East, especially since the Vatican encourages just such a policy of forming nuclei of missionaries of different nationalities to underscore the Church's "catholicity," the West is both vocation-shy and seems at this juncture to be linguistically, if not culturally, unprepared to meet the challenge.

The Italian Bishops Conference is mentioned last and briefly not only for its decision to take particular responsibility for Albania, but also for a type of aid that is becoming increasingly common throughout Europe. Of course, Italian interest in Albania stems from more than geographic proximity or the intent to make reparation for the wartime occupation by Italian fascists. One reason is that Latin Catholics who make up slightly more than 12 percent of this predominantly Muslim country have historically lived in the northern region around Shkodër and, until the advent of communist rule, had often intermarried with Italians.[89] An equally compelling factor is the presence of Albanian minorities in southern Italy, in Calabria and Sicily.[90] Members of an Italo-Albanian Byzantine rite in communion with Rome since 1596, they spearheaded aid to Albanian nationals who, fleeing communist rule in 1991, were so cruelly turned back across the Adriatic by the Italian government.

Between 1990 and 1993, however, some thirty-one instances of *"gemellaggio,"* or "twinning up," have occurred between Catholic parishes in four Italian dioceses, including Bari and Rome, and such Albanian entities as cooperatives, schools, sanitoria, prisons, and universities. Even the national office of Italian Caritas is helping to form branches of the future Albanian national counterpart in the four newly created dioceses of the country.[91]

But "twinning up" was not new to Italy. The Church had extensively experimented with it earlier in Croatia and Bosnia-Herzegovina, and parishes in Trent and Verona are reported to be pairing off with orthodox communities in Russia. "Twinning up" is also a well-developed form of assistance elsewhere in Europe and has been employed assiduously by the churches of Germany, Austria, Switzerland, and Poland, among others. The monetary value of such cooperation and solidarity is impossible to calculate or to centralize, just as the rewards of human fraternity are difficult to measure.

*   *   *

I have reviewed the activity of Europe-wide Catholic philanthropies, of national bishops conferences, and of the Curia in attempting to coordinate their activities. There is one last grouping to be reviewed, the undertakings of the numerous religious orders and congregations and of the laity who form part of the myriad of so-called secular institutes. All operate across the world order and none is not in some way committed to reconstructing the Church in the East. Each tends to work where it had been historically present before the advent of communist rule: the Franciscans in Croatia, the Salesians in the Czech and Slovak Republics and in Poland, the Basilian Fathers (a Uniate order) in Hungary, Slovakia, Poland, and Ukraine.

The Society of Jesus—the Jesuits—offers an example of one congregation's priorities that other religious institutes are likely to share.[92] Highest is the training of new priests; some ninety seminarians from the East are currently completing their studies in Italy, France, Austria, Germany, and England. In the East itself, especially where the Jesuits are more numerous, as in Poland (750) and Croatia (188), but also where their provinces were stripped of possessions, as in the Czech Republic (fewer than 120) and Slovakia (150), the Society conducts retreats. Based on the Ignation exercises, they aim at imparting to the individual a spiritual and intellectual understanding of oneself and of the world around.

Education, the historic area of Jesuit expertise, is also a priority; they have opened their own high school in Kaunas, Lithuania,[93] operate a diocesan lycée in Brno, and direct the interdiocesan seminary in Shkodër. Additionally, as an order especially concerned with mass media and which has run Vatican Radio since its inception, the Society already has Jesuits in key secular and religious broadcasting positions in Warsaw, Prague, and Zagreb. Moreover, they meet periodically to exchange views about developments in media which, for the most part, have remained not only under government control but also in the hands of professionals who were former Communist Party members.

On June 21, 1992, a new Jesuit administrative region was established for all of Russia.[94] There, not surprisingly, the Society—directors of the Russicum and among the intellectual authors of the new PIDCCEE—is concerned with promoting an ecumenical exchange with Orthodoxy. In Moscow, the opening of a branch of the Russian-language theological review, *Simvol*, long edited and published near Paris, is on the agenda. So too is close collaboration in the new Faculty of Philosophy of the State University in Novosibirsk. Finally, since 1991 a Russian Jesuit of Volga-German origin with the rank of bishop has presided from Novosibirsk over the first Roman Catholic Apostolic Administration of Siberia.[95]

Data on lay secular institutes (i.e., organizations of the laity dedicated to full-time religious work) are not as public as those of religious orders. The activities of the highly secretive and theologically conservative Opus Dei in the East are difficult to discern, whereas those of the Charismatic Renewal Movement have been notable and publicly undertaken in the field of mass communications.[96] A prominent member of a Dallas, Texas, community has since 1991 aided episcopacies in several East European countries in purchasing transmitters, furnishing studios, and training personnel. Whether this assistance seeks to further the particular spirituality of the charismatic movement, initially at odds with "liberal" Catholicism and liberation theology but increasingly in harmony with current Vatican priorities, or whether it conforms—as do the many donor episcopacies—to the needs of the new national conferences of bishops, is a moot point.

Conclusion

This chapter has illustrated the direction, the shape, the history, and the institutions of Roman Catholic philanthropy in Central and East Europe since 1947, emphasizing the role of the global church and its material and moral support to the growth and flourishing of communities of faith in countries where they had been limited and suppressed. The argument points to two contradictory trends: Self-generating, "spontaneous" forms of local religiosity are on the increase even as their autonomous nature is compromised by dependency on external assistance. I have also shown the dilemmas posed by the Church's Drang nach Osten. One dilemma surrounded choices in pre-1989 East Europe, where the Church's low-key, almost invisible, exchanges with East German communism encouraged East German churches in time of distress but compromised the Church's principled stand not to work with communist regimes. Another dilemma surrounds choices in Russia, where the new freedom of religion offers new opportunities to Catholicism even while it endangers Rome's ecumenical approaches to the Orthodox Church, which resents the competition.

From the viewpoint of transnational religious regimes, the defining characteristics of Catholicism in our time may well be the sheer multiplicity and variety of official and lay entities within the Roman Catholic Church; the flexible structures that have been created in response to changing needs and the rise of new constituencies; the capacity of these organizations to amplify themselves across the world order; their ability to operate both separately and collectively, as have the numerous national and pan-European philanthropies discussed in this account; and the preeminence in the philanthropic initiatives of actors from the industrialized world. In the particular case of Catholicism, each of the many official and lay entities forms an alternative network of information and resources. But they are also capable of coming together to act in concert, as they did in Eastern Europe and Russia after 1989, executing the common global strategy of a single global institution.

NOTES

The research for this essay was made possible by a fellowship from the German Marshall Fund of the United States. During the academic year 1992–1993 it permitted me to reside and travel in the United States; Germany and Austria; Italy and Vatican City; Slovenia, Croatia, Hungary, Romania, the Czech Republic, Slovakia, and Poland. Supplementary grants were received from the Research Foundation of the City University of New York and from the History Department and the Social Science Division of Queens College, City University of New York. I wish to express my heartfelt thanks to all who gave me welcome, lent an ear, and told their stories during the course of this extraordinary journey.

1. The term "transnational religious regimes" was adopted by the organizers of the Social Science Research Council conference at which an earlier version of this paper was presented. In two recent essays, however, I have preferred to speak of

"trans-systemic" religions; see Ralph Della Cava, "Thinking About Current Vatican Policy in Central and East Europe and the Utility of the 'Brazilian Paradigm,'" *Journal of Latin American Studies* 25 (May 1993):257–281, and "Financing the Faith: The Case of Roman Catholicism," *Journal of Church and State* 35 (1) (Winter 1993):1101–1122. The notion of "trans-systemic" derives from the work of Immanuel Wallerstein on the "modern world-system." I must also acknowledge the work of Juan Linz on the process of democratization in the former peoples' and soviet socialist republics as well as his comparisons, with Alfred Stepan, of these processes with those in South America.

2. Within Wallerstein's framework, these polar terms are really part of the triad, *periphery, semi-periphery,* and *core.* Similarly, in Wallerstein's work, "trans-systemically" would replace "transnationally."

3. See the excellent account by Brian H. Smith, *More Than Altruism: The Politics of Private Foreign Aid* (Princeton: Princeton University Press, 1992). For Brazil, see the illustrative volume by Leilah Landim, ed., *Sem Fins Lucrativos: As organizações não-governmentais no Brasil* (Rio de Janeiro: ISER, 1988). In one important respect, Landim's volume falls short of the mark: It does not reveal the international linkages of the Brazilian NGOs, even though in the case of the most prominent of them, those ties are extensive and largely known. For perhaps the most interesting account of NGOs in Latin America and of the perception of them as the new vehicles for effecting major changes in society and as a fresh alternative for civil society following upon the exhaustion of such historic movements as trade unions and workers' and ideological parties, see the still unpublished essay by Rubem Cesar Fernandes, "The Third Sector in Latin America," A Report for Civicus, mimeo (October 1993), 110; available through the Nucleo de Pesquisas de ISER, Rio de Janeiro.

4. This contention—that the iron curtain proved exceptionally porous—flies in the face of the conventional wisdom about the cold war and about the "persecution of the Church" under communist rule. I recognize, however, there is much truth to the story of persecution, and I fully sympathize with all who paid dearly for the expression of their religious beliefs. The "stories" laid out later on in this chapter refer summarily to the former Yugoslavia, Poland, and the former German Democratic Republic.

5. This early history is by no means forgotten; KIN's official name today is "Kirche in Not/Ostpriesterhilfe." Partly for the sake of brevity, but also because the organization is known in English-speaking lands only as Aid to the Church in Need, it is referred to in this chapter simply as Kirche in Not or KIN.

6. KIN's leaders delineated its new policy toward the East as early as 1952. With the death of Stalin in 1953, uprisings in East Germany and Poland and then in Hungary in 1956, their activities increased. See "We Jumped over the Curtain" and the two subsequent chapters on Central and East Europe in the informative informal history of the organization by its founder, the Dutch-born Norbertine monk from the Flemish abbey of Tongerlo (Belgium), Fr. Werenfried van Straaten, *They Call Me the Bacon Priest,* revised American edition (San Francisco: Ignatius Press, 1991; original edition 1961), 183–226.

7. The systematic dismantling of the Uniate Catholic Church; the imprisonment, torture, and murder of their hierarchs and their faithful; and the confiscation of

their properties and subsequent acquisition by the Orthodox Church took place in 1946 as a consequence of policies dictated by the Soviet Union; see *Die ukrainische katholische Kirche* (Munich: Kirche in Not, 1988 and 1989). On Romania, see *Rumänien* (Munich: Kirche in Not, 1991), part of the series *Christentum in Osteuropa*, no. 1. Oddly enough, the Hungarian Uniate Church, indeed a minuscule minority located primarily in Hajdúdorog and the several neighboring towns on the eastern border, unscathed, primarily because they "were neither numerous nor Slavs," according to His Excellency Keresztes Szilárd, the Uniate Bishop of Hajdúdorog, in an interview by the author in Nyíregyháza, Hungary, May 14, 1993.

8. On the execution of a similarly aggressive policy in Czechoslovakia after 1949, see *Tschechoslowakei* (Munich: Kirche in Not, 1991), part of the series *Christentum in Osteuropa*, no. 2, and *Storia religiosa dei cechi e degli slovacchi*, edited by Luciano Vaccaro (Milan: La Casa di Matriona, 1987).

9. This is not the place to reassess such phenomena in detail or to question at length the nature of the cold war and its unspeakably rigid ideological distortions, which held in thrall many observers and participants in every quarter, including in the Church, until the fall of the Berlin Wall. Such a reassessment, however, is under way.

10. From the Roman Catholic side, my point about the earlier beginnings of "polycentrism" is affirmed, but in a slightly inverted way, namely, as "the earlier beginnings of the Vatican's 'Ostpolitik.'" Not surprisingly, this judgment is found in an article by a noted Croatian ecclesiastical historian, Djuro Koksa, "Linee metodologiche per una lettura della storia religiosa dei Croati," in *Storia religiosa dei popoli balcanici*, edited by Luciano Vaccaro (Milan: La Casa di Matriona, 1983), 181–201: "In sostanza ritengo che la vera Ostpolitik, anche se non sul piano diplomatico, è cominiciata ancora sotto Papa Pacelli [Pio XII, 1938–1958]" [In essence, I consider the true *Ostpolitik*, even if not at the diplomatic level, to have begun under the papacy of Pope Pacelli] (200). It was precisely Pius XII's policy toward the former Yugoslavia, of which Catholic Croatia was then a part, that had helped to reinforce the measure of religious freedom.

11. Vjekoslav Bajsíc remarks, "e questo è il punto forse più importante—la Chiesa nel suo 'ghetto' era libera" [the most important point is—the Church in its 'ghetto' was nonetheless free]; see his "La Chiesa in Croazia durante L'Era Marxista," and France M. Dolimar, "La Chiesa Cattolica in Slovenia," both in *La Fede "Sommersa" nei paesi dell'Est*, edited by Alba Lazzaretto Zanolo (Vicenza: Neri Pozza Editore, 1992), 15–24 and 25–32, respectively. Nevertheless, the imprisonment in 1945 and subsequent house arrest until his death in 1960 of Aloysius Stepinac, Archbishop of Zagreb (Croatia) and later (1953) Cardinal, by the Tito government for alleged collaboration with the wartime pro-Nazi regime in Croatia became a cause célèbre throughout the Roman Catholic world. The story is summarized in Sergio Trasatti (editor-in-chief of *L'Osservatore Romano*), *La croce e la stella: La Chiesa e i regimi comunisti in Europa dal 1917 a oggi* (Milan: Arnaldo Mondadori Editore, 1993), 134–138. After its initial sensationalism, however, the case does not seem to have interfered with the relative freedom of Yugoslav Catholics, provided their religiosity remained confined to church quarters. That, at least, is the consensus of most Croatian and Slovene Catholic sources cited in these notes.

12. See Bajsíc, "La Chiesa in Croazia durante L'Era Marxista," 22.

13. See *Kosciól Katolicki w Polsce, 1918–1990: Rocznik Statystyczny* (Warsaw: Glówny Urzad Statystyczny Zaklad Socjologii Religii SAC, 1991); also Jerzy Kloczowski, "L'Europa Centro-Orientale, la Polonia, e la Chiesa oggi," and Jerzy Kloczowski and Lidia Müllerova, "Le Christianisme polonais après 1945," both in *La Fede "Sommersa" nei paesi dell'Est*, edited by Zanolo, 51–60 and 83–127, respectively.

14. See Hans-Jakob Stehle, *The Eastern Politics of the Vatican, 1977–1979* (Athens: Ohio University Press, 1981); a new edition of this authoritative work, which supposedly brings the story of the Vatican's *Ostpolitik* up to date, recently appeared in Europe under the title *Geheimdiplomatie im Vatikan: Die Päpste und die Kommunisten* (Zurich: Benziger, 1993). Two other excellent recent works are Andrea Riccardi, *Il Vaticano e Mosca: 1940–1990* (Bari, Italy: Editori Laterza, 1993), and Sergio Trasatti, *La croce e la stella*; the latter has an excellent chronology. On Polish criticism, see Stehle, *The Eastern Politics of the Vatican*, 341–356.

15. The ecclesiastical organization of postwar Germany is a rather complicated story, since some of the jurisdictions in the former East Germany, the German Democratic Republic (GDR), pertained to dioceses in West Germany, the Federal Republic of Germany (FRG), while others pertained to former diocesan sees in the East that were incorporated into Poland after the war. Most interesting was the status of the Diocese of Berlin, which in 1976 was granted by the Holy See jurisdiction over the entire Catholic population of East Germany, amounting to about 6 percent of the GDR's 15 million inhabitants. At the moment when the eastern borders of East Germany were recognized diplomatically—West Germany as well as Poland were parties to the agreement—the Holy See permitted a change in the status of the bishops' organization in Berlin from the Berlin Conference of Ordinaries (bishops) (die Berliner Ordiniarienkonferenz), to the Berlin Bishops Conference (Die Berliner Bischofskonferenz). Although the latter had jurisdiction over all of East Germany, it belonged fully at the same time to the (West) German Bishops Conference with its historic see in Fulda (although its government affairs office, Das Katholische Büro, was in Bonn). Documents pertaining to the life of the Church in East Germany are found in *Katholische Kirche—Sozialistischer Staat DDR: Dokumente und Öffentliche Äußerungen, 1945–1990*, edited by Gerhard Lange (Leipzig: Benno-Verlag, 1992). For an East German perspective, based on newly released documents of state of the former GDR, see Bernd Schäfer, "Grenzen von Staat und Kirche—Zur diplomatie zwischen DDR und Vatikan von 1972 bis 1979," *Stimmen der Zeit* 212 (2) (February 1994):121–131. For some insights into German Catholicism in the postwar era (1945–1986), see the essays contained in Actes du Colloque Franco-Allemand, *France-Allemagne: Églises et société, du Concile Vatican II à nos jours*, Bibliothèque Beauchesne: Religions, Sociétés, Politique, no. 13 (Paris: Beauchesne, 1988).

16. For a brief description of the Church in the GDR, see Vicente Cárcel Ortí, *La Chiesa in Europa: 1945–1991* (Milan: Edizioni Paoline, 1992), 159–165.

17. This was alluded to by Fr. Gerhard Lange, former editor of the Catholic weekly *St. Hedwigsblatt* and current director of the Publications Office of the Berlin Diocese, in "Staatliche Kirchenpolitik in der DDR—Versuch einer Bilanz aus

katholischer Zeit," *Die Neue Ordnung* (Walberberg, Germany: Institut für Gesellschaftswissenschaften) 46 (5) (October 1992):326–343, esp. 337–338.

18. Prälat Dieter Grande, currently director of the newly established Katholisches Büro Sachsen and member of the organizing committee for the 92nd Katholikentag (held in Dresden in June 1994), interview by the author, Dresden, January 26, 1993. The founder of Kirche in Not contended: "Economic conditions in the Soviet colonies of Eastern Europe are so bad the Communist authorities are compelled to disavow their own principles for the sake of a little foreign currency. So, for the restoration of church buildings, it is possible to pay a sum of money—in dollars—into a foreign account with a guarantee that the equivalent amount in wood, stone, cement, iron and roof tiles will be placed at the disposal of our brethren behind the Iron Curtain." Quoted in van Straaten, *They Call Me the Bacon Priest*, 190.

19. Fr. Gerhard Lange, interview by the author, in the former East Berlin, January 23, 1993.

20. Vicente Cárcel Ortí notes that conditions and possibilities of action "furono—per espresso riconoscimento degli stessi vescovi—le migliori fra quelle dei Paesi a regime comunista" [were—by the express recognition of the bishops—best with those countries that had a communist regime]. *La Chiesa in Europa,* 160.

21. According to Sergio Trasatti (in his *La croce e la stella,* 138–140), two other factors appear to have played a role in the East German regime's toleration of Roman Catholics. First, they were few in number, only 6 percent of the population. Second, the state held the Vatican to one major demand: that East Germany's ecclesiastical administration be kept separate from West Germany's. In reality, only one of the seven dioceses was entirely confined within the territory of the East; the other six extended over territory in both states. Moreover, newer dioceses were always presided over by apostolic administrators, rather than bishops, armed with full powers of the Holy See, among which was the capability of freely traveling to and fro. Nonetheless, from the vantage point of the German Democratic Republic, these arrangements—which underwent changes over time—were perceived as tantamount to the recognition of the state's sovereignty. As a consequence, Trasatti implies, "there was a margin of tolerance" (140).

22. Bishop Joachim Meisner actually took office on the first Sunday of Lent 1989. His nomination to the archdiocesan See of Cologne was not without controversy, since he was appointed by the pope but not from the list of three candidates originally nominated and submitted to the Holy See, in time-honored tradition, by the clergy of Cologne. On the turbulence within the West German Church, see Francesco Strazzari, *Chiese della Cee all' appuntamento del '93* (Milan: Edizioni Paoline, 1991), 192–245, esp. 210–212.

23. The new national director of Caritas is Prälat Hellmut Puschmann; his views on having Caritas help create like living conditions throughout united Germany and on other issues are expressed in an interview, entitled "Im Gespräch," *Caritas in NRW* 4 (October 1991):17–19. For a brief history of German Caritas from its beginnings to the creation of such specialized agencies as Misereor in 1959, see Erwin Gatz, "Caritas und soziale Dienste," in *Der soziale und politische Katholizismus—Entwicklungslinien in Deutschland, 1803–1963,* edited by Anton Rauscher (Munich-Vienna: Günter Olzog Verlag, 1982), vol. 2, 312–351.

24. Not the least of these reasons was the commitment of German Catholics to fulfill "our responsibility for the commonweal of the entire world. We see this task as an injunction of the Social Doctrine of the Church." Dr. Paul Becher, Chief of the Department for Social Policy and International Tasks of the Zentralkomitee der Deutschen Katholiken, letter to the author, April 24, 1994. Among the seven philanthropic agencies established by the German Bishops Conference in the postwar era were Adveniat and Misereor, intended to support respectively ecclesiastical needs in Latin America and social development projects throughout the developing world. These are entirely independent of and separate from German Caritas. Misereor and German motives are ably discussed in Brian H. Smith, *More Than Altruism*, 83. For a brief sketch of Adveniat, see *20 Jahre Bischöfliche Aktion Adveniat* (Essen, Germany: Adveniat [1981]). For a discussion of German and U.S. "political foundations," see Michael Pinto-Duschinsky, "Foreign Political Aid: The German Political Foundations and Their U.S. Counterparts," *International Affairs* 67 (1) (1991):33–63. For a discussion of the West German government's taxation policy, which allocates a portion of public tax moneys to private religious agencies and foundations, see Knut Walf, "The Church Tax as a Means of Subsistence," in *The Finances of the Church*, edited by William Bassett and Peter Huizing (New York: Seabury Press, 1979), 20–27.

25. For an account of the EHF, see the biography of Carlo Bayer, founder of Caritas Internationalis: Christian Heidrich, *Carlo Bayer: Ein Römer aus Schlesien und Pionier der Caritas Internationalis*, vol. 6, *Arbeiten zur schlesien Kirchengeschichte* (Sigmaringen, Germany: Jan Thorbecke Verlag, 1992), 338–360. For observations on the role of Austrian Caritas, see 170–178 and 339–342. The categories of classification and of analysis, *"Osteuropa"* and *"Südosteuropa,"* correspond to historic and present-day German definitions for Central Europe. In the context of the founding of EHF, the former included Poland and Czechoslovakia, the latter, Yugoslavia, Romania, and Bulgaria. See Heidrich, *Carlo Bayer*, 338.

26. See Werenfried van Straaten, *Where God Weeps* (Sutton, Surrey, England: Aid to the Church in Need, 1970), and the unnumbered chapter entitled "Behind the Iron Curtain," 140–204, esp. 200. For an appreciation of the Vatican stance, compare van Straaten's viewpoint with that of Franz Cardinal König, the Archbishop of Vienna, who personally negotiated the release of Jozsef Cardinal Mindszenty and then personally persuaded him to leave the U.S. Embassy in Budapest for Vatican City: "The Church in the East and the Church in its confrontation with the East knows that it must live with Communism, and Communism knows that Faith is not simply a passing phenomenon. Is that now called co-existence?" From a 1974 radio address cited in Heidrich, *Carlo Bayer*, 344. It must also be remembered that Cardinal König had been engaged in discussions with Cardinal Mindszenty at the express order of the Holy See since 1963; see Stehle, *The Eastern Politics of the Vatican*, 317.

27. The suggestion that the EHF may have "picked up the slack" left by KIN's boycott of Hungary was made by several well-informed sources. On the prevailing sense of betrayal by the Vatican, see Stehle, *The Eastern Politics of the Vatican*, 314–323. On the simultaneous institution of the West German government's *Ostpolitik*, see Walter Laqueur, *Europe in Our Time: A History, 1945–1992* (New York: Penguin Books, 1993), 449–460. See also the recent work by Timothy

Garton-Ash, *In Europe's Name: Germany and the Divided Continent* (New York: Random House, 1994), a view extremely critical of the former West Germany's *Ostpolitik*, its acceptance of the permanence of communist regimes, and its blindness to their inherent weaknesses as well as to the efficacy of internal dissent.

28. Support for such populations was rooted in part in large constituencies in West Germany that were composed of formerly displaced persons and their descendants who had originated in those very same ethnic settlements abroad. Today there are a number of research institutes attached to German universities that specialize in the study of the history and culture of German ethnics abroad, including the Volga-Deutsch in Russia and the highly assimilated German stock in Brazil.

29. Heidrich notes that the German bishops had earlier operated a Katholisches Hilfswerk Büro with headquarters in Rome, while the Austrian bishops operated a similar organization out of Vienna; the EHF was seen as a coordination effort between the two, and each national bishops conference preserved autonomy over the collection and allocation of its donations. Heidrich, *Carlo Bayer*, 340–341.

30. Heidrich, *Carlo Bayer*, 339. The ratio of contributions was said to have been nine to one in Germany's favor. The German share was contributed by the Association of Dioceses of Germany, to which all German dioceses belong, according to Dr. Gerhard Albert, deputy chief of the World Church Department of the German Bishops Conference, in an interview by the author, Bonn, November 19, 1992.

31. Msgr. Hubert Wilschowitz, Director of the EHF, interview by the author, Vienna, December 15, 1992.

32. For a more detailed analysis of both the projects and the EHF methods employed to select them, see Heidrich, *Carlo Bayer*, 343–353.

33. Two Polish Catholic lay movements, the Kraków journal *Znak*, and the Clubs of Catholic Intellectuals (KIK), enjoyed a considerable degree of autonomy from the party in the years prior to Solidarity's establishment. But in no way did they enjoy any like political success.

34. There are dozens of accounts of Pope John Paul II's pontificate; a recent introduction is David Wiley's *God's Politician: John Paul at the Vatican* (London: Faber and Faber, 1992); a more critical account is Constance Colonna-Cesari, *Urbi et Orbi: Enquête sur la géopolitique vaticane* (Paris: Éditions La Découverte, 1992). On Solidarity, see the celebrated accounts of Timothy Garton-Ash, *The Polish Revolution: Solidarity* (Sevenoaks, England: Hodder and Stoughton, 1985), and *The Uses of Adversity: Essays on the Fate of Central Europe* (New York: Viking, 1990). For a prescient perspective on conflicting forces in Polish society, written a full two years before the recent electoral victory of former communists, see David Ost, "Polish Solidarity and the Transformation of Eastern Europe," *Occasional Papers Series*, The New Hampshire International Seminar, March 29, 1991, 29.

35. This information is based in part on the author's interview with Mr. Karl Schinko, secretary-general of the Österreichische Caritaszentrale, in Vienna, December 16, 1992.

36. The role of the Polish Bishops Conference is alluded to in a publication of the Austrian Caritas, which in this same period had organized a major campaign of assistance; see *Caritas: Polenhilfe 1981/85* (Vienna: Caritas Österreichs [1985?]). Prior to communist rule in Poland, there existed a Polish national agency of Caritas. But in January 1950 it was placed under state control with the help of the government-

tolerated PAX (the Polish Progressive Catholic Movement, a pro-government group that nominally attempted to reconcile Catholicism and communism). In reality, PAX thoroughly "acted as a tool of the state in the harassment of the Church," according to Ronald C. Monticone, *The Catholic Church in Communist Poland, 1945–1985: Forty Years of Church-State Relations* (Boulder: East European Monographs, 1986), 15–17. This situation is also addressed by Lucjan Blit in *The Eastern Pretender, Boleslaw Piasecki: His Life and Times* (London: Hutchinson & Co., 1965), 167–170. Consequently, aid to the Church in Poland since 1950 has been distributed through the bishops and through the Commission for Charities of the Polish Bishops Conference and not the national Caritas structure, whose very name spells ignominy to almost all Polish Catholics. To my knowledge, as of 1993, no new Caritas organization had yet been created.

37. Aid was especially forthcoming from West German Catholics, who took up a special collection for Poland in 1982, according to Dr. Gerhard Albert, who at that time was the responsible officer for aid to Poland (interview by the author, Bonn, June 14, 1984). Aid to Solidarity was sent from the U.S. government via the AFL-CIO national headquarters. Additional Church aid was allegedly channeled through the Vatican's bank, Istituto per le Opere Religiose, which in 1982 was publicly involved in the collapse of the Banco Ambrosiano; on this topic, see Della Cava, "Financing the Faith." Austrian Catholic Charities made considerable contributions between 1981 and 1985, no small portion of which was agricultural machinery such as plows, balers, tractors, and so on; they are mentioned in the pamphlet *Caritas: Polenhilfe 1981/85* (Vienna: Caritas Österreichs [1985?]).

38. Many of the churches, almost always on the scale of cathedrals, today stand half finished and likely will remain so for a long time to come as inflation drives building costs skyward, as churchmen are criticized for living in a grandiose way, and as bishops consciously take measures to redirect scarce resources toward the training and mobilization of youth and laity.

39. The information in this section on German efforts was discussed in an interview by the author with Dr. Gerhard Albert, Bonn, November 16, 1992.

40. Though administrative costs of the EHF were paid exclusively by the German and Austrian Bishops Conferences, Swiss Catholics also collaborated with specific projects through donations made to the "Lenten Sacrifice of Swiss Catholics" (Fastenopfer der Schweizer Katholiken). Dr. Gerhard Albert, interview by the author, Bonn, November 16, 1992. See also Knut Walf, "The Church Tax as a Means of Subsistence."

41. The annual collection, a 1993 initiative of Renovabis, the newly created agency to aid the Church in the East, is discussed at length later in this chapter. Of course, annual collections for specific purposes, usually referred to as a "special appeal," were by no means new to German Catholics (or Catholics elsewhere for that matter). Misereor and Adveniat, two important episcopal foundations, were primarily financed by an annual special collection. On the operation of Catholic development agencies in Europe, see Brian H. Smith, *More Than Altruism.*

42. The information in this section is based on the pamphlet *Caritas Internationalis: What It Is, What It Does* (1993); on Caritas Internationalis, *Estatutos y reglamento interno* ([Rome], 1989); and on interviews by the author in Rome with Messrs. Gerhard Meier and Jean-Paul Evrard, respectively CI's secretary-general

and director of operations, March 23 and 24, 1993. For CI's early history, also see Heidrich, *Carlo Bayer*, 123–201.

43. Mimeographed memo entitled "Arbeit im sozialen Bereich über nationale Grenzen hinweg," prepared by Karl Schinko, secretary-general of Austrian Caritas for the ÖKSA-Workshop, held in Bratislava on April 26, 1991 (8). The memo notes that from the 1970s until 1989, Caritas's "permanent" contacts were limited to the former East Germany, Croatia, and Poland. "Single-contacts" with the former Czechoslovakia and Hungary took place only via the three "permanent" nations (2–3).

44. Since the reunification of Germany, the total number of the German Caritas staff has risen to 450,000, according to Msgr. Georges Hüssler, the former secretary-general (1959–1969) and president (1969–1991), in an interview by the author, Freiburg, Germany, June 24, 1994. He was quick to point out that such numbers, excluding unpaid volunteers, were in fact distributed over national, regional (or state-level), and diocese-wide organizations.

45. Undated flyer, entitled "The Pontifical Council 'Cor Unum'" and the rubrics "Ponitifico Consiglio 'Cor Unum'" in *Annuario Pontificio per l'Anno 1993* (Vatican City: Libreria Editrice Vaticana, 1993), 1228–1231 and 1740–1741. Three important goals are spelled out in the latter source: 1. to provide a more equitable distribution of resources; 2. to encourage common charitable enterprises with other religious entities; and 3. to facilitate relations of Catholic institutions with international public organizations that operate in the same area of "aid and progress" (1740).

46. For the fervor of this moment, replicated in Warsaw, Budapest, and Prague, see Timothy Garton-Ash, *The Magic Lantern* (New York: Random House, 1993), originally published as *We the People: The Revolution of 89, Witnessed in Warsaw, Budapest, Berlin, and Prague* (Cambridge, England: Granta Books in association with Penguin Books, 1990).

47. The bibliography is already extensive; a good starting point that places recent events in the context of the postwar era is the new edition of Joseph Rothschild's *Return to Diversity: A Political History of East Central Europe Since World War II*, 2d edition (New York: Oxford University Press, 1993). The best weekly journal is *RFE/RL Research Report* (previously entitled *Report on Eastern Europe* and *Report on the USSR*), and the best daily news roundup, available on-line at no cost through Bitnet, is the *RFE/RL Daily Report* (to subscribe, e-mail LISTSERV@UBVM); all are publications of Radio Free Europe and Radio Liberty, with offices in Munich and Washington, D.C. The bibliography on the former Soviet Union grows by leaps and bounds. One useful overview is *After the Soviet Union: From Empire to Nations*, edited by Timothy J. Colton and Robert Legvold (New York: W. W. Norton, 1992).

48. An excellent starting point is Sabrina P. Ramet, "The New Church-State Configuration in Eastern Europe," *East European Politics and Societies* 5 (2) (Spring 1991):247–267, and Ralph Della Cava, "Thinking About Current Vatican Policy in Central and East Europe." A rather euphoric account of the role of Catholicism in the fall of communist rule may be found in George Weigel, *The Final Revolution: The Resistance Church and the Collapse of Communism* (New York: Oxford University Press, 1992). The only account of the last ten years currently available in book form is that of Sergio Trasatti, *La croce e la stella,* especially chapter 7,

279–362. For current reporting about religion in the region, consult the excellent monthly newsletter, *Informationdienst Osteuropäisches Christentum* (Munich).

49. Sergio Trasatti, *La Croce e la stella*, 363.

50. Thirteen new dioceses were erected in Poland alone, another six in Lithuania; see Anna Sabbat-Sadwicki, "Polish Church Plans Administrative Changes," *RFE/RL Research Report* 6 (March 1992):62–65. Diplomatic relations have been established between the Holy See and all former communist states and the new states of the former Soviet Union; for a chronology of Vatican diplomacy, see Trasatti, *La croce e la stella*, 363–401.

51. I have summarized here the types of projects currently sponsored by U.S. Bishops as recounted to me in an interview in Washington, D.C., October 8, 1992, by Rev. Fr. George Sarauskas, executive director of the U.S. Catholic Conference's Office to Aid the Catholic Church in Central and East Europe.

52. The distinction between "policy" and "operations" as a significant factor of difference between the two international bodies, recognizing full well, however, that each indulged in both, was suggested by Mr. David Holdridge of the East European Desk of Catholic Relief Services, Baltimore, Maryland, in a telephone interview with the author, October 1, 1993.

53. Dr. Hermann Herwig, Chief for Structural and Emergency Aid to East Europe of the German National Caritas Office, interview with the author, Freiburg, Germany, November 23, 1992.

54. Ms. Andrea Scharf, Director of Training Programs in East and Central Europe for Catholic Relief Services, Baltimore, Maryland, telephone interview with the author, October 1, 1993.

55. On the resistance of Russian Orthodoxy to permit other religions to operate freely, see "Orthodox Warn Other Christians on East Europe," *New York Times*, March 17, 1992; "Roman Church and Society of Jesus Confront Obstacles in 'New' Russia," *National Jesuit News*, February 1993; "Russia May Curb Foreign Religions," *New York Times*, July 16, 1993; and "Religion Returns to Russia with a Vengeance," *New York Times*, July 28, 1993.

56. For a description of the nineteen Eastern Catholic churches as well as other Christian Orthodox churches, see Ronald G. Roberson, *The Eastern Christian Churches: A Brief Survey*, revised 4th edition (Rome: Pontificium Institutum Studiorum Orientalium, 1993). For a guide to the separate Codex of Canon Law for the Eastern Churches that governs the nineteen Eastern churches, as distinct from the Code of Canon Law that governs the Latin rite, see Marco Brogi, "Le Chiese sui Iuris Codex Canonum Ecclesiarum Orientalium," *Revista Española de Derecho Canonico* (Salamanca) 48 (131) (1991):517–544.

57. In some Roman and Uniate circles today, the term "Greek Catholic" seems preferable to "Uniate." The Orthodox have apparently pejoratively employed the term "uniate" ever since the Treaty of Brest in 1596, which ratified the "union" of some liturgically orthodox communities to the See of Peter. The change may reflect Rome's new directions toward Orthodoxy and consequently an intention to remove the many obstacles—such as its use of the term "uniate"—to greater understanding between Catholicism and Orthodoxy.

58. On the operations of ROACO in 1990, see *L'Attività della Santa Sede* (Vatican City, 1991), 1139–1145, which cites the 1990 budget. The chief American

donor is the Catholic Near East Welfare Association; among the Germans are the Archdiocese of Cologne, the richest in Europe, Misereor, Missio, and the Europäischer Hilfsfonds.

59. Brother Austin David (Carroll), Director of Programs of the Catholic Near East Welfare Association of New York, telephone interview with the author, September 24, 1993.

60. See *Die ukrainische katholische Kirche*. There is also a Ukrainian Uniate Diaspora of almost 4 million believers who now live primarily in Canada, the United States, and Brazil and who represent an important source of vocations and material donations to the Church in the Ukraine, now in the process of full reconstruction.

61. Trasatti discusses this question at length in *La Croce e la stella*, 351–360. It is covered extensively in English in *The Ukrainian Weekly* (Jersey City, New Jersey). More scholarly treatments can be found in Bohdan R. Bociurkiw, "The Ukrainian Catholic Church in the USSR Under Gorbachev," *Problems of Communism* (November-December 1990):1–19; Grigorij Protopopov, "La Chiesa in Ucraina," in *Cattolici in Russia e Ucraina* (Milan: La Casa di Matriona, 1992), 133–261; "Allocution de l'évêque orthodoxe Vsevolod au Synode ukrainien catholique de Lviv," *Irénikon* 2 (1992):200–206; and Serge Keleher, "Church in the Middle: Greek-Catholics in Central and East Europe," *Religion, State, and Society* 20 (3-4) (1992):289–302.

62. Trasatti, *La croce e la stella*, 351–360.

63. Reunion with Rome was ratified by the Treaty of Brest in 1596; see Sophia Senyk, "L'Unione di Brest," in *Storia religiosa della Russia*, edited by Luciano Vaccaro (Milan: La Casa di Matriona: 1987), 97–111.

64. For a survey of Catholics in the former Soviet Union, see *Die römisch-katholische Kirche in der Sowietunion* (Eichstätt, Germany: Kirche in Not, 1990).

65. On the concept of "sister" church and the papacy's search to restore the unity of the Christian Church as it was prior to the "Great Schism," see Wilhelm de Vries, *Ortodossia e Cattolicesimo*, 2d edition (Brescia, Italy: Queriniana, 1992), 160–162.

66. For insights into the Synod, see the articles by Peter Hebblethwaite published in *The Tablet* (London), under the titles "The Church's Mission to Europe Today," December 7, 1991, 1515–1518, and "The Remaking of Europe," December 14, 1991, 1534–1536; see also the unsigned article, filed from Rome perhaps by the same writer, entitled "What the Gospel Means for Europe Today," December 21–28, 1991, 1601–1603. The minutes of that Synod, including the intervention of the one non-Slavic Orthodox observer who openly criticized Rome on behalf of his confreres, are found in Giovanni Caprile, ed., *Il Sinodo dei Vescovi 1991: Assemblea Speciale per Europa (28 novembre–14 dicembre 1991)* (Rome: Edizioni "La Civiltà Cattolica," 1992).

67. The U.S. government and those of the European Community insisted that such laws were a breach of Russia's commitment to permit freedom of religion and speech.

68. See the document dated June 1, 1992, issued by the Pontifical Commission for Russia (extinct as of January 1993), entitled "Principles and Norms: Evangelization and Ecumenism in Former Soviet Territories," reproduced in *Origins* 22 (17) (October 8, 1992):301–304.

69. See Ann Carey, "The Bishop of Siberia," *Our Sunday Visitor* (Indianapolis, IN), August 16, 1992. The bishop in question is the Jesuit Fr. Joseph Werth, himself a Russian of Volga-Deutsch ethnicity. Also see Boguslaw Steczek, SJ, "Being a Bishop in Siberia," in *Jesuits: Yearbook of the Society of Jesus* (Rome, 1993), 96–97.

70. *Annuario Pontificio 1993*, 1206–1207, and *L'Osservatore Romano* (edizione italiana), February 23, 1993.

71. The pastoral and political grounds for abandoning the policy to "convert" the Orthodox were contemplated as far back as the late 1940s by Fr. Philippe De Régis, SJ. In 1950 he published a "prophetic" article to that effect in the University of Louvain's *La nouvelle revue théologique* (full citation unavailable). Only in the 1990s, however (well after his death in 1955), was the likely original, fuller version—drafted in about 1948—discovered in his papers. In it, he argued insistently that the Orthodox hierarchy had survived World War II intact, even if politically compromised. Consequently, Rome, which had always recognized the legitimacy of the uninterrupted apostolic succession of all bishops within the Orthodox Church and hence the validity of its sacrament of holy orders, must then simply deal with that reality and—revolutionary to Catholic thinking until that point—abandon its idea of setting up a "parallel" church, that is, a Uniate or Greek Catholic Church in Russia. Fr. De Régis authored this position sometime after he had served for a number of years (both before and after World War II) as the director of the Pontificium Collegium Russicum, a Jesuit-run seminary originally established for Byzantine rite priests who were to be sent to convert the Orthodox of Russia. Although this purpose has been radically altered, the Russicum still remains a "collegium," in the European sense.

It may be that one contributing factor in Rome's recent changing of its policy toward Orthodoxy, already beginning in the 1960s and 1970s, was the realization that Catholic candidates available or willing to go to Russia as proselytizers in the Byzantine rite had ceased to come forward. The information in this note is based on interviews by the author in Rome on February 19, 1993, and June 7, 1994, with the Russicum's present Rector, Fr. John Long, SJ, and on March 15, 1993, and June 2, 1994, with Fr. Robert Taft, SJ, a member of the faculty of the Pontificio Istituto Orientale, a master's- and doctoral-level center for the study of Eastern Christianity, also staffed by the Jesuits.

72. According to the *Annuario Pontificio 1993*, the four member congregations of the PIDCCEE are those for the Eastern Churches; Clergy; Institutes of Consecrated Life and Societies of Apostolic Life (i.e., religious orders and lay secular institutes); and the Pontifical Council for the Promotion of Christian Unity. *Annuario Pontificio 1993*, 1206.

73. See, for example, "For the Record: Activists React to Vatican Policies," *The Ukrainian Weekly* (Jersey City, New Jersey), March 21, 1993, 6. The letter, signed by officers of the Ukrainian Patriarchal Society of the USA, "a lay Ukrainian Catholic organization," enumerates a virtual litany of the Papacy's slights against Ukrainian Uniates.

74. See the declaration published after the Balamand conference entitled "Uniatism, Method of Union of the Past, and the Search for Full Communion," reproduced in *Ecumenical Trends* 22 (8) (September 1993):1, 3–7.

75. Rev. Fr. George Sarauskas, telephone interview by the author, October 4, 1993.

76. "Hilfe bei der Erneuerung des Ostens—Katholiken zu Spenden für die Initiative 'Renovabis' aufgerufen," *Frankfurter Allgemeine Zeitung*, April 24, 1993.

77. Renovabis must be seen in the larger context of current German efforts to aid the East. For example, the country's federation of Protestant churches, die Evangelische Kirche in Deutschland (EKD), established an organization of its own on February 27, 1994, called "Hoffnung für Osteuropa" (Hope for East Europe), to coordinate aid projects in East and southeast Europe. At the same time, several of the state governments have established partnerships with successor states or regions of the former Soviet Union: Nordrhein-Westfalen with the Russian Federation, Bavaria with Ukraine, and Sachsen-Anhalt with the administrative region of Omsk. See "Waffenschmidt: Rußland helfen—Aktivitäten der Wirtschaft, der Kirchen und Verbände sowie der Länder," *Frankfurter Allgemeine Zeitung*, January 25, 1994, 6.

Jewish organizations have also been active in Central and East Europe, especially in Russia, where the Jewish population is estimated to be some 2 million. According to "Nationalist Gains Shake Russia's Jews," *New York Times*, February 6, 1994, donations for the "nearly $28 million invested from abroad in the Jewish life of the former Soviet Union in 1993 came from the Jewish Agency, a quasi-official arm of the Israeli Government, for emigration and resettlement. The American Jewish Joint Distribution Committee, a New York–based relief organization, contributed just over $5 million, and $8 million more came from smaller Jewish organizations around the world."

Muslim institutions are also active. The Red Crescent is the most well known. Another is Mercy International (MI), a Muslim humanitarian organization founded in Pakistan in 1986 and financed by Kuwaiti resources to provide medical assistance to Afghan refugees. Recent activities have included humanitarian aid to Bosnia and to Bosnian refugees in other states. In May 1993 I met in Zagreb, Croatia, with the representative of MI, who was charged at that very moment with opening a branch in that capital, and with whom I visited a refugee center on the border with Serbia in which there resided many Muslims. MI's world headquarters moved to Zurich in 1989, and it has branch offices in New York and Toronto as well as Kuwaiti City.

78. For an overview of the Renovabis project, see the "Aktionsheft," a twenty-page publicity brochure entitled *Renovabis: "Du erneuerst das Antlitz der Erde"* (1993) and distributed in parishes prior to the first annual collection in May 1993. Dr. Gerhard Albert indicated, in an interview by the author in Bonn November 17, 1992, that the position toward the Europäischer Hilfsfonds (EHF) with regard to funding was "noncompetitive"; however, in a follow-up interview on November 24, 1992, he left me with the impression that some adjustments were likely going to have to be made regarding the Europäischer Hilfsfonds ("it may need to be restructured") once the creation of Renovabis was decided upon.

Author's note: By midyear 1994, the impression abounded among several officials of Catholic aid agencies in various parts of Europe that the fate of EHF was fairly predictable: For the coming year, it would likely carry out its current and pending commitments and then drastically reduce its efforts over the coming year or two; thereafter, it could conceivably close its doors for good once its current director retires.

One reason for this scenario is the recent decision (late 1993 or in the first semester of 1994) of the German bishops to transfer over the next two years their customary allocation made to EHF through the Association of Dioceses of Germany directly to the newly established Renovabis. Another more significant factor is that the unification of Germany, the collapse of the Soviet Union, and the end of the cold war have meant that the German Church is no longer required to conduct its relations with the East indirectly through a "European" funding agency—EHF, located in Vienna—but rather can now do so directly through a German agency—Renovabis, located in Germany (in Freising, outside of Munich).

79. No small reason for KIN's "relative independence" is that it has raised and continues to raise its own funds from among hundreds of thousands of individual donors, residing today primarily in Germany (many of whom, along with their descendants, were likely to have been among the recipients of KIN's aid immediately after the war), in Belgium, and in Holland. In contrast, the EHF had no resource base of its own, receiving the bulk of its funding from allocations of German bishops.

80. *Author's note:* Two months after this essay was completed, the English-language edition of KIN's bimonthly newsletter, *Mirror,* carried the following comment: KIN's "General Council [convened perhaps in October 1993] had reduced our budget from 78 to 69 million dollars. They took this step because of the high dollar, the economic recession and *the founding of 'Renovabis'—the new German relief agency for Eastern Europe that was launched with the intention of spearheading a pan-European campaign"* (*Mirror* 8 [December 1993]:1; italics are mine). This item surely confirms KIN's perception of Renovabis as a potential competitor for the generosity of German Catholics. In this respect, Renovabis—unlike EHF—will operate exactly like KIN as a direct fund-raiser.

81. See Johannes Liehs, "25 Jahre Versöhnungsbotschaft: Zum polnisch-deutschen Bischofstreffen in Gnesen [Gniezno]," *Ost-West Informationdienst des Katholischen Arbeitskreises für zeitgeschichtliche Fragen* (Bonn: Zentralkomitee der deutschen Katholiken—ZdK) 166 (December 1990):62–76. For a fuller historical discussion, see Monticone, *The Catholic Church in Communist Poland, 1945–1985.*

82. Dr. Paul Becher and Dr. Gerhard Albert, interviews by the author, Bonn, November 17 and 24, 1992.

83. The issue was brought home in 1993 by Boris Yeltsin's original "assent" for the Poles and Czechs to become signatories to and participants in NATO and later, under pressure from the Russian military, his reversal of the same policy. On the issue of boundaries, see Immanuel Wallerstein's paper, "La recomposition perpétuelle des frontières culturelles perçues: L'Europe centrale á l'aune d'aujourd'hui," presented at the international colloquium, "L'Europe Centrale: Réalité, mythe, enjeu—XVIIIᵉ–XXᵉ Siècles," held in Warsaw, September 24–27, 1990.

84. Rev. Fr. George Sarauskas, interview by the author, Washington, D.C., October 8, 1992.

85. According to the *Catholic Almanac* for 1991, the Catholic populations numbered as follows: Czechoslovakia, 10,770,000; the former East Germany, 1,279,000; Hungary, 6,490,000; Lithuania, 2,680,000; Poland, 36,085,000; Romania, 1,382,000; Ukraine, ca. 3,500,000 (exclusive of Uniates among Ukrainians in the Diaspora); the former Yugoslavia (primarily in Slovenia and Croatia),

6,717,000; the data for the Ukraine, today considered short by about a million and a half, are taken from Bohdan R. Bociurkiw, "The Suppression of the Ukrainian Greek Catholic Church in Postwar Soviet Union and Poland," in *Religion and Nationalism in Eastern Europe and the Soviet Union*, edited by Dennis J. Dunn (Boulder: Lynne Rienner Publishers, 1987), 97–119. Most of these figures are based on prewar data and do not take into account the high proportion of purely nominal Church members. Up-to-date analyses are beginning to appear; an excellent example of recent survey data is Adrienn Molnár and Miklós Tomka, "Youth and Religion in Hungary," *Religion in Communist Lands* 7 (3) (Autumn 1989):209–229. For Poland, see *Kosciól Katolicki w Polsce, 1918–1990: Rocznik Statystyczny* (Warsaw: Glówny Urzad Statystyczny Zaklad Socjologii Religii SAC, 1991). In Poland in 1985, there were approximately 20,000 priests in all (4,000 are from religious orders that have an additional 5,000 brothers), resulting in a ratio of 5.8 priests per every 10,000 parishioners; 102 female congregations, consisting of 25,000 sisters, operate 2,500 institutions; see Lidia Müllerowa, "La Chiesa polacca dal 1939 ai nostri giorni," in *Storia religiosa della Polonia*, edited by Luciano Vaccaro (Milan: La Casa di Matriona, 1985), 205–218, esp. 216–217.

86. See Przemyslaw L. Falczynski with Witold Laskowski, "The Silent Polish Mission: Catholicism East of Poland," *The Warsaw Voice: Polish and Central European Review* 25 (243) (June 20, 1993):6.

87. The priest was Fr. Tadeusz Pikus, who was dispatched to Russia as the delegate of the Polish Primate to work there among resident Polish Catholics and as the chaplain of a Polish company contracted to preserve monuments. Poles within the former Soviet Union soon thereafter began to organize "ethnically" and along "cultural" lines in response to Mikhail Gorbachev's policy of allowing ethnic or national cultural organizations to flourish alongside those dedicated to "Soviet culture," according to Fr. Pikus, in an interview by the author, Warsaw, June 11, 1993. His recollections are contained in Tadeusz Pikus, *Bylem Swiadkiem Przelomu—wspomnienia z Moskwy, lata 1990–1992* (Warsaw: Fundacja im. Prymasa Tysiaclecia, 1994).

88. Przemyslaw L. Falczynski with Witold Laskowski, "The Silent Polish Mission," 6.

89. "La Chiesa Cattolica in Albania," an undated flyer published in Rome by Besa (Circolo Italo-Albanese di Cultura). The best historical treatment of religion and society is Roberto Morozzo della Rocca, *Nazione e religione in Albania (1920–1944)* (Bologna: Il Mulino, 1990).

90. *Besa-Fede: Corrispondenza del circolo italo-albanese di cultura* (Rome) 72/1993 (March 1993):2.

91. Msgr. Giuseppe Pasini, Director of Caritas Italiana, interview by the author, Rome, March 31, 1993.

92. Fr. Boguslaw Steczek, SJ [Assistant to the Father-General of the Society of Jesus for Eastern Europe], "La compagnie de Jésus dans les pays de l'Est," *Christus: Revue de formation spirituelle* (Paris) 40 (153) (January 1993):119–126.

93. Anatanas Saulaitas, SJ, "Jesuits in Lithuania," in *Jesuits: Yearbook of the Society of Jesus* (Rome: 1993), 92–93.

94. Stanislaw Opiela, SJ, "Russia: A New Independent Region of the Society," in *Jesuits: Yearbook of the Society of Jesus* (Rome: 1994), 36–37.

95. In addition to Ann Carey's brief biography of Bishop Joseph Wirth, SJ, "The Bishop of Siberia," see also Boguslaw Steczek, "Being a Bishop in Siberia" (both cited earlier).

96. See Ralph Della Cava, "The Ten-Year Crusade Towards the Third Christian Millennium: An Account of Evangelization 2000 and Lumen 2000," in *The Right and Democracy in Latin America*, edited by Douglas Chalmers, Maria do Carmo Campello de Souza, and Atilio Borón (New York: Praeger Publishers, 1992), 202–222.

EIGHT

In Defense of Allah's Realm: Religion and Statecraft in Saudi Foreign Policy Strategy

CARY FRASER

The Contemporary Islamic Resurgence[1]

Scholarly attention has increasingly focused upon the role of religion in the politics of the Middle East since the Iranian Revolution of 1979. Despite the revolution's original and continuing impact upon international relations in the late twentieth century, its role as a catalyst in the transformation of international politics has been underestimated. Its immediate consequence was to confer enormous importance upon religion as a factor in the international and internal politics of countries in the Middle East and Persian Gulf. Iran's revolutionary leaders consolidated their rule and legitimacy by invoking Islam as an ideology of state power. The appeal to Islam has not, however, been restricted to the revolutionaries in Iran. Saudi Arabia and other conservative Arab governments have sought to portray the Iranian Revolution as outside of the mainstream of Islamic culture, both because of its origins among the Shiites, a Muslim minority, and its challenge to existing Islamic authorities. On the other hand, militant Islam has also emerged as a political force in societies as diverse as Egypt, Algeria, and the Palestinian territories where Sunni Islam has been the dominant sect. In these latter societies, the Islamic militants have mounted a vigorous and increasingly violent challenge to existing political authorities, which has further expanded the role of religion in the calculus of states in the region.

The Iranian Revolution also represented a significant watershed in the wider international system by pioneering a revolutionary model that did not have its intellectual roots in the secular ideologies of Western revolutionary traditions. The French, American, and Russian Revolutions provided little inspiration for the Islamic revolution; in fact, the Islamic revolution has constituted an antithesis to the Western traditions that had all consciously sought the secularization of state power and authority.[2] The revolutionaries triumphed in Iran against the Pahlavi regime, which was both a symbol of Westernization in the Islamic world and a major American ally in the Persian Gulf. Their success contributed to the perception that the Islamic revolution portended a major reversal in the influence of the West in the Islamic world. As a revolutionary model, Iran threatened also to contest the applicability of Marxist revolutionary traditions in the non-European world, impugning simultaneously Marxist and liberal modernization theories of social and political development. The subsequent collapse of the Soviet Union and other communist states in Europe, and the continuing resistance to Western strategies of social transformation in the Islamic world, have helped to validate the challenge of the Iranian Revolution.[3]

The major powers' opposition to the Iranian Revolution has not diminished its appeal to political insurgents in the Islamic world. The Soviet invasion of Afghanistan in 1979 was one response to the sense of threat felt by the Soviet Union at the emergence of an Islamic revolutionary regime on its border and in close proximity to the Central Asian Republics, which had long-standing ties to the Islamic world.[4] The Soviet invasion of Afghanistan stimulated a response across the Islamic world that, beyond the provision of military and other support for the Afghan resistance movements, mobilized opinion in favor of Islam and Islamic communities threatened by non-Islamic forces or states.[5] Similarly, the tacit approval by the Western powers of Iraq's ill-conceived effort to inflict military defeat upon the Iranian revolutionary government, as well as the U.S. decision to adopt a close strategic relationship with Israel in the Middle East after the collapse of the Shah's regime, were at best ineffective in containing the appeal of the Islamic revolution in the wider Islamic world. Together, the Iranian Revolution, the Western response to the revolution, and the Soviet invasion of Afghanistan have combined to widen the appeal of the Islamic resurgence across the relationship between Islamic societies and the non-Islamic world. More important, the Iranian Revolution assumed a greater importance within Islamic debates about strategies for the reassertion of the autonomy of Islamic societies from Western and other influence.

Though the Iranian Revolution has had a significant impact upon the wider international system, its influence upon regimes in the Persian Gulf, the Middle East, and North Africa has been evolving in ways that suggest that states and societies in these areas will not be able to escape the redefinition of the politics of Islam that were set in train by the revolution. In Lebanon, the Palestinian territories, and Algeria, the growth of insurgent forces under the umbrella of Islam since 1979 has effectively challenged the basis of existing regimes within a context of escalating violence. Both Afghanistan and Sudan have been in a state of civil war for more than a decade, and a fundamental catalyst has been the impact of the Islamic resurgence, which has rendered political alliances unstable in these countries. The increasing polarization of Egyptian politics since the start of the 1980s demonstrates that the country has become a major terrain for the conflict between Islamicist forces and the secularist republican forces that have dominated Egyptian politics since the 1952 revolution. Given the historic role of Egypt in the Islamic and Arab worlds, it is evident that an Islamist victory in Egypt would have enormous consequences for the politics of the Middle East.[6]

The inability of the secularist Iraqi state to defeat revolutionary Iran, despite the enormous resources provided to it by the superpowers, the European states, and Iraq's Arab allies, has also added to the mystique of the Iranian Revolution. The Iraqi failure has compounded further the problems confronting regimes in the Arab world. By the time of the Iranian Revolution in 1979, neither monarchical nor secular republican regimes had been able to create an Arab center of power within the Arab world. However, the foreign policies of the Qaddafi regime in Libya and the Saudi monarchy had emphasized the growing importance of religion in the statecraft of Arab politics prior to the Iranian Revolution.[7] The Libyan revolutionary government had actively begun to support Islamic groups outside of the Arab world, as in the case of Islamic guerrillas challenging the Marcos government in the Philippines. Saudi Arabia also began to use its oil revenues to consolidate a wider constituency in the Islamic world as a means of countering the influence of Arab challengers to its own influence. However idiosyncratic the activities of Saudi Arabia and the Qaddafi regime may have appeared to observers, in retrospect, their activities before the Iranian Revolution would seem to have helped to set in motion the Islamic resurgence that would begin to assume greater importance after 1979. Further, upon the installation of the Islamic regime in Iran, Libya and Syria were among the Arab states disposed to cooperate with the revolutionary government.[8] Saudi Arabia, for its part, willingly collaborated with Iran in supporting the Afghan resistance forces against the Soviets and their allies in Afghanistan, even as it helped to finance the Iraqi war efforts against Iran. Thus, while the Iranian Revolution provoked further divisions among the Arab states, the Islamic resurgence to which it contributed also served as a vehicle for collaboration among Iran and Arab regimes on a variety of issues, including the challenge to the Soviet efforts to assume greater control over Afghanistan.[9]

In addition to the problems that the Islamic revolution posed for Arab regimes, they continued to suffer from the defeats inflicted upon them by Israel in the 1960s and 1970s. The Arab secularist and revolutionary regimes, as well as Jordan, had seen their appeal as champions of the Arab and/or the Palestinian cause undermined even prior to the Iranian Revolution. The Palestinian issue did little to advance the cause of Arab politics. Arab secularist regimes failed to contain Israel, and they used the Palestinian issue to further their own diplomatic and strategic agendas without commensurate benefit to the Palestinians. The deepening divisions in the Arab world and in the Arab League that had been occasioned by the uneven impact upon Arab societies of the oil price increases of 1973, and the Egyptian decision in 1979 to sign a peace treaty with Israel, were both indications of the far-reaching changes that were occurring in the Arab state system. The lack of momentum on the Palestinian issue; the undisputed military superiority of Israel over its Arab neighbors; the failure of efforts to forge a common Arab position in dealing with external actors, particularly the Soviet Union and the United States; and the expulsion of Egypt from the Arab League as a result of its separate peace with Israel—all were symptomatic of the state of pan-Arab politics by 1979. Individually and collectively the Arab states found themselves besieged by a range of issues for which there were no easy solutions.

Notwithstanding their effective collaboration within the Organization of Petroleum Exporting Countries (OPEC) to manipulate the market and price of oil, the Arab states were unable to demonstrate the same level of cohesiveness on a wider range of issues. This paralysis was actually worsened by the changes in oil prices. Windfall revenues accrued largely to the oil-producing Arab states whose influence within Arab councils was out of proportion to their size and population. Further, given the strategic value of oil in the world economy and the heightened oil dependence of the industrialized states upon the Middle East, external actors increasingly exerted their influence in the politics of the region in ways that further accentuated the divisions among the Arab states. In effect, by 1979 the Arab world was a maelstrom in which many of the regimes appeared to be losing their room for maneuver.

In this context, the Iranian Revolution offered an alternative solution to the stalemate of pan-Arab and other nationalist ideologies in the Middle East. The growth of Islamicist militancy throughout the Arab world after the Iranian Revolution cannot be divorced from the perceived bankruptcy of secularist Arab politics. Iran played a direct role in supporting Hizbullah, the Party of God, in Lebanon, Hamas in the Israeli-occupied territories, and the growth of Islamist militancy in Sudan. However, the Islamic resurgence that has spread beyond Iran was also one response by Islamic populations to other problems that they confront.[10] In any event the Islamic resurgence, whether supported by external actors such as Iran, Saudi Arabia, and Libya or domestically generated, has created new politics in individual societies and occasioned new alliances that transcend the secular nationalist and revolutionary politics that has defined the Middle East for much of the twentieth century.

Saudi Foreign Policy: An Historical Overview

One of the major beneficiaries of the transformation of Arab and Islamic politics as a consequence of the Iranian Revolution and the Islamic resurgence has been Saudi Arabia, the guardian of the holy sites Mecca and Medina. It is startling to recognize that Saudi Arabia, a critical actor in the events that have shaped both the contemporary Islamic and Arab worlds, did not exist at the beginning of the twentieth century.[11] The Saudi royal family has been remarkably astute in using its role as guardian of the holiest sites of Islam to secure the stability of the kingdom. As Wahhabis—strict and puritanical adherents of the oneness of God—who have assumed the symbolic leadership of Sunni Islam, thereby displacing the Hashemite dynasties that had exercised that leadership for several centuries, the Saudis have used their control over the religious sites to consolidate their status as a leader within the Islamic world. They have also used their identity as Arab Muslims, together with their status as guardians of the holy sites and their oil wealth, to counter the growth of Iranian influence in Middle East politics.

Thus one major consequence of the Islamic resurgence has been the full flowering of the Iranian-Saudi rivalry for leadership in the Persian Gulf and the wider Islamic world. As the secular Arab states and smaller monarchies suffered from the lack of consensus on a common Arab agenda, Saudi Arabia has found greater room for maneuver vis-à-vis the major Arab states. At the same time, Iran, though limited by the fact that it is not an Arab state, has emerged as an alternative model for polities in the Arab world. Prior to the Iranian Revolution of 1979, it could be argued that the Iranian monarchy and Saudi Arabia had a tacit alliance to contain the secular and radical Arab states in the wider Middle East while competing for influence among the smaller monarchies in the Persian Gulf. In that context, Saudi Arabia was constrained to play second fiddle to Iran since its own ability to exercise influence in the region was limited by the policies of other Arab regimes, particularly the radical governments in alliance with the Soviet Union. Before the Shah's ouster, the heightened Soviet-American rivalry in the region, Iran's assertiveness, and the divisions among the Arab states had continued to limit the role of the Saudi monarchy in the region even as it had been elevated to unprecedented importance as a result of the oil crisis.

The Saudi reluctance to adopt an activist posture in the politics of the Arab state system has its roots in the rise, collapse, and resurrection of Saudi Arabia over the past two centuries. The foundations of contemporary Saudi Arabia were laid in the mid-eighteenth century by an alliance between Muhammad ibn 'Abd al-Wahhab, founder of the Wahhabi movement, which espoused Islamic revival, and Muhammad ibn Saud, a minor shaykh in central Arabia. By the turn of the century, the Saudi-Wahhabi alliance had brought much of the area of the Arabian peninsula under its control. Despite the death of the two principals (Ibn Saud in 1765 and Ibn 'Abd al-Wahhab in 1792), the conversion to Wahhabi Islam by the family of Ibn Saud had provided the cornerstone of the expansion of the shaykhdom under the original shaykh and his successors. However, by 1819, Egyptian and Ottoman hostility to the Wahhabis resulted in the destruction of the Saudi shaykhdom, the execution in Istanbul of the reigning amir, Abdallah, and the forced exile of a large number of the family. For much of the nineteenth century, rivalries among members of the Saudi family reduced the scope of their authority within the Arabian peninsula and resulted in the fragmentation of the realm. By the final quarter of the nineteenth century, the Rashidis, also Wahhabi Muslims, had displaced the Saudis as the dominant family in the Arabian peninsula.[12]

However, the death of Muhammad ibn Rashid in 1897 and the spread of Anglo-German rivalry over the dismemberment of the Ottoman Empire provided an opportunity for the restoration of Saudi authority within the Arabian peninsula. It was an opening that 'Abd al-'Aziz, commonly known in the West as Ibn Saud, a twenty-year-old scion of the family who was in exile in Kuwait, maneuvered over the next three decades to reestablish the Saudi monarchy and consolidate its rule over the political frontiers of contemporary Saudi Arabia. His leadership of the realm from 1902 to 1953 was a critical element in the survival and expansion of the regime through the collapse of Ottoman rule and two world wars. This was also the period of Arab nationalist struggle against the Ottoman Empire and the European imperial powers which spawned the contemporary Arab state system. 'Abd al-'Aziz's longevity was the anchor of the survival of the Saudi state during a period of immense shifts in the political balances and frontiers in the former provinces of the Ottoman Empire. Even as he began to reassert Saudi-Wahhabi preeminence within the Arabian peninsula, 'Abd al-'Aziz was very deliberate in his choice of allies and strategies in pursuing his goals.

One remarkable feature of 'Abd al-'Aziz's reign was his use of Islam to legitimate the political authority of his family within the realm and, simultaneously, to secure the kingdom from external threats, particularly those posed by other Arab dynasties and states that sought to contest the Saudi monarchy's influence. The initial military campaign against the Rashidis by 'Abd al-'Aziz in 1902 was supported by the Sabah ruler of Kuwait, who sought to exploit the divisions among the Rashidis to establish a wider range of Kuwaiti influence in the Arabian peninsula. While utilizing the Kuwaiti support, 'Abd al-'Aziz began to pursue his own agenda for reestablishing Saudi rule. Over the next two decades he supported the establishment of a religious military force, the Ikhwan, committed to *jihad* on behalf of Saudi-Wahhabi rule over the Arabian peninsula. Those forces, and the religious zealotry they represented, were critical to the military campaigns conducted by 'Abd al-'Aziz as he sought to restore Saudi-Wahhabi rule over the areas lost to other claimants, including the Rashidis. Thus, central to the creation of the contemporary Saudi realm was the pursuit of *jihad* under the mantle of Wahhabi Islam. Following the pattern established by the original Saudi amir, the spread of Wahhabi Islam through *jihad* provided the basis for the expansion of Saudi influence over a large portion of the Arabian peninsula. By 1921, 'Abd al-'Aziz had gained decisive military victories over the Rashidi dynasty, which had ruled much of central Arabia after the decline of the original Saudi realm. During this period of Saudi expansion, he also skillfully exploited Anglo-Ottoman tensions to secure recognition for his military gains against the Rashidis.[13]

Beyond his use of the Ikhwan against the Rashidis and their allies, 'Abd al-'Aziz also systematically sought to secure control over the holy cities of Mecca and Medina in order to legitimate the stature of Wahhabi Islam. His strategy was to secure that legitimacy against the pretensions of the Egyptian monarchy and the Hashemite dynasty, which had been the traditional guardians of the sites. After the disintegration of the Ottoman Empire, the Egyptian monarchy and the Hashemites, who were ensconced in Iraq and Transjordan with British support, were competing for the mantle of leadership in the Arab world. By 1926, after a long military campaign against the Hashemites, 'Abd al-'Aziz took control over the Hijaz, the region encompassing the holy cities of Mecca and Medina. However, he was very careful to eschew any claims to the Caliphate and asserted that the Wahhabis' control of the holy sites was for the benefit of all Muslims. In essence, 'Abd al-'Aziz sought to use Islam and the Saudi role as the guardians of the holy sites as the mantle for the territorial expansion of Saudi Arabia and to secure the realm against other dynastic challengers in the Arab world.[14]

Thus from the outset the contemporary Saudi state has stressed the importance of its role as the leader of Wahhabi Islam for purposes of both domestic legitimacy and foreign policy. The propagation of Wahhabi Islam as an integral element of Saudi identity was important for its unifying effect upon the diverse groupings that had populated the Arabian peninsula. The guardianship of the holy sites helped to legitimize the Saudi-Wahhabi realm over other claimants to that role after the dissolution of the Ottoman Empire. Just as important, the Saudis could exploit that status to secure recognition from the European powers and the non-Arab communities in the wider Islamic world. Wahhabi Islam has, as a consequence, been central to the survival and legitimacy of Saudi Arabia since its founding in the first quarter of the twentieth century.[15]

However, notwithstanding the importance of Wahhabi Islam to Saudi Arabia, 'Abd al-'Aziz and his successors have all demonstrated considerable pragmatism in bridling the zeal of Islamic militants when their activities threaten to harm the interests of the state. Despite their importance to his success in reasserting Saudi-Wahhabi influence over the Arabian peninsula, 'Abd al-'Aziz subsequently suppressed the Ikhwan when its military activity in the Hashemite territories challenged his relationship with the British. On the other hand, the religious authorities have also been involved in mediating tensions within the royal family when such tensions challenge the stability of the state.[16] This interpenetration of Islam and state authority has been the rubric by which the royal family has ruled Saudi Arabia since its establishment. In effect, the religious authorities have served as a mechanism for containing the potential damage of factional conflicts within the royal family and helped to maintain the legitimacy of their rule. As the expansion and consolidation of the Saudi realm over the twentieth century shows, Islam served successfully as an instrument for the consolidation of state authority in the Persian Gulf well before the Iranian Revolution. However, unlike in Iran, there has been an implicit contract between the Saudi royal family and religious authorities that has allowed the royal family to withstand domestic and external challenges to the realm; in return, the religious authorities have acquired a virtual monopoly over social life, which has limited the opportunities for the emergence of independent institutions and "civil society" that are to be found in societies in which there is a wider gap between the sacred and secular realms.

Saudi Arabia and the Arab System of States

While the role of Wahhabi Islam has been the central pillar of the Saudi state and foreign policy, Saudi Arabia's emergence as the largest Arab and Middle Eastern producer of petroleum has transformed the context of Saudi Arabia's existence. Saudi Arabia's oil and the increasing demand for it in the Western world redefined the nature of Saudi relations with the major Western powers. As one of the world's largest oil producers, Saudi Arabia was of immediate importance to the Western countries after 1945. However, the country's relatively sparse population, its enormous geographic spread, and its minuscule state apparatus rendered the kingdom vulnerable to threats from its neighbors. As a consequence, the Saudis sought external guarantors for the kingdom's security even as they began to use their increased revenues to develop the infrastructure to expand the state's control over the country. As in the case of the holy sites, Saudi control over a critical resource did not enhance its security but rather rendered it vulnerable to challenges from its neighbors. The Saudis were forced toward reliance upon extraregional actors to compensate for their vulnerabilities vis-à-vis their neighbors.[17]

Until the discovery of Saudi oil during World War II, the kingdom's principal external patron had been Britain. Increasingly thereafter, the United States replaced Britain in the eyes of Saudi rulers as the most important guarantor of Saudi Arabia's survival. This shift in Saudi strategy would seem to have been one consequence of Britain's continued support for the Hashemite kingdoms in Iraq and its continued role in the Arabian peninsula among the smaller Gulf states during and after World War II. The Saudi rulers again displayed great perspicacity in choosing to side with the emerging major external power in the Middle East against the declining influence of the British. Prior to his death in 1953, King 'Abd al-'Aziz demonstrated in his dealings with both the Ottomans and the British a quality of statecraft that was cognizant of the major shifts under way in the international system.

The burgeoning alliance with the United States became increasingly useful in the 1950s as Egypt, under the impact of the revolution and the accession to power of Gamal Adbel Nasser, sought support from the Soviet Union for its efforts to establish itself as the undisputed leader of the Arab world. Nasser's championship of pan-Arabist ideas; secularist, revolutionary, and antimonarchical politics; and his assumption of leadership of the Arab challenge to Western influence and Israel's presence in the Middle East relegated the Saudis to the margins of the Arab state system and Middle Eastern politics.[18] Given the wide appeal enjoyed by Nasser in the Arab world—his rhetoric had powerful resonance within other Arab societies— the very policies he championed were anathema to the continued survival of the Saudi-Wahhabi regime. The overthrow of the Hashemite monarchy in Iraq in 1958, the emergence of the Front de Libération Nationale (FLN) in 1962 in Algeria, and the formation of the Palestine Liberation Organization (PLO) in 1964 with Egyptian support all pointed to the changing political mood and the growing strength of nationalist sentiment within the Arab state system. The creation of a Marxist government in South Yemen, the establishment of a radical regime in Somalia that courted Soviet support, and the overthrow of the Libyan monarchy in 1969 by young military officers also pointed to the growing legitimacy of Nasserite policies within the Arab world and Middle East. In the two decades after the Egyptian Revolution of 1952, Nasser embodied and defined the major shifts in the Arab state system.

In this context, it was perhaps not surprising that the Saudi royal family would search for allies outside of the Arab state system. The United States, Britain, and Iran provided the strategic partnerships and counterweights to the growing influence of Egypt, the Ba'th party, other radical regimes, and the Soviet Union in the politics of the Middle East. Although Saudi Arabia could not single-handedly reverse the course of politics within the Arab state system, it could serve as an interlocutor within that system for the concerns of its Western allies. Thus, in return for Western recognition and support of Saudi Arabia, the Saudi monarchy could serve as a channel of Western influence upon the politics of the Middle East. However, it was not only through these strategic "partnerships" that the Saudis countered the momentum of anti-Saudi developments within the Arab state system. The Saudis also used their status as guardians of the holy sites to consolidate their presence in the wider Islamic world, supporting the Muslim World League and the Organization of the Islamic Conference.[19] As in its initial competition with the Hashemite dynasty, the Saudis used their religious status to secure the support of the wider Muslim world against threats from within the Arab state system mounted by secularist and radical challengers.

Whereas Nasser's rise in Egypt and the Arab world had helped to keep Saudi Arabia on the margins of the Arab state system, Egypt's defeat in the 1967 war with Israel and Nasser's death in 1970 presaged an extraordinary realignment in the politics of the Middle East and catapulted Saudi Arabia to a central role. One immediate consequence of Nasser's death was a surge in competition among Arab leaders to assume the mantle of leadership in the Arab state system. Leaders like Hafiz al-Assad of Syria, Muammar Qaddafi of Libya, and Saddam Hussein of Iraq—representing a new generation of leaders who saw themselves as heirs to the legacy of Nasser— began to compete for leadership. Though the emergence of these new leaders signaled the continuing fragmentation of leadership within the Arab state system, the legitimacy of the Nasserite agenda—pan-Arabism, secularist and revolutionary politics, and the search for an Arab power center capable of defeating Israel and challenging Western influence within the Arab world—was unquestioned among them.

The fate of Egypt under Anwar Sadat was testimony to the power and legitimacy of the Nasserite agenda in the Arab world. Beginning with his decision in 1972 to expel Soviet military advisers in Egypt, Sadat began to reverse the policies that had been adopted by Nasser. Instead, he sought an alliance with the United States, undertook a separate peace with Israel, abandoned the pan-Arabist strategies and revolutionary rhetoric championed by his predecessor, and provided an opening for a greater role for the Islamist forces within Egypt. This reorientation of Egyptian domestic and foreign policies paved the way for the expulsion of Egypt from the Arab League after its agreement to the U.S.-brokered Camp David accords.

Eventually, Sadat himself would be assassinated by Islamists angered by his pro-Western policies and his new relationship with Israel. Egypt's expulsion from the Arab League signaled its marginalization within the Arab state system for adopting policies antithetical to the Nasserite agenda. Within a decade of Nasser's death, Egypt had moved from its position as the dominant Arab state to a pariah state in the eyes of the Arab world.

Egypt's decline as a major player was hastened by the 1967 and 1973 wars against Israel, which revealed its military weakness and inability to become an independent center of power in the Middle East. The decisive Israeli victory in the 1967 war and Egypt's failure to win either a political or military victory in the Yemeni war had tarnished Nasser's and Egypt's image by 1968. Sadat's willingness to abandon Syria in the 1973 war in his efforts to secure a cease-fire with the Israelis provided further evidence to dispute Egypt's claim to be a champion of the Arab cause. Paradoxically, the Arab oil embargo against the United States and the Netherlands during that war proved to be the most powerful and effective instrument in the Arab arsenal against the West. Moreover, its use and effectiveness were critically dependent upon the decision of the Saudi monarchy to join the other Arab states in confronting the West and particularly the United States over its support for the Israeli war effort.[20] The Saudi decision to support Sadat's decision to wage war against Israel and its support for the use of the "oil weapon" against the West catapulted Saudi Arabia to the center of Arab politics at the expense of an Egypt that became even more dependent on Saudi Arabia and the West after the 1973 war.

The 1973 war and the oil crisis provided vivid testimony of the capacity of the Arab states to change the terms of their relationship with external powers through their control of large supplies of a critical resource—oil. This change in their strategic environment enhanced the autonomy of the Arab oil exporters vis-à-vis both external actors and other Arab states, particularly those not endowed with oil resources. These changes accelerated the process of transformation within the Arab world that had been gathering momentum even prior to Nasser's death. With the massive transfers of wealth to the oil-producing states, the Arab states obtained resources to become more active on a variety of fronts. Saudi Arabia, by virtue of its status as the largest oil producer and exporter in the Middle East, became *the* critical player in international oil diplomacy and in the Arab world, endowed with credible leverage over the Western powers.

However, Saudi Arabia had been only one of several beneficiaries of the oil crisis. Libya, Iraq, and Algeria—all under the sway of radical regimes, and themselves major oil producers—began to play more assertive roles within the Arab system of states as well as on the wider international scene. With the declining influence of Egypt after 1973, Syria, notwithstanding its lack of oil resources, emerged as the principal Soviet ally in the Middle East and the most important Arab state in the Arab-Israeli conflict.[21] The leadership of these states sought to acquire Nasser's mantle in support of pan-Arabist and anti-Western policies in the Arab world, though their competition for it did little to further the development of consensus among them.

Pre-revolutionary Iran, despite its pro-Western orientation, had been a leading proponent of oil price increases within OPEC and began to use its own increased revenues to build its military capabilities. As the major non-Arab oil producer in the region, it also became the principal American ally in the region following the Saudi decision to pursue an agenda supportive of the major Arab states. In the wake of the British withdrawal from the Persian Gulf, Iran had increasingly sought to become the dominant power in the region, in competition with both Iraq and Saudi Arabia. It exploited the fears of the smaller Arab Gulf states to contain both the Saudis and the Iraqis, thus exacerbating the tensions among the Arab states.[22]

The shifts in the politics of the Middle East that followed the 1967 war also resulted in increased visibility for the issue of self-determination for the Palestinians. The Israeli occupation of the Palestinian territories represented both military humiliation for the Arab states and the loss of control over Islamic holy sites in Jerusalem. In the already complex political environment of Middle East politics, the issue of Palestinian nationalism thereafter became intertwined with the Jewish-Muslim struggle for control over Jerusalem as a holy city and center of pilgrimage for both religious groups. Within the Arab world, Jordan's failure to safeguard the part of the city under its control diminished the historic prestige and appeal of the Hashemite monarchy. Consequently, Saudi Arabia, as the guardian of Mecca and Medina, assumed greater importance as a religious leader in the Arab and Islamic worlds. However, neither the Jordanian monarchy nor the Saudi royal family, despite their long-standing rivalry and competing claims to guardianship of the holy sites of Islam, could afford to abandon the Islamic claims to a role within Jerusalem. This religious dimension of the conflict with Israel, and the Jerusalem issue in light of Israeli efforts to unify the city and have it recognized as the capital of Israel, emerged as major obstacles to efforts to reach agreement on the future political status of the city. The Saudis' concern with maintaining the strength of their credentials as leaders of Sunni Islam has been a powerful incentive to support both Palestinian nationalists and the efforts to prevent the unification of Jerusalem under sole Israeli authority.

After the 1967 war, the PLO became increasingly important in Arab councils as the major Arab states sought to exploit the Palestinian issue as a path to leadership within the Arab world. With the Black September uprising in Jordan in 1970, which pitted the PLO's guerrillas against the Jordanian monarchy, it became increasingly evident that the failure to address the Palestinian issue could be a critical source of instability for those regimes playing host to large Palestinian populations. After 1973, the Palestinian issue also served as a vivid reminder to the Arab states that, notwithstanding the enormous shift in influence and power that had occurred as a result of the oil crisis, their influence within the Middle East was constrained by the continued military superiority of Israel.[23] Saudi support for the Palestinian cause, the PLO (notwithstanding its early ties to Nasser), and the restoration of some form of Arab suzerainty over the Islamic holy sites in Jerusalem provided it with the opportunity to forge some common ground with its Arab rivals in adopting an anti-Western and anti-Israeli stance in the region.

The oil crisis also brought a new issue to the agenda of the Arab states—one that has added to the volatility of the region's politics—the issue of redistribution of wealth within and among the Arab states. In the 1970s, the Arab oil producers acquired enormous wealth from the increases in the price of oil. However, a central paradox of the Arab state system is that the oil-producing states—with the exception of Algeria and Iraq—are relatively lightly populated. On the other hand, the more densely populated states do not have comparable oil resources that would provide them with the income enjoyed by their OPEC counterparts. As a consequence, states such as Egypt, Syria, Jordan, and Lebanon, which have all borne the burden of the Arab-Israeli conflict, have sought to use their championship of the Arab cause to exert moral claims upon the wealth of the Arab oil producers. The PLO has similarly sought the financial support of the wealthier Arab states to build and maintain its infrastructure in the Israeli-occupied territories. The disparity in wealth among Arab states has created pressures within the Arab world for the wealthier states to assume greater responsibility for the collective well-being of the Arab system of states. As the major Arab oil producer and wealthiest Arab state, Saudi Arabia has assumed the role of financier to the wider Arab community.[24] Given the role of alms-giving in Islamic culture and Saudi Arabia's status as the guardian of the holy sites, it was incumbent upon the Saudi monarchy to maintain its Islamic credentials by adopting that role. Where other wealthy Arab producers—Kuwait, Oman, Abu Dhabi, and the United Arab Emirates—could limit their largesse, Saudi Arabia's status as a religious leader has made it difficult for the Saudis to limit their role as a provider to the Arab world. Thus, even as the oil crisis enhanced Saudi Arabia's influence within the Arab world, it also created a wider web of responsibilities for the guardian of the holy sites of Islam. The Saudi largesse also provided the opportunity for the Saudis to legitimize their pretensions to leadership within the Islamic world, since its traditional rival, the Hashemite monarchy, was rendered increasingly vulnerable by the shifts in Arab politics and its lack of oil wealth.

If the oil crisis helped to move Saudi Arabia to a position of unprecedented influence in the Arab state system, it also placed the monarchy at the center of the conflicts wracking that system. First, the increasingly assertive Iranian monarchy, with open American support, began to extend its influence over the Persian Gulf, to the discomfiture of both Iraq and Saudi Arabia. For the Saudis, Iran's policies effectively undercut Saudi influence in the Gulf and with the United States. At the same time, Iraq sought Soviet support as a means of countering Iran's increasing influence and thus brought the superpower rivalry into the Persian Gulf.[25] The flowering of the Iran-Iraq rivalry, with their associated superpower patrons in tow, followed upon the creation of a revolutionary regime in the People's Democratic Republic of Yemen, the establishment of a revolutionary state in Ethiopia, and the radicalization of Sudan by the Numeiri regime. Even as it moved to the center of Arab politics, Saudi Arabia found the course of events in neighboring countries moving in a direction inimical to its own security concerns.

Before the expulsion of Egypt from the Arab League in 1979, Saudi Arabia sought to nurture a Cairo-Damascus-Riyadh axis that could serve as a counterweight to Iran, Iraq, and Israel.[26] However, the growing influence of the United States in Sadat's strategy and the Soviet encouragement of Syrian military and strategic dependence provided little room for the consolidation of that axis. Beyond its role as the principal Arab oil producer, Saudi influence within the Arab state system continued to be minimal in terms of its ability to influence the course of events. The competition for leadership among the major Arab states, the marginalization of Egypt, and the growing influence of non-Arab states upon the politics of the Arab world had sharply reduced the room for maneuver available to the Saudis.

As in its earlier response to its rivalry with the Hashemite dynasty and the Nasserite challenge, Saudi Arabia after 1973 moved to secure support from actors outside of the Arab state system to compensate for the adverse circumstances in which it found itself within that system. First, it began to cultivate a much closer strategic relationship with the United States, on the basis of the acquisition of military equipment and training for its own forces from American suppliers. However, it also sought to minimize its dependence upon the United States by purchasing weapons systems from other suppliers as well. In so doing, it circumvented efforts by Israel and its supporters within the United States to impose limits upon the technological sophistication and quantities of weapons sold by U.S. suppliers to Saudi Arabia. This search for the development of an independent military capability has increased the relative weight of military institutions in Saudi politics, but the Saudi royal family has been careful to maintain control over them through the appointment of senior officers who are loyal to, or are members of, various factions of the royal family.[27] In addition, there has also been a calculated strategy of using ethnic divisions within Saudi Arabia to limit the capacity of the military from assuming an independent role

through the establishment of the Bedouin-based National Guard as a counterweight to the regular armed forces.[28] This conscious effort to contain the
influence of the armed services reflects both considerations of patronage as
well as maintaining the balance of power among the various institutions of
state.[29]

This sense of vulnerability that has weighed upon Saudi Arabia has been
exacerbated by the fact that the task of defending the country, given its
small population relative to its geographic expanse, is beyond the capacity
of the country's military forces. Hence the U.S. connection serves also as
the means to secure the country's territorial integrity in the event of a threat
to its borders or to the royal family itself. Given the lack of transparency of
the precise nature of Saudi-American military ties and the studied ambiguity of the scale of the U.S. commitment to the Saudi monarchy, it is not in-
conceivable that this opacity has been useful in providing flexibility to both
parties. Saudi Arabia thus enjoys U.S. protection without the need for a formal treaty arrangement that would require a bruising fight within the U.S.
political system. For U.S. political leaders, the current strategy obviates the
need for public discussion of the Saudi-U.S. relationship and its implications for the U.S. relationship with Israel. As in its earlier policy toward the
British under Saud, the monarchy has sought the support of one of the
major Western powers without formal treaty arrangements that would
compromise its claims to leadership of the Muslim world.[30] The U.S. role in
supporting Israel's strategic policies, often at the expense of the Arab states
and the Palestinians, has helped to define the limits of the Saudi-U.S. relationship. Similarly, hostility to the Islamic resurgence has not improved the
U.S. appeal to political sentiment in the Arab world, and the Arab governments, including Saudi Arabia, continue to be wary of being perceived as
participating in U.S. efforts to confront or undermine Islamist forces.

The Saudi Dilemma:
Surviving the Challenge of Islamic Resurgence

The concern with maintaining the legitimacy of the House of Saud within
the Arab world has also informed the Saudi strategy of containing Iranian
influence in the Persian Gulf and Middle East. Beyond its historic pretensions to dominance in the Gulf, revolutionary Iran has pursued an assertive
foreign policy in support of Islamic groups throughout the Islamic world.
That policy, which has been articulated both in terms of a challenge to the
West and the championship of Islam, constitutes a direct challenge to Saudi
Arabia's pro-Western alignment and its claim to leadership of the Islamic
world through its role as the guardian of the holy sites. The Iranian challenge to Saudi Arabia moved it to become active among Shiite communities
across the Arab world, particularly in Lebanon and Iraq. Even in Saudi

Arabia's eastern province, bordering the Persian Gulf, home to a large community of Shiites, Iran's influence has become a source of concern to the Saudi regime. Hence the Iranian challenge to Saudi Arabia has not only been in the wider Islamic world but also represents a potential threat to the domestic stability of the Saudi monarchy through the exploitation of centrifugal tendencies within the Arabian peninsula.[31]

The Saudi response has been to exploit the tensions and conflict between Iraq and Iran, notably through its financial support for the Iraqi war effort against Iran. However, it has also promoted the establishment of the Gulf Cooperation Council (GCC) as a means of containing the influence of both powers among the smaller states and shaykhdoms in the Persian Gulf. A critical element in this Saudi strategy of containing both Iraq and Iran has been its strategic partnership with the United States, which, for its own reasons, has pursued a similar approach of dual containment of Iran and Iraq as a means of maintaining its role as the dominant military and naval power in the Persian Gulf. The Saudi-U.S. partnership has strengthened the Saudi's leverage over the smaller Gulf monarchies within the GCC, and the latter's dependence upon that partnership provides the Saudis with support within the Arab world for its close relationship with the United States. Thus the Iran-Iraq conflict and their individual challenges to Saudi leadership within the Arab world and Persian Gulf have encouraged the Saudi monarchy to develop a strategic alliance with the smaller Gulf monarchies and the United States, which has served to consolidate Saudi preeminence in the Arab state system.

Notwithstanding its success in exploiting the Iran-Iraq competition to contain these states, Saudi Arabia's ability to withstand the challenge that they both pose to the kingdom's security has been and continues to be tested by that ongoing rivalry. Iraq is a secular republican state with a majority of Shiites among its Arab population and a significant Kurdish minority, ruled as a unified state until the Gulf crisis of 1990–1991 by a secular nationalist government with its base in the Sunni Arab minority. This ethnic diversity has been a source of constant centrifugal pressure in Iraq and in the past has fueled the conflict between Iraq and Iran. With the advent of the Iranian Revolution, the loyalty of the Shiite population in Iraq was questioned by the Ba'thist regime, although Shiite soldiers were to prove their loyalty in the eight-year Iran-Iraq War. However, the fear of an Arab Shiite capture of power, with support from the revolutionary regime in Iran, has been a recurrent fear for Saudi Arabia and its allies in the Arab world. As a consequence, the majority of Arab states supported the Ba'th party in Iraq in its rivalry with Iran for fear of the possible radicalization of their own politics through the influence of the Iranian Revolution. This fear was magnified by the transformation of the politics of Lebanon in the 1980s by the increasing militancy of its Shiite population and Iran's growing involvement in that

process. For the Saudi monarchy, with its own Shiite population, the implications of Shiite militancy in Lebanon and their majority status among
Arabs in Iraq posed a fundamental challenge to perceptions of the internal
stability of the Saudi state. The reassertion of Shiite activism in the Arab
world, as a source of contestation of Sunni-Wahhabi preeminence within
the Islamic world, has forced Saudi Arabia to be very wary of the consequences of its relationship with Iran for its own internal stability and its legitimacy in the Arab state system.

But even as the Saudis have been able to win significant support from the
other Arab states against the religious challenge posed by Iran, its relationship with Iraq has revealed the unease that undergirds its relationship with
the secular nationalist Arab states. Concurrently with the decline of Egyptian influence within the Arab state system, Iraq saw its own star gain increasing prominence. As an Arab oil producer, it enjoyed the windfall revenues that followed the oil price shocks of 1973 and 1979. The Iranian
Revolution and the ensuing Gulf War transformed its strategic weight in
the Arab world and the Persian Gulf as its military capabilities were increased exponentially to support the war against Iran. Following the Saudi
lead, many of the other Arab states, especially Kuwait, supported Iraq's efforts on behalf of the "Arab nation" to inflict a crushing military defeat
upon the Islamic revolutionary regime. The increasing reliance of the Gulf
states upon the Iraqi military shield fed Iraq's long-standing ambitions to
become the dominant power in the Persian Gulf. It also encouraged the
Ba'thists' desire to become an independent center of Arab power—a goal
that had been central to the evolution of pan-Arab nationalist thought
throughout the twentieth century. These ambitions inevitably provoked
strains between Saudi Arabia and Iraq as the respective champions of religious and secularist tendencies within the Arab state system, and these
strains were worsened by differences over production and pricing of oil
within OPEC.

Notwithstanding their ideological and strategic competition, both states
are aware of their vulnerability to pressures from revolutionary Iran. The
Iranian Revolution provoked their fears of an expansionist Iran in the Persian Gulf and the Islamic world and triggered concerns about their own internal stability. Both Iraq and Saudi Arabia have large Shiite populations,
which may constitute serious internal challenges to the existing governments; they are both vulnerable to the resurgence of Iranian military and
naval power in the Persian Gulf; their individual and concerted efforts to
contain or marginalize Iran have not succeeded; and both have cause to
fear Iran's championship of Islam as an instrument of state power and its
ability to exploit tensions within and among states in the Arab world.[32]

For Saudi Arabia particularly, it is this latter dimension of Iran's challenge to its leadership within the Arab and wider Islamic world that poses

the most acute problems. The Iranian Revolution had occurred within a context of far-reaching realignments within the Arab state system that revealed the continuing weaknesses of the principal Arab states.[33] While Saudi Arabia had moved from the margins of the Arab state system in the early post-1945 period to a central role by 1979 (largely as a result of its role as the swing producer in the international oil market), its claims to leadership of the Arab world were contested by other Arab states of a more secular persuasion. Even as its status as the guardian of the holy sites had underscored Saudi legitimacy within the Arab and Muslim worlds, the Arab states were never persuaded that the Saudi-Wahhabi monarchy represented the mainstream of the Arab-Muslim system. This paradoxical status was accentuated by the fact that the changes in oil prices that had increased Saudi leverage within Arab circles had been accompanied by growing disparities within and among the Arab states. These growing disparities and the perception among the disadvantaged Arab populations that the thinly populated Gulf states were less than enthusiastic about the welfare of the wider Arab community did little to improve Saudi Arabia's appeal within the Arab world. Further, after 1973, Saudi Arabia's deepening relationship with the United States, the principal ally of Israel, provided even more evidence of the country's ambiguous status within the Arab system of states.

Thus, even as it became more influential in the politics of the Arab world and the wider international system, Saudi Arabia was unable to translate its role as the guardian of the holy sites into a vehicle for assuming the role of ideological center for Arab and Islamic politics. By the early 1980s the gap between the status and the actual appeal of Saudi Arabia as a leader in the Arab world was particularly obvious. The rivalries among the Arab states had by then effectively dissipated their collective success in undermining international support for Israel and achieving greater control over international oil pricing and production—both of which had come to symbolize the reassertion of Arab autonomy vis-à-vis the West. Egypt's decision to sign a separate peace with Israel, Israel's bombing of the Osirak reactor in Iraq, and the Israeli invasion of Lebanon were symbolic of the reversals that invalidated the assumptions of increased autonomy for the Arab states.

This changing context of politics among the Arab states was the backdrop against which the Iranian Revolution unfolded and began to assume wider significance in the Islamic world. It proved to be more than a triumph of anti-Western political forces against a pro-Western regime. It also signaled the return of Islam as an ideology of state power that explicitly challenged both variants of Western secular ideology, capitalism and socialism. In addition, the revolutionary government championed the reassertion of Islamic autonomy within the international system and portrayed itself as a model for capturing state power in Islamic societies. The triumph of the revolutionary forces had been achieved in the face of strenuous opposition from the United States and considerable disquiet on the part of the Soviet Union. That success vindicated the claims of the leadership that the revolution could redefine the role of Islam and Islamic societies within the international system. As a consequence, the Iranian Revolution provided a boost to the legitimacy of Islamic tendencies within Arab societies which had long coexisted with the Westernizing secularist tendencies in Arab politics in the twentieth century and which had remained in competition with that secularist tradition. In effect, the success of the Islamic revolution, in a context of the perceived weakness of the Arab secular regimes, provided a further stimulus to the Islamic resurgence that continues to shake the wider Islamic world. To be precise, the Iranian Revolution's importance lay in its usurpation of one of the key goals of the Arab nationalist agenda legitimated by Nasser—militant Islamicists had proven their success in effectively challenging and humbling the West. The ouster of the Shah and his peripatetic search for a sympathetic refuge before his death, and the conspicuous efforts of the Western powers to refuse him sanctuary, were only the opening gambit in a complex multilayered game in which Western influence would suffer a series of reverses in the Middle East and the Persian Gulf in the decade following the Iranian Revolution. However, as Iran emerged as the foremost challenger to Western influence in the region, its Arab neighbors confronted the reality that with the expulsion of Egypt from the Arab League, there was no credible Arab counterweight to Iran in the region. The increased efforts by the Gulf monarchies to counter the influence of revolutionary Iran contributed to the further fragmentation of the Arab world. The GCC has functioned both as an alliance of the weaker Gulf Arab states against Iran and a mechanism for securing Western assistance against challenges from within the Arab world. Nonetheless, their individual and collective vulnerability, despite their oil wealth, has been highlighted by the emergence of a revolutionary regime in Iran.

However, the Iranian usurpation of the Nasserite-nationalist agenda was only one of the various ways in which the Islamic revolutionary regime disrupted the politics of the Arab state system. As a model for the capture of state authority by Islamist forces and movements, as well as a center for support of such political forces in the Islamic world, Iran's appeal has assumed pan-Islamic dimensions that have spread beyond its original appeal to Shiite Muslims. The growth of Islamist forces in Arab politics now spans the entire range of those who are willing to contest existing regimes through the electoral system to those pursuing their goals through violence.[34] Further, by seeking to legitimize the establishment of an Islamic state, Iran has also undercut the appeal of secular advocates of revolution and Western-influenced revolutionary ideologies. Again, the call to Islam as an ideology of state authority has served to authenticate the Iranian Revolution as a successful example of the rejection of Western influence in the Islamic world.

It is Iran's transformation into a successful symbol of Islamic resurgence that has posed several problems for the Saudi-Wahhabi monarchy. The Saudi support for the Iraqi military buildup as a counterweight to Iran over the 1980s ultimately created a major Iraqi threat to the Gulf kingdoms once the Iran-Iraq War came to an end. At the same time, the Iranians were free to begin the process of reconstruction and the pursuit of an active diplomacy on several fronts that has helped to provide further momentum for the growth of influence for Islamist forces. The growth of Iranian influence in Sudan, Lebanon, and in the Israeli-occupied territories was accompanied by the increasing strength of Islamist forces in Algeria, Tunisia, and Egypt. The rise of Islamist and/or Iranian influence in these Arab societies has forced further realignment within the politics of the Arab state system and the Middle East. In Sudan, Iran has also emerged as a major external influence upon that country's politics, with negative consequences for Saudi Arabia's influence there. Iran's pursuit of its foreign policy agenda in competition with Saudi Arabia has allowed their supporters to play them against each other.

As the Arab Islamist forces have gained momentum and the Iranian regime has consolidated its authority and become more focused on postwar reconstruction and pursuit of a foreign policy agenda which would expedite the reconstruction, Iran's revolutionary shadow has contracted. Since the end of the war with Iraq, Iran has pursued a foreign policy strategy that has been supportive of Islamist forces but in a context of both competition and collaboration with other actors in the Middle East. The search for an end to the Lebanese civil war required the intervention of Saudi Arabia, Iran, Syria, and Israel to manage the confessional conflict within that country. Iran's role as source of support and inspiration for some of the Shiites in Lebanon has allowed it to adopt a posture of protector of Shiite communities in the Arab world. Such a posture has immediate implications for both Iraq and Saudi Arabia, where large Shiite communities have been subject to disadvantages that have on occasion led to explosions of resentment and repression by the governments. The issue of Palestinian self-determination has provided an opportunity for Iran to demonstrate its support for non-Shiite Arabs while embarrassing both Israel and the major Arab states. As a supporter of both the PLO and Hamas—until 1995 when the PLO-Iranian relationship deteriorated as a consequence of the intensification of the rivalry between the PLO and Hamas—Iran's strategic reach was again extended further into the politics of the Arab state system, since its support for the Palestinians transcended its appeal to Shiite communities in the Arab world. While the Saudis have been a major source of financial and diplomatic support for the Palestinian cause, Iran's increasing involvement helped to fuel the rise of Islamist leadership within the Palestinian resistance movements in the territories. The growing strength of the Islamist forces in the Israeli-occupied territories was undoubtedly one of the critical factors that encouraged Israel to seek a negotiated settlement with the PLO on the future of the West Bank and Gaza.

Iran's foreign policy activism has not been restricted to support for Islamist forces in Arab societies. Iran continues to be a factor in Syria's efforts to contain both Iraq and Israel, and in both Lebanon and the Israeli-occupied territories Iran's support for militantly anti-Israeli factions has complicated the peace process. The Iranian activism suggests that the revolutionary regime continues to pursue the regional power strategy adopted by the Shah, though the context in which this strategy is being implemented has been transformed by the increasing weight of the Saudi-American alliance in the politics of the Persian Gulf.

The Saudi strategy of increased reliance upon the United States has proven to be a double-edged sword. While it represents a continuation of the historic Saudi policy of maintaining ties with the Western powers as a means of countering challenges within the Middle East, this dependence has provoked some doubts about Saudi Arabia's ability to maintain its legitimacy as a leading force in the Islamic world. The Saudi monarchy has had to chart a course that balances its need for the Western security umbrella without undermining its Islamic credentials or leads to Saudi Arabia's being perceived as a party to Western efforts to undermine the Iranian Revolution. Similarly, Saudi policy on the Israeli-Palestinian conflict has had to reflect a careful balance by not appearing to sacrifice Palestinian interests for the protection of its own ties to the Western powers, the principal supporters of Israel.[35] In addition, the U.S. determination to guarantee Israeli military superiority in the region has done little to remove the deeply rooted suspicion of U.S. policies among Arab populations. The Saudis have had to be very cautious in their relationship with the United States for fear of being identified as a supporter of Israel.

Since 1979 Saudi Arabia's role as the central player in Arab politics has been the result of the progressive weakening of other major actors in the Arab world. Egypt and Algeria are both beset by the rise of Islamist forces and economic difficulties, and Syria and Iraq have pursued expensive military strategies that have yet to transform them into alternative centers of power in the Arab world. The weakening of the other Arab states has stimulated Saudi efforts to become more active on its own behalf. In a remarkable and unprecedented step, Saudi Arabia went beyond its traditional strategy of wooing Western support to acquire medium-range missiles from the People's Republic of China to boost its defense capabilities. The Saudi decision to purchase the Chinese missiles represented a significant break with its past weapons procurement strategies and, in the proverbial single stroke, changed the strategic equation in the region. Now armed with missiles capable of reaching both Tehran and Tel Aviv, the Saudi defense capacity has been boosted in a manner that has simultaneously lessened its dependence on Western suppliers and provided an opening for a Chinese role in the region. In addition, the Saudis have demonstrated their ability to circumvent Israeli-backed efforts to limit the quantity and technological sophistication of the weapons supplied to Saudi Arabia by the United States. As in its earlier shift from British to American protection, the Saudi monarchy has again exploited changing circumstances in the wider international system to secure itself from threats to its survival.

The Iraqi invasion of Kuwait in 1990 and the subsequent defeat of Iraq by the U.S.-led military coalition in 1991 demonstrated the continuing predicament facing Saudi Arabia in the contemporary Middle East. Saudi Arabia, Kuwait, and the other Arab Gulf states essentially reaped the whirlwind of Iraq's frustration after its war with Iran and were unable on their own to neutralize Saddam Hussein's military adventurism.[36] The Iraqi military that the Gulf states had helped to build was unleashed against them, and in their desperation they were forced to seek support from the international community, particularly Britain and the United States, to contain Iraq. In the wake of Iraq's invasion of Kuwait, the polarization of the Arab world into camps of supporters and opponents of Iraq was resolved only through the U.S.-led intervention that routed Iraq from Kuwait. The intervention shattered the notion of an autonomous system of Arab states, and the destruction of Iraq's infrastructure and much of its military capability rendered moot the idea of an independent center of Arab power. The collective and individual weaknesses of the Arab states were laid bare. In view of its own military vulnerability, Saudi Arabia, the most important of Arab states and guardian of the holy sites, had been forced to secure the support of non-Islamic forces to protect the holiest sites of Islam; the decision to secure U.S. and other assistance provoked debate about the capacity of Saudi Arabia to be an effective guardian of these sites. Both Iraq and Saudi Arabia were later to invoke holy war against each other with support from different elements within the international Muslim community and with the issue of decrees from the religious authorities sympathetic to their cause.[37]

Notwithstanding the military successes of the Saudi-U.S. alliance in the war over Kuwait, the disquiet and the rifts provoked by the decision to pursue the war against Iraq have provoked some concern over the long-term consequences for Saudi Arabia as a result of its role in the war. One immediate consequence of the war has been the consolidation of the Saudi-U.S. alliance against Iraq and Iran in the Persian Gulf. However, the growth of Islamic sentiment in the region, and in Saudi Arabia especially, continues to complicate the royal family's efforts to use U.S. support to maintain its legitimacy. The wave of arrests of Islamic militants and efforts to undercut appeal of Islamic leaders in Saudi Arabia in September and October 1994 suggest that the royal family is less than sanguine about their image as defenders of the faith.[38] The arrests followed upon the public acknowledgment by the Algerian military leadership that it was opening talks with the jailed leaders of the Islamic insurgency in that country, the decision by Saudi Arabia and other Gulf states to lift their trade embargo on Israel, and the successful efforts of religious leaders in Saudi Arabia and other parts of the Islamic world to block the participation of their governments in the United Nations population conference in Cairo in September 1994.

The Saudis are sensitive to the domestic repercussions of their policy positions. Though the royal family has faced Islamic-based opposition on occasion—notably, at the time of the siege of the Grand Mosque in November 1979—dissent since the Gulf War of 1990–1991 has increased markedly. The regime has placed two junior religious officials—Safar al-Hawali and Salman al-'Uda—under house arrest for their public criticisms of the kingdom's alliance with the United States and its pursuit of un-Islamic domestic policies. For the first time in Saudi history, a well-organized and visible oppositional group makes almost daily and broadly distributed criticisms of the regime. The Committee for the Defense of Legitimate Rights (CDLR) combines a number of elements, including religious officials and relatively liberal middle-class professionals. In communiqués, statements, and journals that are distributed via fax, electronic mail, and post from London, where the group is headquartered, CDLR routinely denounces the royal family for its inability to deal with the pressing problems of a deficit-ridden, militarily vulnerable state:[39] "King Fahd bin Abdul-Aziz will be remembered with the Roman Emperor Nero. Fahd too watches while his realm's economic, social and political problems reduce it to nothingness."[40] The group suggests that the government's harsh treatment of critical religious scholars will have unfortunate consequences: "When the regime assaults the houses of scholars of the calibre of Sheiks Safar and Salman, and many others, regardless of their names, status, tribal affiliations, etc., then the regime brings upon itself the hatred of the people and the society as a whole."[41]

On November 13, 1995, a bomb exploded at a National Guard center in Riyadh that, among other casualties, killed five Americans. Several groups claimed responsibility, including the Tigers of the Gulf, the Movement for Islamic Change, and Organization of the Militant Partisans of God. Though it is not clear who makes up these groups, what they specifically demand, and whether they are composed chiefly of Saudis, this incident, along with the daily criticisms of the CDLR, brings home to the government that its very legitimacy—a matter, as I have argued, that is predicated on the acceptability of its religious credentials—is at the core of its security concerns. In this sense, its foreign policy and domestic politics overlap: Because the regime has proposed itself in effect as the Islamic government, whatever it does at home or abroad will have a discernible impact on how Islamic it seems—to its own people as well as to millions of Muslims worldwide who maintain a proprietary interest in the conduct of *khadim al-haramayn* (the servant of the holy places).[42]

Conclusion

Over much of the twentieth century Saudi Arabia has managed to pursue an effective foreign policy strategy that was premised upon the support of Western powers and Islamic opinion. This strategy has allowed the monarchy to consolidate its authority over the country and to withstand challenges from its rivals in the Arab world. As Saudi influence expanded through its emergence as the dominant producer in the international oil market, its strategy continued to serve it well in increasingly radical Arab nationalist and revolutionary politics in the wake of the Egyptian Revolution. However, Western support for Israel and its expansionist policies has forced the Saudi monarchy to rethink its relationship with the Western powers. The Israeli capacity to influence U.S. and wider Western policy toward the Arab world has forced the Saudis to adopt policies that allowed it to distance itself from the West, as it did in precipitating the 1973 oil crisis that helped to bring about both a cease-fire in the October War and a reevaluation of the Arab-Israeli conflict among the Western powers. Similarly, the failure of Nasser and his successors and rivals to develop an independent center of Arab power has done little to improve the context of Saudi Arabia's existence. It has become the dominant Arab state by default, not through the fulfillment of its own ambition. Its roles as the key to supply and pricing in the international oil market and guardian of the holy sites have conferred upon the kingdom a preeminent status, which, as the second Gulf War showed, is difficult for the kingdom to sustain without significant external assistance.

Iran's emergence as the tribune of the contemporary Islamic resurgence as well as its power potential has redefined the limits of Saudi Arabia's foreign policy strategy. It is possible to argue that Saudi unwillingness to encourage a permanent Western land-based deterrent force in the Persian Gulf has been influenced by Iran's intransigence on this issue.[43] Even as it has usurped the Arab nationalist and revolutionary agenda, Iran's active propagation of the contemporary Islamic resurgence has opened the opportunity to challenge Saudi claims to leadership within the Islamic world.[44] Given this adverse external environment, it is evident that the Saudi royal family will continue to pursue a strategy that marries the use of religion to more pragmatic instruments of state policy to secure its rule from both religious and secular challenges.

NOTES

I would like to thank James Piscatori, Susanne Rudolph, and John Waterbury for their comments on an earlier version of this chapter as well as for their support and encouragement.

1. This term is borrowed from John L. Esposito, *The Islamic Threat: Myth or Reality* (New York: Oxford University Press, 1992), 11. Esposito's book is a masterly survey of the Islamic Resurgence and its multidimensional nature without succumbing to hysterical overstatement of the "threat" that is imputed to the wide range of processes of intellectual and social transformation that it covers.

2. It is this anomalous dimension of the Iranian revolution that has confounded analysts confronted by the legitimacy of the Islamic revolution for millions of Muslims, since its very rejection of Western ideological influences resonates with the wider Third World challenge to Western notions of the inherent supremacy of Western intellectual paradigms and political models. For an interesting comment on the parallels between the rhetoric of Ayatollah Khomeini and Third World nationalists, see "Eric Rouleau Talks About the Peace Process and Political Islam," *Journal of Palestine Studies* 22 (4) (Summer 1993):45–61.

3. For a revealing official Iranian view of both the Islamic resurgence and the implications of the Iranian revolution for that resurgence, see Dr. Kamal Kharrazi, "Iran and Islamic Revivalism," *Middle East Insight* 9 (4) (1993):17–19. Dr. Kharrazi was at the time his country's permanent representative to the United Nations and had been deputy minister for political affairs for the Islamic Republic in 1979 and 1980. According to Kharrazi, "the Islamic Revolution in Iran gave momentum to the Islamic awakening which was already in progress. Undoubtedly, what happened in Iran in 1979 seriously challenged the notion of Western hegemony. It was vivid testimony to the fact that Muslims can overcome militaristic pro-Western regimes if they are devoted. It strengthened all Muslims who were of the view that Islamic communities can change their destinies by themselves. Furthermore, the Islamic Revolution was conducive to the asserting of religion in the main domain of life in non-Muslim communities as well."

4. Though the initial Soviet invasion may have been triggered by the escalation of struggles among factions within the Afghan communist party and the state, the potentially unsettling consequences of the Iranian revolution and the fear of an Islamic resurgence within the Soviet Union's borders were critical dimensions of the effort to deny victory to the Islamic resistance forces and their allies. For a discussion of Soviet policy toward Afghanistan see Raymond L. Garthoff, *Détente and Confrontation: American-Soviet Relations from Nixon to Reagan* (Washington, D.C.: Brookings Institution, 1985), 887–965; Shirin Tahir-Kheli, "The Soviet Union in Afghanistan: Benefits and Costs"; and Edward A. Corcoran, "Soviet Muslim Policy: Domestic and Foreign Policy Linkages," in *The Soviet Union in the Third World: Successes and Failures,* edited by Robert H. Donaldson (Boulder: Westview Press, 1981).

5. One interesting long-term consequence of the mobilization of Islamic sentiment was the decision of Islamic volunteers to go to the assistance of Bosnian Muslims in the former Yugoslavia. See "Muslims from Abroad Join in War Against Serbs," *New York Times*, November 14, 1992. Of even greater interest is the report

that, in Algeria, experienced fighters from the Afghan war have apparently become part of the insurgency against the Algerian government. See "Militant Islam's Saudi Paymasters," *The Guardian,* February 27, 1992.

6. For a discussion of the implications of the escalating conflict between Islamicists and the Egyptian government, see Bradford R. McGuinn, "The Islamic Challenge in Egypt: Has It Reached the Point of No Return?" *Middle East Insight* 9 (1) (1992):61–68.

7. For a discussion of the role of Libya in promoting Islamic solidarity as a foreign policy strategy, see Esposito, *The Islamic Threat,* 79–87. For the Saudi role, see James Piscatori, "Islamic Values and National Interest: The Foreign Policy of Saudi Arabia," in *Islam in Foreign Policy,* edited by Adeed Dawisha (Cambridge, England: Cambridge University Press, 1983), 33–53.

8. Syria also established an informal alliance with Iran in an effort to contain Iraq and to manage relations in Lebanon in response to the growth of Shiite political and military influence in Lebanon. However, that alliance did not constrain the Syrian regime's brutal suppression of the Islamicist forces within Syria, nor did this Syrian action lead to a rupture in relations between Iran and Syria. The pragmatism that has shaped the Syrian-Iranian relationship reflects the multidimensional strategy that has informed Iran's foreign policy even as it has exploited the Islamic resurgence for purposes of revolutionary legitimation.

9. The shared sentiment in the Middle East about the Soviet invasion was probably best demonstrated by the reaction of Iran and Iraq. Even as the two states were in the throes of escalating conflict in late 1979 and early 1980, both openly criticized the Soviet intervention. See Oles M. Smolansky with Bettie M. Smolansky, *The USSR and Iraq: The Soviet Quest for Influence* (Durham, NC: Duke University Press, 1991), 214–229.

10. The Islamic resurgence has not been restricted to those societies in which Muslims are in a majority. The resurgence has resonated with Islamic populations in France and Britain, particularly around issues such as education and the relationship between the state and religious communities. See Esposito, *The Islamic Threat,* 175–181.

11. I have relied extensively upon Nadav Safran, *Saudi Arabia: The Ceaseless Quest for Security* (Cambridge, MA: The Belknap Press of the Harvard University Press, 1985), for information on the evolution of Saudi Arabia over the twentieth century. While Safran's work has an enormous amount of detail on Saudi foreign and security policies, its depiction of Saudi Arabia tends to emphasize the vulnerability and weakness of the country. If the focus is shifted to the ways in which the Saudi-Wahhabi state has played its limited hand and built a series of interlocking relationships with a wide range of powerful actors in the international system, Safran's perceptions would need to be revised to develop a more complex and nuanced assessment.

12. For historical background on the earlier Saudi realm and the rivalry with the Rashidi dynasty, see Madawi Al Rasheed, "Durable and Non-Durable Dynasties: The Rashidis and Saudis in Central Arabia," *British Journal of Middle Eastern Studies* 19 (2) (1992):144–158.

13. For the foreign policy of the Saudi kingdom in the early twentieth century, see Piscatori, "Islamic Values and National Interest," and Safran, *Saudi Arabia.*

14. See Piscatori, "Islamic Values and National Interest," 33–38.

15. Safran, *Saudi Arabia*, 28–72.

16. Ibid., 100

17. Ibid., 28–72, and Piscatori, "Islamic Values and National Interest."

18. This assessment does not imply that Saudi Arabia was unimportant but rather that its capacity to define the political agenda of the Arab world was both limited and inconsequential. For an overview of the course of Arab politics prior to Nasser's death, see William L. Cleveland, *A History of the Modern Middle East* (Boulder: Westview Press, 1994), 304–323. However, the Saudis had already demonstrated by 1950 their sagacity in negotiating with Western oil companies to acquire higher levels of revenue and control over their oil reserves. Their strategy would be adapted by other oil-producing countries, and it paved the way for the creation of OPEC and the oil weapon of the 1970s. For a discussion of Saudi Arabia's deliberate management of its oil resources as a political instrument, see Daniel Yergin, *The Prize: The Epic Quest for Oil, Money, and Power* (New York: Simon & Schuster, 1991).

19. Piscatori, "Islamic Values and National Interest," 40–41.

20. For a discussion of the Saudi decision to participate in the embargo, see Yergin, *The Prize*, 606–610, and Safran, *Saudi Arabia*, 153–155.

21. See Kassem M. Ja'far, "The Soviet Union in the Middle East: A Case Study of Syria," in *Soviet Interests in the Third World*, edited by Robert Cassen (London: Sage/Royal Institute of International Affairs, 1985), 255–283.

22. The U.S. decision to strengthen ties with the Shah was influenced by both Iran's obvious endowments and its decision in 1973 not to join the embargo against the United States. See Yergin, *The Prize*, 645.

23. For an overview of the Palestinian issue and its role in Arab politics, see Eric Rouleau, "Comment les fractures et les surenchères ont affaibli le monde arabe," *Le Monde Diplomatique*, October 1993.

24. For a discussion of Saudi foreign aid, see Piscatori, "Islamic Values and National Interest"; see also "Les financiers de l'intégrisme," *Le Nouvel Observateur,* July 19–25, 1990.

25. For a discussion of the evolution of the Soviet-Iraq relationship, see Smolansky, *The USSR and Iraq*.

26. Safran, *Saudi Arabia*.

27. Mordechai Abir, *Saudi Arabia: Government, Society, and the Gulf Crisis* (New York: Routledge, 1993), 119. Further, according to Safran, the younger members of the royal family have become entrenched in the higher echelons of the army, the public sector, and large private businesses. See Safran, *Saudi Arabia*, 219.

28. James Piscatori was kind to draw this distinction to my attention in his review of this essay.

29. For an overview of the evolution of factional politics within the Saudi royal family, see Alexander Bligh, *From Prince to King: Royal Succession in the House of Saud in the Twentieth Century* (New York: New York University Press, 1984).

30. For details of the Saudi-U.S. relationship, see Ronald D. McLaurin, "Foundations of the Saudi-American Security Relationship," *Middle East Insight* 8 (4) (1992):36–42, and Safran, *Saudi Arabia*.

31. Shiite discontent in the late 1970s and the Saudi monarchy's response to it are treated in Abir, *Saudi Arabia*, 79–89. Abir also addresses the growing assertiveness of religious figures and the sensitivity of the regime to this militancy in recent years; see 155–159.

32. For recent discussions of the changing context of international relations in the Persian Gulf, see James A. Bill, "The Resurrection of Iran in the Persian Gulf," *Middle East Insight* 8 (4) (1992):28–42; Shahram Chubin, "Iran and the Gulf Crisis," *Middle East Insight* 7 (4) (1990):30–35; Olivier Da Lage, "Regain d'activisme dans le golfe: Illusoire sécurité collective sans l'Irak et l'Iran," *Le Monde Diplomatique*, February 1993; and, Shireen T. Hunter, "Persian Gulf Security: Future Challenges," *Middle East Insight* 9 (1) (1992):22–27.

33. For a gloomy assessment of the evolution of inter-Arab politics, see Samir Kassir, "The Princes of Our New Disorder: The Arab World After the Gulf War," *Beirut Review* 5 (1993):3–11.

34. Or, as in the case of Algeria, those who have been denied a political role through the disruption of the electoral process have now embarked on an insurgency against the regime. See Gerard Grizbec, "Sale guerre en Algérie," *Le Monde Diplomatique*, August 1993.

35. See McLaurin, "Foundations of the Saudi-American Security Relationship."

36. See Tom Kono, "The Economics Behind the Invasion," *Middle East Insight* 7 (4) (1990):36–41.

37. For an account of the controversy and the decisions, see "Saudis Decree Holy War on Hussein," *New York Times*, January 20, 1991.

38. See Youssef M. Ibrahim, "Saudi Arabia Arrests 110 Muslim Militants," *New York Times*, September 28, 1994.

39. For information on problems confronting the Saudi regime, see "Saudi Arabia's Future: The Cracks in the Kingdom," *Economist*, March 8, 1995, 21–22, 25.

40. Communiqué of Committee for the Defense of Legitimate Rights, *Monitor*, February 27, 1995, 1.

41. Committee for the Defense of Legitimate Rights, *Monitor* 65 (15 September 1995), transmitted via electronic mail.

42. The level of Saudi sensitivity to criticism of its image has recently been revealed by the British decision to expel the head of the London-based CDLR, Mohammed Masaari. The British decision was reportedly taken as a consequence of Saudi pressures, including a threat to future business with British companies. See "Britain Expels Saudi Dissident," *Washington Post*, January 4, 1996, and "Britain Faces Criticism for Ordering Saudi to Leave," *New York Times*, January 5, 1996. The CDLR's focus on corruption in Saudi Arabia and among members of the royal family has been systematic and aimed at undermining the legitimacy of its Islamic credentials. See "Saudi Trial May Air Allegations of Wide Corruption by Leadership," *Washington Post*, January 2, 1996.

43. The Iranian foreign minister, Dr. Ali Akbar Velayati, referred to conversations with GCC officials in which Iran made it known that it expected to be a full participant in any new security order developed in the Persian Gulf. He also reiterated opposition to the U.S. presence in the region. See "An Exclusive Interview with Dr. Ali Akbar Velayati," *Middle East Insight* 7 (5) (1991):6–9. Iran has also

opposed the Damascus Declaration, which proposed an alliance of the GCC member states and Egypt and Syria with the two non-Gulf states playing a major role in the security arrangements for the Gulf. See M. Zuhair Diab, "The Debate over Gulf Security," *Middle East Insight* 9 (4) (1993):12–16. With Iraq's military capabilities diminished by the war for Kuwait and focused upon maintaining the territorial integrity of the country, Iran has been afforded the opportunity to rebuild its own military forces. A permanent U.S. presence in the region is likely to increase Iran's efforts to bolster its own military forces and escalate tensions with the Gulf states. It would seem that Iran and Saudi Arabia are currently engaged in efforts to find an accommodation that would reduce the need for external involvement in Persian Gulf security arrangements. See Bill, "The Resurrection of Iran in the Persian Gulf," and Hunter, "Persian Gulf Security."

44. Chubin argues that: "The Islamic Republic of Iran has always sought a constituency larger than the Shia of the Muslim world and has seen the emphasis on 'Arabism' as false and unreal." See Chubin, "Iran and the Gulf Crisis," 35. This Iranian activism has made it difficult for the Saudis to withdraw their funding from groups or states even when their policies may be inimical to the interests of the Saudi state. See "Militant Islam's Saudi Paymasters," and Piscatori, "Islamic Values and National Interest."

PART THREE

Reflections

NINE

Dehomogenizing Religious Formations

Susanne Hoeber Rudolph

Religion as Master Variable?

To argue as this volume that religion must be taken into account as a significant determinant in international relations and world politics is not to argue that it is a master variable like the mode of production, overriding all others. Political actors have choices; historical events and ambiguities in the social structure offer them alternatives. Religious identities are part of a bundle of identities defining historical actors. Elements in the bundle acquire greater or lesser saliency depending on the ebb and flow of historical events and actors' attempts to situate themselves.[1] Thus "Iraq" has several possible constructions: national identity (Iraq); religious identity (Muslim); "sectarian" identity (Sunni); ideological/policy identity (secularist-socialist). At particular moments in the contemporary history of Iraq, different elements have defined the field of action. Dominant identifications result from interaction between the subject and historical opportunities. Religion competes for primacy with alternative categories of interest and identification. It is as likely to be used instrumentally to justify other interests as it is to be the dominant interest.

Totalizing explanations are likely to miss more fine-grained interests and motivations that lead to war and peace. Samuel Huntington has suggested that "Civilization identity will be increasingly important in the future, . . . and the most important conflicts of the future will occur along the cultural fault lines separating these civilizations from one another," where civilization is defined primarily in religious terms; this notion sits uneasily with the perspectives of our contributors. That Huntington's nine "civilizations"—North American, European, Confucian, Japanese, Islamic, Hindu, Slavic-Orthodox, Latin American, and "possibly African"—will serve as two ideologies did during the cold war seems improbable. This list provides a curious array of sorting principles: ethnic markers (Japanese, Latin American); territorial markers (North American, European); religious markers (Islamic, Hindu); and the mestizo category, "Slavic-Orthodox."[2]

Such macro-categories, advanced as determinants for international actors, ignore the contest over relevant identities. One can find some support for "Islam" as a unifying transnational political principle among theologians. The late Maulana Mawdudi, an influential and respected Muslim scholar of British India, regarded nationalism as an immoral tyranny imposed by the West. He believed that Muslims had once held common citizenship in an Islamic *umma* of brothers in the faith traveling freely across state boundaries. But his is not a dominant view. "An intellectual consensus developed" among Muslims, writes James Piscatori, "which sees the nation-state as part of the nature of things and perhaps even inherently Islamic."[3] Mawdudi's vision was itself a romantic abstraction from the contest over Islam. Shia-Sunni conflicts, like Catholic-Protestant conflicts of the seventeenth century, remind us that intrafaith differences may be as bloody as those between faiths, especially when they coincide with dynastic or state boundaries—as the history of post-Reformation Europe demonstrates.

Macro-determinants treat states as billiard balls rather than as agents. States are not simply victims of determinants such as "civilization" or "religion." They can and do use them and shape them in policy formulation and strategic choices. It seemed as plausible for Francis I of France to ally with Suleiman and the Ottomans against his fellow Christian Charles V and for Iraq to fight its fellow Muslims in Iran as for either to ally with their co-religionists. "One of the three great contestants was Moslem," writes Eugene Rice of the chief conflict that agitated early sixteenth-century Europe, "yet the fundamental alliance of the period was between the Most Christian King of France and the Infidel Sultan [Suleiman] against their common enemy, the Holy Roman Emperor, the temporal head of Christendom. Even the pope received a Turkish pension, in return for keeping a rebellious brother of the sultan in captivity."[4]

If religiously driven civilizational categories do not help much in understanding cleavages in the recent past of the Middle East, neither will they help to identify critical cleavages of the twenty-first century. In contrast, Cary Fraser's essay in this volume historicizes the categories that have characterized the Middle East. He not only suggests their considerable fluidity but also demonstrates the way in which states as agents use religion. Today's dominant category—Islamic—by which both insiders and outsiders would characterize Middle Eastern states is not the same as that prevalent in the 1960s—"pan-Arabic." Numerous nonreligious categories have functioned to structure solidarities in the Middle East, a fact that seems to have dropped from memory as observers focus mainly on religious identities.

Pan-Arabism and Islamic solidarity are alternative ways of defining the regional state system of the Middle East. Pan-Arabism, at its high point with the preeminence of Nasser's Egypt, stood forth as anti-imperial, antimonarchical, nationalist, secular, socialist, and populist-authoritarian. "Islam" has revealed a variety of sociopolitical faces, some of which reflect the radical side of the superseded pan-Arabism. The new militant Islam valued by Algeria and Iran has transformed the anti-imperialism of the 1960s into a diffuse, religiously tinged anti-Westernism. Khomeini-inspired Islamists and those of the Front Islamique du Salut (FIS) suspect secularism as an antireligious stance,[5] hold to antimonarchical and populist authoritarian propensities, and opt for what one might call private socialism, that is, the egalitarian thrust of socialism without its statist implications.[6]

Whereas pan-Arabism and Islam are alternative ways of conceptualizing the Middle East state system, a significant contest for the definition of Islam divides what one might call the old and the new Islam. Saudi Arabia and Iran confront each other as the traditionalist and conservative protector of the holy shrines of Islam on the one hand and the leader of a populist, radical Islam on the other.[7]

The term *religion*, as the foregoing reveals, has an illusory quality. In characterizing Middle Eastern religious solidarities, one employs a whole set of descriptors that have very little to do with religion. "Religion" is the carrier and summary of wider, more diffuse identifications. For the socialist agnostics who helped to found Israel, Judaism was a cultural and historical trope more than a "religion." Or witness the Greek political struggle over the significance of "Orthodoxy"—a signifier only partly impregnated with religious meaning. Greeks opting for solidarity with Europe skirt Orthodoxy and identify with a rationalist Hellenism. Greeks who want to embrace a Balkan or even Asian identity deny Hellenism, explore Orthodox solidarity with Serbia and Russia, or dream of Constantinople and the empire of the East.[8]

The uses to which a religiously defined concept of "civilization" can be put recall the problems of previous intellectual totalizations. In retrospect, it is generally recognized that the category "communism" obscured many aspects of policy choice that might have served the cause of peace. The insistence that Vietnamese communists were an organic component of a metaphysically constructed whole that included the Soviet Union, China, and Vietnam veiled the divisions between Southeast Asian and East Asian nationalisms and between China and the Soviet Union. A more particularizing vision might have seen that Vietnam's relationship with China resembles Pakistan's with India. Recognition of diverging tendencies might have dictated different alliances and acts of strategic balancing than did the focus on a "communist" totality.[9]

Categories affect security by the way they define threats and opportunities. Recognizing that categories are contested and internally differentiated is more fruitful than using static, totalizing wholes such as "Islam," "Christianity," or "Orthodoxy." An account of how such wholes are constantly disrupted may yield a better understanding of present and future alliance patterns than an account of timeless civilizational homogeneity.

Is Religion Part of Civil Society? Theoretical Questions

How should we think about the relationship of "religion" to the concept of "civil society," whether transnational or domestic? Is religion part of the "civil"? Is the concept of civil society universal, or is it peculiarly Western? In this volume Ousmane Kane, himself in part an inheritor of French rationalist traditions, defends the proposition that religion in a non-Western society—here the Tijaniyya (Sufi) orders in West Africa—can be construed as components of civil society. Don Baker, in his account of how East Asian states deal with religion, raises the possibility that in the "East" there is no autonomous space for civil society and that religion does not create such space.

Few would challenge the claim that nonstate actors such as environmental and human rights NGOs operating in world policy space and multinational industrial, financial, and service firms operating in a global economy are components of transnational civil society.[10] But modern mentalities often perceive religious actors in transnational space as a different breed, a different order of being from NGOs and multinational firms.[11] NGOs and multinationals are seen as denizens of modern society; NGOs are seen as occupying public space, while religions reside—or ought to reside—in private. The definitions of religion created by enlightenment polemics are read as natural. For modern enlightenment rationalists, religion invokes at best the nonrational, transcendent, and "otherworldly," and at worst the irrational, superstitious, and magical.

The modern sociological imagination objects to the idea that religious formations are components of civil society on other grounds, that religious affiliations are assigned by ascription, that they are inherited identities rather than chosen ones.[12] Sociological theories of ascription offer nonbiologistic ways of perpetuating biological determinism—inheritance is destiny. But is acquiring a religious identity at birth really the same as—or even like—acquiring blue eyes, a five-foot-three-inch stature, or left-handedness? Such attributes are said to be genetic and in that sense "natural" and beyond choice. But religious identities are different. They are subject to individual, collective, and institutional construction and reconstruction. Persons by themselves or in a variety of contexts can and do reshape the religions into which they were born by acts of interpretation and praxis.[13] In that sense religious formations are, like other organized forms of social life in civil society, intentional.

Before the onset of modernization processes in the second half of the twentieth century gave new life and meaning to religion, the nineteenth-century United States provided dramatic evidence of how religious formations helped to shape civil society. Both Alexis de Tocqueville and Max Weber, observing America's low stateness seventy-five years apart, noted the proliferation of voluntary associations, clubs, and marching societies.[14] Weber especially noted the role that sectarian movements had played in laying the basis for American associationalism.[15] Both men stressed the religious dimension of America's remarkable associational life.

Is civil society a "Western" cultural construct and therefore inappropriate for theorizing non-Western contexts? Don Baker's account in this volume of the relationship between states and religions in East Asia suggests that Asian state doctrines and practice do not recognize a separate space for religion. "There was no word for religion as a separate and distinct sphere of life," he writes, and religions were not "seen as inherently different from other forms of communal activity." Furthermore, they "were expected to recognize that the locus of ultimate authority was the state. The little autonomy religious communities did enjoy, they enjoyed only because of neglect or indifference by the state, and this autonomy could be violated by the state at any time the state chose to do so."[16] The lack of an autonomous space for religion suggests a weak articulation of civil society.

Baker tells us that East Asian states granted some autonomy to what they called worldwide religions but did so as a consequence of international threats and unequal treaties made by Western imperial powers. Eventually all three East Asian countries, China, Japan, and Korea, de-transnationalized the "World Religions" (Buddhism, Christianity, Islam), that is, they brought them within state corporatist regimes. They allowed them to operate on the condition that they sever foreign connections and communicate abroad only through state channels, accepting state control of appointments and finances. Rather than being representatives of transnational bodies, their leaders became delegates of the sovereign nation-state to the international arena.

At the same time, though, recent analyses of East Asia examine more seriously some of the religious communities that were earlier ignored or scorned.[17] Dissident or rebellious popular religiosity associated with Buddhism, Taoism, and the pervasive secret societies in China now commands considerable scholarly attention. Evidently religiosity carved out unlicensed and unregulated spaces beyond the state's reach. Such voluntaristic, state-challenging formations make credible recent scholarly claims that East Asian countries too were sites of "civil society."

Recent reports from the People's Republic of China confirm both Baker's account of state-entwined religious corporate formations and accounts of a civil society populated in part by extensive dissident religiosity.[18] The PRC officializes religions by recognizing and monitoring Buddhist, Taoist, Protestant, Roman Catholic, and Islamic formations. Parallel to these official churches are underground churches and private worship. In the 1990s they are said to have proliferated widely. Estimates of Christians, for example, ran from 8 or 9 million, the government figures, to 80 million, the figure given by Christians.[19] In early 1994 the government tried to check the tide by barring underground worship, allowing services only in sanctioned churches, and barring foreign religious activity.[20] The precautions suggest that in China, as in South Korea and Japan, religion is becoming an important part of civil society, sustained in part by transnational civil society.

Effect of "High" and "Low" Religion on State-Society Relations

Regardless of whether the model is storefront Pentecostalism in Latin America, Singapore, or Moscow, or the educational, devotional, and social service organizations of Islam in Egypt, London, New Jersey, and Sudan, acephalous religion from below is clearly as visible and influential a force as religion from above. Variations among religious formations suggest that civil society can take diverse forms. Self-generating, self-inventing forms of religiosity are proliferating, initiated and propagated by the local devout through informal, loosely coupled networks. These forms prevail as much as the religion of imams or bishops and the high orthodoxy of certified religious discourses.

What implication has this proliferation for the relationship between states on the one hand and domestic and transnational civil society on the other? Are bureaucratic and centralized forms more powerful agents of diffusion domestically and across state lines, or informal and local religious associations? How spontaneous, how guided, are transnational religious movements? To what extent are they "agents" of Rome/Mecca/Washington/Dallas? When and why do states and transnational religion collaborate? When and why do they conflict?

At an early meeting of the panel that led to this volume, James Kurth reminded us of the "original metaphor" of religious transnationalism that often furnishes the minds of Western observers when they imagine the organization of high religion: the (Catholic) Universal Church, its national churches with their conferences of bishops, and the Church's ambassadors to the outer world, its religious and lay orders, Jesuits, Franciscans, Opus Dei. The model is one of hierarchy, guided development, and leadership from a "center."[21] It is the model that animates Ralph Della Cava's and

José Casanova's essays on the "new" Universal Church in this volume.[22] Yet most world religions have spread without dependence on hierarchy and guidance and have no center. Mecca and Benares are sacred cities. They are not the seats of hierocrats in charge of a sacred bureaucracy. The major force in the propagation of Islam was not the high Islam of urban orthodoxy, its ulema and Arabic exegesis. It was the peripatetic Islam of unregulated entrepreneurs, of the Sufi orders, lineages, and individual Sufis who propagated the faith most assiduously, guided by an inner vocation or a conventional proselytizing routine rather than a formal structure.

The Weberian and modernist bias in the social sciences asserts that centralized, "rationalized" organizational structures are more likely to be effective than loose and disarticulate ones, "effective" here referring to the capacity widely to diffuse a religion. In a Festschrift dedicated to Juan Linz's approach to religion, Brian H. Smith summarizes one view of the power of rationalized bureaucracies: "[W]orld religions with very little organizational depth are less effective in sustaining political action over time." He worries that Hinduism, for example, cannot provide "a ready conduit for ... ideas out into wider society since it lack[s] a network of church buildings and schools to spread [the] message."[23] It is a bewildering assertion, given the wide proliferation of Hinduism across Southeast Asia to Indonesia.

Ralph Della Cava's essay in this volume, which features the forays of the major European and U.S. Catholic philanthropies into the Eastern European arena in the wake of communism, takes a similar position. Della Cava doubts that religious formations arise spontaneously and autonomously, or that spontaneous diffusion can be effective. A certain amount of institutional engineering from the top, he insists, is important for religious success. "Today, global church networks of material and religious support and of available qualified personnel influence significantly both the ability of and the terms on which so-called 'spontaneous' or 'grassroots' communities of faith survive and flourish."[24]

Della Cava articulates the perceived strengths of "High Catholicism." When Daniel Levine, David Stoll, and Danièle Hervieu-Léger attend to Catholicism, they speak about religion from below, as does Dale Eickelman in his account of Islam. The former emphasize the more disaggregated, disarticulated nature of Catholic charismatic movements in Europe, of basic ecclesiastical communities spawned by liberation theology in Latin America, and of the new Protestant fundamentalist churches everywhere. Small modules are more adaptable, more responsive, and hence more durable. "Structural flexibility is enhanced by the historically fissile character of Protestant growth, and by the extent to which the Protestant scheme of things accommodates and facilitates personal mobility."[25] Stoll and Levine's account of liberationism and evangelicalism follows the spectacular explosion of evangelical Christianity in Latin America, following on and often flowing into the same spaces as were occupied by liberation theology.[26]

I have spoken of "low" religion as popular, self-invented, local, implying that it is the product of spontaneous processes. But to what extent is it spontaneous? To what extent is it generated by the activity of transnational religious organizations in collaboration with the political interest of distant states?

The wave of evangelical Protestantism that swept over Latin America in the 1980s is often pictured as intentionally engineered by a combination of calculating and entrepreneurial forces, including well-financed U.S. missionary organizations, many of which were seen to be allied with the Reaganite U.S. state. Brazilian Catholic bishops sent the Vatican a report suggesting that the Central Intelligence Agency (CIA) stood behind sectarian infiltration in Latin America.[27] Bishop Mario Enrique Ríos Montt told journalists in 1982, "Don't forget the United States was founded by Protestants. The Catholic Church south of Texas is regarded as too large, too strong. Because we cannot be confronted or fought directly, we must be weakened and divided otherwise. . . . Protestants and Marxists are both against us—Protestantism as the arm of conservative capitalism; Marxism as the arm of atheistic Communism."[28]

In the Montt example, "low" religion is pictured as orchestrated; the "center" is said to be a foreign state. But societal forces may also constitute a "center" and provide leadership. "Church planting" became a major activity of the Overseas Crusades ministries and numerous other American evangelical organizations that in the 1980s and 1990s set goals for the size of the evangelical community in Latin America. These were societal, not state initiatives. Thus the American television evangelist Jimmy Swaggart alone is said to have provided 40 percent of the funding and materials for the Assemblies of God medical and educational program in Honduras, and $6 million to the Assemblies in El Salvador.[29] In the 1980s, such social organizations trained, staffed, and funded both overseas missionary activity and local pastoral recruits.[30] But the boundaries of civil society and state soon melted. Major funding for and efforts by U.S. evangelical organizations became related to the Reagan offensive against communist and other radical forces in Central America. After 1984, when Congress cut off aid to the Nicaraguan contras, evangelical churches helped the private support network organized by Oliver North, a member of the Church of the Apostles, with the authorization of the White House.[31]

This peculiar alliance of evangelical centers in the United States with the Reagan administration's anticommunist activities shaped many observers' understanding of religion as a nonautonomous feature of transnational civil society, as a statist project laundered through a societalist front. It provided an image of religious formations manipulated by a control board in Florida or Texas or southern California, parallel to the image of an Islamic conspiracy that emerged out of the Iranian activities of the early 1980s. Though elements of the alliance of the 1980s persist, the passing of the Reagan administration, the discrediting of the contras, and the fall of several televangelists active in Latin America weakened the switchboard from the United States even while the Latin American Protestant churches started moving well beyond the reach of their U.S. supporters. Protestantism in Latin America is increasingly generated locally, by diffusion, and from below. "We must also acknowledge," writes Levine, "the emergence of a corps of independent churches, leaders and preachers throughout the region. . . . As North American evangelism encountered growing difficulties by the late 1980s, these groups have moved to increasing fiscal and ideological independence."[32]

Hervieu-Léger likewise emphasizes the spontaneous nature of the new religiosity from below. Her exemplar is nonobservant French Catholicism. The "institutional deregulation of religious beliefs" turns out to be favorable to "syncretic homemade beliefs" similar to those arising out of the Latin American local control of Bible reading and religious praxis. American variants of such youthful, populist, and charismatic Catholicism create phenomena such as the gathering the *New York Times* called "Popestock," or World Youth Day, in which 400,000 young celebrants descended on Denver in the summer of 1994.[33] The World Youth Day in January 1995 in Manila, again graced by the pope but generated from below, attracted celebrants from all over Asia.[34]

The autonomy of transnational civil society and its engagement with or guidance by states is further complicated by the role of radio and television. The electronic media have had contradictory effects on the pattern of religious diffusion, enabling greater centralization and state control on the one hand and greater "spontaneous" proliferation on the other. Both of the major "fundamentalisms" that Martin Riesebrodt compares, of the U.S. and Iran, display a powerful enthusiasm for the latest in cassette, video, and radio diffusion.[35] The media provide a form of communications that is increasingly difficult for nation-states to control—whether they are television programs broadcast over satellite or small cassettes carried in a vest pocket. Dale Eickelman, in a discussion of religious disputation between Oman and Saudi clergy over the nature of Islam, in which the Saudi imam attacked the interpretation of the Omani mufti, notes that it was carried on to a large extent over Saudi and Omani state television, evidently with the support of the two states. Oman regularly broadcasts Friday sermons; it issued cassettes recording the Omani side of the television "debate."[36]

Here state leadership played a role. But television and other media are now often beyond the capacity of states to control. The well-funded television preaching of the southern evangelical churches in the United States played a significant leading and guiding role in the early spread of evangelicalism to Latin America, often from beyond the border and in the face of opposing states. Jim Bakker, Jimmy Swaggart, and Pat Robertson achieved significant television exposure both in states where they were welcome—Pinochet's Chile—and where they were not—Sandinista Nicaragua.

In summary, religious formations as an aspect of transnational civil society demonstrate a wide variety of forms and a range of relationships to states. The most striking development with respect to form is the proliferation of popular religion from below, spreading in the Atlantic community among both Catholics and Protestants, propagated through informal and self-repro-ducing religious networks. They represent phenomena very different from re-ligion emanating from a "center" dominated by professional religious practi-tioners—such as "Rome." Catholic liberationism was no initiative of Rome; *tabliqhi* (revitalization) movements are no initiative of "Mecca." Latin Amer-ican Pentecostalism becomes less and less an initiative of "Dallas."

From the point of view of the state, elite-controlled religion is more pre-dictable and manipulable, but religion from below less so. High religion lends itself more readily to formal or informal pacts with the state—be-tween Orthodox Christianity and Soviet communism; between the papacy and Mussolini's Rome; between certified Buddhism and Chinese commu-nism; between Jimmy Swaggart and Augusto Pinochet. Religion from below is amorphous, "formed from networks of trusted neighborhood and school acquaintances and devoid of complex hierarchies,"[37] hard for states to monitor, to control, or to bring into a regularized relationship. Uncerti-fied underground churches in China and the basic ecclesial communities of liberation Catholicism escape state supervision. They elaborate autono-mous social spaces beyond the reach of the state. In contrast, centralized and "high" religion can offer concentrated opposition to the state—as did the Polish Catholic Church—that is hard for "low" religion to approxi-mate. As Stoll and Levine make clear, self-founded and locally sustained forms of religion from below may not be able to engage the state in conse-quential fashion.

The relationship of religious formations to states takes place along a con-tinuum from autonomy to incorporation. Religious movements go mission-izing across state boundaries, sometimes in alliance with supportive states, sometimes in the face of resistant states. And sometimes they move in a space in which states fade from sight, driven by spiritual enthusiasms that have social and transcendental meanings, creating networks and communi-ties of which the state scarcely knows.

Tightly Held or Loosely Coupled: Cross-national Transfer of Religious Resources

Many of the functions associated with a modern welfare state have tradi-tionally been performed by institutions sponsored by pious laypersons and religious orders. To what extent these institutions represent the virtues of generosity and fellow feeling and to what extent they represent institutional and political self-interest is often unclear. Associated with the difference between religion from below and from above is a difference between tightly held, centralized modes of transnational religious formations on the one hand and informal, loosely coupled modes on the other. The distinction is apparent in the way Catholics and Muslims organize the transnational transfer of religious resources—"charity."

Catholic charitable organizations are formally constituted components of a hierarchical structure, often created by the central episcopacy, and when by the laity, in harmony with a center. They rely on institutional channels for resources—in Europe, church collections as supplements to the proceeds of church taxes, and in the United States, church collections.

Islamic philanthropies, on the other hand, which have a wide reach across lands where Islamic peoples live, are more spontaneously founded and funded, not part of a hierarchy or a monocratic system. Organizations "spring up" sharing a vague but commonly held understanding of an *umma*, a community of the devout, instead of being "planted" by the representatives of a formal institution. A well-known set of models—mosques, *madrasas* (religious schools), hospitals, bookstores—is replicated in segmentary fashion by disparate actors on the basis of individual and institutional funding. They often rely on the compliance of individual pious Muslims with the Quranic imperative to offer *zakat*—charitable donations.

Della Cava's account of the transnational philanthropic initiatives of the Catholic Church illustrates the strategies of a complex, formally organized religion at work. The fall of the Berlin Wall and the accessibility of East Germany, and then the turn of events in the Soviet Union itself, placed enormous transnational opportunities and responsibilities before the Church. Catholic philanthropy at the European level, fashioned to deal with the refugee flows of World War II, turned east and adapted to internal political conditions in Poland, East Germany, Yugoslavia, and other Balkan states.[38] The institutions that took advantage of these opportunities functioned at different unit levels—national, European, and worldwide: (1) *nationally* based philanthropies supported by national bishoprics, such as Caritas Germany, with its staff of 300,000 employees "a virtual ministry of social welfare";[39] (2) *pan-European* laity-founded philanthropies (Kirche in Not; Europäischer Hilfsfonds); and (3) a *global* coordinating body, Cor Unum, created by the Holy See's pontifical council within the Roman Curia to deal with the complexity of the Church's aid in Europe, Asia, and Africa.

These structures constitute a component of transnational civil society when entities in many states recognize one another as belonging to a transnational moral, social, and utilitarian community. The West European Catholic churches united across state boundaries to conduct an *Ostpolitik* on the basis of this commonality. They sustained East European co-religionists in their struggle with states repressive of religion, succoring them in their effort to reconstitute domestic civil society once those repressive regimes fell.

Islam also can appear as the emanation of tightly held, centralizing structures, but that is not its most prevalent form. Dale Eickelman speaks of a sort of Islamic Leninism: "Muslim activists have been attracted by the 'highly structured, cadre-based' organization of communist movements," and cites a survey that "indicates that 60 percent of Hamas activists in Gaza . . . acknowledged prior membership in Marxist organizations."[40] Such emanations come in revolutionary and moderate variants. The revolutionary face was characterized in the 1970s and 1980s by state-directed Islamic radicalism issuing from Libya, Syria, Iran, or the Abu Nidal organization. The more moderate variant of centralized initiatives was characterized by Saudi Arabian plantings of Wahhabi Islam, establishing a strong base in Nigeria in the 1960s, for example, through charitable institutions.[41]

Locally generated, nonstatist networks with loose ties to philanthropic organizations and to private philanthropic donors are more prevalent in Islam. In a careful journalistic essay for the *Washington Post*, Steve Coll and David Hoffman examined the relative spontaneity and lack of coordination among Islamic religiously based institutions, acephalous, loosely coupled centers of activity that spread by diffusion. A philanthropic template, known from practice as much as by formal organizational leadership, is emulated by pious Muslims to produce and reproduce institutions, mosques, hospitals, schools, legal clinics in myriad diverse places. In Egypt alone there are 2,000 Islamic charitable societies registered.[42] In Zagreb there are 22. The *Post* article used a map to suggest the extensive and busy reach of these institutions, spreading out from Croatia in the north through Sudan in the south, to Pakistan in the east. One might suggest further extensions to New Jersey, Chicago, and Denver, or Lanzhou, in Qinghai Province of China.[43]

Islamic charities are dependent on wealthy donors. The 2.5 percent *zakat* expected of the pious Muslim has no national boundaries. The motivation of donors does not differentiate sharply between "purely charitable" and more diffuse political or even militant objectives, which are seen to be interwoven. Wealthy Saudis or rich businesspeople from the Gulf countries give to "Palestine" in the spirit in which many American Jews give to "Palestine"—though the receiving country is differently imagined. Honor, piety, and polity are intertwined. The head of a *zakat* fund that paid for a hospital, mosque, and kindergarten complex for the poor in the West Bank explains his supporters' motives: "It is also a matter of prestige. The donor says, 'I donated for Palestine' and asks for a certificate to put on the wall."[44]

Peaceful, service-oriented, religious, and welfare institutions to some extent fill in the gaps where state activity does not suffice and is unable to meet the economic and social needs of migrants, refugees, and newly urbanized rural peoples. They provide security for the needy and uprooted, the refugees from war and ethnic and religious strife. But though their main thrust is philanthropic and social, the Islamic philanthropic foundings also serve as homelands and fronts for political objectives, and for militancy and violence. Militants were recruited through social service and refugee centers in Peshawar and Brooklyn and sponsored to fight in the Afghan war or to disrupt the lives of unbelievers. The accused in the 1993 New York World Trade Center bombing were so recruited.

If the fragmented, nonhierarchical, and multipurpose style of these organizations defies the capacities of states to discover and repress them, modern technologies—telephones, fax machines, cassettes—enable the diffusion of ideas and purposes without the aid of organized associations. Their militant face endangers the security of whatever population is identified as inimical—and these identifications have very little to do with national boundaries. The Afghan war that was waged against Soviet occupation took on the aura of an Islamic "Spanish Civil War," attracting young men driven by a belief in the virtue and daring of a cause, participating in what they saw as an international relief corps. The former Afghan war armies have since become the recruitment source for similar enterprises, such as the bitter struggle by Islamic militants in Kashmir against the Indian state. This malign dispersion of militants is used, but not caused, by states.

Whether the more peaceable of these varied Islamic associations should be regarded as the forerunners of a more liberal civil society or the heralds of repressive theocracy is disputed. To Gilles Kepel, it is likely that they prepare the ground for theocratic totalitarianism.[45] To others, the answer seems more ambiguous as they observe the creation under authoritarianisms of parallel institutions that can resist repressive states. Notable are the networks elaborated by the Muslim Brotherhood in Egypt, but others exist in Algeria and Tunisia. Carrie Rosefsky Wickham sees them as "an alternative domain in which new values are being cultivated and new styles of participation are being forged. This Islamic sphere calls to mind the 'parallel polis' or 'parallel society' of Central and Eastern Europe."[46] At worst, the choice could be one between two evils: the authoritarian state's repression of civil society versus repression of alternatives by dominant elements of civil society. At best, as Eickelman cautiously ventures, both may evolve in the direction of a tentative civic pluralism.

Conclusion

Religious formations have joined issue- and interest-oriented transnational epistemes and communities—human rights associations, environmentalists, public health professionals, multinationals—to constitute a transnational civil society that carries on a world politics. This society creates an arena of belief, commitment, and practice alternative to the state, draining affect and action from it without replacing it. The state fades, thins out, even while persisting. The various communities may have authority and even power and may challenge the monopoly of the state, but they do not claim sovereignty. They are not identified with territory or geographic boundaries.

Transnational civil society does not have statelike qualities. It is not the locus of agreed-upon, common, let alone enforceable norms—although particular communities may create rule-governed arenas within and among themselves. It is the locus of political mobilization, conflict, and negotiation, not of statelike governance.

"Security," a noun now highly contested that entered into the launching of this volume, has to do with two kinds of survival, physical and cultural. Population increases, environmental degradation, the incapacity of the globe to accommodate its denizens, have taken their place by the side of nuclear and conventional warfare as threats to physical survival. But cultural survival has become a leading security issue in the 1990s, and religion is a leading definer of culture. Civil war based on cultural identities has come to rival international war as a cause of death. While most participants in religious and ethnic conflicts are merely hapless victims, thousands risk physical extinction lest they suffer cultural extinction. Humans seek cultural survival because religious and ethnic frameworks supply the basic parameters and patterns of their lives, patterns without which life loses its meaning.

Religious communities straddle the space between inside and outside, between domestic and international politics. They make apparent the role that the domestic plays in constituting the international sphere. They reveal the significance of networks and organizations that reach across national boundaries, disregarding or contravening the principle of national sovereignty. Religious formations may squeeze the state between their domestic and international manifestations. They may also be used by states for their own purposes.

Civil society may be uncivil. The same forces that make for peace make for war. The shared norms and practices that generate community with like persons may generate opposition to unlike. Transnational religious formations organize humans in communities that can live in harmonious pluralism or violent competition. Over historical time, and depending on the constellation of political and social forces within which they are situated, harmonious and disharmonious possibilities may alternate, or be caused to alternate, in the same regions or states. They may provide structure and meaning to uprooted and deprived peoples, giving them the equanimity to adapt to adversity or the strength and courage to change it.

Religion is no master variable that will determine the political cleavages that lead to war or the solidarities that promote peace. Religions are themselves internally contested—Vatican Catholicism and liberationism; modernist and fundamentalist Islam; nationalist and supranational arenas of faith. Religion provides one division among the many social cleavages that will influence the patterns of alliance that civic and state actors will choose. We may not give up the tedium of investigating particulars for the comfort of totalizing hypotheses that may prove to be as ephemeral as those which failed to anticipate and account for the Soviet collapse.

NOTES

1. For an elaboration of a theory of ebb and flow, see my "Now You See them, Now You Don't: Historicizing the Salience of Religious Categories" (paper presented at the Panel on Modern Religion and the State, conference on "Religious Forces in the New World (Dis)order," University of California at Santa Barbara, February 23, 1995). Another aspect of the same problem is addressed in Lloyd I. Rudolph and Susanne Hoeber Rudolph, "Modern Hate," *New Republic*, March 22, 1993.

2. Samuel Huntington, "The Clash of Civilizations," *Foreign Affairs* 72 (Summer 1993):22–49. The article was explicitly meant to offer a substitute for the cold war paradigm: "Civilizations are the natural successors to the three worlds of the Cold War," p. 187 in "Discussion," *Foreign Affairs* 72 (November-December 1993): 186–194. For criticism of the "Civilization" argument, see "Comments," *Foreign Affairs* 72 (September-October 1993):2–26. For more fine-grained political and geopolitical perspectives on religious homogeneity, see Leon T. Hadar, "What Green Peril?" and Judith Miller, "The Challenge of Radical Islam," both in *Foreign Affairs* 72 (Spring 1993):27–42 and 43–56, respectively. For a wider perspective on the politics of "Islam" that also reaches beyond the Middle East, see James P. Piscatori, *Islam in a World of Nation-States* (Cambridge, England: Cambridge University Press, 1986), and Daniel Brumberg, *Islam and Democracy: A Complex Encounter* (unpublished report prepared for the U.S. Agency for International Development [AID], Washington, D.C., June 1992). For another account that inquires into the substitutability of religious discourse for the cold war paradigm, see Mark Juergensmeyer, *The New Cold War? Religious Nationalism Confronts the Secular State* (Berkeley: University of California Press, 1993).

3. Piscatori, *Islam in a World of Nation-States*, 76.

4. Eugene Rice, *The Foundations of Early Modern Europe, 1460 to 1559* (New York: Norton, 1970).

5. See T. N. Madan, "Secularism in Its Place," *Journal of Asian Studies* 46 (4) (1987):747–759, and also his "Religion in India," *Daedalus* 118 (4) (1989):115–146.

6. For a characterization of Islamic economics, see Deborah Harrold, "Im/moral Economies and (Un)Civil Society: Liberalization and Private Accumulation in Algeria" (South Asia Middle East Workshop paper, February 24, 1994).

7. The categories dominating the Middle East have been populated over time by different players with conflicting definitions of sociocultural purposes. The

Pan-Arabists include Egypt, Iraq, the PLO, FLN-Algeria, Qaddafi's Libya, and Yemen. The Old Islamists include Saudi Arabia, Kuwait, Morocco, and the United Arab Emirates. The New Islamists include Iran, FIS-Algeria, Libya, and Egypt.

8. See, for example, speeches by George Kassimeris, founder of Political Spring— a so far not very successful Greek political party. He speaks, on the one hand, about an "Orthodox Arc" from Cyprus to Russia and, on the other, about links to Iran and Syria. He is searching for a religious formulation of the national interest. *The European*, September 16–19, 1993, 11. See also George Gavrilis, "The Politics of Greece's European Identity in the Context of the Macedonia Impasse" (B.A. Paper in Political Science, University of Chicago, Spring 1994). On the nineteenth-century creation of Hellenism, see Michael Herzfeld, *Ours Once More: Folklore, Ideology, and the Making of Modern Greece,* 1st edition (Austin: University of Texas Press, 1982).

9. For a historically oriented critique of methodologies that failed to anticipate or explain the Soviet collapse, see John Gaddis, "International Relations Theory and the End of the Cold War," *International Security* 17 (3) (Winter 1992–1993):5–58.

10. For samples, see Gareth Porter and Janet Welsh Brown, *Global Environmental Politics* (Boulder: Westview Press, 1991); David Korten, *Getting to the Twenty-first Century: Voluntary Action and the Global Agenda* (West Hartford, CT: Kumanian Press, 1990); Henry Steiner, "Diverse Partners: Non-Governmental Organization in the Human Rights Movement," Cambridge, MA: Harvard Law School/Human Rights Internet, 1991.

11. For a philosophically oriented account (and critique) that suggests that modernism and postmodernism converge in their conceptions of the secular and the transcendent, see Daya Krishna, "Secularism: Sacred and Profane," in *Culture and Modernity: East-West Philosophic Perspectives,* edited by Eliot Deutsch (Honolulu: University of Hawaii Press, 1991).

12. I am grateful to James Piscatori for encouraging me to clarify this point.

13. Elsewhere, Lloyd Rudolph and I have asserted that social formations do not fit the binary schemes of post-Enlightenment social theory. We argued so in connection with what some would regard as the strongest case for inherited social identities—caste in India. We emphasized that voluntary and inherited elements overlapped and coexisted in the creation and transformation of caste. Human agents in historical contexts have continually reconstructed this allegedly most determined of social formations. This argument may be transferred to the understanding of religious identities. See Lloyd I. Rudolph and Susanne Hoeber Rudolph, *The Modernity of Tradition: Political Development in India* (Chicago: University of Chicago Press, 1967), part one. In retrospect, it might be argued that the distinction between ascription and achievement, or involuntary and voluntary solidarities, was itself the product of a particular historical moment. Social continuity and lack of communication and mobility made social identities sufficiently durable that they appeared to be a matter of biological processes rather than subject to social construction.

14. Alexis de Tocqueville, *Democracy in America* (New York: Vintage Books, 1959), volume 2, second book, chapter 5, "Of the Uses Which the Americans Make of Public Associations in Civil Life," 114–118.

15. Weber, "The Protestant Sects and the Spirit of Capitalism," in *From Max Weber: Essays in Sociology*, edited by Hans Gerth and C. Wright Mills (New York: Galaxy, 1958), 302–322.

16. Don Baker, "World Religions and National States: Competing Claims in East Asia," in this volume. One way to read the fact that state and religion are not differentiated is to say that the differentiation is a product of East Asian cultural formulations and to label the state-society distinction as a fruit of Western liberal thought. Another way of reading it, which focuses less on the cultural discourse and more on praxis, is to emphasize that on the ground some (unlicensed) religions were always differentiated from the state. The discourse that declared religions as nondifferentiated was state discourse, and it referred to the entities that had succumbed to state licensing.

17. For example, see Joseph W. Esherick, *The Origins of the Boxer Uprising* (Berkeley: University of California Press, 1987).

18. Three million Catholics are among the eight million registered with the Beijing authorities, but the Catholic Church supports clandestine worshippers in China who pursue their faith outside official bounds. Alan Cowell, "Pope Offers the Chinese a Deal on the Church's Role," *New York Times*, January 15, 1995.

19. Nicholas Kristof, "Christianity Is Booming in China Despite Rifts," *New York Times*, February 7, 1993.

20. Ari Goldman, "Religion Notes," *New York Times*, February 12, 1994. During Pope John Paul II's visit to Manila in January 1995 for World Youth Day, he offered a bargain to Beijing: He would acknowledge the Patriotic Association (the official Catholic Church, until then unrecognized by Rome) in return for recognition of the Vatican's spiritual supremacy and its right to appoint bishops. Cowell, "Pope Offers the Chinese a Deal."

21. See also James Kurth, "Things to Come: The Shape of the New World Order," *The National Interest,* no. 24 (Summer 1991):3–12.

22. Both also attend to the pluralization of the Church that parallels its centralization.

23. Brian H. Smith, "Religion and Politics: A New Look Through an Old Prism," in *Society and Democracy: Comparative Studies; Essays in Honor of Juan J. Linz,* edited by Alfred C. Stepan and Houchang E. Chehabi (Boulder: Westview Press, 1995). The proliferation of Hinduism throughout Southeast Asia all the way to Indonesia (Bali) and its active and successful absorption of "tribal" people internal to India suggest a process of extensive diffusion without formal organizations. For an argument that organizational and interest group theories routinely overestimate the significance of "rational" bureaucratic interest groups, see the discussion of demand groups in Lloyd I. Rudolph and Susanne Hoeber Rudolph, *In Pursuit of Lakshmi: The Political Economy of the Indian State* (Chicago: University of Chicago Press, 1987), 247–258.

24. Ralph Della Cava, "Religious Resource Networks: Roman Catholic Philanthropy in Central and East Europe," in this volume.

25. Daniel H. Levine, "Protestants and Catholics in Latin America: A Family Portrait," in *Fundamentalisms Comprehended,* edited by Martin E. Marty and R. Scott Appleby (Chicago: University of Chicago Press, 1995), 160.

26. Pablo A. Deiros, "Protestant Fundamentalism in Latin America," in *Fundamentalisms Observed,* edited by Martin E. Marty and R. Scott Appleby (Chicago: University of Chicago Press, 1991).

27. David Stoll, *Is Latin America Turning Protestant?* (Berkeley: University of California Press, 1992), 32. For an extended account of CIA support and funding of

the sectarian struggle against the Sandinistas, see Margaret Randall, *Christians in the Nicaraguan Revolution* (Vancouver, BC: New Star Books, 1983).

28. Stoll, *Is Latin America Turning Protestant?*, 34.

29. Ibid., 322. Stoll cites Resource Center, *Private Organizations with U.S. Connections: Honduras* (Albuquerque, NM, 1988), and *Private Organizations with U.S. Connections: El Salvador* (Albuquerque, NM, 1988).

30. Stoll, *Is Latin America Turning Protestant?*, 125.

31. Ibid., 323–328.

32. Levine, "Protestants and Catholics in Latin America: A Family Portrait," 167. As Stoll notes, "Even if North American money has been important at certain junctures, it is far from the complete explanation. . . . Where evangelical churches are successful, they proliferate far beyond the buying power of mission subsidies. With little or no training and without financial backing, people equipped with little more than Bibles are starting their own churches, beginning with their families and neighbors, then proselytizing vigorously for enough followers to make a living." Stoll, *Is Latin America Turning Protestant?*, 12–13.

33. "For Young Catholics, Two Days of Faith and Music," *New York Times*, August 15, 1994.

34. Alan Cowell, "Up to 4 Million Turn Out for Pope's Mass in Manila," *New York Times*, January 16, 1995.

35. Martin Riesebrodt, *Pious Passion: The Emergence of Modern Fundamentalism in the United States and Iran* (Berkeley: University of California Press, 1993).

36. Dale F. Eickelman, "National Identity and Religious Discourse in Contemporary Oman," *International Journal of Islamic and Arabic Studies* 6 (1) (1989):1–20.

37. Dale F. Eickelman, "Trans-state Islam and Security," in this volume. On the other hand, Eickelman notes that even Hamas is "less . . . a single, coherent organization with a central command than a loosely organized movement in which several independent affinity groups compete with one another for leadership and support."

38. The extent to which the Church penetrated Eastern Europe beginning in 1956 is striking. This was a time when both official Church pronouncements and official policy in NATO and the Western alliance generally averred that no such penetration was possible. See Della Cava, "Religious Resource Networks," in this volume.

39. Della Cava, "Religious Resource Networks."

40. Eickelman, "Trans-state Islam and Security," in this volume.

41. Daniel Brumberg, "Nigeria: Reformist Islam in a Multi-ethnic Society," in *Islam and Democracy: A Complex Encounter* (unpublished report prepared for the U.S. Agency for International Development [AID], Washington, D.C., June 1992).

42. "Islamic Warriors," second installment of a two-part series in the *Washington Post*, August 2 and 3, 1993. Coll and Hoffman use as a source for these figures Dennis Sullivan, *Private Voluntary Organizations in Egypt: Islamic Development, Private Initiative, and State Control* (Gainesville: University Press of Florida, 1994).

43. Lloyd Rudolph and Susanne Hoeber Rudolph, *China Diary, 1989* (unpublished manuscript, Chicago, 1989). Islamic charitable and missionary efforts also extended to South India. The conversion to Islam of South Indian untouchables, who found that improvement of their economic condition in the late 1980s did not soften the caste barrier was often attributed, especially by Prime Minister Indira Gandhi, to "Gulf money." For an account that attributes the conversions to status

issues, see Abdul Malik, *Conversion to Islam: Untouchables' Strategy for Protest in India* (Chambersburg, PA: Anima, 1989), 71.

44. Steve Coll and David Hoffman, "Radical Movements Thrive on Loose Structure, Strict Ideology," *Washington Post,* August 2, 1993. Most recently, several states in the Middle East have moved to intervene and assert state regulation over the private networks of transnational donors who fund radical movements. In April 1993 the Saudi government announced that all private charitable transnational donations would have to be cleared. A year later, in April 1994, it revoked the citizenship of Usama bin Laden, who bankrolled Egyptian, Saudi, Jordanian, Palestinian, Algerian, and other Arab volunteer fighters. Youssef M. Ibrahim, "Saudis Strip Citizenship from Backer of Militants," *New York Times,* April 10, 1994.

45. Gilles Kepel, *The Revenge of God: The Resurgence of Islam, Christianity, and Judaism in the Modern World,* trans. Alan Braley (University Park: Pennsylvania State University Press, 1994).

46. Carrie Rosefsky Wickham, "Beyond Democratization: Political Change in the Arab World," *PS: Political Science and Politics* 27 (3) (September 1994):507–509. See also Eva Bellin, "Civil Society: Effective Tool of Analysis for Middle East Politics?" 509–510, in the same issue.

About the Book and Editors

Focusing on the dilution of state sovereignty, this book examines how the crossing of state boundaries by religious movements leads to the formation of transnational civil society. Challenging the assertion that future conflict will be of the "clash of civilization" variety, it looks to the micro-origins of conflicts, which are as likely to arise between states sharing a religion as between those divided by it and more likely to arise within rather than across state boundaries. Thus, the chapters reveal the dual potential of religious movements as sources of peace and security as well as of violent conflict.

Featuring an East-West, North-South approach, the volume avoids the conventional and often ethnocentric segregation of the experience of other regions from the European and American. Contributors draw examples from a variety of civilizations and world religions. They contrast self-generated movements from "below" (such as Protestant sectarianism in Latin America or Sufi Islam in Africa) with centralized forms of organization and patterns of diffusion from above (such as state-certified religion in China). Together the chapters illustrate how religion as bearer of the politics of meaning has filled the lacuna left by the decline of ideology, creating a novel transnational space for world politics.

Susanne Hoeber Rudolph is William Benton Distinguished Service Professor of Political Science at the University of Chicago and director of the South Asia Area and Language Center. She is author, with Lloyd I. Rudolph, of *The Modernity of Tradition: Political Development in India* (1996), *In Pursuit of Lakshmi: The Political Economy of the Indian State* (1987), and other books on comparative politics.

James Piscatori is fellow in Islamic Studies, Oxford Centre for Islamic Studies. Before going to Oxford in 1996, he headed the Muslim Studies Project at the New York Council on Foreign Relations and was professor of international relations at the University of Wales, Aberystwyth. He is author with Dale Eickelman of *Muslim Politics* (1996), *Islam in a World of Nation-States* (1986), and numerous books on Middle Eastern politics.

About the Contributors

Don Baker holds the Canada-Korea Business Council Chair of Korean Studies in the department of Asian studies at the University of British Columbia in Vancouver, Canada. He has a Ph.D. in Korean history from the University of Washington and has published numerous articles on Korean religion. His most recent publication is the coedited *Sourcebook of Korean Civilization* (1996).

José Casanova is associate professor of sociology at the New School for Social Research in New York City. He is author of *Public Religions in the Modern World* (1994), and *The Opus Dei and the Modernization of Spain* (forthcoming).

Ralph Della Cava is professor of history at Queen's College, City University of New York, and senior research fellow at the Institute of Latin American and Iberian Studies, Columbia University. He has written widely on ecclesiastical politics in Europe and Brazil and is currently researching the restoration of religious life in the former Soviet Union.

Dale F. Eickelman is Ralph and Richard Lazarus Professor of Anthropology and Human Relations and director of the Asian studies program at Dartmouth College. His most recent book, coauthored with James Piscatori, is *Muslim Politics* (1996).

Cary Fraser is assistant professor of African and African American Studies at Pennsylvania State University in University Park, Pennsylvania. He is an historian of international relations in the nineteenth and twentieth centuries whose current research is on the impact of the civil rights movement on U.S. foreign policy since 1941. He is author of *Ambivalent Anti-colonialism: The United States and the Genesis of West Indian Independence, 1940–1964* (1994).

Danièle Hervieu-Léger is Director d'Etudes at Ecole des Hautes Etudes en Sciences Sociales (Paris) in the Centre d'Etudes Interdisciplinaires des Faits Religieux. She is currently preparing a book on the problem of religious transmission in modern secularized societies.

Ousmane Kane teaches political science at the University of Saint-Louis, Senegal. An Islamicist, Dr. Kane is coeditor of *Islam et islamismes contemporains au sud du Sahara* (1996). He has published several articles on contemporary Islamic movements in West Africa in scholarly journals. He has also contributed entries in many reference works on Islam, including the *Encyclopedia of Islam*, published by E. J. Brill, the *Oxford Encyclopedia of the Modern Islamic World*, and the Fundamentalism Project sponsored by the American Academy of Arts and Sciences.

Daniel H. Levine is professor of political science at the University of Michigan. He has published widely on issues of religion and politics, and on politics and social change in Latin America generally. His most recent books are *Popular Voices in Latin American Catholicism* (1992) and *Constructing Culture and Power in Latin America* (1993).

David Stoll received his doctorate in anthropology from Stanford University. His research has been supported by the Harry Frank Guggenheim Foundation, and the Woodrow Wilson International Center for Scholars. His works include *Is Latin America Turning Protestant?* (1990), *Between Two Armies in the Ixil Towns of Guatemala* (1993), and, with Virginia Garrard Burnett, *Rethinking Protestantism in Latin America* (1993).

Index